A Companion to Hemingway's *Death in the Afternoon*

*Studies in American Literature and Culture*

Camden House Companion Volumes

The Camden House Companions provide well-informed and up-to-date critical commentary on the most significant aspects of major works, periods, or literary figures. The Companions may be read profitably by the reader with a general interest in the subject. For the benefit of student and scholar, quotations are provided in the original language.

Hemingway chose Juan Gris' *El Torero*, which he owned, as the frontispiece for *Death in the Afternoon*, but this beautiful painting is absent from the paperback printings of the book and from the translations. Two contributors to this *Companion*, Nancy Bredendick and Amy Vondrak, discuss *El Torero*.

© 2003 Artists Rights Society (ARS) New York / ADAGP Paris.

# A Companion to Hemingway's
# *Death in the Afternoon*

Edited by
Miriam B. Mandel

CAMDEN HOUSE

Copyright © 2004 by the Editor and Contributors

*All Rights Reserved.* Except as permitted under current legislation,
no part of this work may be photocopied, stored in a retrieval system,
published, performed in public, adapted, broadcast, transmitted,
recorded, or reproduced in any form or by any means,
without the prior permission of the copyright owner.

First published 2004 by Camden House
Reprinted in paperback 2009
Converted to digital printing 2016

Camden House is an imprint of Boydell & Brewer Inc.
668 Mt. Hope Avenue, Rochester, NY 14620, USA
www.camden-house.com
and of Boydell & Brewer Limited
PO Box 9, Woodbridge, Suffolk IP12 3DF, UK
www.boydell.co.uk

Hardcover ISBN-13: 978–1–57113–202–4
Hardcover ISBN-10: 1–57113–202–3
Paperback ISBN-13: 978–1–57113–409–7
Paperback ISBN-10: 1–57113–409–3

Library of Congress Cataloging-in-Publication Data

A companion to Hemingway's Death in the afternoon / edited by Miriam B. Mandel.
  p. cm. — (Studies in American literature and culture)
  Includes bibliographical references and index.
  ISBN 1–57113–202–3 (alk. paper)
  1. Hemingway, Ernest, 1899–1961. Death in the afternoon.
  2. Bullfights—Historiography. I. Mandel, Miriam B. II. Title.
  III. Series.

GV1107.H4 2004 (Commentary)
791.8'2—dc22
                                                         2004008904

A catalogue record for this title is available from the British Library.

This publication is printed on acid-free paper.
Printed in the United States of America.

Cover images — Front: Juan Gris, *El Torero* (1913) © 2003 Artists Rights
Society (ARS), New York / ADAGP, Paris; Back: Courtesy of Hemingway
Collection, John F. Kennedy Library, Boston.

## In Memoriam

Paul Bauer (1915–1963)

Gertrude S. Bauer (1914–1975)

Marianne B. Axtmayer (1913–2001)

Emilia García (1901–2003)

and

Paul Smith (1925–1996)

# Contents

| | |
|---|---|
| Acknowledgments | xi |
| Hemingway Works That Address the Bullfight | xiii |
| A Note on the Text of *Death in the Afternoon* | xvii |
| Introduction<br>    Miriam B. Mandel | 1 |

## Composition, Sources, and Backgrounds

| | |
|---|---|
| The Composition, Revision, Publication, and Reception of *Death in the Afternoon*<br>    Robert W. Trogdon | 21 |
| "Devout Again by Cynicism": Lord Byron and *Don Juan* in *Death in the Afternoon*<br>    Lisa Tyler | 43 |
| "I like you less and less": The Stein Subtext in *Death in the Afternoon*<br>    Linda Wagner-Martin | 59 |
| Subject and Author: The Literary Backgrounds of *Death in the Afternoon*<br>    Miriam B. Mandel | 79 |

## Reading Texts, Paratexts, and Absence

| | |
|---|---|
| "The Real Thing"? Representing the Bullfight and Spain in *Death in the Afternoon*<br>    Peter Messent | 123 |

"Very Sad but Very Fine": *Death in the Afternoon*'s
Imagist Interpretation of the Bullfight-Text 143
    *Beatriz Penas Ibáñez*

"Far from Simple": The Published Photographs
in *Death in the Afternoon* 165
    *Anthony Brand*

Deleted "Flashes": The Unpublished Photographs
of *Death in the Afternoon* 189
    *Anthony Brand*

"¿Qué tal, hombre, qué tal?": How Paratexts
Narrow the Gap between Reader and Text
in *Death in the Afternoon* 205
    *Nancy Bredendick*

## On Authorship and Art

"Prejudiced through Experience": *Death in the
Afternoon* and the Problem of Authorship 237
    *Hilary K. Justice*

"The Sequence of Motion and Fact": Cubist Collage
and Filmic Montage in *Death in the Afternoon* 257
    *Amy Vondrak*

## And What Came After

The Legacy of *Death in the Afternoon*:
Norman Mailer and Barnaby Conrad 283
    *Keneth Kinnamon*

Works Cited 301

Notes on the Contributors 319

Index 323

# Acknowledgments

I WOULD LIKE TO THANK my contributors for all that they taught me during the making of this book. I would also like to thank James Hardin, who was so quickly convinced of the necessity for it and who so patiently waited for it to be finished. I would also like to thank the Artists Rights Society (the U.S. copyright society) and ADAGP (the French copyright society that directly represents Juan Gris) for their generous permission to present Gris's *El Torero* as our frontispiece; and the John F. Kennedy Library for making available the bullfight photographs we reproduce here. Anthony Brand selected and organized the photographs; James Walker (of Camden House) and James B. Hill (Audiovisual Archives of the John F. Kennedy Library, Boston) did all the technical work. And finally I would like to thank my brother and my daughters, who, like this book, got me through the hard times.

M. B. M.
Ra'anana
Israel
April 2004

# Hemingway Works That Address the Bullfight

THIS LIST PRESENTS THOSE OF Hemingway's published and unpublished works that deal, wholly or in part, with the bullfight. Published works are listed first; they are presented according to genre and publication date, and they clarify that Hemingway treated this theme often and in a variety of genres. Some of the work was published posthumously; some still remains unpublished. In some of the items, the bullfight theme dominates; in others, it forms part of the background.

## Published Works

### Long Fiction

    1926 — *The Sun Also Rises*

    1940 — *For Whom the Bell Tolls*

### Short Fiction

    1923 — "The First Matador Got the Horn" (*The Little Review*)

    1924 — Six Chapters of *in our time:*

        Chapter 2: "The first matador got the horn"

        Chapter 12: "They whack-whacked the white horse"

        Chapter 13: "The crowd shouted all the time"

        Chapter 14: "If it happened right down the close"

        Chapter 15: "I heard the drums coming"

        Chapter 16: "Maera lay still"

    1925 — Six Interchapters of *In Our Time:*

        Chapter IX: "The first matador got the horn"

        Chapter X: "They whack-whacked the white horse"

        Chapter XI: "The crowd shouted all the time"

Chapter XII: "If it happened right down close"

Chapter XIII: "I heard the drums coming"

Chapter XIV: "Maera lay still"

"The Undefeated" (*Men Without Women*)

1927 — "Banal Story" (*Men Without Women*)

1933 — "The Mother of a Queen" (*Winner Take Nothing*)

1936 — "The Horns of the Bull" (*Esquire*); rpt. as "The Capital of the World" (*The Fifth Column and the First Forty-nine Stories*, 1938)

1951 — "The Faithful Bull" (*Holiday*)

1990 — "A Lack of Passion" (*The Hemingway Review*)

## Long Nonfiction

1932 — *Death in the Afternoon*

1960 — *The Dangerous Summer* (*Life* magazine)

1986 — *The Dangerous Summer* (book form)

## Short Nonfiction

1923 — "Bull Fighting is Not a Sport — It is a Tragedy" (*The Toronto Star Weekly*)

"Pamplona in July" (*The Toronto Star Weekly*)

"Tancredo Is Dead" (*The Toronto Star Weekly*)

1924 — "Pamplona Letter" (*the transatlantic review*)

1930 — "Bull Fighting — Sport and Industry" (*Fortune*)

1934 — "The Friend of Spain" (*Esquire*)

1959 — "A Matter of Wind" (*Sports Illustrated*)

**Poetry**

1924 — "The Soul of Spain with McAlmon and Bird the Publishers" (*Der Querschnitt*)

"Part Two of The Soul of Spain with McAlmon and Bird the Publishers" (*Der Querschnitt*)

1979 — "Part Three of The Soul of Spain with McAlmon and Bird the Publishers" (*Complete Poems*)

"Part Four of the Same Story" (*Complete Poems*)

"Part Five Follows" (*Complete Poems*)

"Part Six A Serious and Vivid Account of a Dramatic Moment in the Cruel Sport" (*Complete Poems*)

"Some Day When You Are Picked Up" (*Complete Poems*)

"The Poem Is By Maera" (*Complete Poems*)

"To a Tragic Poetess" (*Complete Poems*)

## Unpublished Works

These manuscripts and fragments deal with the bullfight or with Spain, or are otherwise connected to *Death in the Afternoon*. They are in the Hemingway Collection, John F. Kennedy Library (Boston), whose curator, James Roth, generously helped me compile this list. The items range from a few phrases to several pages. Additional fragments may exist in other archives.

The Death of Angel C. Carratalá (JFK, Item 681a)

From Top of Bull Arena (JFK, Item 414)

It Is a Strange Country (JFK, Item 24)

Luis López (Chanito) (JFK, Item 560)

My Life in the Bull Ring with Donald Ogden Stewart (JFK, Items 590 and 590a; *see also* Item 546.5)

Nacional II Was a Bullfighter (JFK, Item 596)

Photographs (JFK, Items 30 and 48)

Revolution (JFK, Item 239a)

There Were Only a Few Good Trout Streams (JFK, Item 737)

There's One in Every Town (JFK, Item 743)

Very Few Men Are Killed in the Bullring (JFK, Item 805)

When We Traveled Together (JFK, Item 831)

With the First Money (JFK, Item 506)

You Could Not Be One (JFK, Item 849)

## Composition Dates

For the composition dates of the novels, see Michael Reynolds's five-volume biography; for the composition dates of the short fiction, see Paul Smith, *A Reader's Guide to the Short Stories of Ernest Hemingway* (Boston: G. K. Hall, 1989). Additional details about the differences between *in our time* and *In Our Time* were supplied by Milton Cohen (University of Texas at Dallas) in email correspondence (March 2004). For the composition dates and history of *Death in the Afternoon,* see Robert Trogdon's essay, pages 21–41 in this volume. For the composition history of *The Dangerous Summer,* see Albert John DeFazio's *The "HemHotch" Letters: The Correspondence and Relationship of Ernest Hemingway and A. E. Hotchner* (Ph.D. dissertation, University of Virginia, 1992) or Miriam B. Mandel's *Hemingway's "The Dangerous Summer": The Complete Annotations* (forthcoming from Scarecrow Press). The composition of the short nonfiction is discussed by Hemingway's biographers, most reliably by Carlos Baker in *Ernest Hemingway: A Life Story* (1969; New York: Collier / Macmillan, 1988) and by Michael Reynolds (but see also *Ernest Hemingway: Dateline: Toronto* and *By-Line: Ernest Hemingway,* both edited by William White). For composition dates of the poems, see Nicholas Gerogiannis's *Ernest Hemingway: Complete Poems* (Lincoln and London: U of Nebraska P, 1992).

# A Note on the Text of *Death in the Afternoon*

THE ESSAYS IN THIS *COMPANION* refer to the first edition of *Death in the Afternoon* (New York: Scribner's, 1932). This is generally compatible with subsequent American versions, which are reprints of the first edition. These American versions (Scribner Library of Contemporary Classics, Scribner Library Lyceum Editions, Collier, and Halcyon House) all carry the same pagination for the twenty chapters of the text (pages 1–278), but thereafter page numbers vary.

## Differences in Pagination

The 1932 first edition presents the book's final item, the "Bibliographical Note," on page 517, but in some other versions the same material appears on page 487. The thirty-page difference is due to a more compressed presentation of the photographs and their captions. Readers with the "shorter" version need only subtract 30 from the page references given in the *Companion* (for page numbers above 278) in order to find the same material in their own books.

## Differences in Illustrations, Captions, and Attributions

In the 1932, 1937 (Halcyon House), 1953, and 1961 (Scribner's) versions, the photographs and their captions were allotted 128 pages, with the right-hand page 279 carrying the heading "Illustrations" and pages 280–407 carrying the captions (on the left-hand, or even-numbered pages) and the eighty-one black-and-white visuals (on the right-hand, odd-numbered pages). This separates the words from the pictures, making it easier for the reader to flip through from photo to photo without paying too much attention to the captions, which usually name the bullfighters, the events, or the bullring, and sometimes tell the readers how to respond, whether with scorn or with admiration, to what they are seeing.

Immediately following the illustrations, on page 408, the 1932 Scribner's hardback first edition (and several subsequent Scribner's hardbacks) gives credit for the illustrations to two photographers, who are identified simply as Vandel and Rodero. This acknowledgment cites page numbers which all together account for seventy-eight of the eighty-one photographs (three photos, one on page 299 and two on page 389, are not attributed). The note also mentions that the Knudsen printing process was used.

In the Scribner Library of Contemporary Classics or Scribner Library Lyceum Editions, the paperbacks that most readers use, page 279 also carries the heading "Illustrations," but the next page is blank, the first photograph and its caption both appearing on unnumbered page 281, and the last photograph appearing on unnumbered page 375. In these versions, where the caption and the photograph often appear on the same page, there is a much stronger connection between word and image. Another difference is that in the 1932 Scribner's first edition, the photographs are sometimes vertical, sometimes horizontal (requiring the reader to turn the book ninety degrees) and, on twelve occasions, two or more photographs (up to four) appear on the same page (*DIA,* 295, 297, 301, 307, 309, 313, 347, 385, 389, 391, 393, and 403). But in the more compressed Scribner's paperback versions, all the photographs are vertical, and no page presents more than two photographs. In addition, the photographs have been cropped differently, which alters their focus and mood.[1] All these differences, in the positioning, cropping, and grouping of photographs, make the experience of looking at the illustrations in the hardback versions quite different from the experience of looking at them in subsequent, more compressed or "shorter" paperback versions.

These "shorter" versions also lack the acknowledgment to the photographers Juan Pacheco (Vandel) and Aurelio Rodero.

**Glossary**

The "Illustrations" are followed by "An Explanatory Glossary." Because in some versions of *Death in the Afternoon* the pages of the Glossary are unnumbered, this *Companion* also provides the Glossary heading (e.g., *DIA,* 473, s. v. *Reglamento;* or Glossary, s. v. *Reglamento*) to enable all readers to find the pertinent section in their own books. For readers with the more compressed paperback version, which is thirty pages "shorter," the same material would appear on page 443.

**Other Differences**

The post-1932 American versions, although produced from the same typesetting, show other differences. The 1937 Halcyon edition omits the photo credit (page 408) and the tissue guard for the Juan Gris frontispiece; the Scribner paperbacks (the Scribner Library Lyceum Editions and the Scribner Library of Contemporary Classics) have different cover designs and omit not only the tissue guard but the frontispiece itself; and the Collier reprints (1938, 1942) omit the frontispiece, the "Illustrations," "Some Reactions of a Few Individuals to the Integral Spanish Bullfight," and "Dates on Which Bullfights Will Ordinarily Be Held." These omissions, like the compression of the photographs, made the book less expensive to produce; the consequent lower price undoubtedly increased its readership.

The British first edition (Jonathan Cape, 1932) is missing the dedication, the Table of Contents, and the photo credits; by the 1960s, the frontispiece had also disappeared. The title page does not display the bull that is seen in the Scribner's versions; and the alterations in spelling and other details, such as the occasional replaced word, indicate that the Cape editors adapted the text to British usage and sensibilities.

## Notes

[1] In the photograph captioned "Joselito, at eighteen, watching a Miura bull," the paperback is missing the hindquarters of the bull (unnumbered page 321), which appear quite fully in the hardback, as do the heads of two bullfighters in the foreground and some of the audience in the background (unnumbered page 335). More strikingly, in the photograph captioned "Maera citing the bull for the second of four pairs of banderillas" (hardback unnumbered page 319, paperback unnumbered page 312), the paperback photograph is missing part of the top (removing quite a bit of audience) and of the sides, particularly of the right-hand side of the photograph. In the paperback, the left-hand part of the photograph shows a bullfighter and a photographer at the *burladero,* where calmness prevails: the bullfighter is not rushing in to help Maera, and he seems unconcerned about the photographer next to him, whose presence in the arena is both illegal and dangerous. All this reassures the viewer that Maera is doing very well. In the hardback, however, the photograph is not as closely cropped, enabling us to see more rows of audience, at the top, left, and particularly on the right-hand side of the picture, which presents several more segments of the *barrera,* as well as two bullfighters in the *callejón* who seem to be rushing towards the *burladero* (where the photographer, even if he is scrambling to get out the way, will become an obstacle) so that they can enter the ring in case Maera needs help. Whereas the paperback photo minimizes the audience and gives little indication of danger, the hardback version emphasizes both and is thus more congruent with caption: "the audience were all shouting together 'No! No! No! No!' begging him not to take such risks." These differences are significant. My thanks to Anthony Brand, who first pointed out the differences in cropping and then helped me understand their implications.

# Introduction

*Miriam B. Mandel*

> *Hemingway's nonfiction continues to be the most neglected part of his canon.*
> Michael S. Reynolds

IT HAS BEEN SAID, both in praise and as criticism, that anyone can read the work of Ernest Hemingway — and indeed, one does not need a graduate degree in literary theory or cultural studies or cross-cultural studies or philosophy or semiotics or history to enjoy his books. Still, the scholars who have been trained in these various disciplines can help us identify and explore complexities that, like the trout that lurk in Hemingway's fictional waters, are not readily visible. This is the function of criticism: to open up the text, to reveal the questions it raises, to suggest answers, to enrich our reading, to raise the prize fish so that it is visible and ours.

Over the years, a growing number of casebooks and companions have helped professional readers — teachers, scholars, critics, researchers — explore Hemingway's fiction. At last count, there were five such collections on *The Sun Also Rises,* another five on *A Farewell to Arms,* a lesser number on *For Whom the Bell Tolls* and *To Have and Have Not,* and a few on his collections of short stories and even on his "neglected short fiction." But no such collections or companions are available to students of his nonfiction, which includes at least seven books: two volumes of journalism (*Dateline: Toronto* and *By-Line: Ernest Hemingway*), two African books (*Green Hills of Africa* and *True at First Light*), two Spanish books (*Death in the Afternoon* and *The Dangerous Summer*), and a memoir of his Paris years (*A Moveable Feast*).[1] This *Companion to Hemingway's "Death in the Afternoon"* is a groundbreaking publication, in that it is the first such book to focus on a volume of Hemingway's nonfiction.

*Death in the Afternoon* is the right book to launch what should become an avalanche of casebooks on the nonfiction. It is his longest book and the one that took him longest to produce: nine years of travel, research, writing, and revising passed between his first essay on the bullfight in 1923 and the book's publication in 1932. And it is a notoriously difficult book: not difficult to read, but almost impossible to define. It looks like a nonfiction essay on bullfighting, but it strays away from that subject to offer travel literature, biography, lexicography, literary theory, and philosophy. It mixes genres: sections of it are dramatized, there are poetic passages, and it offers a complete short story that is not about bullfighting, and discusses another, which is.[2] In addition, its emphasis on the visual — it presents two paintings (one on the cover, one as a frontispiece), several word paintings, and eighty-one carefully captioned photographs — requires us to examine the relationship between the visual arts and the written text — or texts, since this book offers us not only drama, short fiction, and poetry,[3] but also an annotated calendar, a glossary, and several biographical sketches. This curious mix is communicated by a first person narrator whose travels, wives, sons, military adventures, and literary creations are so similar to Ernest Hemingway's own that we are, in addition to all our other readerly options, invited to classify this book as autobiography — a classification which its content challenges.[4]

In very important ways, this decentered, contradictory performance is a natural consequence of Hemingway's biography. His background and childhood were destabilized by conflict and contradictions, by discrepancies between old values and new, between announced agenda and private behavior, between what was public and obvious and what was unspeakable but perhaps even more powerful. Driven as it is by contradictory needs to affirm and deny, to reveal and conceal, Hemingway's modernist art is as decentered as any postmodern work.

The surface of Hemingway's childhood looks nice and smooth. He was born into a prosperous midwestern family that lived in large houses, dressed handsomely but modestly, attended church regularly (some became missionaries), and were proud of themselves and their village, Oak Park, which was near enough to Chicago to enable them to taste urban sophistication but far enough to shield them from urban ills. But this comfortable Victorian world was disintegrating even as Ernest Hemingway entered it in 1899, and its clear rules were being subverted not only by his neighbors, but by his own parents and grandparents.

The Hemingway and Hall grandparents expected their children — Ernest's parents, aunts, and uncles — to be, like their elders, patriotic, pious, well educated, sociable, and hardworking. But these conformist demands were complicated by an aggressive individualism, particularly strong among the family's women. While both of Hemingway's grandfathers were quite conventional (they were Civil War veterans and successful businessmen), his two grandmothers did not follow the traditional mold, having acquired more education than was usual for women of their generation. And his mother, Grace Hall-Hemingway, was a wage-earning professional at a time when women did not get paid for their work. She earned considerably more than her husband did, designed and paid for their homes, stayed out of the kitchen (where her husband enjoyed making pies and pickles), and generally relished her financial independence. She was tall, proud, physically strong, and talented: she sang, taught singing and music, and painted. Her less aggressive husband, Dr. Clarence Edmonds (Ed) Hemingway, seldom collected fees from his patients, made unwise investments, ignored his own diabetes, and finally committed suicide. Like their parents, Grace and Ed advocated "Victorian morality, sentimental piety," and patriarchal patterns (Grimes, 37), but the psychological and financial facts of their lives contradicted these ideals. In fact, Oak Park as a whole was riddled with contradiction. Hemingway early saw the incongruity between public proclamations of abstemiousness, chastity, democracy, and equality with his neighbors' indulgence in the occasional cocktail, the racist and sexist language that was standard for their day, and the occasional illicit affair that inevitably became public knowledge.[5]

The Hemingway children were removed from this complicated environment for at least two months every summer. At the family's lakeside cottage in Horton Bay, in Charlevoix County, Michigan, Ernest fished, hiked, swam, hunted, read, grew vegetables, daydreamed, and made friends with the Ojibway Indians. He experienced a rural leisure more typical of the nineteenth century than of the twentieth. Over the years, as more families built summer homes, as logging decimated the forests, and as the Indian population was increasingly impoverished and marginalized, Horton Bay found it more difficult to maintain its distance from the racism and commercialism that white middle-class Oak Park practiced even as it decried it. But Hemingway never forgot those Edenic summers and, in a passage cut from *Death in the Afternoon,* he mourns the loss:

> Michigan I loved very much when I lived in it, and when I was away from it, but as I grew up each time I returned to it it was changed. It was a country of forests, lakes and streams and small farms with hills and pastures, always with a background of woods. There was no place in upper Michigan where you could look across open land and not see the forest and you were never far away from running water. They cut down the forests, the streams lost their water, the lakes had their levels lowered and raised by the taking or not taking of water to float sewerage from Chicago down the drainage canal; they built concrete motor roads across all the country and around the lakes; the motorists caught all the fish out of the streams and as the young men went to Flint or Detroit to work and prices made it impossible for farmers to make a living, they abandoned the farms. Now the second growth is coming back [. . .] and people seeing the second growth believe that they know what the forest was like. But it was not like that and you will never know what it was like if you did not see it. Nor will you know what the heart of a country was after it is gone. (Qtd. in Beegel, *Craft of Omission,* 52–53)

Just as Horton Bay lost its pristine beauty, so Oak Park found it increasingly difficult to maintain its desired identity as an idyllic, old-fashioned village. When Hemingway was born, Oak Park's population stood at about ten thousand; by the time he left home eighteen years later, it had more than tripled. The automotive revolution, women's suffrage, and the modern fashions — drinking, smoking, short hair, a certain openness about sex — were played out against the moral and social strictures Hemingway's parents both evaded and advocated, and which he necessarily internalized. Not only Oak Park, but the United States itself became increasingly unable to maintain its virtuous distance from the unpleasantness that walked abroad: in April 1917, the United States entered the First World War, which signaled the real beginning of the twentieth century.

Hemingway brought his parents' nineteenth-century complexities into his twentieth-century life and art. In many ways, his entire adult life was an attempt to free himself from their values, which seemed so irrelevant in the postwar world. His rejection was clear in principle but, like his parents' principles, it was blurred by noncompliance. He abandoned their Protestantism, for example, but could not abandon the need to believe in something, be it horse chestnuts, rabbits' feet, luck, or Catholic dogma. He abandoned their complacent American Midwest to live, in restless succession, among people his parents and their neighbors disapproved of: expatriates in Paris, bullfight aficionados in Spain, big game hunters in Kenya, and fishermen, pelota players, and other sportsmen — sometimes wealthy, often disreputable — whom he sought out in Montana, Idaho, Key West, and Cuba. Having left home, he never really settled down. He never had what his parents would call a "proper" job or a "respectable" life style, but, like them, he always worked hard, earned well, lived in small towns where he had comfortable large houses, made sure he had a private space to work in (just as his mother had had a music room and his father an office), spent several months of almost each year away from home, and conventionally married the women he slept with. He may have escaped Oak Park and his parents, but he lived their patterns.[6]

Hemingway's life was further complicated by inherited physical problems. Both parents were troubled by insomnia, headaches, and unspecified, undiagnosed, and therefore untreated attacks of "nerves" or "nervous complaints," Victorian euphemisms for psychological or psychiatric problems. Harassed both by their illnesses and by the need to deny them, Grace and Ed took occasional and unconventional sabbaticals from family. Grace went so far as to build a separate summer cottage for herself, to which she invited a female companion her husband disliked; and Ed, although devoted to his family, occasionally spent his summers alone in Oak Park while they were in Michigan, or absented himself from Oak Park for what the couple called a course in specialized medical training but was probably psychiatric treatment. During their separations, they wrote each other daily to reassure themselves and each other that they were coping and that their marriage, family, and ideals were whole, coherent, and intact.

Kay Redfield Jamison, an expert on bipolar disease, recognizes that "'assortative mating,' the intermarriage of individuals with similar temperaments and genes," may be one of the reasons that "Ernest Hemingway's family [...] was filled with depressive and manic-depressive illness" (230, 228). She recounts "the unnerving number of suicides — four, in just two generations of the family: Hemingway's father, brother, sister, and Hemingway himself" (230). Ernest Hemingway's heavy drinking, insomnia, high blood pressure, "black ass" depressions, periods of intense creativity, and tendency to lose and gain considerable amounts of weight identify him as a victim of bipolar disease. His life experiences did not ameliorate his genetic inheritance: perhaps because of his weak eyes (inherited from his mother), he was accident-prone, suffering several broken bones and more than ten serious concussions over the course of his life. Like his father, he denied his adult-onset diabetes. All his life, he struggled for the physical and mental health that were necessary to his self-image. He carefully tracked his weight and spoke of being or getting healthy, and he exposed himself to physical danger, emotional stress, and alcohol as if he were immune to their harmful effects. Like his parents, he tried to deny his own suffering, pain, loss of control, and unresolved conflicts.

Hemingway's adventurous life (two African safaris, three wars, four marriages, much Spanish carousing) produced a tough *macho* image that has led to much simplification and flattening of both the man and his work. A barrage of biographies, movies, and television documentaries perpetuate the tough-talking, hard-drinking Hemingway while relegating his troubles, his weaknesses, and his revolutionary art, which is the reason we remember him in the first place, to silence.[7] Like nothing else, the posthumously published *The Garden of Eden*, with its gender crossovers, has led to a more thoughtful evaluation of Hemingway's work, which is as complex and transgressive as were Oak Park, his parents' lifestyles, and his own conflicted self. After *The Garden of Eden*, we could see more clearly that these complexities had lurked in much of the earlier work. Nothing was as smooth as it seemed; there were no answers, no consistency, no monolithic persona or reading, no code hero that reappeared in book after book. Hemingway warned us, "never think one story represents my viewpoint because it is much too complicated for that" (qtd. in Baker, 337), and one of his biographers said much the same thing about him: "Anything you can say about him, you can also say almost the opposite" (Reynolds, qtd. in Delling, 22).

Hemingway's narratives questioned, smudged, and even worked to erase the distinctions between masculine and feminine, ideals and reality, individual and society, private and public, the center and the periphery, facts and fictions. Such narratives naturally give rise to critical controversy: almost every one of his war narratives has been read as being both pro-war and anti-war; different critics, looking at the same female character, have read her as strong and as weak; the same male character has been seen as exemplifying and subverting stereotypical masculinity, or as a powerful insider and a weak outsider; women have been found to exemplify the characteristics frequently attributed to the male code hero; his most important Jewish character has been read both as despicable and as a center of value; and so on, in an increasingly sophisticated discussion of basic issues like gender, power, nationality, and identity. Over the years, critics have helped us recognize that Hemingway's work, from beginning to end, has been courageously complex, resisting classification, recognizing and questioning boundaries.

*Death in the Afternoon* is a confusingly transgressive book, for it blurs the distinctions between genres. Hemingway had actually been doing that all along, though never as blatantly. In 1916 and 1917 he published two essays and two poems in his high school newspaper, *Trapeze*, and four more poems and three short stories in the school's literary magazine, *Tabula*.[8] This early writing is curiously intertwined: the poetry was based on current events, as if it were journalism; the fiction was historically and autobiographically informed, as if it were nonfiction; and the journalistic reports were exaggerated, dramatized, and generally enlivened by humor and imagination. As Elizabeth Dewberry notes, "there is evidence that moving among journalism, creative nonfiction, and fiction [Dewberry fails to mention poetry] stimulated all his writing, that his work in each genre informed and enriched his experience in the others. [. . .] [T]hroughout his career Hemingway tends to blur distinctions between fiction and nonfiction as well as between the concrete and imagined realities they purport to represent" (16). Even for the young Hemingway, genre, style, and content were not necessarily or exclusively linked: any subject could be treated in any way, using a mix of facts and fictions, techniques and styles. We can see here, in his high school production, the generic iconoclasm that blossomed so richly in *Death in the Afternoon*.

After graduating high school, Hemingway worked as a cub reporter for the *Kansas City Star*, whose style sheet he found so congenial that he would apply its journalistic strictures — short sentences, clear language — to his long and short fiction. He also wrote articles for *The Cooperative Commonwealth: The Weekly Magazine of Mutual Help*,[9] but a more important connection was *The Toronto Star Weekly* and its companion publication, *The Toronto Daily Star*, for which he wrote journalistic articles and feature stories from 1920 until 1924. Some of them were autobiographical, some political, but all reflected his opinions, wit, and tendency to dramatize and fictionalize himself (sometimes as "I" and sometimes as "we") and to construct a fictional "you" that invites his reader to identify with him. These techniques are visible, for example, in an article whose subject (German inflation) and place of publication (a daily newspaper) suggest that it will be a fact-filled analysis of the contemporary economic situation, and not the engaging, dramatic presentation of human interaction that it actually is. In fact, Hemingway transferred the situation and phrasing of some of his *Toronto Daily Star* articles into his fictions: parts of "A Silent, Ghastly Procession" (20 October 1922) and "Refugees from Thrace" (14 November 1922) reappear in "On the Quai at Smyrna," the opening short story of *In Our Time* (1930), and some of the descriptions and definitions of bullfighting that appear in "Bullfighting a Tragedy" (20 October 1923) and "Pamplona in July" (27 October 1923) will sound familiar to readers of *The Sun Also Rises* (1926).

*The Toronto Daily Star* seems to have been as tolerant of Hemingway's generic crossovers as Oak Park's *Trapeze* and *Tabula*. In addition to publishing Hemingway's fictionalized journalism, the newspaper also published five of his poems.[10] Hemingway published another six poems, grouped together under the title "Wanderings," in *Poetry: A Magazine of Verse* (January 1923), whose editor, Harriet Monroe, described him as "a young Chicago poet now abroad who will soon issue [...] his first book of verse" (qtd. in Gerogiannis, xi). This "first book of verse" was *Three Stories & Ten Poems* (Paris: Contact, 1923), which, as its title announces, also contained short fiction. Paul Smith notes that in the summer of 1923 Hemingway "was [...] placing bets on both genres [fiction and poetry]" (xvi), but in fact he was working with three, for he did not quit *The Toronto Star* until late December 1923.

Even within his fiction, Hemingway rejected the generic distinction between short story and novel. In 1925, when he published the interconnected stories and numbered interchapters of *In Our Time,* he created what D. H. Lawrence termed a "a fragmentary novel" and what Joseph M. Flora defined as a "composite novel."[11] These were not the uncertain crossovers of an artist who had not yet found his niche. As Michael Reynolds has pointed out, "Ernest Hemingway was experimenting with structure, genre, and style [from the beginning] to the very end of his life" ("Ernest Hemingway," 272).

Hemingway's early work dealt with basic contemporary and human problems: war and its psychological aftermath (e.g., "Soldier's Home"), problematic relations between fathers and sons ("Indian Camp"), between same-sex friends ("The Three-Day Blow"), between men and women ("Cat in the Rain"), between the individual and his society, between the old-fashioned and the modern. His themes — lack of communication, isolation, social pressure, the variety of erotic possibilities, the effects of sexuality, couplehood, marriage, and parenthood — were set against the midwestern and Parisian backgrounds that were then meaningful to him. And then, early in 1923, Hemingway found another arena upon which to work out his themes. When Mike Strater, Gertrude Stein, and Alice B. Toklas spoke to him about bullfighting, he immediately recognized its literary possibilities. So strong was its attraction that he wrote "The First Matador Got the Horn," a short piece that was composed in March 1923 and published in April, *before* he saw his first bullfight. The piece reads like an objective, journalistic eyewitness account, but it is a mix of hearsay, imagination, and reading, a crafted exercise in voice and point of view.[12]

Two months after writing this piece, Hemingway went to Spain to see the country and the bullfight for himself. Both captivated him, perhaps because they seemed simpler and more honest than the contradictions and denials that formed his own background. Spain was still very traditional and hierarchical, less industrialized and motorized than the United States, and not traumatized by the First World War or the sexual revolution. And the bullfight is, of course, a powerful spectacle.

Hemingway treated Spain and the bullfight in all the genres he had already practiced. The bullfight appeared in a series of short journalistic essays, three of them published in 1923 ("Bull Fighting Is Not a Sport — It Is a Tragedy," "World's Series of Bull Fighting a Mad, Whirling Carnival," and "Tancredo is Dead"), one in 1924 ("Pamplona Letter"), and a fifth, much longer one appearing in 1930 ("Bullfighting, Sport and Industry"). Five poems about the bullfight also precede *Death in the Afternoon*;[13] the speaker of one of them, "This Poem is by Maera," also appears as a character in an interesting prose piece called "Maera Lay Still" (1923), which graphically described Maera's death (as the result of being gored) before Maera really died (of tuberculosis, in 1924).[14] The bullfight spilled over into Hemingway's fiction, both long and short, from *The Sun Also Rises* through "The Undefeated," "Banal Story," and "The Mother of a Queen."[15] In short, Hemingway wrote a good deal about the bullfight, in several genres and with great inventiveness, before he produced the masterpiece which is *Death in the Afternoon*. Perhaps that is why *Death in the Afternoon* is so powerful and so puzzling: more aggressively and insistently than any of his earlier work, it mixes, blurs, and finally breaks through the limits implicit in concepts like subject, style, genre, experience, research, and invention.[16]

Such a work, identified as nonfiction for lack of a more accurate term, demands at least as much critical attention as has been bestowed upon Hemingway's fiction. A necessary first step is a scholarly edition that takes into account the various stages of writing and revision. Fortunately for us, Hemingway's papers survived his peripatetic life: the holograph manuscripts and the typescripts for *Death in the Afternoon* are available both at the Harry Ransom Humanities Research Center, University of Texas, Austin, and in the Hemingway Collection at the John F. Kennedy Library at Columbia Point (Boston). A set of galleys marked by Hemingway is at the JFK; another marked set (with pencil notations throughout, in an unidentified hand, apparently a transcription of the corrections and revisions Hemingway made on the JFK set) is at the Cohn-Hemingway Papers in Special Collections at the University of Delaware. Several unmarked sets of galleys are also extant.[17]

A scholarly edition would document not only the stages of composition but could also comment on, though not "correct," the book's deviations from fact and standard usage (e.g., giving the wrong name of a town, omitting or misplacing accents, misspellings, inaccuracies of quotation or translation) and indicate at what stage they were introduced — whether in manuscript, typescript, or galleys — and by whom — by writer, typist, reader of typescript, typesetter, copy editor, or any other person involved in the production of this book. As Beegel notes, "The Hemingway manuscripts are full of delectable problems to delight the heart of any documentary editor or textual scholar" ("On Editing Hemingway," 29).

Also desirable, when *Death in the Afternoon* comes into public domain in 2027, would be the addition of hypertextual links to the already available electronic (but read-only) edition (e-book). These links would connect the reader of *Death in the Afternoon* not only to manuscripts and other textual materials but also to the many places, people, events, and arts mentioned in the text. It is difficult to isolate *Death in the Afternoon* from Hemingway's encyclopedic reading, his own experiences in Spain, the archives that hold Hemingway materials, and the many other archives and museums, scattered throughout Spain, which hold journals, newspapers, leaflets, photographs, and the other taurine and political memorabilia that flavored Hemingway's opinions as he prepared to write *Death in the Afternoon*. Other video and audio links could recover "lost" historical information — the things that Hemingway knew and that we, so many decades later, do not — and provide commentary and interpretation in the form of early reviews, bibliographies, interviews, critical articles, and so on.

The critical work that precedes this *Companion* falls into roughly three categories. A handful of critics — Spaniards, Spanish-speakers, Hispanists, and other explicators of Spain, the bullfight, and the bull — focus on the corrida itself.[18] A few other scholars — not enough — have done valuable textual and intertextual work;[19] and recent interest in gender studies, sparked by Mark Spilka, Nancy Comley, Robert Scholes, and others, has attracted two more scholars, Michael Thurston and Thomas Strychacz, to *Death in the Afternoon*. None of this work, important as it is, is reprinted in this *Companion*, because the *Companion* offers only original, previously unpublished work. All twelve essays of this *Companion* engage this earlier work, apply a variety of theoretical models, and offer important new insights.

In the first essay, Robert W. Trogdon carefully traces the book through the various stages of its composition and publication, paying particular attention to the changes made in galley proofs, the critical reception, and the book sales that, although healthy enough, disappointed Hemingway. Trogdon's essay, based on archival materials and on the Hemingway-Perkins correspondence, expands upon and completes the work begun by Robert W. Lewis in 1984.

The next three articles deal with influences and sources that can be detected in *Death in the Afternoon*. Several critics have shown us how crucial Hemingway's reading is to his fiction,[20] but it is equally basic to *Death in the Afternoon*. Lisa Tyler and Linda Wagner-Smith continue the work begun by Gerry Brenner, Nancy Bredendick, and others, to help us understand how Hemingway coded, acknowledged, denied, quoted, paraphrased, translated, mistranslated, and sometimes misrepresented his sources in *Death in the Afternoon*. They discuss not only the presence of two very dissimilar figures (a male nineteenth-century English poet and a female twentieth-century American prose stylist), but also the complicated personal and intertextual politics Hemingway performed as he strove to establish his independence as a man of letters. Tyler recovers the unacknowledged presence of Lord Byron in *Death in the Afternoon,* and Wagner-Martin focuses on Gertrude Stein, who is named in the opening pages of *Death in the Afternoon* but is nameless in the later sections, which attack her. My own bibliographical essay facilitates the search for other sources: its first bibliography lists the many English-language works on Spain and on the bullfight that preceded *Death in the Afternoon,* and its second one identifies Hemingway's voluminous pre-1932 reading, in Spanish and in English, in both these areas.

The next five essays address the unconventional content and form of *Death in the Afternoon*. Two essays deal with cross-cultural matters, an important topic in the work of this very American author who set most of his novels and nonfiction outside the United States. Peter Messent moves the discussion into the theoretical planes of the translation of culture, and Beatriz Penas, a semiotician, reads Hemingway's use of Spanish history, as it is embedded in bullfighting, to critique modern America and as a source of metaphors on modern imagist writing.

Messent and Penas focus mainly on the twenty chapters of *Death in the Afternoon,* but these occupy only 287 of the book's 517 pages. Other sections of the book, largely neglected heretofore, are explored by the next three essays. Anthony Brand offers two approaches to the hundreds of photographs Hemingway collected for *Death in the Afternoon*. His first essay focuses on the organization and significance of the eighty-one photographs that Hemingway finally chose for publication, and the second displays and analyzes thirteen of the unpublished photographs; in a way, these are part of the submerged seven-eighths of that section of the book called "Illustrations." In an equally groundbreaking and very wide-ranging essay, Nancy Bredendick examines the paratexts of *Death in the Afternoon:* the title, the dust jacket, the frontispiece, the dedication, the table of contents, and the postface, or "Bibliographical Note." Bredendick writes out of her broad acquaintance with the bullfight literature that preceded and helped shape *Death in the Afternoon*. As this important section of the *Companion* demonstrates, Hemingway communicated to his readers through every detail — present and absent — of *Death in the Afternoon*.

The *Companion*'s tenth and eleventh essays define the literary and artistic breakthroughs that Hemingway achieved as he explored the problem of producing the desired awareness and responses in his various audiences. Hilary Justice discusses the theoretical issues surrounding authorship, arguing cogently that Hemingway distinguished between the artist working on his art (the writer) and the more compromised figure (the author) that interacts with the public and, in particular, with the critics. Amy Vondrak continues this focus on the audience by examining two modernist artistic techniques, one taken from painting and the other from film, that Hemingway employed in order to create the desired effect on his readers. She thus answers, in part, Reynolds' appeal for an examination of "the intersection between Hemingway's texts with the performing and fine arts," particularly "the influence of motion pictures on his narrative" ("Ernest Hemingway," 279).

In the book's final essay, Keneth Kinnamon reflects upon the influence of *Death in the Afternoon* on subsequent authors who wrote, in English, about the bullfight. In another venue, Kinnamon discussed the influence of *Death in the Afternoon* on Richard Wright's 1957 book, *Pagan Spain*, but for our *Companion* he focuses on Norman Mailer and Barnaby Conrad, whom he identifies as the leading post-Hemingway writers on the bullfight.

These twelve articles not only expand the existing discussions of *Death in the Afternoon*, but testify, in their separate and collective performance, to the rich rewards that a careful examination of Hemingway's nonfiction yields. Two books have dealt with the nonfiction in a general way — Robert O. Stephens' *Hemingway's Non-Fiction: The Public Voice* (1968) and Ronald Weber's *Hemingway's Art of Non-Fiction* (1990) — but this *Companion* is the first book to scrutinize an individual volume of that large body of Hemingway's work. It is an answer to Reynolds' challenge, which I quoted at the beginning of this Introduction and which bears repetition: "Hemingway's nonfiction continues to be the most neglected part of his canon" ("Ernest Hemingway," 277).

# Notes

[1] There is also a volume of *Selected Letters,* edited by Carlos Baker; several more volumes of correspondence are being prepared for publication, under the general editorship of Sandra Spanier. Three of the nonfiction books have been annotated: *A Moveable Feast*, by Gerry Brenner; and *Death in the Afternoon* and *The Dangerous Summer*, by Miriam B. Mandel.

[2] The genre issue was raised by contemporary reviewers and later addressed by (among others) Brenner, who argued for Izaak Walton's *The Compleat Angler* as a

source and pattern for *Death in the Afternoon* ("A Compleat Critique," 65–69), and Thurston, who reads *DIA* as "an anatomy, a logical dissection on the order of Nash's *Anatomy of Absurdity* or Lily's *Euphues* or Burton's *Anatomy of Melancholy* [that incorporates] various generic markers and discursive fragments" (47); Thurston finds that the book's "decorative excesses" represent "forcible sodomy and [. . .] moral decadence" (55).

[3] Junkins transcribes parts of chapter 20 of *Death in the Afternoon* "lined as individual poems"; he does the same for sections that Hemingway cut from the manuscript and typescript ("The Poetry of the Twentieth Chapter," 115).

[4] *Death in the Afternoon* suggests, for example, that its narrator saw Joselito perform, but Joselito died in 1920, three years before Hemingway ever saw a bullfight.

[5] The architect Frank Lloyd Wright, Oak Park's "other" famous son, emphasized the hearth, which he saw as a symbol of family life, in several of the houses he designed for Oak Park residents; but then he abandoned his own hearth and family in order to elope with the wife of one of his clients. Reynolds points that "the notable event went unmentioned in the newspaper" (*The Young Hemingway*, 52).

[6] Reynolds writes, "Ernest may have left Oak Park in 1919, but he carried a piece of the village with him always. [. . .] [H]e took with him Oak Park culture and standards, which, for good or ill, had become a part of him" ("Oak Park Before the Great War," 34).

[7] Moddelmogg discusses the public's need for a *macho* Hemingway in her book, *Reading Desire*, particularly 23–57.

[8] These early poems are reprinted in *Ernest Hemingway: Complete Poems* (6–13). The three short stories are "Judgment at Manitou" (February 1916), "A Matter of Colour" (April 1916), and "Sepi Jingan" (November 1916). They have been reprinted in Constance Cappel Montgomery, *Hemingway in Michigan* (Waitsfield: Vermont Crossroads, 1977); in *Ernest Hemingway's Apprenticeship*, ed. Matthew J. Bruccoli (Washington: NCR Microcard Editions, 1971); and in *Hemingway at Oak Park High: The High School Writings of Ernest Hemingway 1916–1917*, ed. Cynthia Maziarka and Donald Vogel (published by Oak Park and River Forest High School, 1993).

[9] *The Cooperative Commonwealth: The Weekly Magazine of Mutual Help* was a publication of The Cooperative Society of America, based in Chicago, a venture that collapsed when its owner was found to have embezzled $15 million (Mandel, *Reading Hemingway*, 58). Hemingway wrote for *The Cooperative Commonwealth* in September and October 1921, the last months of its existence, and was aware of the scandal. The contradiction between the magazine's proclaimed idealism and its owner's corrupt behavior echoed the situation Hemingway had grown up with.

[10] The five poems are: "On Weddynge Gyftes" (as part of an article by the same title), "I Like Americans," "I Like Canadians," "The Big Dance on the Hill," and "The Sport of Kings" (*Complete Poems*, 38, 65, 66–67, 68, 69; see also *Dateline: Toronto*, 84, 370, 377, 414, and 415–16). Hemingway also published a few poems in other venues, like the *Double-Dealer*, in 1922, and *Der Querschnitt*, in 1925.

[11] Lawrence wrote, "*In Our Time* calls itself a book of stories, but it isn't that. It is a series of successive sketches from a man's life, and makes a fragmentary novel" ("*In

*Our Time:* A Review," 19). Flora argues that another one of Hemingway's collections of short stories, *Men Without Women,* is, like *In Our Time,* a "composite novel."

[12] The piece was published by Jane Heap in the *Little Review* in April 1923. Reynolds reports that "Only one of the six pieces [that Jane Heap published] came from his own experience [. . .]. The other five pieces came from friends or out of the newspapers. One of them was Mike Strater's voice telling of a Spanish bullfight where the first two matadors were both gored badly; the last matador, a young kid, had to kill all five bulls. On the fifth bull he kept missing with the sword" (*The Paris Years,* 114). Reynolds dates the composition of the pieces to early March (*An Annotated Chronology,* 31); the pieces were published in April; Hemingway saw his first bullfight on 27 May 1923 (Mandel, "The Birth of Hemingway's *Afición,*" esp. 142–43). The six pieces were incorporated into *In Our Time* (1925 and 1930), with "The first matador got the horn" appearing as Chapter IX.

[13] The five poems were "The Soul of Spain with McAlmon and Bird the Publishers" and "Part Two of the Soul of Spain with McAlmon and Bird the Publishers"; both were composed in 1923 and published *Der Querschnitt* in 1924. "The Poem is by Maera," composed in 1925, was unpublished in Hemingway's lifetime, and two other unpublished poems also mention the bulls: "[Some day when you are picked up . . .]," written in 1924; and "To a Tragic Poetess," composed in 1926. All appear in *Complete Poems,* 70–71, 72–73, 78–79, 75, 87–89.

[14] "Maera lay still" was published as Chapter XIV of *In Our Time.*

[15] Smith dates the composition of "The Mother of a Queen" to 1931–32 (that is, before the publication of *Death in the Afternoon*), but it was not published until October 1933, when it appeared as part of the short story collection *Winner Take Nothing* (*A Reader's Guide,* 264–65).

[16] Hemingway's impulse to blur the boundaries between experience and research, between fact and fiction, and between fiction and nonfiction continued throughout his lifetime. In the 1930s, his experiences and reading about the Spanish Civil War produced journalism, stories, a play, and a novel, all of which bear a strong family resemblance. And the same story about a fisherman who lost his huge fish was published both as a journalistic account (1936) and as a short novel (1952).

[17] One set of unmarked galleys is in the Scribner Archives, at Princeton University; another set, of eighty-eight galleys (chapters 1–20, with a long section marked for deletion in chapter 20), is held by the University of Virginia Library, Special Collections; and the Monroe County Public Library, Key West, claims to have three copies, including duplicate proofs for the author's file; they are probably unmarked.

[18] Bilger's 1955 dissertation was titled "Corrida, Corrida: The Meaning of *Death in the Afternoon,*" and Norris's 1985 book included a chapter on "The Animal and Violence in Hemingway's *Death in the Afternoon.*" Additional information and interpretation has been offered by Broer, Capellán, Castillo-Puche, Josephs, Junkins, and Kinnamon, scholars whose own *afición* occasionally leads them to take an engagingly personal or anecdotal approach. Phillips discussed why Hemingway was attracted to bullfighting and examined the pattern and purity of the bullfight in terms of Hemingway's writing in other areas, like fishing and hunting.

[19] Lewis wrote on "The Making of *Death in the Afternoon*," Junkins explored the poetry in chapter 20, Mandel indexed and annotated *Death in the Afternoon* and *The Dangerous Summer*, and others have done valuable work on a variety of texts: Brenner and Thurston on unacknowledged sixteenth- and seventeenth-century English sources, Bredendick on an early twentieth-century Spanish source, and Comley and Scholes on Hemingway's reference to the contemporary German art critic, Julius Meier-Graefe.

[20] Spilka's fine book, *Hemingway's Quarrel with Androgyny*, discusses, among other things, how Hemingway's parents were influenced by their reading, and how that affected the atmosphere in which Hemingway grew up. Tyler has read *A Farewell to Arms* against *Wuthering Heights*, and Wilkinson discusses *Hemingway and Turgenev: The Nature of Literary Influence*. See also Wagner-Martin's comprehensive essay, "The Intertextual Hemingway," in *A Historical Guide to Ernest Hemingway*. Other critics have traced the settings, characters, and events that appear in his fiction to nonfictional sources: Reynolds, for example, traces sections of *A Farewell to Arms* to the British historian G. M. Trevelyan (*Hemingway's First War*, 107, 142–43). Hemingway also uses, without attribution, Eric Edward Dorman-Smith's conversation about his experiences in the First and Second World Wars, as well as those of other friends, like Charles Lanham. They supplied materials that Hemingway's own limited participation in these two conflicts could not provide.

# Works Cited

Baker, Carlos. *Ernest Hemingway: A Life Story*. New York: Collier / Macmillan, 1969.

Beegel, Susan F. *Hemingway's Craft of Omission: Four Manuscript Examples*. Ann Arbor: UMI Research P, 1988.

———. "On Editing Hemingway Badly or Not at All: Cautionary Reflections." *Documentary Editing* 20.2 (1998): 29–34.

Bilger, Martin. *Corrida, Corrida: The Meaning of "Death in the Afternoon."* DAI 55.07 (1955): 1951A.

Bredendick, Nancy. "*Toros célebres:* Its Meaning in *Death in the Afternoon*." *The Hemingway Review* 17.2 (1998): 64–73.

Brenner, Gerry. "A Compleat Critique: *Death in the Afternoon*." In his *Concealments in Hemingway's Works*. Columbus: Ohio State UP, 1983. 65–80.

———. *A Comprehensive Companion to Hemingway's "A Moveable Feast."* 2 vols. Lewiston, NY: Edward Mellen Press, 2000.

Broer, Lawrence R. *Hemingway's Spanish Tragedy*. University, AL: U of Alabama P, 1973.

Capellán, Angel. *Hemingway and the Hispanic World*. Ann Arbor: UMI Research P, 1977, 1985.

Castillo-Puche, José Luis. *Hemingway: Entre la vida y la muerte.* Barcelona: Ediciones Destino, 1968.

Comley, Nancy R., and Robert Scholes. *Hemingway's Genders: Rereading the Hemingway Text.* New Haven: Yale UP, 1994.

Delling, Dianna. "Michael Reynolds: Getting Hemingway Right" (interview). *Book* (July / August 1999): 21–22.

Dewberry, Elizabeth. "Hemingway's Journalism and the Realist Dilemma." In *The Cambridge Companion to Hemingway.* Ed. Scott Donaldson. Cambridge and New York: Cambridge UP, 1996. 16–35.

Flora, Joseph M. "*Men without Women* as Composite Novel." *North Dakota Quarterly* 68.2–3 (2001): 70–84.

Gerogiannis, Nicholas. "Introduction." *Ernest Hemingway: Complete Poems.* Rev. ed. Lincoln and London: U of Nebraska P, 1992. xi–xxviii.

Grimes, Larry. "Hemingway's Religious Odyssey: The Oak Park Years." In *Ernest Hemingway: The Oak Park Legacy.* Ed. James Nagel. Tuscaloosa: The U of Alabama P, 1996. 37–58.

Hemingway, Ernest. "Bull Fighting Is Not a Sport — It Is a Tragedy." *The Toronto Star Weekly* (20 October 1923). Rpt. in White 340–46.

———. "Bullfighting, Sport and Industry. *Fortune* (March 1930): 83–88, 139, 140, 150.

———. *By-Line: Ernest Hemingway: Selected Articles and Dispatches of Four Decades.* Ed. William White. New York: Scribner's, 1967.

———. *Death in the Afternoon.* New York: Scribner's, 1932.

———. *Ernest Hemingway: Complete Poems.* Rev. ed. Ed. Nicholas Gerogiannis. Lincoln and London: U of Nebraska P, 1992.

———. *Ernest Hemingway: Dateline: Toronto: The Complete "Toronto Star" Dispatches, 1920–1924.* Ed. William White. New York: Scribner's, 1985.

———. "Pamplona Letter." *the transatlantic review* 2.3 (1924): 300–302.

———. "Tancredo is Dead." *The Toronto Star Weekly* (24 November 1923). Rpt. in White 381–83.

———. "World's Series of Bull Fighting a Mad, Whirling Carnival." *The Toronto Star Weekly* (27 October 1923). Rpt. in White 347–54.

Jamison, Kay Redfield. *Touched with Fire: Manic-Depressive Illness and the Artistic Temperament.* New York: Free Press / Simon & Schuster, 1993.

Josephs, Allen. "Beyond *Death in the Afternoon:* A Meditation on Tragedy in the Corrida." *North Dakota Quarterly* 65.3 (1998): 105–19.

———. "*Death in the Afternoon:* A Reconsideration." *The Hemingway Review* 2.1 (1982): 2–16.

---. "La Plaza de Toros: Where Culture and Nature Meet." *North Dakota Quarterly* 64.3 (1997): 60–68.

Junkins, Don. "Hemingway's Old Lady and the Aesthetics of *Pundonor*." *North Dakota Quarterly* 62.2 (1994–95): 195–204.

---. "The Poetry of the Twentieth Chapter of *Death in the Afternoon*: Relationships between the Deleted and Published Halves." In *Hemingway in Italy and Other Essays*. Ed. Robert W. Lewis. New York: Praeger, 1990. 113–21.

Kinnamon, Keneth. "Wright, Hemingway, and the Bullfight: An Aficionado's View." In *Richard Wright's Travel Writings: New Reflections*. Ed. Virginia Whatley Smith. Jackson: UP of Mississippi, 2001. 157–64.

Lawrence, D. H. "*In Our Time*: A Review." 1927; rpt. in *Hemingway: Seven Decades of Criticism*. Ed. Linda Wagner-Martin. East Lansing: Michigan State UP, 1998. 19–20.

Lewis, Robert W. "The Making of *Death in the Afternoon*." In *The Writer in Context*. Ed. James Nagel. Madison: U of Wisconsin P, 1984. 31–52.

Mandel, Miriam B. "The Birth of Hemingway's *Afición*: Madrid and 'The First Bullfight I Ever Saw.'" *Journal of Modern Literature* 23.1 (1999): 127–43.

---. *Hemingway's* Death in the Afternoon: *The Complete Annotations*. Lanham, Maryland, and London: The Scarecrow Press, 2002.

---. "Index to Ernest Hemingway's *Death in the Afternoon*." *Resources for American Literary Study* 23.1 (1997): 86–132.

---. *Reading Hemingway: The Facts in the Fictions*. Metuchen: Scarecrow, 1995.

Moddelmog, Debra A. *Reading Desire: In Pursuit of Ernest Hemingway*. Ithaca and London: Cornell UP, 1999.

Norris, Margot. "The Animal and Violence in Hemingway's *Death in the Afternoon*." In her *Beasts of the Modern Imagination: Darwin, Nietzsche, Kafka, Ernst, & Lawrence*. Baltimore: Johns Hopkins UP, 1985. 195–219.

Phillips, Steven R. "Hemingway and the Bullfight: The Archetypes of Tragedy." *Arizona Quarterly* 29 (1973).

Reynolds, Michael S. "Ernest Hemingway." In *Prospects for the Study of American Literature*. Ed. Richard Kopley. New York: New York UP, 1997. 266–82.

---. *Hemingway: An Annotated Chronology*. Detroit: Omnigraphics, 1991.

---. *Hemingway: The Paris Years*. Cambridge: Basil Blackwell, 1989.

---. *Hemingway's First War: The Making of "A Farewell to Arms."* 1976. New York and Oxford: Basil Blackwell, 1987.

---. "Oak Park Before the Great War." In *Ernest Hemingway: The Oak Park Legacy*. Ed. James Nagel. Tuscaloosa: The U of Alabama P, 1996. 23–36.

———. *The Young Hemingway*. New York: Basil Blackwell, 1986.

Smith, Paul. *A Reader's Guide to the Short Stories of Ernest Hemingway*. Boston: G. K. Hall, 1989.

Spilka, Mark. *Hemingway's Quarrel with Androgyny*. Lincoln: U of Nebraska P, 1990.

Stephens, Robert O. *Hemingway's Non-Fiction: The Public Voice*. Chapel Hill: U of North Carolina P, 1968.

Strychacz, Thomas. "'The Sort of Thing You Should Not Admit': Hemingway's Aesthetics of Emotional Restraint." In *Boys Don't Cry? Rethinking Narratives of Masculinity and Emotion in the U.S.* Ed. Milette Shamir and Jennifer Travis. New York: Columbia UP, 2002. 141–66.

Thurston, Michael. "Genre, Gender, and Truth in *Death in the Afternoon*." *The Hemingway Review* 17.2 (1998): 47–63.

Tyler, Lisa. "Passion and Grief in *A Farewell to Arms:* Ernest Hemingway's Retelling of *Wuthering Heights*." *The Hemingway Review* 15.2 (1995): 79–96.

Wagner-Martin, Linda. "The Intertextual Hemingway." In *A Historical Guide to Ernest Hemingway*. Ed. Linda Wagner-Martin. New York: Oxford UP, 2000. 173–94.

Weber, Ronald. *Hemingway's Art of Non-Fiction*. New York, St. Martin's, 1990.

White, William, ed. *Ernest Hemingway: Dateline: Toronto: The Complete "Toronto Star" Dispatches, 1920–1924*. New York: Scribner's, 1985.

Wilkinson, Myler. *Hemingway and Turgenev: The Nature of Literary Influence*. Ann Arbor: UMI, 1986.

# Composition, Sources, and Backgrounds

# The Composition, Revision, Publication, and Reception of *Death in the Afternoon*

## Robert W. Trogdon

AFTER PUBLISHING *A FAREWELL TO ARMS* IN 1929, Ernest Hemingway turned his attention almost wholly to nonfiction. While he did write several short stories and supervised (to a limited extent) the 1930 republication of *In Our Time*, from 1930 to 1932 his attention and interest were focused almost entirely on the long treatise on bullfighting that would eventually be titled *Death in the Afternoon*. By the time the book was published, however, it had expanded beyond its original focus on bulls and bullfighters: *Death in the Afternoon* was Hemingway's first and most complete essay on art and his first public articulation of his opinions on writers and writing. He worked harder on *Death in the Afternoon* then he had worked or would work on any book published in his lifetime. *Death in the Afternoon*, therefore, deserves special attention for what it shows of Hemingway's views on art as well as what it shows of the way his publisher, Charles Scribner's Sons, handled what was until then an atypical book for one of its star fiction writers to produce.

Writing a guide to bullfighting had been a dream of Hemingway's at least since 1925. In his first letter to Maxwell Perkins (his editor at Scribner's), dated 15 April 1925, Hemingway had written, "I hope some day to have a sort of Doughty's Arabia Deserta of the Bull Ring, a very big book with some wonderful pictures" (qtd. in Bruccoli, 34). His interest was revived in November 1929 when his friend, the poet Archibald MacLeish, asked him to contribute an article on bullfighting as an industry to *Fortune*, a new magazine owned by Henry Luce; MacLeish had taken an editorial job with the business magazine, which agreed to pay Hemingway $1,000 for the 2,500-word article (Baker, 205–6). The article, titled "Bullfighting, Sport and Industry," appeared in the March 1930 issue. Focused almost exclusively on bullfighting as a business, the article addressed the economic plights and rewards for the promoters, bull breeders, and bullfighters, and bore little resemblance to *Death in the Afternoon*.

It is not clear exactly when Hemingway began writing *Death in the Afternoon*. In 1953, he gave his clearest statement about its composition to Charles Poore, reviewer for the *New York Times* and editor of *The Heming-*

*way Reader* (1953): "I wrote Death In The Afternoon in Key West, the ranch near Cooke City, Montana all one summer, Havana, Madrid, Hendaye and Key West. It took about two years. The glossary I remember I wrote at Hendaye. It was a bastard to do" (*Selected Letters,* 799). If Hemingway can be trusted with the facts, late February 1930, after his return to Key West from Paris, was the probable start of the writing of the book.

While Hemingway was writing, Scribner's had acquired the rights to *In Our Time* from Boni & Liveright, the firm that had first published the book in 1925. Perkins's attempts to get Hemingway actively involved in the collection's reissue were met with increasing resistance. He refused to write an introduction for the new edition, suggesting that Edmund Wilson do so instead. His only contributions were to revise "A Very Short Story" (to protect himself from a libel suit), to ask that the version of "Mr. and Mrs. Elliot" that had appeared in *The Little Review* be substituted for the bowdlerized version published by Boni & Liveright, and to submit "On the Quai at Smyrna" as his "Introduction by the Author" (Bruccoli, 144–46). His work for the republication was slight, as "On the Quai at Smyrna" was probably written in the winter of 1926–27 (Smith, 189–90). On 12 August 1930, Hemingway wrote Perkins about these additions to the volume and about his progress on the new book:

> Am going well on the new book — Have something over 40,000 words done — Have worked well 6 days of every week since got here. Have 6 more cases of beer good for 6 more chapters — If I put in an expense account on this bull fight [*sic*] book it would be something for the Accounting Dept to study. (Qtd. in Bruccoli, 146)

Again, Hemingway's first priority was the book in progress, not the reissue of the one he had published five years earlier. On 3 September, he told Perkins that he had done all he would do on the old book because he wanted to concentrate on the bullfight book: "I'm on page 174 of the book I'm writing and have had it knocked out of my head for two days working on this In Our Time again and I've no interest in publishing it now, will take no risks and give no guarantees against libels nor slanders" (qtd. in Bruccoli, 147). Perkins seemed to understand his author's concerns, wiring him on 24 September that proof could be read at Scribner's.[1]

With most of the worries about *In Our Time* out of his way, Hemingway made good progress on *Death in the Afternoon*. On 28 September, he wrote Perkins that he had nearly two hundred pages of manuscript and would probably need to go to Spain the next summer to get the photographs for the book (PUL). One month later, he reported to Perkins, "Am on page 280 on my book. Nearly through. 2 more chapters and the 4 appendice [*sic*] to do at Piggot" (28 October, PUL; underlining in the original).

Hemingway's plans, however, had to be reformulated. On 1 November, Hemingway wrecked his car outside of Billings, Montana. The car's passengers, John Dos Passos and Floyd Allington, were unharmed, but Hemingway had severely broken his right arm. The injury forced him to curtail most of his writing for nearly six months (Baker, 216–21). The book was very nearly finished at the time of the accident, but Hemingway still needed to provide the endings of chapters 2, 7, 8, 17, and 18. He had written only a small portion of chapter 19, and chapter 20 was still unwritten. "A Natural History of the Dead" had not yet been incorporated into the book (Lewis, 34–37), which at this point dealt almost exclusively with bullfighting. It was in the later additions at the ends of the chapters that Hemingway gave his views on writing and aesthetics.

Hemingway wrote Perkins on 28 December, "I'll let you read some of it when you come down to Key West, if you want to, and are a very good boy in the meantime" (PUL). During the first week of March 1931, Perkins made his third trip to Key West, but there is no clear evidence that the still recuperating Hemingway let his editor see any of the work-in-progress. On 27 April, Hemingway wrote Perkins that he had two possible stories for the August issue of *Scribner's Magazine:* "A Sea Change" and "A Natural History of the Dead." The latter story, Hemingway noted, Perkins had read during his visit to Key West (Bruccoli, 155–56). Neither of these stories appeared in the magazine. Hemingway did not relate in any of his subsequent correspondence with Perkins why or when he decided to insert "A Natural History of the Dead" as the conclusion to chapter 12 of *Death in the Afternoon*. In May of 1931, Hemingway departed for Spain to get the photographs and to view the current bullfight season. Before he left, he wrote Perkins that he was having the manuscript typed out and was leaving a carbon copy in Key West. He added that it should be finished by the fall, but he did not like the idea of publishing in the spring of 1932 (PUL).

Throughout the summer and fall of 1931 Hemingway kept Perkins appraised of his progress on the book. From Paris on the first of August, he wrote he would finish the glossary by the end of the week and would then have only two chapters left to write (PUL). After returning to Spain, he cabled that "ALL ILLUSTRATIONS BOOK COMPLETE" (PUL, 14 September, capitals in the original). Back in Kansas City, where Pauline was giving birth to her second son, Gregory, the author reported on 20 October, "Rewriting going excellently and whipping it into shape and cutting out the crap" (PUL). By mid-November, Hemingway wrote more fully about the book and his schedule for completion. He told Perkins that the manuscript was approximately 75,000 words long and included five appendices and a glossary. He then added that he was still working on the last chapter and the translation of the *Reglamento* (the Spanish government's rules that regulate the bullfight).[2] He expected to have typed setting copy ready for Perkins before Christmas and asked if serializing a few chapters in *Scribner's Magazine* would help promote the work (PUL). Hemingway's estimate was off: it would be nearly two months before he got setting copy to Perkins. But with the conclusion of rewriting seemingly so near at hand, Perkins addressed the idea of running some of the book in *Scribner's Magazine.* On 25 November, he wrote his author that he too had considered publishing portions in the firm's magazine and suggested that Hemingway send a copy of the manuscript so that he and Alfred Dashiell (the periodical's editor) could decide what parts to publish (PUL). Perkins may have hoped to duplicate the success of *A Farewell to Arms* by publishing some parts of the new book in the magazine.

Hemingway wrote his editor on 5 and 6 January 1932 to explain his delay in delivering the book. He was beset by problems, from having workmen in the house to a variety of illnesses affecting nearly every member of the household, including himself. Pessimistically, he added that Archibald MacLeish and John Dos Passos could clean up the manuscript "if anything should happen to me" (qtd. in Bruccoli, 157). The next week, on 14 January, he wired Perkins that he had finished his revisions and would send the book at the first of the next week (PUL). The same day Perkins wrote that William Lengle of *Cosmopolitan* was bothering him about the possibility of serializing *Death in the Afternoon* in that periodical (Perkins, 77–78). Hemingway responded on 21 January that he did not want *Cosmopolitan* to have the book. He added that Scribner's was not to use the photo of him with a sick steer in its publicity (PUL).

Perkins wrote on 20 January that the typescript setting copy had arrived (PUL). Perkins apparently could not give it his immediate attention, but did respond more fully five days later:

> I read the book all yesterday — Sunday — and after it I felt good. I went to bed happy for it in spite of innumerable troubles (not so bad really, I guess). The book piles upon you wonderfully, and becomes to one reading it — who at first thinks bull fighting only a very small matter — immensely important.
>
> I'll write you about practical matters. It's silly just to write you that it's a grand book, but it did do me good to read it. That about America, the corn, is utterly right. And I think of corn as in New Jersey in the winter, — the most unlikely time and place for corn. (Qtd. in Bruccoli, 158; underlining in original)

The passage about the corn and America, which originally appeared early in chapter 20, was later cut from *Death in the Afternoon.*[3]

Most of the subsequent correspondence between Hemingway and Perkins dealt with the book's format (the page size of the book, the number of illustrations, and the way in which they would be reproduced),[4] Hemingway's use of obscene words, whether or not to excerpt parts for magazine publication, and whether or not to place it with the Book-of-the-Month Club. Perkins's main concern was the price of the book. As an editorial in the 12 November 1932 issue of *Publishers' Weekly* noted, the Great Depression was affecting book publishing:

> It has been increasingly clear as the fall publishing developed that the list prices of books in non-fiction areas have shown a very marked decrease since a year ago. Publishers, since last spring, have had time to review their programs and to plan their campaigns on lines that include the closest possible economies in all publishing costs in order that their books as they reached the bookseller's counters might show an appreciable decline in list prices. ("Fall Book Prices Are Lower," 1866)

On 5 February, both Perkins and Dashiell wrote Hemingway about another important question: whether or not parts of the book should be run in *Scribner's Magazine*. Perkins did not want to pull out all of the best parts of the book for magazine publication, although he acknowledged that running some articles would "from the commercial standpoint [. . .] help" the book's sales (qtd. in Bruccoli, 159). Dashiell's plan was to run four articles, one each in the May, June, July, and August issues. The first would be part of chapter 2; the second a section from chapter 11 on fighting bulls; the third would be an article on the bullfighters Maera, Gallo, Gitanillo, and Zurito; and the fourth would be an abridgement of chapter 20 (PUL).

The idea of publishing only parts and abridgments of chapters was unacceptable to Hemingway. On 7 February, he wrote Dashiell that the price offered ($2,000 for all four articles) was too low and that he did not like the idea of cutting up chapters to make articles since each chapter was designed to have its own unity (PUL). To Perkins, Hemingway repeated the points he had made to Dashiell, adding "Max you know truly that while I'm often wrong in personal matters I've always been right about the handling of my own stuff — literarily speaking — and I feel awfully strongly about this" (qtd. in Bruccoli, 160). Hemingway's attitude killed the plan. On 15 February, Dashiell wrote the author that while they could probably come to some agreement about the make-up of the articles, the magazine could not pay the $3,600 that Hemingway wanted (PUL).

In February and March, Perkins worked on the format problems and the proofs of the book. The problem, as he explained to Hemingway on 2 February, was that the book needed to be big enough to present the photographs properly, but not too big as to drive up the list price (PUL). By 2 April, Perkins had settled on a page size of 6-3/8 by 9 inches. Perkins also mentioned that placing *Death in the Afternoon* with the Book-of-the-Month Club might bring the book a measure of free publicity, as well as a guaranteed amount of money for the author and the publisher: With business conditions so bad at the time, Perkins thought that the promotion the club could offer and the $14,000 it would pay for the rights (with Hemingway and Scribner's each receiving half) would outweigh the possibility of decreased sales for Scribner's edition (PUL).

Hemingway opposed this plan for several reasons. First, he believed that if Scribner's was guaranteed $7,000 from the Book-of-the-Month Club they would not "make as much of an effort to sell the book in times like these as the writer had to make to write it in the same times." Secondly, he was convinced that the book club would pressure him to cut out obscene words and passages.[5] Near the end of his response to Perkins, he summarized his views:

> If the publishers need a sure 7,000 from that source all right — but I have to see that two things are not imperilled [sic]; the further sale, which helps you as much as it does me, and the integrity of the book which is the most imprtant [sic] thing to me. If anyone so acts as to put themselves out as a book of the month they cannot insist in ramming the good word shit or the sound old word xxxx down the throats of a lot clubwomen but when a book is offered for sale no one has to buy it that does not want to — and I will not have any pressure brought to bear to make me emasculate a book to make anyone seven thousand dollars, myself or anyone else. Understand this is all business not personal. I'm only trying to be as frank as in talking so you will know how I stand and so we won't get in a jam and if I write too strongly or sound too snooty it is because I'm trying to make it frank and honest and clear as possible. So don't let me insult you Max nor find any insults where none is intended but know I am fond of you and that we could not quarrel if we were together and if I'm rude I apologise [sic] sincerely. (Qtd. in Bruccoli, 163–64)

Perkins agreed: "As for the Book Club, we don't like it any more than you do" (qtd. in Bruccoli, 165). The plan was dropped.

Although *Death in the Afternoon* was very heavily revised in galley proofs, Perkins played a very small role in the actual editing. Hemingway revised the proofs in Havana between mid-April and 2 June (Reynolds, *Chronology*, 67). John Dos Passos, who had read some of the typescript and admired it, made several suggestions for editing:

> The Bullfight book — is absolutely the best thing can be done on the subject — I mean all the description and the dope — It seems to me an absolute model for how that sort of thing ought to be done — And all the accounts of individual fighters towns etc, are knockout. I'm only doubtful, like I said, about the parts where Old Hem straps on the longwhite [sic] whiskers and gives the boys the lowdown. I can stand the old lady — but I'm pretty doubtful as to whether the stuff about Waldo Frank (except the line about shooting an owl) is as good as it

ought to be. God knows he ought to be deflated — or at least Virgin Spain — (why not put it on the book basis instead of the entire lecturer?) and that is certainly the place to do it. And then later when you take off the make up and assure the ladies and gents that its [*sic*] really old Uncle Hem after all and give them the low down about writing and why you like to live in Key West etc. I was pretty doubtful — Dont [*sic*] you think that's all secrets of the profession — like plaster of paris in a glove and oughtn't to be spilt to the vulgar? I may be wrong — but the volume is hellishly good. (I'd say way ahead of anything of yours yet) and the language is so magnificently used — (why right there sitting in Bra's boat reading the typewritten pages I kept having the feeling I was reading a classic in the Bohn library like Rabelais or Harvey's Circulation of the Blood or something and that's a hell of a good way to feel about a book not even published yet) that it would be a shame to leave in any unnecessary tripe — damn it I think there's always enough tripe in anything even after you've cut out — and a book like that can stand losing some of the best passages — After all, a book ought to be judged by the author according to the excellence of the stuff cut out. But I may be packed with prunes with all this so for God's sake don't pay too much attention to it — the Books [*sic*] damn swell in any case. (*The Fourteenth Chronicle*, 402–3)

On 26 March, Hemingway answered: "I will work hard on my proofs and try to cut the shit as you say — you were damned good to take so much trouble telling me" (*Selected Letters*, 355). By mid-April he wrote Dos Passos, "Am working hard. Cut a ton of crap a day out of the proofs" (*Selected Letters*, 356).

Dos Passos's contributions to the editing of *Death in the Afternoon* must, however, be evaluated carefully. Dos Passos's suggestions were very tentatively worded. In fact, on 7 June, Dos Passos asked Hemingway to send him, if he could, a set of the galleys: "I'd like to read them over as I didn't read it all in Key West — due to lack of time and want to read it more slowly —" (*The Fourteenth Chronicle*, 410). And, in spite of his initial grateful responses to Dos Passos, Hemingway did not adopt all of his suggestions, and he revised sections on which Dos Passos did not comment at all. In fact, he revised far more extensively than Dos Passos suggested. To say, then, that Dos Passos helped Hemingway revise the book is to overstate the case: Dos Passos made some general suggestions, a few of which Hemingway accepted. On 30 May, Hemingway wrote his friend,

> Have gone over book 7 times and cut out all you objected to (seemed like the best to me God damn you if it really was) cut 4 1/2 galleys of philosophy and telling the boys — cut all the last chapter except the part about Spain — the part saying how it wasn't enough of a book or it would have had these things. That is OK.

> Left Old Lady in and the first crack early in book about Waldo Frank's book — cut all other references to Frank. Believe old Lady stuff O.K. — or at least necessary as seasoning. (*Selected Letters*, 360)

The four and a half galleys cut were part of chapter 20. This cut appears to be what Hemingway thought Dos Passos disliked.

The galley proofs of *Death in the Afternoon* would seem to verify that Hemingway did put in as much work as he told Dos Passos he did. He reworked the book more extensively at this stage than he did any of his previous or subsequent books. His marked galleys show that he made 405 substantive emendations and 461 emendations of punctuation and spelling in the text.[6] His revisions were so extensive that the firm charged him $145.25 for the alterations that had to be made to the type (Bruccoli, 185).[7]

Hemingway received the first nineteen pages of galley proof for *Death in the Afternoon* on 1 April and sent most of them, "revised — cut and corrected," to Perkins on 2 June (qtd. in Bruccoli, 161, 167).[8] These first nineteen galleys correspond to the first three pages of chapter 7 (as printed in the first edition), which introduce the Old lady. Most of the revisions in this batch of proof are small: additions and deletions that tighten the prose or add more specific information and detail for the reader. For example, in galley 12 (*DIA*, chapter 4, 40), Hemingway added the phrase, "there will be a special bus leaving from the Calle Victoria opposite the pasaje alvarez [*sic*]," thus adding important information for anyone using *Death in the Afternoon* as a guidebook to Spain. In galley 14, he adjusted his description of dancing to the Bombilla by adding the following to the end of the sentence: "there in the leafyness of the long plantings of trees where the mist rises from the small river" (48). The revision is minor in the context of the book, but it gives the reader a more specific account of what it is like to be in Spain. Some changes make the prose more accurate and graceful, as when Hemingway changed the phrase, "crowd empties the ring" (galley 18) to "crowd goes from the ring, leaving it empty" (*DIA*, 58).

The most extensive revisions to this first batch of proofs, however, are in the latter part of chapter 5 (galley 16) where Hemingway cut or modified three passages about Waldo Frank, as Dos Passos had suggested. On what became page 52, Hemingway deleted the sentence ridiculing the fact that Frank produced *Virgin Spain* (New York: Boni & Liveright, 1926) less than a year after his first visit to the country. He added to the second sentence (*DIA*, 53) and changed the third from "it was an interesting mechanical experiment if only the vision of those writers had been a little more interesting and developed when say, not so congested" to the more pointed phrasing, "it was an interesting mechanical experiment while it lasted, and full of pretty phallic images drawn in the manner of sentimental valentines, but it would have amounted to more if only the vision of these writers had been a little more interesting and developed when, say, not so congested" (53–54). In spite of his remarks to Dos Passos, Hemingway did not go easier on Frank.

Hemingway made the most extensive revisions in galleys 20 through 84 (the last part of chapter 7 through chapter 20). Many of the emendations add specific detail, as in chapter 8, where Hemingway changed the description of Gitanillo from "had only been a servant to a gypsy family" (galley 23) to "had only worked as a horse-trader for a gypsy family" (*DIA,* 76). Others bring the work up-to-date. On galley 25, for example, Hemingway added a new detail to his description of Valencia II: "a badly sewn wound at the corner of one eye has distorted his face so that he has lost his cockiness" (chapter 9, 84–85). Later in this same chapter (galley 26; *DIA,* 88), he inserted a phrase to describe Niño de la Palma's cowardice ("its fat rumped, prematurely bald from using hair fixatives, prematurely senile form"), which probably reflects his observation of that bullfighter's performances at the 1931 fights in Pamplona (Reynolds, *The 1930s,* 73).

Most of the extensive modifications occur during the "Author and Old Lady" exchanges and at the end of chapters, where Hemingway shifted from descriptions of bullfighting to matters of aesthetics and writing. Some of the emendations add to the humor of passages. In galley 41, for example, in the middle of "A Natural History of the Dead," Hemingway added the following exchange after his witty distortion of Andrew Marvell's "To His Coy Mistress":

I learned to do that by reading T. S. Eliot.

*Old lady:* The Eliots were all old friends of our family. I believe they were in the lumber business.

*Author:* My uncle married a girl whose father was in the lumber business.

*Old lady:* How interesting. (139–40)

This addition, which adds little to the story, serves mainly to present Hemingway's attack on Eliot, and to do so in a humorous way.

The most extensive revisions occur in the last four chapters. The original conclusion of chapter 17 was "Do you want conversation? No. All right, we will let it go to-day." Hemingway replaced this with a three-page typed insert on Goya, Velázquez, and El Greco (203–5). He also inserted the conclusion of chapter 18 (228–31), which deals with the "four new matadors promoted in 1932." These revisions show that Hemingway wanted to create not only an up-to-date history of contemporary bullfighting, but also a work that could be used as a guidebook to the broader culture of Spain.

No part of the book was altered as radically as its last two chapters. The original chapter 20 (galleys 78 through 84) was longer than the final published version. On one set of galleys, Hemingway revised the section dealing with peninsulas and corn that Perkins had admired (galleys 78 and 79), but on another set he gave the instruction to "Omit" this material (both of these sets of galleys are in the John F. Kennedy Library). Some material from the galleys of chapter 20 (the last quarter of galley 81 and the first half of galley 82) was turned into the conclusion of chapter 19. What was eventually printed as chapter 20 consisted of material that was originally galley 80 (excluding only the first six lines), the first three quarters of galley 81, and a three-page typed insert.

Galleys 83 and 84, the original conclusion of *Death in the Afternoon*, move the focus of the book wholly away from bullfighting and Spain towards the craft of writing and Hemingway's views on the profession of authorship. (There are two sets of galleys 83 and 84 — one with Hemingway's corrections, the other set marked "Omit.") In this section, Hemingway claims that writers and painters must leave their native land in order to create their art. Otherwise, the writer becomes merely a local-color writer. The artist creates rather than describes the country, and could do so anywhere. He then states that once a writer has written of something as well as he can, he should not do so again. An author's personal flaws, Hemingway adds, do not matter; he is an honest writer if he does not lie to himself about what or why he writes. In the concluding paragraph of this statement of aesthetic principles, Hemingway explains how the economic aspect of writing traps writers. He claims that while a writer has a right to make a living any way he wants and may be lucky enough to do so through his writing, if he does profit from one book there will be pressure to write another for money in order to maintain his standard of living. When a writer changes any part of his work because of economic pressure, he becomes a commercial writer and ceases to be an artist (galley 84). Hemingway had said as much before, when the subject of selling serial rights to an unfinished novel had been advanced (Bruccoli, 91). He was no doubt also thinking about the implications of the great success of *A Farewell to Arms*. Conventional wisdom would have Hemingway capitalize on this successful novel by writing another, similar novel. But Hemingway the artist balks at the idea of giving the public what it supposedly wanted. In these galleys, the original conclusion of *Death in the Afternoon*, Hemingway shows that he wanted to set the trend in literature and not merely to pander to the public's desires. Exactly why Hemingway deleted this section from the book is not known. Perhaps he was influenced by Dos Passos's remarks, or perhaps he felt that the critics would use this kind of material against him. In a 7 June 1932 letter to Hemingway, Dos Passos worried about Hemingway's cutting this passage, whose removal Dos Passos himself had recommended:

> It sure makes me feel uneasy to hear you've been taking my advice about plucking some of the long white whiskers out of the end of Death in the Afternoon — I may be wrong as Seldes — A funny thing happened about that stuff I've been trying all week to write a preface to the 97 cent edition of "Three Soldiers" — and yesterday found it pouring out in fine shape — What do you think it was on rereading? Your remarks and the stuff about what you'd liked to have put in the book — and about the lit. game almost word for word — shows there must be something in it to have it stick in just a natural born preface —. (*The Fourteenth Chronicle*, 409–10)[9]

On 2 June, Hemingway sent the corrected proof to Perkins, pointing out the changes:

> Have cut a lot of text — With what is gone the book may be less fashionable (all this stating of creeds and principles which does not belong in literature at all by people who have failed in or lost belief in or abandoned writing the minute it got tough to save their bloody souls). But it will be permanent and solid and about what it is about — I will save what I cut and if it proves to be of permanent value you can publish it in my Notebooks —

Hemingway added that he would be sending the estimate of Sidney Franklin and would not include the *Reglamento* since a new one would be out soon. He also included a projected layout for printing some pictures on the same page and addressed the issue of obscene words. He instructed Perkins,

> About 4 letter words — See your lawyers — If you are unwilling to print them entire at least leave 1st and last letters — You say that's legal — I'm the guy who has been the worst emasculated of any in publishing [*sic*] It's up to you to keep out of jail and from being suppressed [*sic*] I write the books — You publish them — But dont [*sic*] get spooked. (Qtd. in Bruccoli, 167–69)

Perkins responded on 11 June, telling Hemingway that it would be fun to publish his notebooks, and reporting on his meeting with the firm's lawyer and what he believed Scribner's could safely do:

> I did what you suggested about the <u>words</u>. I got our lawyer up here and talked to him. He would have infuriated you, and in fact I ended with quite an argument, — but then broke it off because I saw it was foolish. His advice was against the words, of course, and he suggested that "damn" could be used just as well as one of them, and that was where we got into trouble, for I began to try to show him how it couldn't. But further discussion was confined to the legal aspect of the matter which amounts to this: — the words are literally illegal, but much more latitude is now allowed than formerly, and the courts do

not consider the words by themselves, but in their context and in their general intent and bearing on it all. But there is a serious danger, since this is the first time in a book of any consequence in which these words have been printed in full, that Mr. Sumner [secretary of the New York State Society for the Suppression of Vice] or some of these Prohibitionistic people, would make a fight on the matter in order to stop any further progress that way. Lawyers are mighty careful what they say, but I really think he thought that if they did, we could probably win in court, but not until after sales had been held up and publication suspended, etc. His advice was strongly in favor of the omission of the two middle letters, at least. — Even that, he thought would show that an attempt to meet the law had been made, and would be in our favor. You will understand all about it, I guess. I have simply sent back the proof as it was because we can change those few instances in the page proof. So I shall send it to you as it stands, and we can look at it all in final form. There is no doubt that these words do seriously interfere with library sales. But that does not amount to very great numbers. It is a good sale though, and it gives a book a permanence and finality to which this book is entitled. This book is even a reference book. (Qtd. in Bruccoli, 169–70)

This idea was acceptable to Hemingway, who answered, "If you decide to cut out a letter or two to keep inside the law that is your business —" (qtd. in Bruccoli, 172). Hemingway apparently did not make these alterations as they appear only on the marked set of galley proofs in the Cohn Collection. In addition to transferring Hemingway's revisions, this unknown copy editor emended *fuck* and *fucking* to *f—k* and *f—king*. However, the word *shit* was not changed. Despite these emendations, Hemingway was allowed more latitude than he had enjoyed previously. No legal action resulted from the book's publication.

Hemingway must have been feeling very touchy by the end of June, when he received galley proofs for the short sections at the end of the book. He wired Perkins, "DID IT SEEM VERY FUNNY TO SLUG EVERY GALLEY HEMINGWAYS DEATH OR WAS THAT WHAT YOU WANTED HAVE BEEN PLENTY SICK" (qtd. in Bruccoli, 171; capitals in the original). Since all of the galley proofs, most of which Hemingway had revised in April and May, had been similarly slugged, it seems strange that he had just noticed this notation. Perhaps he was just tired of working over the book and used the headline as an excuse to blow off steam. In any event, Perkins wrote him on 7 July to apologize and to say that he would have had the galleys slugged a different way if he had noticed (Bruccoli, 172). In this same letter, Perkins acknowledged receipt of all the page proof and added that he had hoped that Hemingway would have handled Waldo Frank more gently (173). Hemingway noted in his response of 15 July that he had cut all but one reference to

Frank and would cut no more, noting that Perkins had never asked Frank to tone down anything he had written about Hemingway (PUL). Perkins let the remaining reference about Frank stand without further comment.

Hemingway was intensely concerned with the marketing of the book. Rather than merely wanting more and bigger advertisements, he worried that Scribner's claim that the book was about more things than bullfighting would expose to attack. Scribner's first promotion efforts, aimed at booksellers, consisted of the salesman's dummy and the description in the firm's Fall 1932 catalogue. On 28 June, Perkins wired that the booksellers were responding favorably (PUL). The dust jacket illustration for the dummy was Roberto Domingo's *TOROS,* which was retained for the jacket of the trade edition. Four photographs and the first four pages of chapter 1 were reproduced. The actual descriptions of the book's contents were printed on the front and back flaps of the jacket. The back flap copy mainly quoted from the text, specifically Hemingway's account of how he became interested in bullfighting. On the front flap wider claims for the book were made:

> In bringing into focus all that is important and interesting about bullfighting — the bravery and cowardice, the bull, the costume and theatre and personality and craftsmanship and history (all of it beneath the Spanish sun and in the midst of men *consumed with a passion* for bullfighting) — Mr. Hemingway has also brought into focus a great deal that is significant about human living and dying, and about the trade called literature, which attempts to depict human living and dying.
>
> The author has discovered, and put into this book, the profound and subtle reasons why bullfighting is so wonderful to so many men, for so many centuries, why it is so moving and important and exalting. By virtue of an undismayed and undeceived honesty he has been able to see what *actually* happens during moments of overwhelming emotion, when the exact cause of the exaltation is usually unnoticed.
>
> There is much collateral information in this book, about life and letters and what it takes to be an artist — a real one. There are dicta about writing so honest and true they will very likely become common axioms, so vivid and sincere and convincing is their presentation. There are also episodes of gorgeous comedy and satire, deliberately injected into the discussion and description of bullfighting and bullfighters. (Cohn Collection)

A similar presentation of the book was made in the firm's catalogue of its Fall 1932 list. Along with a small reproduction of the book's frontispiece (Juan Gris's *The Bullfighter*), the publisher ran the following description:

> If this were only the first complete book by an American writer about the bullfight, bullfighters, and bulls — as it is, and that American the one who knows more about the subject than any other — it would be

supremely worth reading. But it is very much more than that. Blended into its pages are several short stories, one of them, "The Natural History of Death [*sic*]," among the finest that Hemingway has done: there is a chapter on writing in America that contains the author's literary credo stated fearlessly and with smashing directness: there are gorgeously funny dialogues on divers subjects with a hypothetical old lady whose mind finally becomes so depraved that she is dismissed from the story: and there are resounding pages in which Mr. Hemingway enters the arena of current literature and plunges sharp critical banderillas into the sensitive sides of some of the bulls of American letters. It is lavish with color, wisdom, humor, tragedy, and life.

But primarily "Death in the Afternoon" is about the art of bullfighting — "a decadent art in every way, reaching its fullest flower at its rottenest point, which is the present." Here are described and explained the technic and the emotional appeal of the bullfight, "the emotional and spiritual intensity and pure classic beauty that can be produced by a man, an animal, and a piece of scarlet serge draped on a stick." There are chapters about bullfighters, men who live every day with death — Joselito, "to watch him was like reading about d'Artagnan as a boy"; Maera, who with his wrist dislocated killed a bull "made of cement," and many others are vividly delineated. And there are pages about bulls, whose bravery is the primal root of the bullfight and who when they are really brave are afraid of nothing on earth. There is something interesting and vital on every page of this book — one that every admirer of Hemingway will enjoy to the end. ("*Death in the Afternoon* Sales Description," 6)

Perkins's role in developing advertising copy for *Death in the Afternoon* is not known. However, Scribner's clearly saw Hemingway as a literary artist — a writer of fiction — and its employees were afraid that American readers would not be interested in a technical book about bullfighting; the book, therefore, had to be presented as a discussion of other subjects as well.

Hemingway reacted angrily to this strategy. On 28 June, he wrote his editor to correct the firm's advertising:

> What you will do is get everyone disappointed — I put all that stuff in so that anyone buying the book for no matter what reason would get their money [*sic*] worth — All that story, dialogue, etc is thrown in extra — The book is worth anybodys [*sic*] 3.50 who has 3.50 as a straight book on bull fighting — If you go to advertising [*sic*] that it is so many damned other things all you will do is make people disappointed because it hasnt [*sic*] a cook book and a telephone directory as well.
>
> If you try to sell it as a great classic Goddamned book on bull fighting rather than some fucking miscellany you may be able to sell a few — Let the critics claim it has something additional — But suppose

all chance of that is gone now with that lovely Hauser stuff — If you want to try to find someone to speak well of it ask Dos Passos — [. . .]

If they feel disappointed and still want my "literary Credo" in a book on bull fighting they can run an insert saying "F—ck the whole goddamned lousy racket." (Qtd. in Bruccoli, 171–72)

Hemingway had obviously seen the catalogue copy by this point, as his reference to his "'literary Credo'" makes clear. By 15 July, he had also seen the dust jacket, and he asked Perkins to discontinue making similar claims on the jacket copy since, he claimed, reviewers reviewed the blurbs and he wanted them to read the book (PUL). Nearly a month later, he wrote Perkins that the now revised jacket was "fine" as the revised blurbs "Seem restrained, to make no false promises, and know what the hell it is about." But he added that Scribner's would have to back the book strongly to insure a large sale:

> If you advertise [*sic*] like hell and realize there is a difference between Marcia Davenports [*sic*] Mozart etc (nice though they must be) you can sell plenty. If you got spooked or yellow out on trying to sell them naturally they will flop in these times — You will have to stick with it hard, <u>as though it were selling big</u>, through Christmas no matter <u>how</u> it goes. Like Sun also. Then it will go. It is really a swell book. (Qtd. in Bruccoli, 176; underlining in original)

This was Hemingway's familiar advice when publication of a book was near; Perkins had heard it often before.

Hemingway's instructions must have arrived before copy was ready for Scribner's prepublication advertisements in *Publishers' Weekly*. The firm ran two notices in the trade periodical for *Death in the Afternoon*. The first, in the 10 September 1932 issue, is a one-page spread for Hemingway's book and for James Truslow Adams's *The March of Democracy*. The copy refers only to bullfighting and mentions the many photographs in the book ("Scribner's advertisement," 826). The second advertisement, in the 17 September issue, is part of the firm's two-page announcement for its fall books. The description emphasizes the book's strengths:

> Bullfighting, bulls and bullfighters plus much collateral observation on life and letters. Drama, color, action, humor, *and* 80 amazing pictures. Every Hemingway admirer is a sure sale [. . .] and it will interest a public that his novels hasn't [*sic*] touched. ("Scribner's advertisement," 1007)

However, the statement is vague about the types of "collateral observations" and exactly who the Hemingway admirers are. Although the publisher had an extensive nonfiction list, it seems that they were having a difficult time deciding how to present a work of nonfiction by a writer who was known almost exclusively for his fiction.

*Death in the Afternoon* was published on 23 September 1932 and sold for $3.50. The first printing by the Scribner's Press consisted of 10,300 copies (PUL). The book was widely reviewed. Between the date of publication and June 1933, fourteen reviews appeared in major American newspapers and magazines. Hemingway's scrapbook contains clippings from some sixty-five reviews or notices from American publications (JFK). Most of the major reviewers admired the breadth and detail of the treatise. The reviewer for *Time* called it a "complete, compendious, and appreciative guide" (47). Laurence Stallings, writing in the *New York Sun,* described it as "a superbly colored and capricious essay on human pride" (34). Nearly all the reviewers liked the style; the *Saturday Review of Literature* reviewer, Ben Ray Redman, wrote that the descriptions in the book were "couched in a prose that must be called perfect" (121). Some reviewers, however, such as R. L. Duffus in the *New York Times Book Review* and Curtis Patterson in *Town & Country,* thought the style was too dense and not as good as it had been in Hemingway's previous work. Many reviewers, like *The New Yorker*'s Robert M. Coates, also disparaged Hemingway for his attacks on other writers and for his use of "obscene" language, which was H. L. Mencken's only criticism in his review in the *American Mercury*. The reviews on the whole can be described as good, though not overwhelmingly positive.

Scribner's advertising campaign for the book was extensive, but probably not as extensive as Hemingway would have wanted. In addition to the notices in *Publishers' Weekly,* Scribner's ran prepublication advertisements in *Retail Bookseller* and *Book Dial* — advertisements aimed primarily at booksellers — and in *Scribner's Magazine, The Saturday Review of Literature, The New York Herald,* and *The New York Times* — advertisements aimed primarily at book buyers.[10] The firm bought notices for *Death in the Afternoon* until February 1933, but most of its advertisements ran from September to December of 1932 (only four ran in 1933). In all, Scribner's purchased 178 notices for the book. Most of the ads — seventy-eight — appeared in New York newspapers. Twenty-seven of the advertisements were in book-trade publications. Thirty-one appeared in general circulation magazines like *Harper's Monthly, The Forum,* and *Atlantic Monthly.* The rest appeared in newspapers: thirteen in Boston papers, eight in Philadelphia, nine in Chicago, two in California, and four in Ivy League alumni magazines like the *Princeton Alumni Weekly* and *The Yale Review.* Perhaps because they did not expect large sales, the firm made little effort to promote the book outside the Northeast. The total expenditure for these advertisements was $8,581.14. In contrast, between September 1929 and December 1930, the firm had spent $20,578.17 to promote *A Farewell to Arms.*

Examination of the advertisements for *Death in the Afternoon* does show that Scribner's attempted to push the book but did not have a clear idea of how to do so. From 25 September to 18 December 1932, Scribner's advertised *Death in the Afternoon* every week in the *New York Times Book Review*.[11] In all but four of these notices (23 October–13 November), Hemingway's book had to share the spotlight with other Scribner's books. These advertisements also show a shift in Scribner's strategy. Initially, the firm described the book only as a guide to bullfighting, with quotes from reviewers appearing at the beginning of the advertisement for 9 October. By 13 November, however, Scribner's began describing the book as a "best seller" in "New York Chicago Philadelphia and points West." These claims gave way in December to advertisements that, against Hemingway's wishes, promised a book with many "digressions into literature and life."

These shifts in focus indicate something that the printing records and Perkins's letters bear out: *Death in the Afternoon* was not selling. Scribner's had ordered an initial printing of 10,300 copies. Between September and 1 November, three more printings added 9,780 copies — altogether, 20,080 copies for these four printings. The next, and last, printing for this edition was on 27 August 1934 — seven hundred copies.[12] Two weeks after publication, the sales outlook was good: more than twelve thousand copies had been sold (PUL). The first hint of trouble came on 3 November when Perkins wrote his author that sales had started dropping off two weeks earlier (PUL). Nine days later, Perkins explained more fully what problems the book faced: although sales had been good in cities like New York and Chicago, book buyers in most of the smaller towns and cities were not interested in bullfighting. While this disinterest had also been the initial reaction among the book-buying public in New York and Chicago, Perkins claimed that advertising and reviews had been able to change their minds and promote sales. But since Scribner's did not promote the book as aggressively in other markets, bookstores were not able to sell the book and were returning many copies to the publisher (PUL). The sales situation seemed so hopeless, as Perkins reported to Hemingway on 21 November, that the firm adopted a direct mail campaign, sending two circulars[13] — the first to 161,000 people, the second to 10,000 — in hopes of stirring interest (PUL). This effort seems to have had little effect.

*Death in the Afternoon,* then, had two equally difficult obstacles to overcome: the harsh economic conditions caused by the Great Depression and the indifference of the so-called common reader to bullfighting. This view appeared in a letter to the editor of the *New York Times Book Review* (9 October 1932):

> If we are to believe Mr. Hemingway, high adventure and a lust for blood fuse in the Castilian bullring. One might question wherein a bullfight differs from a dogfight, or a cocking main, or terriers in a rat-pit, or shooting at pigeons from a trap, save, indeed, that a bullfight endangers human life. Certainly there is a mean between baiting the

bull and "bedside mysticisms" as there is between bulldogging and the study of sex eugenics.

But it certainly is a non sequitur to infer that the aficionados at an actual bullfight are more redblooded than the spectators of a moving picture featuring gangster warfare. Both assay as bleacher fans simon pure. Neither play the game; neither are in added fear of, or in increased love with, death by violence. And the theories advanced by Mr. Hemingway as to tauromania simply recall the brainstorms born of the Thaw trial at the beginning of this century.[14]

I have never so much as seen the cover of one of the 2,000-odd Spanish books and pamphlets bearing on the subject, nor, after reading the utter maudlin tosh distilled by Mr. Hemingway, do I desire to do so. My strong impression is that a peerless short-story writer wrote "Death in the Afternoon" purely to put across a sensational book which would find a ready market. (Howard, 25)

The "ready market" was not there. Faced with such resistance, Hemingway could not hope that this work would be as successful as his fiction had been. If all of the 20,780 copies were eventually sold, Hemingway would have made only $10,909.50.[15] This was a respectable amount for 1932, but a far cry from the $47,712.50 that the sale of 101,675 copies of *A Farewell to Arms* had netted Hemingway in 1929.

The final insult came in March of 1933, when the first royalty report for *Death in the Afternoon* was sent to Hemingway. Included in the report was a charge of $145.25 for excess corrections of the galley proofs. Hemingway reacted angrily: he cited the $600 he had spent on photographs and his reasonable requests for advances as proof that he had been fair with the firm (Bruccoli, 185–86). As usual, Perkins gave in to Hemingway's demands, writing his author on 3 April, "I thought that you would not feel that the cost of the corrections was fair, and we shall cancel it. Corrections are frightfully expensive things and really unreasonably so, and due to union charges. They seem particularly hard to bear under present conditions" (PUL).

This essentially marked the end of the story of the publication of Hemingway's first nonfiction book. *Death in the Afternoon,* especially after the great success of *A Farewell to Arms,* must have been a great disappointment to him and Perkins in terms of sales and reception. The public did not want such books from Hemingway. As the 1930s wore on, both Hemingway and Perkins would become convinced that the Hemingway works that sold were fiction — especially novels. But Hemingway would not produce another novel until he had tried his hand at another nonfiction work: *Green Hills of Africa.*

## Notes

[1] Maxwell Perkins to Ernest Hemingway, 24 September 1930, typed cable draft, 1 p., Hemingway Files, Scribner's Archive, Princeton University Library, Princeton, NJ. Other unpublished material from this archive will be cited parenthetically in the text as "PUL."

[2] The translation did not appear in *Death in the Afternoon*. Hemingway may have decided not to finish it, because a new *Reglamento* was about to supersede the one he was translating (see Glossary, s. v. *Reglamento*).

[3] This material is quoted and discussed by Beegel (51–67) and Junkins (113–21).

[4] For a discussion of the layout and use of photographs in *Death in the Afternoon*, see Anthony Brand's essay, "Far from Simple" (pages 165–87 in this volume).

[5] Since the Book-of-the-Month Club shipped books through the mail, they were subject to strict U.S. Postal Service regulation regarding obscene material.

[6] *Death in the Afternoon*, galley proofs (2–117), JFK; the first galley is missing from the JFK set. Another set of marked galleys, in addition to the salesmen's dummy, is held in the Cohn Collection at the University of Delaware, subsequently cited parenthetically in the text as "Cohn Collection." The Cohn set seems to be the one onto which a Scribner's copy editor transferred Hemingway's revisions; it is complete.

[7] Hemingway's contract for *Death in the Afternoon*, dated 20 September 1932, included the following clause: "Expenses incurred for alterations in type or plates, exceeding twenty per cent. of the cost of composition and electrotyping said work, are to be charged to the AUTHOR's account" (PUL; capitals in the original). This clause was standard for all contracts the firm issued at this time.

[8] Although he spent much of those two months fishing for marlin near Havana, Hemingway did spend a great amount of time on the revisions (Reynolds, *The 1930s*, 91–95).

[9] Dos Passos, in his "Introduction" to the Modern Library edition of *Three Soldiers*, addresses the same concerns that Hemingway had in the deleted sections of *Death in the Afternoon*'s twentieth chapter and uses similar language and phrases:

> Making a living by selling daydreams, sensations, packages of mental itching-powders, is all right, but I think few men feel it's much of a life for a healthy adult. You can make money by it, sure, but even without the collapse of capitalism, profit tends to be a wornout motive, tending more and more to strangle on its own power and complexity. No producer of the shoddiest five and ten cent store goods, can do much about money any more; the man who wants to play with the power of money has to go out after it straight, without any other interest. Writing for money is as silly as writing for self-expression. The nineteenth century brought us up to believe in the dollar as an absolute like the law of gravitation. History has riddled money value with a relativity more scary than Einstein's. The pulpwriter of today writes for a meal ticket, not for money. [. . .]

> Well you're a novelist. What of it? What are you doing it for? What excuse have you got for not being ashamed of yourself?
>
> Not that there's any reason, I suppose, for being ashamed of the trade of novelist. A novel is a commodity that fulfills a certain need; people need to buy daydreams like they need to buy icecream or aspirin or gin. They even need to buy a pinch of intellectual catnip now and then to liven up their thoughts, a few drops of poetry to stimulate their feelings. All you need to feel good about your work is to turn out the best commodity you can, play the luxury market and to hell with doubt. (vi, vii)

Whether Hemingway read Dos Passos's preface is not known.

[10] Information on advertisements for *Death in the Afternoon* (price and location of notices) is in the files of the Advertising Department in the Scribner's Archive (PUL).

[11] Advertisements for *Death in the Afternoon* appeared in the following issues of the *New York Times Book Review:* (25 September 1932): 13; (2 October 1932): 16; (9 October 1932): 15; (16 October 1932): 20; (23 October 1932): 19; (30 October 1932): 21; (6 November 1932): 22; (13 November 1932): 24; (20 November 1932): 11; (27 November 1932): 15; (4 December 1932): 13; (11 December 1932): 15; and (18 December 1932): 13.

[12] Printing card for *Death in the Afternoon,* Scribner's Press, 1 p., PUL. The Scribner Press also printed copies for the Halcyon House edition (October 1937) using the same plates.

[13] These circulars have not been located.

[14] In 1906, Harry Thaw shot architect Stanford White, who Thaw believed had had an affair with his wife, former chorus girl Evelyn Nesbit. The press covered the scandal extensively. After two lengthy trials, Thaw was declared sane and set free.

[15] This figure based on Hemingway's royalty rate, as stipulated in the *Death in the Afternoon* contract: 15 percent of list price for the first 25,000 copies, 20 percent for every copy thereafter.

## Works Cited

Baker, Carlos. *Ernest Hemingway: A Life Story.* New York: Scribner's, 1969.

Beegel, Susan F. *Hemingway's Craft of Omission: Four Manuscript Examples.* Ann Arbor: U of Michigan Research P, 1988.

Bruccoli, Matthew J., ed., with the assistance of Robert W. Trogdon. *The Only Thing That Counts: The Ernest Hemingway-Maxwell Perkins Correspondence 1925–1947.* New York: Scribner's, 1996.

Coates, Robert. Rev. of *Death in the Afternoon. The New Yorker* 8 (1 October 1932): 61–63.

"*Death in the Afternoon* sales description." *Scribner's Fall Books 1932.* New York: Scribner's, 1932. 6. Microfilm copy, Collection of Matthew J. Bruccoli, Columbia, SC.

Dos Passos, John. *The Fourteenth Chronicle: Letters and Diaries of John Dos Passos*. Ed. Townsend Ludington. Boston: Gambit, 1973.

———. "Introduction." *Three Soldiers*. New York: Modern Library, 1932. v–ix.

Duffus, R. L. Rev. of *Death in the Afternoon*. *New York Times Book Review* (25 September 1932): 5, 17.

"Fall Book Prices Are Lower." *Publishers' Weekly* 122: 20 (12 November 1932): 1866.

Hemingway, Ernest. *Death in the Afternoon*. New York: Scribner's, 1932.

———. *Ernest Hemingway: Selected Letters: 1917–1961*. Ed. Carlos Baker. New York: Scribner's, 1981.

Howard, A. E. "Ernest Hemingway." *New York Times Book Review* (9 October 1932): 25.

Junkins, Donald. "The Poetry of the Twentieth Chapter of *Death in the Afternoon*." In *Hemingway in Italy and Other Essays*. Ed. Robert W. Lewis. New York: Praeger, 1990. 113–21.

Lewis, Robert W. "The Making of *Death in the Afternoon*." In *Ernest Hemingway: The Writer in Context*. Ed. James Nagel. Madison: U of Wisconsin P, 1984. 31–52.

Mencken, H. L. "The Spanish Idea of a Good Time." Rev. of *Death in the Afternoon*. *American Mercury* 27 (December 1932): 506–7.

Patterson, Curtis. Rev. of *Death in the Afternoon*. *Town & Country* 87 (15 October 1932): 50.

Perkins, Maxwell. *Editor to Author: The Letters of Maxwell E. Perkins*. Selected and edited by John E. Wheelock. New York: Scribner's, 1950.

Redman, Ben Ray. Rev. of *Death in the Afternoon*. *Saturday Review of Literature* 9 (24 September 1932): 121.

Review of *Death in the Afternoon*. *Time* 20 (26 September 1932): 47.

Reynolds, Michael. *Ernest Hemingway: An Annotated Chronology*. Detroit: Manly / Omnigraphics, 1991.

———. *Hemingway: The 1930s*. New York: Norton, 1997.

"Scribner's advertisement." *Publishers' Weekly* 122: 11 (10 September 1932): 826.

"Scribner's advertisement." *Publishers' Weekly* 122: 12 (17 September 1932): 1007.

Smith, Paul. *A Reader's Guide to the Short Stories of Ernest Hemingway*. Boston: G. K. Hall, 1989.

Stallings, Laurence. Rev. of *Death in the Afternoon*. *New York Sun*, 23 September 1932, 34.

# "Devout Again by Cynicism": Lord Byron and *Don Juan* in *Death in the Afternoon*

*Lisa Tyler*

IN THE COURSE OF *Death in the Afternoon*, Ernest Hemingway refers to an astonishing host of writers and their work: Miguel de Cervantes (73), Jean Cocteau (71), T. S. Eliot (139), William Faulkner (173), Ronald Firbank (73), Richard Ford (53), Waldo Frank (53–54), Andre Gide (205), Dashiell Hammett (228), W. H. Hudson (133), Aldous Huxley (190), Henry James (467), Christopher Marlowe (73), Andrew Marvell (139), Guy de Maupassant (102), Mungo Park (134), Raymond Radiguet (71–72), Shakespeare (73, 102), Bishop Stanley (133), Gertrude Stein (1), Stendhal (204), Lope de Vega (73), Gilbert White (133), Walt Whitman (205), John Greenleaf Whittier (133, 144), Oscar Wilde (205), and Virginia Woolf (106). He also alludes obliquely to Alexandre Dumas (212–13), Sigmund Freud (53), O. Henry (182), Henry Wadsworth Longfellow (266), Leo Tolstoy (180), and very likely other writers as well — an impressive tour de force for a writer who also declares, in the course of the same work, that a good writer should not be "anxious to make people see he is formally educated, cultured or well-bred" (*DIA*, 192).

Perhaps most interesting of all, in this extraordinarily allusive work that is about writing as much as it is about bullfighting, is its author's unacknowledged indebtedness to Lord Byron in general and to his masterpiece, *Don Juan*, in particular. Nancy R. Comley and Robert Scholes have argued that in the Meier-Graefe and Huxley passages of *Death in the Afternoon* Hemingway both acknowledged and concealed his sources (116), and Robert Paul Lamb has observed, in reference to Henry James, that Hemingway was "loath to acknowledge any influence (which was his usual response to any writer who had truly mattered in his development)" (477). It does seem that the more Hemingway was indebted to a writer, the more likely he was to obscure his sources — hence, Byron is never explicitly named in *Death in the Afternoon*. But his presence is nevertheless everywhere in this highly personal work. Even in the intertextuality of *Death in the Afternoon*, Hemingway follows Byron, whose "*Don Juan* is marked by a mode of incessant but curiously casual, apparently inconsistent, allusion" (Manning, 201).[1]

Hemingway's lifelong fascination with the life and work of the nineteenth-century British poet began as early as 1914, when fifteen-year-old Ernest memorized Byron's poem "The Destruction of Sennacherib" (which famously begins, "The Assyrian came down like the wolf on the fold") for his Oak Park High School English class (Reynolds, *Hemingway's Reading,* 106). In November 1922, Hemingway visited Lausanne, Switzerland, and toured the Castle of Chillon, including its dungeon where, as Michael Reynolds points out, "the name Byron was carved into the third stone pillar where once Bonivard, the Prisoner of Chillon, was chained" (*Paris Years,* 20). Because Hemingway was still carrying shrapnel in his knee, Peter Griffin reconstructs the visit from that perspective: "Ernest imagined the poet [who had a clubfoot], resting his bad leg on a chair, at work on *The Prisoner of Chillon*" (36–37). In a 1926 letter to Maxwell Perkins, Hemingway mentions Byron in passing as a "great writer about whose life, personal and literary, books have been written" (*Selected Letters,* 209), and Perkins in turn recommends a recently published book, Edward John Trelawny's *The Adventures of a Younger Son,* "for [its] material on Shelley and Byron" (Reynolds, *Hemingway's Reading,* 193).

Before he wrote *Death in the Afternoon,* then, Hemingway was no stranger to books by and about Byron. The inventories of his libraries indicate that he owned the complete works of Byron in several editions, as well an impressive collection of his letters, journals, and diaries, and at least eight volumes of biography: Harold George Nicholson's *Byron, The Last Journey, April 1823–April 1824;* Andre Maurois' *Byron;* Iris Origo's *The Last Attachment;* Peter Quennell's *Byron: The Years of Fame* and *Byron in Italy;* Ethel Colburn Mayne's *Byron* and *The Life of Lady Byron;* and Leslie Marchand's three-volume *Byron: A Biography.*[2]

Well read in Byron's life and work, Hemingway was surely aware that many factors linked him to Byron. Critics have also noted the parallels (one of the earliest was Clifton Fadiman, in his 1933 review of *Death in the Afternoon*), as did biographers (most notably Jeffrey Meyers), creating a wide-ranging list of similarities. Both men, for example, owned boats and loved animals. Both were affected by physical handicaps (Byron's clubfoot and Hemingway's defective vision and war-torn knee), yet both were vigorous, athletic, and given to physical confrontation. Both were good-looking and attractive to women, both became world-famous in their twenties, both rebelled against conventional morality and bourgeois culture, and both left their homelands for adopted nations. Both became disillusioned with war after an initial infatuation with its possibilities for honor and glory, and both wrote about this disillusionment.[3]

Meyers also notes similarities in character and in their personal relationships: "Both had a frank and open character, abused their intimates and quarreled with their friends. Both had devoted servants and cultivated the company of inferiors rather than equals. Both were brilliant talkers as well as attentive listeners" (564). Fadiman, who branded Hemingway "An American Byron," sees in both writers a fascination with sexual transgression. He compares Byron's fascination with incest to Hemingway's with homosexuality (63–64), although the vaguely incestuous quality of Hemingway's then-unwritten short story "The Last Good Country" suggests an even closer parallel.

Michael Reynolds, the most thorough and perceptive of Hemingway's biographers, has suggested that Byron was a personal role model for Hemingway: "From d'Annunzio, T. E. Lawrence of Arabia and Lord Byron, Hemingway gradually developed a public role for the writer in his time: a physical, passionate, active life balanced against the contemplative life while actually writing" (*Young Hemingway*, 211). The biographer Peter Griffin, who consistently blurs the distinction between life and art, elaborates: "Ernest was fascinated by Byron — the handsome, talented aristocrat, irresistible to women, contemptuous of death — and by his poems. Unique in the literature Ernest knew, Byron had portrayed the hero as living just the sort of emotional life Ernest believed his had been" (36–37). Reynolds pointedly notes that Hemingway "did not object" to being called "the American Byron" (*Final Years*, 180),[4] although from the beginning to the end of his career Hemingway consistently and sharply repudiated any suggestion of literary indebtedness, most notably to Sherwood Anderson or Gertrude Stein. That he relished the comparison with Byron is very revealing.

Examining Byron's influence on Hemingway helps us see the importance of Hemingway's reading to his writing and his use of literary sources, an astonishingly underdeveloped area in Hemingway studies. More importantly, it corroborates the work of earlier scholars who have sought to show Hemingway's roots in Romanticism — including Richard K. Peterson's 1969 argument for Hemingway as a Romantic (213–16), Mark Spilka's discussion of Emily Brontë's influence on Hemingway (125–56), my own essay on Brontë and Hemingway (Tyler), and Steven M. Lane's presentations linking Hemingway's writings with the poetry of Wordsworth and Byron. In *Death in the Afternoon*, Hemingway's sensibility and perhaps especially, as Lane observes, his aesthetic are as consistent with Romanticism as with high Modernism.

The Byronic influence has been identified both early and late in Hemingway's career. His first novel, the 1926 *Torrents of Spring*, has been seen as "a prosaic descendant of Byron's *English Bards and Scottish Reviewers*, which could also have been cut to advantage" (Baker, *Writer as Artist*, 39). Reynolds has proposed a passage from Byron's letters as a source for the implausible "fornication in the gondola" in *Across the River and into the Trees* (*Final Years*, 203), a novel in which Hemingway explicitly mentions Byron

(48). Parallels have also been drawn in terms of tone ("Hemingway's irony corresponds to the Byronic irony" [Warren, 51]) and in terms of the so-called Hemingway code: "the character with the code of the tough guy, the initiate, the man cultivating honor, gallantry, and recklessness, represents the Byronic aristocrat" (Warren, 51–52). Or, as Griffin puts it, "The Byronic hero, a born idealist, learns early and through pain that faith in anything or anybody usually ends with betrayal. He survives by force of will and comes 'to love despair'" (36–37). And in fact some of the critical comments regarding Byron's work apply equally well to Hemingway's: "the man who does not permit himself to be deluded, who does not acquiesce in spells and charms and deliriums, suffers like a martyr for his integrity from the pain of encountering a fallen world face on" (Ridenour, 97).

*Death in the Afternoon* might seem an unlikely vehicle for arguing Byron's influence on Hemingway, given that it is an introduction to bullfighting. Yet Byron, who had seen a bullfight in Cadiz (Grosskurth, *Byron*, 89), anticipated Hemingway's subject matter when he depicted a bullfight in *Childe Harold's Pilgrimage* and even commented, as Hemingway was to do more than a century later, on the fate of the horses:

> One gallant steed is stretch'd a mangled corse;
> Another, hideous sight! Unseam'd appears,
> His gory chest unveils life's panting source [. . .] (I.LXXVII).

In his review of *Death in the Afternoon*, Fadiman also saw a kinship between Hemingway's matadors and the princes, giaours, and corsairs that appear in so many of Byron's poems.

But it is *Don Juan* to which *Death in the Afternoon* is more heavily indebted. Byron's epic satire opens with a heartfelt cry for "a hero," discusses the publicity that panders to this need, and refers to the disappointments of "the age" when the much-heralded "hero" fails to deliver:

> I want a hero, an uncommon want,
> When every year and month sends forth a new one,
> Till after cloying the gazettes with cant,
> The age discovers he is not the true one. (I.1.1–4)

Hemingway was keenly aware of the human need for "a hero," and in Spain's taurine public, he saw that need writ large. José Gómez Ortega (Joselito), born and bred to be a bullfighter and arguably the best bullfighter of all times, had been killed in 1920, and in 1923, when Hemingway first came to Spain to see bullfights, the country was still mourning the loss. Its press hailed each promising bullfighter as "the successor to Joselito," the "Messiah of the year" (*DIA*, 166), or the "Redeemer of bullfighting" (74, 166, 167–68). In short, Hemingway echoes Byron's lament: "There are always new phenomenons [read: heroes] in bullfighting. There will be newer ones by the time this book comes out. Watered by publicity they sprout each season on the strength of one good afternoon in Madrid with a bull that was kind to them; but the morning glory is a floral monument of lasting endurance compared to these one-triumph bullfighters" (226).

Other important matters in *Death in the Afternoon* also echo Byron. Hemingway responded to the conservatism of his age, and particularly its hypocrisy about physical pleasures, by foregrounding these pleasures in print — much as Byron did in *Don Juan,* when he wrote, "Let us have wine and woman, mirth and laughter, / Sermons and soda water the day after" and added, "Man being reasonable must get drunk; / The best of life is but intoxication" (II. 178.7–8, 179.1–2). Similarly, Hemingway enthusiastically proclaims in *Death in the Afternoon* that "Wine is one of the most civilized things in the world and one of the natural things of the world that has been brought to the greatest perfection, and it offers a greater range for enjoyment and appreciation than, possibly, any other purely sensory thing which may be purchased" (10).[5]

Both *Don Juan* and *Death in the Afternoon* devote considerable space to the pleasures of sex, and both expand upon the conservatism which leads to censorship in this matter. Certainly Hemingway would have warmed to Byron's character when he read of his upbringing. Because Juan's mother was deeply concerned that "his breeding should be strictly moral" (I.39.4), he had been allowed to read only carefully expurgated versions of the classics. As a consequence, "he was much and deeply read / But not a page of anything that's loose / Or hints continuation of the species / Was ever suffered, lest he should grow vicious" (I.40.4–8). Of course, such extended innocence has the opposite effect. Hemingway comments satirically upon the "citizens who, in college, were great moral influences, but after coming out into the world discovered the joys of immorality [. . .]. They believed this was this great new thing that they had just discovered and were most joyously promiscuous until their first experience with disease" (*DIA,* 101–2). And in the appendix cataloguing some reactions to bullfighting, he carefully notes that "Mrs. S. T.," who had been given a "convent education," is now an "alcoholic nymphomaniac" (498). As Byron puts it, "no branch was made a mystery / To Juan's eyes, excepting natural history" (I.39.7–8), which may have been precisely the reason he developed as he did.

By "natural history," Byron meant, of course, human sexuality, but Hemingway expanded the concept to include, in Huxley's terms, other "Lower Things" (Huxley's phrase is ironically quoted in *DIA,* 190), such as the blown-apart bodies of women, the changes suffered by dead bodies, the indecorous death of victims of Spanish Influenza, and the "highly indecorous" activities involved in procreation (135–39). The catalogue is part of Hemingway's interpolated short story, "A Natural History of the Dead"

(133–44), in which he, too, discourses on material that has been carefully expurgated from the writings of the naturalists popular in his day.

Hemingway shared Byron's anger over the grotesqueries of the battlefield and, like Byron, was unafraid to describe these things in his published work. Byron himself wrote of "The groan, the roll in dust, the all-white eye / Turned back within its socket — these reward / Your rank and file by thousands" (VIII.13.5–7). His description of pointless battlefield mayhem is uncompromising:

> Thus on they wallowed in the bloody mire
> Of dead and dying thousands, sometimes gaining
> A yard or two of ground, which brought them nigher
> To some odd angle for which all were straining;
> At other times, repulsed by the close fire,
> Which really poured as if all hell were raining,
> Instead of heaven, they stumbled backwards o'er
> A wounded comrade, sprawling in his gore. (VIII.20)

Compare that to Hemingway's ironic observation about "a withdrawal having been forced and an advance later made to recover that ground lost so that the positions after the battle were the same as before except for the presence of the dead" (*DIA*, 137), whose decomposing corpses he describes in vivid detail: "in the heat the flesh comes to resemble coal-tar, especially where it has been broken or torn, and it has quite a visible tarlike iridescence" (137).

*Don Juan* offers not only men dying in battle, but several stanzas in which Byron describes in abundant detail how the men on board ship reacted to its imminent sinking:

> Some lashed them in their hammocks; some put on
> Their best clothes, as if going to a fair;
> Some cursed the day on which they saw the sun
> And gnashed their teeth and howling tore their hair;
> And others went on as they had begun,
> Getting the boats out, being well aware
> That a tight boat will live in a rough sea,
> Unless with breakers close beneath her lee. (II.45)⁶

Hemingway offers similarly graphic descriptions of the varied reactions of bullfighters who face a violent and horrible death: he details Gitanillo de Triana's unbearable pain and resulting physical humiliation (*DIA*, 218–20), Maera's fierce denial of his own suffering (79–81), the night terrors of an unnerved former "phenomenon" (226), and the gory disemboweling of José Gómez Ortega (Joselito, 242).

Hemingway also followed Byron's lead in presenting a cynical view of heterosexual romance. Byron sardonically writes of the end of a marriage through death, "Sad thought! to lose the spouse that was adorning / Our days, and put one's servants into mourning" (III.7.7–8). Elsewhere he compares Suwarrow's arrival to a bridal celebration: "The whole camp rung with joy; you would have thought / That they were going to a marriage feast. / (This metaphor, I think, holds good as aught, / Since there is discord after both at least.)" (VII.49.1–4). He concludes that "Love and Marriage rarely can combine" (III.5.3). Less profoundly disillusioned, Hemingway cheerfully suggests that Ronda "is where you should go if you ever go to Spain on a honeymoon or if you ever bolt with any one," adding dryly, "if a honeymoon or an elopement is not a success in Ronda it would be as well to start for Paris and both commence making your own friends" (*DIA*, 42–43). He writes extensively, if euphemistically, of the prevalence of venereal disease among the risk-taking, thrill-seeking bullfighters.

While skeptical about heterosexual romance, both authors are curiously preoccupied with transgressive sexual practices. Byron writes primarily of cross-dressing: first Julia, and then Haidée and Zoe, cover Juan with female clothes, and later Baba orders Juan to dress as a woman in Canto V (73–80) so that he can usher Juan safely in to Gulbeyaz. The Duchess of Fitz-Fulke masquerades as a (ghostly) friar so that she can gain sexual access to Juan. Byron also presents his characters in androgynous terms: Juan is described as "a most beauteous boy" (IX.53.1) with a "half-girlish face" (I.171.8) that is "feminine in feature" (VIII.52.8). Empress Catherine is "handsome" and "fierce" (IX.63.3). Hemingway is not far behind. Performing a certain pass, he writes, the bullfighter's cape "billows out like an apron on a pregnant woman in a breeze" (*DIA* Glossary, s. v. *Delantal*). The matador Juanito Martín Caro (Chiquito de la Audiencia) "has the pretty, pretty look of a young girl" (228; see also 276). Another matador, Manuel Jiménez (Chicuelo), has "the long eyelashes of a girl" (74), and Nicanor Villalta's "voice is a shade high sometimes" (70). Although matadors are "most manly chaps" (70), androgyny surfaces in Hemingway's *Death in the Afternoon* as it does in Byron's *Don Juan*.[7]

Not only androgyny, but homosexuality as well surfaces in the work of these two writers. Byron refers to homosexuality only obliquely, by naming Sappho (II.205.4).[8] Hemingway is able to be much more direct: Chicuelo is depicted as overtly homosexual in "A Lack of Passion," a short story Hemingway alludes to briefly in *Death in the Afternoon* (273). In his Glossary, he defines *Maricón* and points out that "A man who is said to work from the back is a sodomite" (s. v. *Espalda* and *Maricón*). St. Sebastian, he comments, is invariably portrayed as "queer" (204). Hemingway offers the interpolated story of a homosexual rape that results in the victim's apparent conversion to homosexuality, pointedly indicated by the coded reference to his hennaed hair (180–82), and then, in a spectacularly homophobic passage, links the sixteenth-century artist El Greco with the French author André Gide, the turn-of-the-century English author Oscar Wilde, and the American poet Walt Whitman in a sort of parade of gay artists (205). Interestingly, many of those to whom Hemingway alludes throughout *Death in the Afternoon* are writers he knew to be homosexual or bisexual (for example, Christopher Marlowe, Raymond Radiguet, Jean Cocteau, Ronald Firbank, and Gertrude Stein) or writers whom he would probably have considered at least sexually ambiguous (Shakespeare, Virginia Woolf, and Henry James).

For all that they daringly exploited forbidden territory, both Byron and Hemingway acknowledged that in general they were working with traditional subjects rather than wholly original material. Both valued originality and so were sensitive to the challenges posed by canonical literature. For the motto to Cantos I through IV of *Don Juan,* Byron takes a quotation from Horace that translates as "It is hard to treat in your own way what is common" (Byron, 562). Hemingway expresses a parallel awareness of the weight of tradition upon modern performance, be it bullfighting or writing: "The individual, the great artist when he comes, uses everything that has been discovered or known about his art up to that point [. . .] and then the great artist goes beyond what has been done or known and makes something of his own" (*DIA,* 100). Hemingway acknowledged that there were at least "2077 books and pamphlets in Spanish dealing with or touching on tauromaquia, to the authors of all of which the writer of this book wishes to acknowledge his deep indebtedness" (517)[9] and distinguishes his work as the first serious book on the subject in English (4). Treating traditional materials in an original way, as Horace and Byron pointed out, "is hard": it goes much beyond translation. One has to master the tradition but not be overwhelmed by it; one has to "Make it new," to distinguish one's self from it: "I was trying to write then and I found the greatest difficulty, aside from knowing truly what you really felt, rather than what you *were supposed* to feel, and *had been taught* to feel, was to put down what really happened in action; what the actual things were which produced the emotion that you experienced" (2, italics added).

Perhaps what distinguishes both works is their digressive form. The self-conscious narrator of *Don Juan* acknowledges this tendency in himself: "If I have any fault, it is digression, / Leaving my people to proceed alone, / While I soliloquize beyond expression" (III.96.1–4). As he later, more simply, observes, "I rattle on exactly as I'd talk / With anybody in a ride or walk" (XV.19.7–8). Byron has his narrator ingenuously seem to lose track of his own tale, at times: "But to my subject — let me see — what was it" (III.81.5), he muses to himself, acknowledging later, "I meant to make this poem very short / But now I can't tell where it may not run" (XV.22.3–4). Drawing on Aristotelian aesthetic theory, the narrator comically proclaims that "poems must confine / Themselves to unity, like this of mine" (XI.44.7–8).

Aristotelian unity, of course, is the last claim anyone could make for *Don Juan*. It would be similarly difficult to argue for such unity in *Death in the Afternoon*, which besides including text, photographs, a glossary, several appendixes, and a bibliographical note, encompasses much more:

> a word painting, romantic descriptions of landscape; graphic descriptions of natural and unnatural deaths; political commentary; a series of portraits ranging from the affectionate and familial to the harsh and cynical; an extended calendar of events in Spain, France, and Portugal, and most of the countries of Central and South America; a statement of his own literary philosophy; and even an account of what he liked to eat and drink. (Mandel, 89)

The work was so spectacularly *dis*unified that the bewildered reviewer for the London *Times Literary Supplement* "demanded in an angry parenthesis what the literary conversations with the Old [l]ady were 'doing in this galley,' as though they were some sort of printer's error" (Welland, 20).

Both authors indulge in what might be termed metatextual commentary and self-consciously mock their own literary reputations. "I won't describe; description is my forte," the narrator of *Don Juan* blandly tells us (V.52.1). "What we want in a book by this citizen is people talking; that is all he knows how to do and now he doesn't do it," writes Hemingway (*DIA*, 120). The narrator of *Don Juan* also mentions his "conversational facility" (XV.20.3), and it is true that both works are written in an informal, conversational tone.

Both authors vigorously attacked contemporary writers they viewed as inferior. Their attacks seem particularly petty in hindsight, given their own prominence and the relative obscurity of some of their targets. That's not true, of course, of William Wordsworth, whom Byron describes as "unintelligible" (I.90.8), later complaining, "Wordsworth's last quarto, by the way, is bigger / Than any since the birthday of typography — / A drowsy frowzy poem called *The Excursion,* / Writ in a manner which is my aversion" (III.94.5–8). Attacks on other writers often took on strong overtones of sexual inadequacy. In fact, Byron's "Dedication" was originally suppressed because its content was considered too inflammatory. In its third stanza, Byron criticized Britain's then poet laureate, Robert Southey, who ironically is now best known as the author of *Goldilocks and the Three Bears*, for what Byron saw as his overweening arrogance:

> You, Bob, are rather insolent, you know,
> At being disappointed in your wish
> To supersede all warblers here below,
> And be the only blackbird in the dish,

> And then you overstrain yourself, or so,
> And tumble downward like the flying fish
> Gasping on deck, because you soar too high, Bob
> And fall for lack of moisture quite a dry Bob.

The editors of the Penguin edition of *Don Juan* helpfully explain the sexual *double entendre* that closes the stanza:

> The pun on "Bob" associated Robert Southey's name with the meaning of "dry bob" in Regency slang: coition without emission [Marchand, 2: 763 n.]. Byron scorned in Southey the self-contradiction of a straining pretentiousness that produced only lifelessness. (Byron, 565n)

Hemingway similarly attacked earlier as well as contemporary writers, and he also adopted Byron's practice of linking his rivals' bad writing to their sexual habits and orientations. In *Death in the Afternoon*, he attacked the openly homosexual writer Ronald Firbank by suggesting that his subject matter was limited — he "was, let us say, a specialist" (73) — by his sexual orientation. Like Byron's attack on Southey, Hemingway's attack on the now-forgotten Waldo Frank also seems excessive in hindsight. But Frank was much admired in Hemingway's day, and Hemingway expected that his own book would be compared unfavorably to *Virgin Spain*. And so he writes disparagingly of what he called Frank's "bedside mysticism" and develops a facetious theory of what he calls "erectile writing" in which he blames the book's aesthetic failures on the author's sexual congestion. And he attacked his most serious competition, William Faulkner, for both his productivity and his sexual subject matter (173; see also 179).

Such attacks on fellow authors are, of course, defensive maneuvers. Both Byron and Hemingway were defensive in face of expected or imagined rejection by their readers, whom both authors constructed as being more conservative than they are. In an example of what Peter Manning calls "Byron's deference to the sham purity of his audience" (208), Byron's narrator tries to preempt criticism:

> If any person should presume to assert
> This story is not moral, first, I pray,
> That they will not cry out before they're hurt,
> Then that they'll read it o'er again and say
> (But doubtless nobody will be so pert)
> That this is not a moral tale, though gay.
> Besides, in canto twelfth, I mean to show
> The very place where wicked people go. (*Don Juan*, I.207)

In the poem's fourth canto, the narrator complains that he might have described Juan's resistance to temptation in greater detail, but "several people take exception / At the first two books having too much truth" and in a typically irreverent biblical allusion, quotes his publisher as saying, "Through needle's eyes it easier for the camel is / To pass than those two cantos into families" (IV.97.7–8). In the seventh canto, the narrator is shocked (*shocked!*) into incoherence by the indignant response of his readers: "They accuse me — me — the present writer of / The present poem of — I know not what — A tendency to underrate and scoff / At human power and virtue and all that" (VII.3.1–4).

Hemingway, too, fully expected his audience to condemn his work as immoral — hence his pre-emptive attack on the critics who pillory living writers (like himself) while aggrandizing dead ones (like Byron), who used some of the same language, themes, and techniques for which Hemingway expected to be attacked — and suggested that "a serious book on such an unmoral subject may have some value," elaborating:

> So far, about morals, I know only that what is moral is what you feel good after and what is immoral is what you feel bad after and judged by these moral standards, which I do not defend, the bullfight is very moral to me because I feel very fine while it is going on and have a feeling of life and death and mortality and immortality, and after it is over I feel very sad but very fine. (*DIA*, 4)

Both men defend their work chiefly on the grounds that it accurately represents their world. "I sketch your world exactly as it goes," the narrator of *Don Juan* defiantly tells his scandalized readers (VIII.89.8). As Steven M. Lane observes, "Like so many of the Romantic poets, Hemingway insisted on 'the truth,' even if it was unfashionable or unconventional or offensive."

Both writers expressed disgust with the erosion of words' meanings. Byron refers cynically to "groves, so called as being void of trees"; "prospects named / Mount Pleasant, as containing nought to please / Nor much to climb"; and "'Rows' most modestly called 'Paradise', / Which Eve might quit without much sacrifice" (XI.21.1–4, 7–8). In turn, Hemingway's narrator tells the Old lady, "all our words from loose using have lost their edge" (71). Ironically, Hemingway arguably perpetrates this sin himself, saying of the Café Fornos that "there is no wholesomer place in the Peninsula," only to declare four lines later that the "Fornos is a café frequented only by people connected with the bullfights and by whores" (64).

There is a final resemblance between the structures of the two works. Manning believes that "A complete vision of Juan's life is never given, and this is not merely a function of the poem's unfinished state," attributing it instead to "the Romantic mode of imitating the fullness of experience by a suggestive rather than summary close" (221). Its unfinished state recalls the many Romantic poems that, although apparently finished to the author's satisfaction, are nevertheless deliberately styled as "fragments." Similarly,

Hemingway's catalogue of what his book could *not* contain suggests that the fullness of his experience in Spain cannot be captured in any book, no matter how expertly written. Chapter 20 laments his so-called failure to write "enough of a book" and thus suggests that *Death in the Afternoon*, like *Don Juan* before it, should be styled a fragment.[10]

Clearly Hemingway was attracted to Byron's lifestyle and to his poetry, but perhaps he was also drawn to that excessive moodiness and volatility which both men shared and which would now probably be diagnosed as bipolar affective disorder (more familiarly known as manic depression). In *Touched with Fire: Manic-Depressive Illness and the Artistic Temperament*, Kay Redfield Jamison (a scientific researcher who herself has battled this mental illness) devotes a chapter of more than forty pages to Byron (149–90) and later spends a couple of pages on Hemingway, whose history is better known (228–30). It is almost certainly not coincidental that Byron was haunted by the suicide of his grandfather (much as Hemingway was tormented by his own father's suicide) and believed he had inherited a predisposition toward melancholia (or what we would call depression), mental instability, and suicidal tendencies (Jamison, 159–60). Yet both writers created great art despite their battles with manic depression. Perhaps because the disease was not diagnosed or acknowledged, difficult mood shifts which affect an artist's life, his performance, or even his ability to perform, are discussed in veiled terms. Hemingway writes of the spirituality of the young matadors he has met:

> At the start of their careers all are as devoutly ritual as altar boys serving a high mass and some always remain so. Others are as cynical as night club proprietors. The devout ones are killed more frequently. The cynical ones are the best companions. But the best of all are the cynical ones when they are still devout; or after; when having been devout, then cynical, they become devout again by cynicism. (59)

It is easy to imagine that in writing that passage Hemingway might well have had in mind a personal hero, a thirty-six year-old man who had experienced enough to make any man cynical (including childhood sexual molestation, incest, and adultery, not to mention homosexuality at a time when it was considered both a sin and a crime), yet who maintained sufficient idealism, or devoutness, to volunteer to support Greece in its fight for freedom. It's almost impossible not to share Hemingway's admiration and respect for a man who could parody the Ten Commandments in one stanza (I.205) and a few stanzas later write nostalgically and with evident sincerity of "The love of higher things and better days, / The unbounded hope and heavenly ignorance / Of what is called the world and the world's ways" (XVI.108.1–3). Hemingway, who risked his life and reputation to publicly oppose fascism during the Spanish Civil War, would surely have known what Byron meant.

## Notes

[1] In *Don Juan* Byron mentions three literary passages that are among Hemingway's favorite quotes. He alludes to the preacher's assertion in Ecclesiastes that all is vanity (VII.6.1), which Hemingway used as an epigraph to *The Sun Also Rises*. In writing "'tis true that man can only die once" (II.39.7), Byron alludes to a line from Act III, Scene 2 of Shakespeare's *Henry IV, Part II* that turns up in "The Short Happy Life of Francis Macomber" as well as in Hemingway's introduction to *Men at War*. And Byron refers to "that rather somewhat misty bourn, / Which Hamlet tells us is a pass of dread" (VIII.41.3–4); Hemingway considered titling his Spanish Civil War novel *The Undiscovered Country* in an allusion to a later line in that same Shakespearean passage (Baker, *Life*, 348), and Bourne, the last name of David and Catherine in *The Garden of Eden*, is believed to have been inspired by Shakespeare's use of the term.

[2] For more on Hemingway's interest in books by and about Byron, see Reynolds's *Hemingway's Reading* and Brasch and Sigman's *Hemingway's Library*.

[3] See Meyers's *Hemingway: A Biography* and Fadiman's "Ernest Hemingway: An American Byron." Others who have remarked on the correspondences between Hemingway and Byron are Donaldson (3), Stanton (xi), McConnell (195–96, 201–2), and Bloom (4–5). In *Hemingway in Germany*, Wayne E. Kvam adds Teutonic critics Gotthilf Dierlamm and Adalbert Schmidt to the long and distinguished list (22, 87).

[4] Not just Hemingway's life but his phrasing as well can be compared to Byron's. The blurb Hemingway wrote for the cover of *Men without Women* — "The softening feminine influence is absent — either through training, discipline, death, or situation" (qtd. in Lynn, 369) — is indebted to a phrase taken from Byron's letters: "There is something to me very softening in the presence of a woman, — some strange influence, even if one is not in love with them, — which I cannot at all account for, having no very high opinion of the sex. But yet — I always feel in better humour with myself and every thing else, if there is a woman within ken" (*BLJ*, 3: 246). While these blurbs were sometimes drafted by Scribner's publicists, it seems unlikely this one was, since it appears in Hemingway's 14 February 1927 letter to Maxwell Perkins outlining the writer's proposed plans for *Men without Women* (*Selected Letters*, 245).

[5] Hemingway expands upon the interdependent pleasures of food and drink in the Glossary, s. v. *Cerveza* and *Mariscos*.

[6] As the narrator later points out, storms frighten seamen: "They vow to amend their lives, and yet they don't / Because if drowned, they can't — if spared, they won't" (V.6.7–8). The passage's cynical depiction of human nature is neatly echoed in Chapter VII in Hemingway's *In Our Time*, where a soldier promises Jesus "If you'll only keep me from getting killed I'll do anything you say. I believe in you and I'll tell every one in the world that you are the only one that matters." After he survives the war, however, "he never told anybody."

[7] Comley and Scholes also discuss the themes of androgyny and homosexuality in *Death in the Afternoon* (118 ff.).

[8] Byron's interest in cross-dressing presumably stems from his own apparent bisexuality, which has been examined at greatest length in Louis Crompton's *Byron and Greek Love*. Interestingly, Crompton points out that in *Sexual Inversion* Havelock Ellis suggested that Byron's feelings for some of the men in his life may have been homosexual; Hemingway was reading another book by Ellis as early as 1920 (Lynn, 114), corresponded with Hadley about Ellis's *Psychology of Sex* early in 1922 (Diliberto, 54–55), and might well have read *Sexual Inversion* as well. Both Andre Maurois and Peter Quennell, whose biographies of Byron Hemingway owned, acknowledged Byron's bisexuality, so it is likely Hemingway was aware that there was at least speculation about the issue. Hemingway's own interest in cross-dressing and androgyny is perhaps owing to his mother's dressing him in girl's clothes until he was five, long past the age when most boys of his generation would have switched from dresses to short pants (Lynn, 38–42).

[9] Nancy Bredendick discusses Hemingway's indebtedness to his Spanish sources in "*Toros célebres:* Its Meaning in *Death in the Afternoon*" (*Hemingway Review* 17.2 [1998]: 64–77) and in her article in this volume, see pages 222–23.

[10] He makes a similar point with respect to Goya's paintings (*DIA*, 205).

# Works Cited

Baker, Carlos. *Ernest Hemingway: A Life Story.* New York: Scribner's, 1969.

———. *Hemingway: The Writer as Artist.* 3rd ed. Princeton, New Jersey: Princeton UP, 1963.

Bloom, Harold. "Introduction." In *Ernest Hemingway.* Ed. Harold Bloom. New York: Chelsea House, 1985. 1–5.

Brasch, James D., and Joseph Sigman. *Hemingway's Library: A Composite Record.* New York: Garland, 1981.

Byron, George Gordon, Lord. "Childe Harold's Pilgrimage." In *The Complete Poetical Works of Lord Byron.* Ed. Paul Elmer More. Boston: Houghton Mifflin, 1905. 1–83.

———. *Don Juan.* Eds. T. G. Steffan, E. Steffan, and W. W. Pratt. New York: Penguin, 1987.

Comley, Nancy R., and Robert Scholes. *Hemingway's Genders: Rereading the Hemingway Text.* New Haven: Yale UP, 1994.

Crompton, Louis. *Byron and Greek Love: Homophobia in 19th-Century England.* Berkeley: U of California P, 1985.

Diliberto, Gioia. *Hadley.* New York: Ticknor & Fields, 1992.

Donaldson, Scott. *By Force of Will: The Life and Art of Ernest Hemingway.* New York: Viking, 1977.

Fadiman, Clifton. "Ernest Hemingway: An American Byron." *The Nation* 136 (18 January 1933): 63–64. Rpt. in *Ernest Hemingway: The Critical Reception*. Ed. Robert O. Stephens. New York: Burt Franklin, 1977. 124–28.

Griffin, Peter. *Less Than a Treason: Hemingway in Paris*. New York: Oxford UP, 1990.

Grosskurth, Phyllis. *Byron: The Flawed Angel*. Boston: Houghton Mifflin, 1997.

Hemingway, Ernest. *Across the River and into the Trees*. New York: Scribner's, 1950.

———. *Death in the Afternoon*. New York: Scribner's, 1932.

———. *Ernest Hemingway: Selected Letters, 1917–1961*. Ed. Carlos Baker. New York: Scribner's, 1981.

Jamison, Kay Redfield. *Touched with Fire: Manic-Depressive Illness and the Artistic Temperament*. New York: Free Press, 1994.

Kvam, Wayne E. *Hemingway in Germany: The Fiction, the Legend, and the Critics*. Athens, Ohio: Ohio UP, 1973.

Lamb, Robert Paul. "Hemingway and the Creation of Twentieth-Century Dialogue." *Twentieth Century Literature* 42 (1996): 453–80.

Lane, Steven M. "Child Hemingway's Pilgrimage: Byron, Hemingway, and Authority." Paper presented at the International Hemingway Society. Bimini, the Bahamas. 3–9 Jan. 2000. http://www.mala.bc.ca/~lanes/english/hemngway/ehbyron.htm.

———. "A River Runs Through It: Recollection, Return, and Renovation in Hemingway's *In Our Time* and Wordsworth's *Prelude*." Paper presented at the International Hemingway Society. Sun Valley, Idaho. 20–27 July 1996. http://www.mala.bc.ca/~lanes/river.htm.

Lynn, Kenneth S. *Hemingway*. New York: Simon and Schuster, 1987.

Mandel, Miriam B. "Index to Ernest Hemingway's *Death in the Afternoon*." *Resources for American Literary Study* 23.1 (1997): 86–132.

Manning, Peter J. *Byron and His Fictions*. Detroit: Wayne State UP, 1978.

McConnell, Frank. "Stalking Papa's Ghost: Hemingway's Presence in Contemporary American Writing." In *Ernest Hemingway: New Critical Essays*. Ed. A. Robert Lee. Totowa, New Jersey: Barnes & Noble, 1983. 193–211.

Meyers, Jeffrey. *Hemingway: A Biography*. New York: Harper & Row, 1985.

Peterson, Richard K. *Hemingway: Direct and Oblique*. Paris: Mouton, 1969.

Plimpton, George. "The Art of Fiction: Ernest Hemingway." *Paris Review* 5 (1958): 60–89. Rpt. in *Conversations with Ernest Hemingway*. Ed. Matthew J. Bruccoli. Jackson: UP of Mississippi, 1986. 109–29.

Reynolds, Michael. *Hemingway: The Final Years*. New York: Norton, 1999.

———. *Hemingway: The Paris Years*. Cambridge, Massachusetts: Basil Blackwell, 1989.

———. *Hemingway's Reading 1910–1940: An Inventory*. Princeton: Princeton UP, 1981.

———. *The Young Hemingway*. New York: Basil Blackwell, 1986.

Ridenour, George M. *The Style of Don Juan*. New Haven: Yale UP, 1960.

Spilka, Mark. *Hemingway's Quarrel with Androgyny*. Lincoln: U of Nebraska P, 1990.

Stanton, Edward F. *Hemingway and Spain: A Pursuit*. Seattle: U of Washington P, 1989.

Tyler, Lisa. "Passion and Grief in *A Farewell to Arms:* Ernest Hemingway's Retelling of *Wuthering Heights*." *The Hemingway Review* 14.2 (1995): 79–96.

Warren, Robert Penn. "Ernest Hemingway." In *Ernest Hemingway*. Ed. Harold Bloom. New York: Chelsea House, 1985. 35–62.

Welland, D. S. R. "Hemingway's Reputation in England." In *The Literary Reputation of Hemingway in Europe*. Ed. Roger Asselineau. New York: New York UP, 1965. 9–38.

Wolfson, Susan J. "'Their She Condition': Cross-Dressing and the Politics of Gender in *Don Juan*." *ELH* 54 (1987): 586–617. Rpt. in *Romantic Poetry: Recent Revisionary Criticism*. Eds. Karl Kroeber and Gene W. Ruoff. New Brunswick, NJ: Rutgers UP, 1993. 267–89.

# "I like you less and less":
# The Stein Subtext in *Death in the Afternoon*

## Linda Wagner-Martin

IT IS NO COINCIDENCE THAT Gertrude Stein makes her appearance on the first page of Hemingway's treatise about the bullfights, their rituals, and their matadors. Had it not been for Stein, Hemingway might never have gone to Pamplona at all; might never have invested the Spanish art (and, by extension, the Spanish and Catholic cultures) with the kind of high seriousness he gave them. But in the manner that came to be typical of Ernest Hemingway, the very fact that he owed Stein some thanks for this introduction to the art of bullfighting made her suspect.[1] Throughout *Death in the Afternoon,* the author-as-character shows his antipathy toward the Old lady figure who, without much of a stretch, seems to be a surrogate Gertrude. In the author-persona's use of references, names, sexual innuendoes, and comments about writing, he establishes a covert text about Stein's friends, aesthetic principles, and personal mannerisms.

Hemingway's homage to bullfighting had begun, of course, with several columns he had written for the *Toronto Star*.[2] In limning the exotic — the places and scenes beyond the headily familiar aspects of postwar Paris — he drew on both his coverage of the Turkish War (and on his other European and Continental travels) and on his own leisure time activities: fishing, drinking in the cafés, skiing, and, most exotic of all, going to bullfights. As a journalist, Hemingway knew that writing about different experiences was a way to insure some publication. If those experiences were new or obscure enough, writing about them was also a way to avoid correction or contradiction.

It also seemed as if Hemingway moved under a neon sign that flashed whenever he was occupied in ways that would have most disturbed his mother, the ever-proper Grace Hall-Hemingway of Oak Park, Illinois. Going to the bullfights would have been high on her list of disreputable pastimes. We know that drinking fell into that category too, and we can imagine where Hemingway would have assumed that Grace would have listed his and Hadley's experimental lovemaking. Once Grace had moved her older son out of the family cottage,[3] a year before he married Hadley Richardson, much of his physical and psychic behavior was aimed at getting back at his mother, at instructing her about activities she could not presume to understand. Part of Hemingway's real problem in relating to the usually benevolent Gertrude Stein, who certainly cared about his talents as writer as well as his bonhomie as young American husband and friend, was that she uncannily resembled Grace Hall-Hemingway. Both women were sure of themselves, with a certainty that bordered on the egotistic; both were full bosomed and imperious in appearance; and both were given to conveying instructions that might well be taken to be orders.[4]

There is another layer to Hemingway's treatment of the Stein figure in *Death in the Afternoon:* the presence of Stein's 1922 book, *Geography and Plays.* This book collects much of the writing — in portraits, poems, and the markedly short dramas — which Stein had done since her first books were published. Her first published work, *Three Lives* (1909), had marked the end of her realistic mode, although she used some of the same stylistic insistence in *The Making of Americans* (written during 1910–1912, but not published until 1925).[5] *Tender Buttons,* her three-part poem collection which appeared in 1914, placed Stein with the Dadaist and Surrealist European artists. The rest of her writing had seldom seen publication, partly because of the First World War and partly because few publishers would risk bringing out writing that was so difficult to comprehend. So what appeared within the covers of *Geography and Plays* were Stein's attempts to write about the bullfights, the culture of Spain, the war, her relationship with Alice B. Toklas, and her break with her brother Leo. According to Michael Reynolds, Hemingway read this book, including Sherwood Anderson's introduction, in typescript,[6] and after its publication, he, like the rest of her circle, followed the reviews with interest. It is possible to see Stein's wide-ranging 1922 *Geography and Plays* as a kind of practice text for *Death in the Afternoon.* But by 1931, when he was writing *Death in the Afternoon,* the now arrogant and successful Hemingway had decided that if all Stein really knew about Spain, the bullfights, and war appears in her 1922 volume, then he would show the world that his education had been much more complete than hers, and that he could write about these subjects much better than she.

It is this convoluted relationship between Hemingway as apprentice writer and Stein as published author that makes the insulting repartee between the male author-persona and the unidentified character of "Old lady" credible. Of all the insults possible, calling the doyen of Paris salons "Old lady" was surely the worst. First, "old ladies" are nonentities in culture: they are the maiden aunts, cousins, sisters, women who cannot even support themselves and are stereotypically burdens to their families. No one thinks twice about some old lady, although his use of "lady" rather than "woman" ironically suggests a higher class persona. (Stein was always lecturing Hemingway about what people of a certain class did and knew — we remember that she judged his early story "Up in Michigan" *inaccroachable,* as she did his sometimes coarse language and his heavy drinking.)

To relegate Stein to this feminized and powerless category is an amazing stroke of meanness; it is transgressive of her announced homosexuality — in which role she saw herself as genius and as masculine — and it also emphasized the respective ages of both the mentor, Stein, and her pupil, Hemingway. Even though Stein was nearly fifty when Hemingway met her, she prided herself on her fascination for the young men of her circle, many of whom were half her age. As I have written elsewhere, Stein imagined that she had created for herself the allure of George Sand, and she may also have been imagining for herself a situation like that between the aging Sand and the young and brilliant Frederic Chopin.[7] Stein may have seen herself as a possible courtesan to some men of her circle, and part of Toklas's watchfulness and hostility to several of those men, Hemingway included, may have stemmed from the existence of such an imaginative canvas. Hemingway's rubric, "Old lady," deflates Stein's sense of herself as an attractive, independent figure, whether female or male.[8]

The questions Hemingway assigns to the "Old lady" mark her as someone completely out of her element. They are clearly an insult to Stein, who prided herself on her intellect; after all, she had graduated *magna cum laude* with a B.A. in philosophy and psychology from Radcliffe College. She had been the prize pupil not only of William James but also of Hugo Münsterberg and George Santayana, and she had published two pieces in the *Harvard Psychological Review*. She had also been a valued assistant to Llewellys Barker, who had sponsored her essay and drawings on the development of the human brain after she had left medical school. Hemingway, who had never gone to college, was touchy on the matter of education. Stein's academic qualifications, and particularly her scientific work, aroused his jealousy. Even without a formal degree, he considered himself well trained in the methods of science and saw himself as a naturalist. As Susan Beegel has shown, he often worked from naturalist methodology,[9] as he does throughout *Death in the Afternoon*, and in the short story, "A Natural History of the Dead," an ironic commentary about war which is significantly centered at the heart of this bullfighting project. Stein was a quick study in the academic sense, but so was Hemingway, mastering languages with no formal training, studying economics and politics, and, like Stein, reading at least a book a day. More importantly, during the previous twenty years Stein had become a leading art collector (and writer) on the international scene. In contrast, "Old lady" as Hemingway creates her in *Death in the Afternoon* is scattered, imperceptive, dumb. Her questions (to his always-superior knowledge) mark her as, truly, someone out of her element. She sounds like the stereotypical "old lady" tourist: ignorant of much of what surrounds her and, worse, more interested in the bodies of the young bullfighters than in their consummate art.

But in addition to the sexual innuendoes that run throughout *Death in the Afternoon,* "Old lady" is presented as an object of ridicule because she is so slow to catch on to everything in life that she seems seriously impaired. The Stein character is almost retarded in her behavior, her level of comprehension, and her actions. Once Stein had read Hemingway's *Death in the Afternoon,* there would be no turning back into even a tentative friendship.[10] There is no record of Stein's response to *Death in the Afternoon* if, indeed, she did read it. We know she owned it: Hemingway had sent her a copy in angry answer to her portrait of him as a writer who "looks like a modern" but who "smells of the museums."[11] Hemingway dedicated that gift copy, writing "To Gertrude Stein / from her pal / Ernest Hemingway." But separating the first of those lines from the rest, he added "A Bitch Is a Bitch Is a Bitch Is a Bitch." These words, which appear in a circular pattern, echo Stein's by-then well-known motto, "Rose is a rose is a rose is a rose." Just as Stein's "rose" motif was sexual, appearing throughout her love poems to Alice B. Toklas, so was the two-line quotation Hemingway placed at the bottom of his inscription page: "Before the fruits of marriage came, / marriage came."[12] Whatever meaning those lines from Stein may have had for her and Hemingway, they are certainly sexually suggestive, a combined inquiry into the meaning of the ambiguous word *fruits* (which could refer to intercourse without benefit of wedlock, or, very impolitely, to a gay person) and the word *marriage* (always defined during the 1920s and 1930s as heterosexual). In case any confusion existed about Hemingway's intentions in the text of *Death in the Afternoon,* his inscription made those inordinately plain.

### Stein in the Text of *Death in the Afternoon*

Although the name *Gertrude Stein* appears on the first page of Hemingway's book, she and her companion Alice B. Toklas are never named again. The only other women writers who are named within *Death in the Afternoon* are Mrs. Gaskell (in the Huxley quote) and Virginia Woolf, a key modernist figure with whom Hemingway also had conflicts. But once Hemingway had decided to use the scatological (and very out-of-place) passages of dialogue between the author-persona and the ridiculous "Old lady," the reader is never far from the character of Gertrude Stein. Her contrived presence may not dominate the book, but narratively the interchanges between author-persona and "Old lady" become more interesting than yet another supposedly informed description of this picador or that one. (In point of composition, *Death in the Afternoon* mimics the 1925 book Hemingway might well have learned from, his nasty satire on both Sherwood Anderson and Stein, *The Torrents of Spring,* which was published by Scribner's as a way of breaking Hemingway's contract with Liveright; and it looks ahead to the posthumously published *A Moveable Feast,* another book fueled by the venom of Hemingway's personal hatred.[13])

Innocuously identified as the person who "spoke of her admiration for Joselito" (a bullfighter who will figure prominently in Hemingway's discussion of the art), Stein then becomes the woman showing off her photographs: one of Joselito but another, underscoring Hemingway's objection to Stein's "personal" style, of herself and Toklas "sitting in the first row of the wooden barreras at the bull ring at Valencia with Joselito and his brother Gallo below" (*DIA,* 1–2). What changes the tenor of this descriptive sentence is the fact that Stein and Toklas are clearly just observers, and to make that point, Hemingway's sentence does not end but runs on further, leaving the image of Stein and Toklas as pleasure-seekers and moving abruptly to the figure of Hemingway as war correspondent. The juxtaposition makes the point: it is Hemingway who knows about conflict, war, life. The sentence continues with references to "his brother Gallo below, and I had just come from the Near East, where the Greeks broke the legs of their baggage and transport animals and drove and shoved them off the quay into the shallow water when they abandoned the city of Smyrna, and I remember saying that I did not like the bullfights because of the poor horses" (2). Blended into this strange passage are two elements Stein would have understood clearly. One of her criticisms of Hemingway's writing was that he used the same episodes over and over. She said this first in relation to the several fishing scenes that occurred in his early stories, particularly his use of such detailed scenes in the monumental "Big Two-Hearted River."[14] In the lines quoted here, then, repeated from his news stories and from his 1925 *In Our Time,* is the quai at Smyrna, complete with those maimed animals. Doubly effective as a contrast to the goring the unpadded horses took in the early days of bullfighting is this scene of countless animals being wounded so that they would drown helplessly: the bullfight tragedy seems slight when compared with the unquestioned brutality of war. This segue adds another personal note, because Stein liked to tell about the way she had educated Toklas about bullfighting, since it was Toklas who could not bear to see the horses injured. Hemingway's assumption of this prudish stance mischaracterizes him as the experienced bullfight aficionado, adding irony to the description.

The second paragraph of *Death in the Afternoon,* which runs for two pages in stream-of-consciousness style and becomes a discourse on Hemingway's aesthetic of writing (interwoven with that of Henry James — see comments on "the real thing" — as well as that of Stein), includes many of his often-quoted comments about art, such as "I was trying to learn to write, commencing with the simplest things, and one of the simplest things of all and the most fundamental is violent death" and "the sequence of motion and fact which made the emotion" (*DIA,* 2). That these comments occur in a highly ironic context, spoofing both James and Stein, is seldom mentioned. The fact that Hemingway can write a two-page-long paragraph using only ten sentences seems to be another stylistic tour de force, to which he calls attention by opening the third paragraph with a more precise, Hemingway-like sentence, "So I went to Spain to see bullfights and to try to write about them for myself" (3).

Ironic from the start, then, *Death in the Afternoon* accommodates a number of asides and digressions that any treatise by a natural historian would not allow. Rather, the science of Hemingway's book about Spain is that of the literary critic, a somewhat sly literary critic, and the work rides on currents of emotion and characterization that were established from the beginning. During the next seven or eight paragraphs (which are, again, long and rambling), Hemingway discusses a number of topics that were intellectualized at length during the 1920s: the morality of art, the place of the humanist (a term often capitalized), comments about a culture's "values," the responsibility of the well-educated person, the riddle of "taste," and the best wines (after which digression he comments, "This seems to have gotten away from bullfighting, but the point was that a person with increasing knowledge and sensory education may derive infinite enjoyment from wine" [11]). Setting the tone for elite conversation, then, this opening chapter says almost nothing about bullfighting until the last paragraph, when he quotes from the Spanish and insists, in English, that "The sun is the best bullfighter" (15). This non sequitur completes the mimicry of what erudite, polite conversation at Stein's salon might have sounded like (and recalls in turn how often she used the non sequitur in her writing). The even tone of voice, the assumptions of a great many attitudes, the pronouncements of people who have lived very little (as, for instance, in discussions of war and tragedy) — here Hemingway records his ironic recollections before turning, in chapter 2, to the bullfight. The discourse of *Death in the Afternoon* has already been established as the discourse of pupil to mentor, of Ernest Hemingway to Gertrude Stein.

Although chapters 2 through 6 are about the bullfights, they also include a number of satiric comments: references to "women's" behavior, for example, and a consistent privileging of the author's intimate acquaintance with war, death, suicide (rather than Stein's secondhand information about those topics); commentary about places in Spain which have little reason to be mentioned except that Stein had visited them. But in chapter 7, the whole mood of the idiom changes when the "Old lady" makes her first appearance, appropriately speaking from the back of the room in order to ask questions of the acknowledged expert, the author-persona.

*An old lady in the back of the room:* What is he saying? What is that young man asking?

*Some one near her:* He's asking if any one liked the bullfight.
*Old lady:* Oh, I thought he was asking if any of us wanted to be bullfighters.
Did you like the bullfight, madame?
*Old lady:* I liked it very much.
What did you like about it?
*Old lady:* I liked to see the bulls hit the horses.
Why did you like that?
*Old lady:* It seemed so sort of homey. (*DIA,* 64)

The scene continues, leading to a scatological interchange in which the woman wants to find live bullfighters so that she can enjoy seeing their bodies. She has gone from being a hard-of-hearing and confused tourist to a lascivious predator; the reader is only temporarily diverted by her use of the word *homey,* which suggests that goring animals might be behavior she understands as occurring within her own social circles. What seems most surprising about the critical treatment of interchanges like this, and there are another half-dozen such extended passages in the book, is that the character of Old lady has been accepted — simply — as an interlocutor figure for the Hemingway text.[15]

Other dialogues with Old lady center on discussions of the highly charged term *decadence,* one of the touchstones for Wyndham Lewis's extensive criticism of what he saw as Hemingway's immoral art (52–55), and on the philosophy of using words as words in literature. With overtones of Laura Riding Jackson, as well as Santayana and Stein, Hemingway as author discusses the problems of developing skill in using words rather than using certain words that are said to have significance.[16] In this highly philosophical section, he brings the text back to the sexual by telling the story of Raymond Radiguet, Jean Cocteau's lover who betrayed Cocteau by keeping a woman as his mistress (71–72).[17]

This "dirty" story feeds the notion that our author-persona is a lower-class boor, someone who does not understand what is appropriate for salon conversation. It is not the first sexual gaffe in *Death in the Afternoon*. The author-persona had earlier described Villalta's surprisingly high voice, and had discussed the virility of matadors, in response to Old lady's worry that they might have been "affected with mumps" (94). The long interchange about the mating practices of bulls and cows (one bull to service fifty or more cows [120–22]) takes the Old lady's interest in sheer sexual matters to an absurd point. And Hemingway further insults Stein by praising Ronald Firbank (one of her obscure favorites) as a writer so great he might be said to have inherited the mantles of both Shakespeare and Marlowe (73).[18]

As Hemingway's author-persona weaves more and more information about the bullfights into his text, he continues to rely on commentary that links his information with attitudes that would have been familiar to people who knew Gertrude Stein. The story of Manuel García (Maera), for example, who worked his way up from poverty to become a matador, is given parallels with the narrative of the young American artist of the wrong class — Hemingway[19] — and the parable is intensified because both Maera and Hemingway insist on using crude language. Injured beyond saving, Maera continues to fight, using the unmentionable word to his handlers: "F—k the wrist," Maera said, and later "go f—k yourselves" (80, 81). At the end of a long interchange between Old lady and author, one of the most comic in the book, the author himself is similarly guilty of inappropriate language, when he points out that "it may well be that we are talking horseshit."

*Old lady:* That is an odd term and one I did not encounter in my youth.

*Author:* Madame, we apply the term now to describe unsoundness in an abstract conversation or, indeed, any over-metaphysical tendency in speech.

*Old lady:* I must learn to use these terms correctly. (95)

By this point in the book, the reader accepts the fact that, in Hemingway's view, Old lady has become a docile pupil, ready to learn attentively from anything author-Hemingway cares to say. It must have given Hemingway great satisfaction to have created such a role for Gertrude Stein.

## "A Natural History of the Dead" in *Death in the Afternoon*

As *Death in the Afternoon* progresses, an increasing sexual tension develops between Old lady and the author (the references to Radiguet, Cocteau, and Firbank are important to this strand of insult). In discussions of honor and bravery (in which Hemingway comments on the amount of hair on a brave man's chest), qualities of machismo are contrasted with qualities of true valor. The next several chapters emphasize the difference between genders, first through a disquisition on matadors' sexuality (the number of women they bed, their roles as husbands, and the challenge to Stein that she could never write from a wife's point of view because she would never be a wife) and then through a long comparison of bulls, cows, and steers. That section begins "The fighting bull is to the domestic bull as the wolf is to the dog" (105), and a later reference to Virginia Woolf deepens the pun. In a chapter filled with tales of mad and destructive killer bulls, Hemingway builds to the story that is placed at the exact center of *Death in the Afternoon,* the section that he later published as a separate short story, "A Natural History of the Dead." In *Death in the Afternoon,* however, it is preceded by a cynical discussion about "love" and interrupted, comically and irreverently, by dialogues between the Old lady and author. The chief use of Old lady in this context is as an irritant. "I don't care for the title," she says initially (133). "You wrote about those mules before," she complains, linking this section to the beginning of *Death in the Afternoon* (135).

Because Hemingway had prefaced "A Natural History of the Dead" by saying it would take its place in popular culture as a kind of John Greenleaf Whittier *Snow Bound,* implying a pastiche of sentimental reassurances, Old lady is purposefully antagonistic about his accounts of the carnage of war — among both animals and people (the latter defined, to carry on his gender discourse, as men: "In war the dead are usually the male of the human species" [134]).

Even before the most graphic (if objective) descriptions of the bloated dead bodies on the field of battle, Old lady says abruptly, "This is not amusing" (137). To her interruption, the author replies, "Stop reading it then. Nobody makes you read it. But please stop interrupting" (137). The long description of mutilated and rotting bodies continues, with no comment from Old lady. Perhaps she has stopped listening: what follows is much worse than anything Hemingway had previously written.

The dialogues between Old lady and author disappeared when the story was published separately, and there are several other differences between the two versions. One of the most interesting of these changes occurs during the grim description of death: "most men die like animals, not men," says the narrator of *Death in the Afternoon* (139), and he plays on the word *natural* in a subsequent sentence: "The only natural death I've ever seen, outside of loss of blood, which isn't bad, was death from Spanish influenza. In this you drown in mucus, choking, and how you know the patient's dead is: at the end he shits the bed full" (139). Followed by a highly formal discourse about "decorum" and language choice, the final five words of the sentence have an intensified impact. In the later publication as independent story, the eight words after the colon disappear completely and are replaced with a construction of proper, polite phrasing: "and how you know the patient's dead is: at the end he turns to be a little child again, though with his manly force, and fills the sheets as full as any diaper with one vast, final, yellow cataract that flows and dribbles on after he's gone."[20] "A Natural History of the Dead" ends with another devastating narrative, this one about a military doctor whose brutal treatment of a wounded man is incomprehensible. (It also makes use of six incidences of the "f—k" word, which Hemingway knew offended the entire reading world, not only Gertrude Stein.)

To counter the relentless horror that Hemingway has charted, the dialogue that concludes the section is useful. The irritable Old lady now responds, "Is that the end? I thought you said it was like John Greenleaf Whittier's *Snow Bound.*" The author's reply is "Madame, I'm wrong again. We aim so high and yet we miss the target." Somewhat justifiably, Old lady then says, "You know I like you less and less the more I know you." To which the author ironically replies, "Madame, it is always a mistake to know an author" (144).

The last dialogues between Old lady and author in *Death in the Afternoon* focus on homosexuality, including the story of a young man, corrupted irrevocably by his sexual initiation, even to the point of dying his hair red and joining the homosexual circles in Paris. The most aberrant use of this Old lady-author interchange occurs here. The section begins with a sexual metaphor:

> *Old lady:* I would not say your book is that bad, sir.
> Thank you. You encourage me, but is there nothing I can do to keep your interest from flagging?
> *Old lady:* It does not flag. It is only that I get tired sometimes.
> To give you pleasure then.
> *Old lady:* You give me pleasure.
> Thank you, Madame, but I mean in the way of writing or conversation. (179)

Pleasuring the old woman is an explicitly sexual phrase and combined with the play on "flagging," clearly marks the passage. Again, the Old lady is the one who must be restrained; the author would rather devote their time to "writing or conversation." As the narrative continues (in her tiredness, she wants to hear a simple story), the author-persona gives details with relish of the young homosexual's seduction, including his (overheard) words, "'I didn't know it was that. Oh, I didn't know it was that! I won't! I won't!' followed by what the newspaperman [the witness who told the story to the narrator] described as a despairing scream. He hammered on the wall and the noise ceased, but he could hear one of the friends sobbing" (181). It is the naïve young man who later "hennaed" his hair and became complacent with his life, "wearing well-tailored clothes, looking clean cut as ever" (182).

Before this passage, Hemingway's author-persona adds in a more personal insult by defining *old* as "between forty and fifty" (156; this was Stein's age when she and Hemingway first met). Hemingway ascribes his own failure as a novice bullfighter to being "too old, too heavy and too awkward. Also my figure was the wrong shape, being thick in all the places where it should be lithe" (171). The sensitive Stein, careful to appear taller than she was by sitting in ornate and statuesque chairs, would have quickly recognized this description of her stocky body.

Physical insult coupled with sexual joke makes this section of *Death in the Afternoon* unrelievedly personal. After these passages, however, there is a respite of more than a hundred pages without dialogue. As the author tells the reader, "What about the Old lady? She's gone. We threw her out of the book, finally. A little late you say. Yes, perhaps a little late. What about the horses? They are what people always like to talk about in regards to the bullfight. Has there been enough about the horses? [. . .] Should we try to raise the general tone? What about higher things?" (190).

Hemingway's bitter questions about morality and class — those "higher things" — in some ways testify to the continuing influence of the Old lady, even after the author removed her from the text. The next section of *Death in the Afternoon* returns to the craft of writing, which has always been the subtext of the writer's antagonism toward the Old lady (not a writer, she seldom understands anything about his craft) and here it builds from the author's disagreement with "Mr. Aldous Huxley." In this comparatively long section, discussions of method and style reaffirm the author Hemingway's ability to draw character, to shape dialogue, and to write selectively. His first expression of the now-classic iceberg theory appears in this passage (192), after which *Death in the Afternoon* returns to its announced role of instructing readers about the bullfights. A lengthy section of photographs, a glossary of bullfight terms, an appendix that describes viewers' reactions to the bullfight (and particularly to the goring of the horses), a profile of the American matador Sidney Franklin, a calendar of bullfights throughout the world, and a "Bibliographical Note" complete the book.

### Stein's Writings in the Text of *Death in the Afternoon*

As a number of Hemingway critics have recently pointed out,[21] Hemingway liked to work intertextually, even though he tried to disguise or deny the parent texts for his embroideries and his outright borrowings. In the case of Gertrude Stein's 1922 *Geography and Plays*,[22] he needed less secrecy than usual because the book had sold poorly.[23] Esoteric as Stein's writings were, there were titles that signaled her interest in Spain, bullfights, and war: "I Must Try to Write the History of Belmonte," "In the Grass (On Spain)," "Mallorcan Stories," "Susie Asado," "Tourty or Tourtebattre. A Story of the Great War," "Accents in Alsace," and "Johnny Grey" are the most visible, although works like "Sacred Emily" (usually considered one of Stein's love lyrics) also contain references to war.

One of the most important of Stein's profiles collected in *Geography and Plays,* and the one that relates most directly to the First World War (and consequently to such of Hemingway's writings about the war as "A Natural History of the Dead") is "Johnny Grey."[24] This dialogue of non sequiturs returns repeatedly to the speaker's resentment at the futility of his having ever made plans. War disrupts lives, the portrait insists in this bedside tableau, where whoever speaks with the wounded Johnny Grey reassures, cajoles, orders ("Eat it"). In response, the laconic voice says only "I am not going to talk about it, I am not going to talk about it" (Stein, *Geography,* 167).

The poignancy of the man's refusal — a young man, judging from the effect of the diminutive form of his name — cuts through the trivia imposed by the person, or people, trying to care for him:

> He was so thirsty.
> They asked him.
> Please.

There is the sense early in the nine-page portrait that the caregiver is writing a letter for Johnny Grey, but subsequent sections shatter into single-word lines, which disrupt any sense of traditional meaning (or, perhaps, of a traditional or a womanly response to those wounded in war). For instance,

> He said it.
> It's wonderful.
> Target.
> They don't believe it either.
> Call it.
> That.
> Fat. Cheeks.
> By.
> That.
> Time.
> Drenched.
> By.
> That.
> Time.
> Obligation.
> To sign. [. . .] (170)

The marks of illness and exhaustion, juxtaposed with the "obligation" to join up, suggests the soldier's dilemma: to fight (and probably die) or to disappoint the older generation, which includes parents, friends, and onlookers like Stein and Toklas. The falsity of patriotism that Hemingway wrote about so dramatically in *A Farewell to Arms* is here only fleetingly and fragmentarily suggested.

Still recognizable as "portrait," "Johnny Grey" maintains its ostensible focus. By 1919, the date Stein gives for "Tourty or Tourtebattre" and "Accents in Alsace," her interest had shifted from the war itself to her life, driving the supply Ford (Pauline) for Alice Toklas's work at various of the American Fund for the French Wounded stations (their reason for being in Alsace shortly after the end of the First World War). A strange melange of impressions, the twenty-one parts of "Alsace" — some described as "Act in America" or "Act 425," others as "Scene," "Interlude" or "III" — are barely connected to any war. The closing section, identified by the title "The Watch on the Rhine," combines the exoticism of American men's being abroad with what regularly become Stein's most memorable lines, those having to do with women's physical love. It is from that last passage that Hemingway earlier "borrowed" the line he made famous in "Soldier's Home": "In the photograph the Rhine hardly showed."[25] In Stein's context, the sentence is an ambiguous and clearly unrelated deflection of the sexual; that section opens "Sweeter than water or cream or ice. Sweeter than bells of roses. Sweeter than winter or summer or spring. Sweeter than pretty posies. Sweeter than anything is my queen and loving is her nature." It closes "In the midst of our happiness we were very pleased" (415).

For Hemingway, who took all war and its resultant killing very seriously, Stein's treatment was not only ineffectual, it was immoral. As he wrote a decade later, in his introductory essay to *Men at War* (1942), "I have seen much war in my lifetime and I hate it profoundly." But, he continues, the knowledge of war, and the truths that knowledge mandates, is one reason for living through the experience: "the people always finally know in the end because enough of them have been there" ("Introduction," 20). That is the role of the writer, of course: "A writer's job is to tell the truth. His standard of fidelity to the truth should be so high that his invention, out of his experience, should produce a truer account than anything factual can be" (Introduction, 7).

Hemingway's conviction about the writer's moral responsibility is one of the primary reasons he takes Stein so sternly to task in *Death in the Afternoon*. By 1930, when he began writing the bullfight treatise, he had learned that escaping Stein's influence, or the perception that he remained under her influence, was nearly impossible. His second major novel, *A Farewell to Arms,* was admitted to be a masterpiece. Although it was a love story, it was most definitely a novel about the First World War, and Hemingway aimed for it to become the *Red Badge of Courage* for that conflict, just as Stephen Crane's novel had encapsulated an individual's fear and honor on the field of America's civil conflict. Yet one of the first reviews of *A Farewell to Arms* published in the French press (in October of 1929) was a reprint of Fanny Butcher's *Chicago Tribune* review. It claimed that

> Ernest Hemingway is the direct blossoming of Gertrude Stein's art. Whether he consciously was influenced by her no one, of course, can say. But he does in "A Farewell to Arms," what Gertrude Stein did in "Three Lives," except that he does it in a longer, more complicated medium and with more certain power. There are whole pages in the new book which might have been written by Gertrude Stein herself, ex-

cept that, even in their most tortuous intricacies, the reader is perfectly clear about what Mr. Hemingway is saying and why he is saying it that way. (Qtd. in Reynolds, *The 1930s*, 28)

It had happened throughout his comparatively short career: Hemingway was continuously linked with both Stein and Sherwood Anderson, and the pattern of such linkage had itself become a stereotype. The comparison with Stein struck Hemingway as particularly inept: a woman known for her obscurity, her *un*intelligible narrative, was being held up as *his* teacher. Would critics never stop thinking that repetition (which Stein called "insistence") of any kind marked him as a Stein disciple? Would they continue to limit his poetic passages, those in which the arts of the poem underscored the effects of his deft prose, to some kind of obscure borrowing? Hemingway was sure that his writing was the epitome of clarity, in contrast to her obfuscation. As the author insisted to Old lady in *Death in the Afternoon*, "Be patient, can't you? It's very hard to write like this" (135).

Michael Reynolds has concluded that the Old lady and her dialogues with the author were added to the galley proofs of *Death in the Afternoon*, and so date to 1932 (*The 1930s*, 83–84). Their inclusion adds another three weeks to Hemingway's usual timetable for reading the galleys, and allows John Dos Passos, who was visiting him and Pauline at that time, to read most of the book. Dos Passos's response to Hemingway's creation of the Old lady character was less than enthusiastic. A person who cared about his friends and their writing, "Dos [Passos] has to tell Ernest that the attacks on living people are unnecessary and the philosophizing, at times, tedious" (*The 1930s*, 85)."[26] Perhaps the few changes Hemingway made in answer to his friend's objections saved the book from more savage criticisms: one of the sections Hemingway had at first added to the galley proofs (and then deleted) read, "It takes a long time to be a good whore and receiving visitors is a form of whoring" (qtd. in Reynolds, *The 1930s*, 86). It would have been easier for readers to identify Gertrude Stein as one who received visitors than to recognize her in the ignorant and lustful Old lady of *Death in the Afternoon*.

Within the volume *Geography and Plays*, Hemingway would have also seen, and quite correctly, that Stein was creating the same kind of dismissal for her themes of Spanish life and bullfighting as she had for topics about war, even in her piece on Juan Belmonte. Although Stein called him a man "of talent and plenty" (*Geography*, 71), she is frustratingly vague about Belmonte's status, his wounding (something to do with his foot, she says, or above his foot), and his character. In fact, as the portrait builds to what appears to be its climax, Stein spends most of her attention on the seaweed, and on the iodine it contains, which were used to treat Belmonte's injury. She then concludes the piece with a sentence that appears to dismiss the entities Hemingway finds of crucial importance: "I forget war and fear and courage and dancing" (74). Not surprisingly, Hemingway's last story within "A Natural History of the Dead" borrows the iodine, which the egotistic physician uses to blind the already wounded lieutenant who comes to him for care. Stein's iodine as poultice becomes Hemingway's iodine as weapon, and the analogy works to express what he sees as her excessively personal use of the bullfight — and of everything she writes about — for her self-aggrandizement.

This illustration of what Hemingway refers to as "the personal" foregrounds a great deal of his aesthetic of good writing. His references to Stein's propensity to enjoy what she calls "conversation" — and to judge people on how well they speak in her salon — pepper his commentary. Hemingway's *Death in the Afternoon* is shaped to set Stein's personal involvement, her subjective judgments of people, and her dismissal of many of his touchstone themes against his own hard-won knowledge about both bullfighting and writing. "Prose is architecture, not interior decoration," he contends, "and the Baroque is over. For a writer to put his own intellectual musings, which he might sell for a low price as essays, into the mouths of artificially constructed characters which are more remunerative when issued as people in a novel is good economics, perhaps, but does not make literature. People in a novel, not skillfully constructed *characters*, must be projected from the writer's assimilated experience, from his knowledge, from his head, from his heart and from all there is of him" (*DIA*, 191).

Above all, Hemingway implies, readers had to be able to understand what was being written about. Clarity was the key to meaning, and meaning went before understanding. And in his judgment, Gertrude Stein showed in most of her writing that she had never learned what to Hemingway were the primary, the basic, and the essential principles of modernist art.

# Notes

[1] The incidences of Hemingway's ingratitude and downright spite are legion — for example, his treatment of F. Scott Fitzgerald, Ford Madox Ford, and Gertrude Stein in *A Moveable Feast,* as well as his commentary on both Fitzgerald and John Dos Passos elsewhere. Scott Donaldson has discussed Hemingway's literary jealousy in *Hemingway vs. Fitzgerald* and "Dos and Hem"; see also Susanna Egan, Marc Dolan, and Michael Reynolds.

[2] Besides the three columns in the *Toronto Star Weekly* for 1923, Hemingway wrote about bullfighting in his 1926 novel, *The Sun Also Rises,* in "Pamplona Letter" (*transatlantic review,* 1924), and in "Bullfighting, Sport and Industry" (*Fortune,* March 1930); and see Robert O. Stephens, throughout.

[3] Westbrook discusses the involvement of both of Hemingway's parents in this much-written-about event (19–40).

[4] Wagner-Martin, "*Favored Strangers,*" 168–78.

[5] Enthusiastic about Stein's writing, and prompted by the good reviews of the 1922 *Geography and Plays,* Hemingway carefully typed out segments from her manuscript of *The Making of Americans* and urged Ford to publish them in *transatlantic review* (for payment). This exposure led to the work's publication as a whole. For reviews, see Ray Lewis White.

[6] Reynolds, *Hemingway's Reading,* 187. Reynolds also found evidence that Hemingway may have read *Three Lives* "as early as 1920" although he borrowed the book (again?) from Sylvia Beach in 1929; from Beach he borrowed Stein's *Composition as Explanation* in November of 1926, the month it was published, and returned it in late February, 1927; and he owned a signed copy of "Portrait of Mabel Dodge at the Villa Curona" and number 117 of 200 numbered copies of Stein's 1926 *Descriptions of Literature* (*Hemingway's Reading,* 187–88).

[7] See Wagner-Martin, "*Favored Strangers,*" 163–65. See also Daniel, 16–18; and Imbs, *passim.*

[8] Hemingway's penchant for naming characters to give them layered and often private meanings was by this time well-established — the name of "Jacob Barnes" in *The Sun Also Rises* suggests Hemingway is responding to Virginia Woolf's war novel, *Jacob's Room* (Wagner-Martin, "Intertextual," 186); the various levels of "Nick Adams," related to Henry Adams, among others; and the Frederic of Frederic Henry (a combination of Adams — representing the intellectual — and Chopin — representing the sensual) in *A Farewell to Arms.* "Frederic Henry" may also refer to Flaubert's Frédéric Moreau, in *L'Education Sentimentale* (Mandel, *Reading Hemingway,* 487). The name "Frederic" in each case is spelled without a *k*.

[9] Beegel remarks upon his rigorous training in the Agassiz method at the hands of his father and of his high school teachers (67–71).

[10] Wagner-Martin, "Racial and Sexual Coding in *The Sun Also Rises,*" 39–41.

[11] Stein, *The Autobiography of Alice B. Toklas,* 873. As Reynolds notes: "smarting from Gertrude Stein's portrait of him in *The Autobiography* [. . .], Hemingway had threatened to set the record straight with his own memoirs" (*The Final Years,* 46).

[12] Hemingway's inscription is in the copy of *Death in the Afternoon* held by the Lilly Library, Indiana University, Bloomington; Hobhouse says that Hemingway sent Stein the copy in retaliation for her *Autobiography of Alice B. Toklas* (167).

[13] In the case of *The Torrents of Spring,* the friend Pauline Pfeiffer rather than the wife Hadley thought it was clever and appropriate; and in the case of *A Moveable Feast,* Mary Hemingway as its editor tried hard to subdue the book into a reasonable — but still heavily flawed and heavily fictionalized — memoir. Brenner discusses both the changes and the psychological implications of Mary's editing (297–311).

[14] See Daniel, 17; and Wagner-Martin, "*Favored Strangers,*" 171.

[15] Mandel summarizes the readings of "Old lady," identifying her as, among other things, a literary descendant of Richard Ford's "venerable harridan" from his *Gatherings in Spain,* as Grace Hall-Hemingway, and as a "little" innocent (*Complete Annotations,* 314–16).

[16] Jackson, 240–60.

[17] Donaldson reports that Fitzgerald had recommended Radiguet, as well as Hemingway, to Maxwell Perkins, his editor at Scribner's (*Hemingway vs. Fitzgerald*, 54–55). Hemingway's anecdote about Radiguet may have been prompted by pique at this "equation" between himself and Radiguet. Reynolds adds another reason for the appearance of the Radiguet anecdote: Lincoln Kirstein, editor of *Hound & Horn*, had in August of 1932 published Laurence Leighton's comment that Hemingway was lazy, and had no history of traditional writing behind him — as, supposedly, did Radiguet. It was Radiguet, says Leighton, who knew how to use this inherited tradition (Reynolds, *The 1930s*, 99).

[18] In *A Moveable Feast*, Hemingway wrote, "I cannot remember Gertrude Stein ever speaking well of any writer who had not written favorably about her work or done something to advance her career except for Ronald Firbank and, later, Scott Fitzgerald" (27).

[19] See Wagner-Martin, "*Favored Strangers*," 166–82.

[20] Hemingway, "A Natural History of the Dead," *The Short Stories of Ernest Hemingway*, 445.

[21] See Wagner-Martin, "The Intertextual Hemingway," 173–74.

[22] *Geography and Plays* was republished in 1993 by the University of Wisconsin Press, but its contents are not included — except fragmentarily — in the two-volume American Library edition.

[23] Pondrom, however, compares *Geography and Plays* to T. S. Eliot's *The Waste Land* and James Joyce's *Ulysses* (all published in 1922); see her introduction to the 1993 republication.

[24] Stein in "Bibliography" spells the piece "Johnie Grey" and dates it 1915, along with "Pink Melon Joy." Most of the Spanish pieces come from 1916 on, and the other war portraits are circa 1919.

[25] When Hemingway used the line, he phrased it "The Rhine does not show in the picture." It punctuates the returning soldier's ironic set of memories about his war experiences, and deflates any glamorization Krebs might suggest ("Soldier's Home," 145).

[26] In February 1932, Dos Passos wrote Hemingway, "I may be wrong — but the volume is so hellishly good (I'd say way ahead of anything of yours yet) and the language is so magnificently used [. . .] that it would be a shame to leave in any unnecessary tripe" (JFK).

# Works Cited

Anderson, Sherwood. "The Work of Gertrude Stein." (Introduction to the 1922 ed. of *Geography and Plays*). Rpt. in *Geography and Plays*. By Gertrude Stein. Madison: U of Wisconsin P, 1993. 5–8.

Beegel, Susan F. "Eye and Heart: Hemingway's Education as a Naturalist." In *A Historical Guide to Ernest Hemingway*. Ed. Linda Wagner-Martin. New York: Oxford UP, 2000. 53–92.

Brenner, Gerry. "Are We Going to Hemingway's *Feast*?" In *Ernest Hemingway: Six Decades of Criticism*. Ed. Linda W. Wagner. East Lansing: Michigan State UP, 1987. 297–311.

Daniel, Alix Du Poy. "The Stimulating Life with Gertrude & Co." *Lost Generation Journal* 6 (1979): 16–18.

Dolan, Marc. *Modern Lives, A Cultural Re-reading of "The Lost Generation."* West Lafayette, IN: Purdue UP, 1996.

Donaldson, Scott. "Dos and Hem: A Literary Friendship." In *Ernest Hemingway: Six Decades of Criticism*. Ed. Linda W. Wagner. East Lansing: Michigan State UP, 1987. 41–59.

———. *Hemingway vs. Fitzgerald: The Rise and Fall of a Literary Friendship.* Woodstock, NY: Overlook Press, 1999.

Egan, Susann. "Lies, Damned Lies, and Autobiography: Hemingway's Treatment of Fitzgerald in *A Moveable Feast*." *Auto-Biography Studies* 9 (1994): 64–82.

Hemingway, Ernest. "Bull Fighting Is Not a Sport — It Is a Tragedy." *Toronto Star Weekly*, 20 October 1923, 33.

———. "Bullfighting, Sport and Industry." *Fortune* 1 (March 1930): 83–88, 139, 140, 150.

———. *Death in the Afternoon*. New York: Scribner's, 1932.

———. Introduction. *Men at War*. Ed. Ernest Hemingway. New York: Crown, 1942. 5–20.

———. *A Moveable Feast*. New York: Scribner's 1964.

———. "My Own Life." (subtitled segment: "The True Story of My Break with Gertrude Stein"). *New Yorker* (12 February 1927): 23–24.

———. "A Natural History of the Dead." *The Short Stories of Ernest Hemingway*. New York: Scribner's, 1938. 440–49.

———. "Pamplona Letter." *the transatlantic review* 2.3 (October 1924): 300–302.

———. "Soldier's Home." *The Short Stories of Ernest Hemingway*. New York: Scribner's, 1938. 145–53.

———. "World's Series of Bull Fighting a Mad, Whirling Carnival." *Toronto Star Weekly*, 27 October 1923, 33.

Hobhouse, Janet. *Everybody Who Was Anybody*. New York: Putnam's, 1975.

Imbs, Bravig. *Confessions of Another Young Man*. New York: Henkle-Yewdale, 1936.

Jackson, Laura Riding. "The Word-Play of Gertrude Stein." In *Critical Essays on Gertrude Stein*. Ed. Michael J. Hoffman. Boston: G. K. Hall, 1986. 240–60.

Lewis, Wyndham. "Tests for Counterfeit in the Arts" and "The Prose-Song of Gertrude Stein." In *Critical Essays on Gertrude Stein*. Ed. Michael J. Hoffman. Boston: G. K. Hall, 1986. 52–55.

Mandel, Miriam B. *Hemingway's "Death in the Afternoon": The Complete Annotations*. Lanham, MD: Scarecrow, 2002.

———. *Reading Hemingway: The Facts in the Fictions*. Metuchen: Scarecrow, 1995.

Pondrom, Cyrena N. "An Introduction to the Achievement of Gertrude Stein." *Geography and Plays*. By Gertrude Stein. Madison: U of Wisconsin P, 1993. vii–lv.

Reynolds, Michael S. *Hemingway: The Final Years*. New York: Norton, 1999.

———. *Hemingway: The 1930s*. New York: Norton, 1997.

———. *Hemingway's Reading 1910–1940, An Inventory*. Princeton, NJ: Princeton UP, 1981.

Stein, Gertrude. *The Autobiography of Alice B. Toklas*. In *Gertrude Stein, Writings 1903–1932*. Eds. Catharine R. Stimpson and Harriet Chessman. New York: Literary Classics of the United States, 1998. 653–913.

———. "Bibliography." *transition* 15 (February 1929): 47–55.

———. *Geography and Plays*. 1922. Madison: U of Wisconsin P, 1993.

Stephens, Robert O. *Hemingway's Nonfiction, The Public Voice*. Chapel Hill: U of North Carolina P, 1968.

Wagner, Linda W., ed. *Ernest Hemingway: Six Decades of Criticism*. East Lansing: Michigan State UP, 1987.

Wagner-Martin, Linda. *"Favored Strangers": Gertrude Stein and Her Family*. New Brunswick, NJ: Rutgers UP, 1995.

———, ed. *Hemingway: Seven Decades of Criticism*. East Lansing: Michigan State UP, 1998.

———, ed. *A Historical Guide to Ernest Hemingway*. New York: Oxford UP, 2000.

———. "The Intertextual Hemingway." In *A Historical Guide to Ernest Hemingway*. Ed. Linda Wagner-Martin. New York: Oxford UP, 2000. 173–94.

———. "Racial and Sexual Coding in Hemingway's *The Sun Also Rises*." *The Hemingway Review* 10.2 (1991): 39–41.

Westbrook, Max. "Grace Under Pressure: Hemingway and the Summer of 1920." Rpt. in *Ernest Hemingway: Six Decades of Criticism*. Ed. Linda W. Wagner. East Lansing: Michigan State UP, 1987. 19–40.

White, Ray Lewis. *Gertrude Stein and Alice B. Toklas: A Reference Guide*. Boston: Hall, 1984.

Woolf, Virginia. "An Essay in Criticism." 1927. In her *Granite and Rainbow*. London: Hogarth, 1958. 85–92.

# Subject and Author: The Literary Backgrounds of *Death in the Afternoon*

*Miriam B. Mandel*

> *Life is too short to learn bullfighting.*
> A Castilian gentleman[1]

READERS COME TO *Death in the Afternoon* for two major reasons: they are interested in its subject, or they are interested in its author and his art. The first group ranges from tourists preparing for a trip to Spain, to serious students of the bullfight, and to other scholars whose interests somehow or other lead them to the bullfight. The bullfight might, for example, become an important concern to students of Goya's paintings, Benlliure's sculpture, García Lorca's poetry, DeFalla's music, and Bizet's operas. The bullfight is also germane to the study of urban architecture, medieval jousting, material culture, the history of aggression, crowd psychology, genetics and selective breeding, violence and the ethics of violence, legal codes, folklore studies, marketing and advertising, and the influence of the Roman Catholic church. Historians of publishing who are interested in translations, bilingual publications, illustrated publications, transcultural studies, travel writing, biography, autobiography, technical manuals, lexicography, or authorship would find rich materials within the extensive literature of bullfighting. That is, a variety of areas of interest might lead readers to the bullfight, and to read about the bullfight is to come in contact with *Death in the Afternoon*.

As a treatise on bullfighting, *Death in the Afternoon* has practically no rival. In Spain, it was immediately recognized as a significant work. Spain was well-aware of foreign interest in the bullfight, as evidenced by titles like "En beneficio de los extranjeros" (1899) and *Los ingleses y los toros* (1926). But these were humorous and pedagogical pieces, nothing like the respectful review, by one of Spain's leading taurine critics, that hailed *Death in the Afternoon* as "algo extraordinario, muy merecedor de los mayores encomios" (an extraordinary book, worthy of the highest praise).[2] Among those who know the subject, that evaluation still holds.

*Death in the Afternoon* has been translated more frequently than any other book on the bullfight (into eight languages, at last count),[3] and it dominates subsequent literature on the subject. In 1957, Angus McNab recognized that "After twenty-five years, Mr. Ernest Hemingway's *Death in the Afternoon* remains the standard work of literature in the English language on the subject of bullfighting, and it is difficult to see how it could well be dislodged from that position. No doubt it is an easy book to raise secondary objections to, but on the permanent, unalterable things Hemingway has said what was to be said, once and for all" (xi). In 1961, Barnaby Conrad, introducing his own *Encyclopedia of Bullfighting*, acknowledged that *Death in the Afternoon* was "still splendid" (xii). Even John McCormick, whose anti-Hemingway bias is quite clear (he felt that Hemingway paid insufficient attention to the bull in general and to the bullfighter Domingo Ortega in particular), had to concede that "*Death in the Afternoon* [. . .] remains the best work on the subject in the language" (31). And in 1999, a scholarly volume dealing with economics, social history, and commercialism, clearly capitalized upon Hemingway through its title, *Death and Money in the Afternoon: A History of the Spanish Bullfight*, even though it failed to acknowledge Hemingway's 1930 article, "Bullfighting, Sport and Industry," or those sections of *Death in the Afternoon* that also discuss economics.[4] Whether avoiding, praising, or criticizing *Death in the Afternoon*, later authors necessarily work in its shadow.

But the literature of the bullfight did not begin with Hemingway's book, and it is part of the scholarly enterprise, no matter the discipline that brings the reader to *Death in the Afternoon*, to analyze its backgrounds. *Death in the Afternoon* was preceded by a (to me) surprisingly long and varied list of memoirs, histories, biographies, short stories, novels, and travel books, many of them beautifully illustrated, that deal with Spain and bullfighting in one way or another. Much more had been written about the bullfight in Spanish, of course, but the English-language bibliography available before *Death in the Afternoon* is far from inconsiderable.

The earliest listing seems to be Antoine de Brunel's *A Journey into Spain* (1670), of which only eight copies are now extant; many other items are similarly rare and valuable. Some, like Frances Elliot's *Diary of an Idle Woman in Spain* (1884), are personal accounts; others, like Henry Day's *Observations on Spain, Its History and Its People* (1884), or Albert E. Calvert's *Spain: An Historical and Descriptive Account of Its Architecture, Landscapes and Arts* (1911), or Sidney Lee's study of *Bearbaiting, Bullbaiting and Cockfighting* (1916), are wider ranging. But all devote a few pages or chapters to the bullfight, without which an understanding of Spain was thought — and quite rightly so — to be incomplete.

In the first two decades of the 1900s, at least sixty books on Spain and the bullfight were published in English; a similar number appeared in the 1920s; and the two years preceding *Death in the Afternoon*, 1930 and 1931, added twenty more titles. Many of these books were published both in

Britain and the United States, sometimes with a year's difference, more often in the same year, and frequently by mainstream publishers whose names we still recognize: Macmillan, Dutton, Harper, and Houghton Mifflin. Hemingway's own publisher, Scribner's, had published at least nine books on Spain and bullfighting before issuing *Death in the Afternoon* (Hemingway owned two of them, Salvador de Madariaga's *Spain* and Stoddard's *Spanish Cities*). Many of these books were reprinted, or revised, expanded, and reissued, testifying to the growing interest among the English-language book-buying public in topics associated with Spain and the bullfight. The first of the two bibliographies that follow will enable researchers interested in these matters to discern the shape of the relevant literary backgrounds over four centuries.

While many readers come to *Death in the Afternoon* to learn something about the bullfight, many others want to learn something about Hemingway, his art, his craft, his style, his literary theories, his process of composition, his relationship to other authors, and other matters pertaining to his position as man of letters. We often quote *Death in the Afternoon*'s pronouncements on life, death, love, sex, and the Iceberg Theory. But as this *Companion* reveals, *Death in the Afternoon* is not merely a stepping stone to help us interpret Hemingway's life or his other work. It is not background, but foreground: a complex book that richly rewards critical and textual analysis — and such an analysis requires us to examine the text's backgrounds and sources. We know that Hemingway did not merely go to war or to the bullfights and then write down what he learned and saw there: it was always his habit to research his topics carefully. The study of the reading that preceded *A Farewell to Arms* has yielded several important scholarly books and articles, and a similar crop could be reaped from a study of the research that produced *Death in the Afternoon*.

By 1932, Hemingway owned or is known to have read well over one hundred books and several journals on Spain and the bullfight, a few of them in French, many in English, most of them in Spanish. The oldest of the forty or so books that Hemingway read in English were probably Madame d'Aulnoy's *Travels into Spain* (ca. 1800), Washington Irving's *Tales of the Alhambra* (1832), Richard Ford's *Gatherings from Spain* (1846), and John Hay's *Castillian Days* (1871). In the 1920s, as he traveled through Spain and attended bullfights, he read at least a dozen contemporary volumes of Spanish history and travel literature, ranging from the general (e.g., Henry Dwight Sedgwick's *Spain: A Short History of Its Politics, Literature, and Art,* Havelock Ellis' *The Soul of Spain,* Dorothy Giles' *The Road Through Spain,* Martin Hume's *The Spanish People,* Robert McBride's *Spanish Towns and People,* Julius Meier-Graefe's *The Spanish Journey*) to the regionally specific (e.g., Aubrey FitzGerald Bell's *Spanish Galicia* and Somerset Maugham's *Andalucia*). And he collected books that focused directly on the bullfight, like J. Morewood Dowsett's *The Spanish Bullring* and Roy Campbell's *Taurine Provence: The Philosophy, Technique and Religion of the Bullfight*.

Many of the American and English authors that Hemingway read were ill informed, unsympathetic to the bullfight, blind to its philosophical significance, and apparently unaware of the differences among bullrings, bulls, matadors, audiences, and local customs. A few, like Waldo Frank and Richard Ford, were reasonably open to the foreign art, but many of them, like Dowsett, were so staunchly pro-horse that they lost all sympathy for the bullfight in the very first *tercio*. Reading their reports, we see that Hemingway's serious, sympathetic, and technically and historically well-informed treatment constitutes a major advance in the English language literature of a topic that, although often discussed, was generally slighted and dismissed.

Hemingway falls more easily in the Spanish than into the English tradition of writing about the bullfight. He took the trouble to learn Spanish, collected about seventy books in Spanish, and subscribed to more than a dozen Spanish journals and newspapers that dealt with Spain, the bullfight, and related topics. His pre-1932 Spanish-language taurine library is orthodox, scholarly, and remarkably complete. He owned classic reference works such as Sánchez de Neira's two volume taurine dictionary (1879), historical surveys like that of the Conde de las Navas (1899), explanations of the bullfight like that of Antonio Fernández de Heredia (1904), and the great bibliography of Graciano Díaz Arquer (1931). He also collected practical works like the *consultores* (professional directories) of José Becerra y Alvarez (Capotito) and Angel Carmona (Camisero), and important technical works like the *tauromaquias* of Francisco Montes (Paquiro) and Rafael Guerra (Guerrita) — although that of José Delgado (Pepe-Hillo), which he mentions in the Glossary of *Death in the Afternoon* (s. v. *Tauromachia*), is strangely absent from the inventories of his bookshelves.

Libraries reveal their owners. Hemingway owned, for example, three detailed book-length studies of Rafael Guerra,[5] as well as Guerra's *Tauromaquia*. The spectacular Guerra retired in 1899 and was, in Hemingway's day, a still-living representative of the *toreo* that had been irrevocably altered by Joselito and Belmonte; Hemingway's interest in him reveals both his concern for reputation and his strong historic bent. Hemingway also owned several books of and about taurine drawings and illustrations, including a two-volume collection of Goya's illustrations, Daniel Perea's album (1895), and Pedro Vindel's *Estampas de toros,* which reproduced important illustrations of the eighteenth and nineteenth centuries. Taken together with his own collection of paintings (one of which was used as the dust jacket of *Death in the Afternoon* and another as the frontispiece), these books reveal his highly developed visual sense.

As he wrote *Death in the Afternoon,* Hemingway continued to collect and read new books at an impressive pace, acquiring seventeen volumes published in 1930 and 1931. Twelve of these were highly detailed and technical examinations of his subject, that is, professional literature written by and for the committed taurine public. In short, by 1932, Hemingway owned an up-to-date library, with more than a dozen annual surveys of contemporary bullfight seasons, written and edited by knowledgeable critics (see the entries for Calvo Martínez, Minguet, Orts-Ramos, Rivera, and Uriarte). Many of their statistics, evaluations, predictions, anecdotes, and opinions show up, unacknowledged, in *Death in the Afternoon*.

Scholarly discussion of the influence of all this reading on *Death in the Afternoon* has barely begun, perhaps because Hemingway took such clever care to minimize or conceal it. He vaguely alludes, at one point, to "all the different sources I have read," but he soon undercuts this indebtedness by suggesting parenthetically that he was merely looking for statistics: "(I've looked up the weights and the photographs)" (243). The Glossary's entry for *Revistas* lists several journals with which he was familiar, but the listing is incomplete. The "Bibliographical Note" claims to "acknowledge his deep indebtedness" to all of the 2077 unnamed and unidentified authors listed in Díaz Arquer's bibliography, but such an obviously exaggerated generalization hides rather than reveals his sources. Occasionally Hemingway does mention a particular title, like *Virgin Spain* or *Toros célebres*, though without identifying its author; or he mentions an author, like Julius Meier-Graefe or Richard Ford, without identifying the particular book he is referring to. We need to identify and examine Hemingway's reading so that we can discuss how *Death in the Afternoon* internalized, transformed, and outperformed its predecessors. Tomás Orts-Ramos perceptively noted that Hemingway's reading can be detected most readily in his repetition of the "errores históricos y técnicos" (historical and technical errors) that had marred earlier works ("Libros de toros," 2–3), but there are other techniques for recovering embedded and absent sources. We have applied these techniques in our reading of Hemingway's fiction; it is just as necessary to apply them to the large body of his nonfiction. Some of this work has been done (see, for example, the essays by Linda Wagner-Martin and Lisa Tyler, in this volume), but much more remains undone.

To facilitate this work, I offer the following two bibliographies, both of which take 1932, the date of the publication of *Death in the Afternoon*, as their cut-off point. The first, broader one, lists English-language works about Spain and the bullfight and identifies those that Hemingway owned with an asterisk. The second list, which itemizes and annotates Hemingway's reading on these topics, contains journals and books in Spanish, French, and English.

## Note

The first bibliography relies on the 1931 bibliography of Graciano Díaz Arquer; on *Libros y folletos de toros: Bibliografía taurina,* which lists books in several languages, including English; and on *La Busca,* the publication of Taurine Bibliophiles of America, particularly volumes 9 (1973), 12 (1976), 16 (1980), 20 (1984), and 30 (1994). When these sources provided incomplete or conflicting data, I consulted *The National Union Catalogue Pre-1956 Imprints* and its *Supplements* (for books in English) and *La Fiesta Nacional: Ensayo de bibliografía taurina,* the *Catálogo Núm. 9: Catálogo de libros, folletos, revistas y carteles de asuntos taurinos,* and the *Catálogo de la biblioteca taurina de don Antonio Urquijo de Federico* (for books in Spanish).

The second bibliography, which lists Hemingway's reading, devolved from the listings compiled by James Brasch and Joseph Sigman, in *Hemingway's Library: A Composite Record* (New York: Garland, 1981); by Michael S. Reynolds, in *Hemingway's Reading, 1910–1940: An Inventory* (Princeton: Princeton UP, 1981) and "A Supplement to *Hemingway's Reading, 1910–1940*" (*Studies in American Fiction* 14.1 [1986]: 99–108); by Noel Fitch, in "Ernest Hemingway — c/o Shakespeare and Company" (*Fitzgerald-Hemingway Annual* [1977]: 157–81); and by Richard Layman, in "Hemingway's Library Cards at Shakespeare and Company" (*Fitzgerald-Hemingway Annual* [1975]: 191–207).

My thanks to Albert John DeFazio III, Anthony Brand, and Nancy Bredendick, three inveterate aficionados of bibliographies, who answered my many questions and offered suggestions and information.

## I: English-Language Books on Spain and Bullfighting, Pre-1932

(The list includes translations from other languages into English. Items owned or read by Ernest Hemingway are marked by an asterisk; they reappear on the second list, where many are annotated.)

Amicis, Edmondo de. *Spain and the Spaniards.* Trans. from the Italian. New York: G. P. Putnam's Sons, 1881; Philadelphia: H. T. Coates & Co., 1895.

Andersen, Hans Christian. *In Spain and a Visit to Portugal.* New York: Riverside Press, 1870.

Andujar, Manuel. *Spain of Today from Within.* New York: Revell, 1909.

Anon. *The Attache in Madrid.* New York: D. Appleton & Co., 1856.

———. *Bullfights in Mexico and Spain: Full explanation and rules, Illustrated with many engravings.* 2nd ed. Mexico: Tipografía y litografía "La Europea," 1910. This thirty-two page pamphlet is a guide for "Americans and foreigners generally" (5), and is prepared by unnamed Mexican experts. It presents a glossary, a historical survey, an explanation of the three acts of the bullfight, a discussion of bull breeding and economics, and brief biographies of "famous modern bullfighters," including two Mexicans, Vicente Segura and Rodolfo Gaona, then twenty-four and twenty-two years old. Most of the illustrations feature Gaona. Like Jones' *Bull Fighting Illustrated*, this is a serious, well-informed treatment of the subject — one of the very few such items pre-1932. It points out the difference between those publications prepared by knowledgeable aficionados and those produced by tourists, travel writers, or experts in fields other than bullfighting.

———. *Daniel Webster and His Contemporaries: Sketches and Adventures in Madeira, Portugal, and the Andalusias of Spain*. New York: Harper Bros., 1856.

Asquith, Margot. *Places and Persons*. London: Thornton Butterworth, 1925.

*Aulnoy, Madame d'. *Travels into Spain*. Ca. 1800. Rpt. London: George Routledge, 1930.

Aurousseau, Marcel. *Beyond the Pyrenees*. New York: A. H. King, 1931.

———. *Highway into Spain*. London: P. Davies, 1930; New York: A. H. King, 1931.

*Baedeker, Karl. *Spain and Portugal: Handbook for Travelers*. Leipzig: Baedeker, 1913.

Baerlin, Henry. *Mariposa*. New York: Boni & Liveright, 1924.

Baring-Gould, S. *In Troubadour Land*. London: W. H. Allen & Co., 1891.

Barretti, Joseph. *A Journey from London and Genoa*. London: T. and L. Davies, 1760.

Bates, Katherine Lee. *Spanish Highways and Byways*. New York: The Chautauqua Press, 1905, 1920; New York: Macmillan, 1900, 1901, 1907.

Batson, Alfred. *Vagabond's Paradise*. Boston: Little, Brown & Co., 1931.

Bécquer, Gustavo Adolfo. *Romantic Legends of Spain*. Trans. from the Spanish by Cornelia Frances Bates and Katharine Lee Bates. New York: T. Y. Crowell & Co., 1909.

Bell, Aubrey FitzGerald. *The Magic of Spain*. London: John Lane Bodley Head, Ltd., 1912; New York: John Lane Co., 1912.

———. *A Pilgrim in Spain*. Boston: Little, Brown & Co., 1924.

*———. *Spanish Galicia*. New York: Duffield & Co., 1923.

Bensusan, S. L. *Home Life in Spain*. With twelve illustrations. London and New York: Macmillan, 1910.

Blanco y White, José María (Leucadio Doblado). *Letters from Spain*. London: Henry Colburn & Co., 1822. The author was Spanish, from Seville, but lived in England. His *Letters* are written in the first person plural, to express his intimate connection with the country he describes. His Fourth Letter, which focuses on Seville and the bullfight, begins with a discussion of various types of training for the aspirant bullfighter: *toreo de salón* (practice with a mechanical contraption that acts as a bull), *tientas* (testing of the calves on the ranch), and *mataderos* (slaughterhouses where animals could be caped before being killed). He then describes Seville's bullring, the bulls' arrival at the ring, and the subsequent events: the clearing of the ring, the ceremonial entrance of the performers, the entrance of the bull, the pic-ing, the death of two horses and the wounding of four (related with a minimum of gory detail), the banderillas (including *banderillas de fuego*), and the performance of the local hero, the matador Pepe Illo, and the removal of the dead bull. The author clearly loves the bullfight, finding the bloodshed an acceptable price to pay for such a heightened emotional experience. He refers to an earlier reporter, Joseph Townsend, whose description of the bullfight he admires.

*Blasco Ibáñez, Vicente. *Blood and Sand*. Trans. from the Spanish by Mrs. W. A. Gillespie. New York: E. P. Dutton Co., 1919. There are other translations: by Douglas, 1911; by Campbell, 1911; by Cushing, 1921.

*———. *La Corrida / The Bullfight*. Abridged bilingual edition. English translation by C. D. Campbell. Philadelphia: David Mackay, 1911, 1919.

Blichfeldt. E. H. *A Mexican Journey*. New York: Thomas V. Crowell, 1912; New York: The Chautauqua Press, 1919.

Bishop, W. H. *Old Mexico and Her Lost Provinces*. New York: Harper & Bros., 1887.

*Borrow, George Henry. *The Bible in Spain*. 1843. London: Murray, 1923.

Brown, Irving H. *Nights and Days on the Gypsy Trail*. New York: Harper & Bros., 1922.

Browne, Edith A. *Spain*. London: Macmillan, 1910.

Brunel, Antoine de. *A Journey into Spain*. London: H. Herringman, 1670. *See also* Moore, Thomas Ewing.

Bryant, William C. *Letters of a Traveler*. 2nd Series. New York: D. Appleton & Co., 1859.

Burnett, Frances Hodgson. *The Pretty Sister of José, A Spanish Love Story*. Illustrated by C.S. Reinhart. New York: Charles Scribner's Sons, 1889, 1910; Leipzig: B. Tauchnitz (Collection of British Authors), 1891.

Byrne, Mrs. William Pitt. *Cosas de España, Illustrative of Spain and the Spaniards as They Are*. New York and London: Strahan, 1866.

*Byron, George Gordon, Lord. *Childe Harold's Pilgrimage*. In *Complete Poetical Works of Lord Byron*. Boston: Houghton Mifflin, 1905. 1–83.

Callin, Rodney. *Palms and Patios*. London: Heath Cranton, Ltd., 1931.

Calvert, Albert E. *Madrid: An Historical Description and Handbook of the Spanish Capital*. London: John Lane, 1909.

———. *Spain: An Historical and Descriptive Account of Its Architecture, Landscapes and Arts.* 2 vols., over 1700 illustrations. London: J. M. Dent & Co., 1911.

*Campbell, Roy. *Taurine Provence: The Philosophy, Technique and Religion of the Bullfight.* London: Desmond Harmsworth, 1932.

Carelton, George. *Memoirs.* London: n.p., 1808.

*Cervantes, Miguel de. *Don Quijote de la Mancha.* This book has been translated into English numerous times.

Chapman, Abel, and Walter J. Buck. *Unexplored Spain.* London: Edward Arnold, 1910.

*———. *Wild Spain: Records of Sport with Rifle, Rod and Gun; Natural History and Exploration.* London: Gurney & Jackson, 1893.

Chapple, Joe Mitchell. *Vivid Spain.* Boston: Chapple Publishing Co., 1926.

Chatfield-Taylor, H. C. *The Land of the Castanet.* Chicago: Herbert Stone & Co., 1896.

———. *Tawny Spain.* Boston: Houghton Mifflin, 1927.

Clark, Keith. *The Spell of Spain.* Boston: The Page Co., 1914.

Clarke, Edward. *Letters Concerning the Spanish Nation, Written at Madrid During the Years 1760 and 1761.* London: T. Becket and P. A. de Hondt, 1763. The Seventh Letter describes a bullfight that took place in the Plaza Mayor, Madrid, 1760, in the presence of King Charles III and the royal family. Mariano Tomás provides additional details, including the fact that Juan Romero, the father of Pedro Romero, was among the performers (*Los extranjeros en los toros,* 36). Clarke is impressed by the richness of the vestments, the size and enthusiasm of the crowd, the power of the animals, and the skill and valor of the performers. He finds that the bullfight is not only a beautiful spectacle, one of the handsomest in the world, but also an acknowledgment of the fierceness in our own nature, an example of how to face fear, and a lesson in how to help our fellows when they are injured or in danger. He reports going to see another bullfight, in Madrid's *plaza de toros.*

*Colvil, Helen Hester. *In the Footsteps of a Saint and Other Sketches from Spain.* London: Burns, Otis & Washbourne, 1931.

Cooper, Clayton. *Understanding Spain.* New York: Frederick A. Stokes, 1928.

Cox-McCormack, Nancy. *Pleasant Days in Spain.* New York: J. H. Sears, 1927.

Crealock[e], Lt. Col. [Henry] Hope. *What I Saw at a Bullfight in Madrid.* London: n.p., n.d. (ca. 1880).

Crockett, S. R. *The Adventurer in Spain.* London: Isbister & Co., Ltd., 1903; New York: Frederick A. Stokes, 1904.

[Cutter, Mrs. Norman]. "Six Bulls to Die." By the author of "In the Time of the Cherry Viewing." With pictures by Louis Loeb. *The Century Magazine* 46.5 (September 1893): 659–76. Towards the end of this interesting narrative, the story's three main characters (a young bride, her husband, and her former suitor) see a bullfight in Mexico. The husband, Mr. Phelps, turns "white with indignation" at the treatment of the horses; the suitor, Mr. Crawford, understands that financial and psychological attractions may draw men to bullfighting but feels that "the brutes [the bullfighters] deserve to be gored for their bungling work"; his sympathies lie with the "poor frightened brute of a horse" (673). Both men, fascinated but appalled by all they see, are surprised that sweet, sympathetic, and delicate Mrs. Phelps is absolutely unaffected by the afternoon's shocking events; indeed, it is she who keeps the threesome in the ring, bull after bull. When the matador narrowly escapes being gored by the sixth bull, the two men are "half unnerved [. . .] by such wantonness of torture and trifling with death [. . . and turn] instinctively [. . .] to hurry Mrs. Phelps from a scene so pitiless." She, however, is as unruffled, attentive, and cheerful as always, and they hear "the familiar click of the [K]odak button firmly pressed by her little white, well-manicured thumb" (673). Her "unfeminine" detachment leads them to reevaluate themselves and their responses to her. The story's generally accurate and straightforward description of the varied events of the bullfight contains some interesting details: it uses the word *capeador* for the bullfighters who cape the bull (today they are called *banderilleros*), two of the bulls leave the ring alive (one in shame [670] and one apparently *indultado* [671]), the horses wear "grim leather aprons which protect the breasts of the blindfolded and reluctant horses" (668; this sounds like a harbinger of the *peto,* which was not formally adopted in Spain until the 1920s, two decades after the story was published), and a banderillero, running to the barrera after placing the banderillas, drops his "cloak" as he runs (670) — an anomaly, since the man placing the banderillas does so without using his cape.

d'Aulnoy, la Comtesse. *See* Aulnoy, Madame d'.

D'Avillier, Baron Charles. *Spain*. London: Bickers & Sons, 1881.

Day, Henry. *From the Pyrenees to the Pillars of Hercules: Observations on Spain, Its History and Its People*. New York: G. P. Putnam's Sons, 1883. 2nd ed., 1884.

de Amicis, Edmondo. *See* Amicis, Edmondo de.

de Brunel, Antoine. *See* Brunel, Antoine de.

de Madariaga, Salvador. *See* Madariaga, Salvador de.

Doblado, Leucadio. *See* Blanco y White, José María.

*Dos Passos, John. *Rosinante to the Road Again*. New York: George H. Doran, 1922.

Downes, William Howe. *Spanish Ways and By-Ways with a Glimpse of the Pyrenees*. Boston: Cupples, Upham Co., 1883.

*Dowsett, J. Morewood. *The Spanish Bullring, being Some Account of the Spanish Bull Fight from its Earliest History and To-day.* London: Bale, 1928.

Dubourg, M. *Bullfighting.* London: Edward Orme, 1813.

Edwards, George Wharton. *Spain.* Philadelphia: Penn Pub. Co., 1926.

Edwards, Matilda B. *Through Spain to the Sahara.* London: Hurst and Blackett, Ltd., 1868.

Eliot, George. *The Spanish Gypsy.* New York: Tichnor & Fields, 1868.

Elliot, Frances. *Diary of an Idle Woman in Spain.* 2 vols. London: n.p., 1884; Leipzig: Bernhard Tauchnitz, 1884.

*Ellis, Havelock. *The Soul of Spain.* Boston and New York: Houghton, Mifflin & Co., ca. 1908, 1923; New York: G. P. Putnam's Sons, 1923.

Elsner, Eleanor. *Romantic Spain.* London: Thornton Butterworth, Ltd., 1924.

———. *Spanish Sunshine.* New York: The Century Co., 1925.

Erskine, Mrs. Stuart. *Madrid.* New York: E. P. Dutton & Co., n.d.

———. *Madrid, Past and Present.* London: John Lane, 1922.

Ewing Moore, Thomas. *See* Moore, Thomas Ewing.

Fetridge, W[illiam] Pembroke. *The American Travelers Guide: Hand-Book for Travelers in Europe.* New York: Harper Bros., 1862.

Field, Henry M. *Old Spain and New Spain.* New York: Scribner's, 1888. The author traverses Spain from north to south, discusses important buildings, events, and cities, avoids bullfights, describes only the crowds entering and leaving the plaza, deplores the sight of dead animals (282–84).

Field, Kate. *Ten Days in Spain.* Boston: Houghton Mifflin, 1886.

Finck, Henry T. *Spain and Morocco.* New York: Scribner's, 1891.

Fish, Horace. *Terassa of Spain.* New York: Mitchell Kennerly, 1923.

Fisher (or Fischer), Frederick. *Travels in Spain.* London: n.p., 1797.

Fitz-Gerald, John D. *Rambles in Spain.* New York: Thomas V. Crowell, 1910.

Flitch, John Ernest Crawford. *A Little Journey in Spain.* London: Grant Richards, Ltd., 1914.

———. *Idler in Spain: The Record of a Goya Pilgrimage.* New York: Robert M. McBride & Co., 1914.

———. *Mediterranean Moods, Footnotes of Travel.* New York: E. P. Dutton & Co., 1911.

*Ford, Richard. *Gatherings from Spain.* London: John Murray, 1846, 1851, 1861; London: J. M. Dent, [1906]; New York: E. P. Dutton & Co., 1906, 1913, 1927. Also issued under the title *The Spaniards and Their Country.*

London, 1847; New York: Wiley and Putnam, 1847; New York: G. P. Putnam, 1848, 1850, 1852, 1854.

———. *The Handbook for Travellers in Spain and Readers at Home*. 2 vols. London: John Murray, 1845. This was followed by several revised and corrected editions, the ninth and last appearing in 1898 (all published by John Murray).

*Foreign Field Sports, Fisheries, Sporting Anecdotes &c &c From Drawings by Messrs. Howitt, Atkinson, Clark, Manskirch &c, with a Supplement of New South Wales Containing One Hundred and Ten Plates*. London: H. R. Young, 1819.

Franck, Harry A[lverson]. *Four Months Afoot in Spain*. New York: Garden City Publishing Co., 1911.

*Frank, Waldo. *Virgin Spain: Scenes from the Spiritual Drama of a Great People*. New York: Boni and Liveright, 1926.

*Frazer, James George. *The Golden Bough: A Study in Magic and Religion*. New York: Macmillan, 1922.

Gallichan, Catherine. *See* Hartley, Catherine Gasquoine.

Gallichan, Walter M. *The Story of Seville*. London: J. M. Dent & Co., Ltd., 1903, 1910.

Garstin, Crosbie. *The Coasts of Romance*. New York: Frederick A. Stokes, 1922.

Gasquoine, Hartley C. *See* Hartley, C. Gasquoine.

Gautier, Theophile. *A Romantic in Spain*. English translation, New York: Alfred A. Knopf, Inc., 1926.

———. *Wanderings in Spain*. English translation, London: Ingram Cook & Co., 1843, 1853, 1859. Gautier objects to the pic-ing and the fate of the horses (he describes the disemboweling and death of one horse in vivid detail), but has a good appreciation of the bullfight, calling it one of the most beautiful spectacles one can imagine (Tomás, *Los extranjeros en los toros*, 116). He rightly informs his fellow Frenchmen that the word *toreador* is incorrect, the proper term being *torero*. Gautier follows the usual pattern, first describing the crowds in the streets of Madrid, then the plaza itself, the clearing of the plaza, the *paseo* (with careful detail about the clothes and equipment of the participants), and the entrance of the bull. Gautier is specific, not generic; he describes the picadors Francisco Sevilla (as Prosper Mérimée did, ten years earlier) and Antonio Rodríguez, a bull with a *querencia*, the banderillero Majarón, the matador Juan Pastor and so on: these details enable Tomás to date this corrida to 27 April 1840 (*Los extranjeros en los toros*, 127). Gautier also discusses *banderillas de fuego*, the use of dogs (to worry and wear down the bull), the *media-luna* (crescent-shaped blade on a pole, used to hamstring a difficult bull), and the sorry effects of an inaccurate sword-thrust. In another section, he discusses the plaza, the heat, and the women of Málaga; he witnessed the death of twenty-four bulls and forty-six horses during the three days of the Málaga fiesta, which starred Francisco Montes (Paquiro). Gautier touches upon many of the same points as Mérimée, whom he may have read.

*Giles, Dorothy. *The Road Through Spain*. Philadelphia: Penn Pub. Co., 1929.

Gordon, Jan, and Cora Gordon. *Poor Folk in Spain*. Illustrated by the Authors. London: John Lane The Bodley Head Ltd., 1922. Written in the first person by Cora, this book reports the adventures of a British couple who go to Spain to sketch. They see one small-town bullfight that features four bulls and two bullfighters. Cora, who has a generally open mind, recognizes the deficiencies of both the bulls and the bullfighters and is not moved to admire either. She repeatedly and unfairly compares the event to British sports, and in a peculiarly heartless statement says that "For us bullfighting would begin to be a serious sport if the men and the bull stood on the same conditions" (102).

———. *Two Vagabonds in Spain*. New York: McBride & Co., 1923.

Green, Francis L. *The Bullfight: A Short Handbook Containing Some Accounts of Spain*. Madrid: Ricardo Fe, 1898.

Gwynne, Paul. *See* Slater, Ernest.

Hale, Edward E. *Seven Spanish Cities*. Boston: Roberts Bros., 1883.

———, and Susan Hale. *Spain*. New York: Putnam's Sons, 1898.

Hale, Susan. *A Family Flight Through Spain*. Boston: Roberts Bros., 1883.

Hall, Trowbridge. *Spain in Silhouette*. New York: Macmillan, 1923.

Halsey, Francis W., ed. *Seeing Europe with Famous Authors*. 10 vols. New York: The Chautauqua Press, 1914. Contains "A Bull Fight," by Kate Field.

Hare, Augustus. *Wandering in Spain (with illustrations)*. New York: George Routledge & Sons; London: Strahan, 1873.

Harrigan, M[ildred] H[ornsby]. *Traveling Light: How to See Spain and Morocco, A Practical Guide for Economical People*. New York: Brentano's, 1928.

Harris, Frank. *Montes the Matador and Other Stories*. London: Grant Richards, 1900; London: Alexander Moring, Ltd., 1906. Although there is no evidence that Hemingway owned this particular book, he did own several Harris volumes and may have read some of these short stories in a magazine or anthology. Wagner-Martin considers Harris a probable influence on two Hemingway stories ("The Undefeated," "The Killers") and on *Death in the Afternoon* ("The Intertextual Hemingway," 182).

Harris, Miriam C. *A Corner in Spain*. Boston: Houghton Mifflin, 1898.

Harrison, James A. *History of Spain*. Chicago: The Werner Co., 1895; N.p.: n.p., 1903.

Hart, Jerome. *Two Argonauts in Spain*. San Francisco: Payot, Upham, & Co., 1904. Presents a series of humorous, rambling "pen-sketches" or letters originally published in the San Francisco *Argonaut*. Contains the usual description of crowds going to bullfights, water and orange sellers, and other details. Hart declares "I do not intend here to describe a bull-fight" (107) but mentions two unusual events: an *espontáneo* vaulting in and out of the arena (107–8) and a horse kicking a bull, which the author quite approves, adding that "If he had kicked the head off a bull-fighter or two, I would not have shed a tear" (108–9). Hart considers the bullfight "a very disgusting spectacle" (109).

Harte, Bret. "The Devotion of Enriquez." With pictures by Gilbert Gaul. *The Century Magazine* 51.1 (November 1895): 37–50. The story, set in California, filters the courtship of Miss Mannersley, a well-educated, well-bred Bostonian, and Enriquez, the self-confident, graceful, and romantic young man whose Spanish is better than his English, through a rather obtuse and condescending first-person narrator. One scene takes place at a local bullfight, and the narrator rejoices "that I am able to spare the reader the usual realistic horrors, for in the Californian performances there was very little of the brutality that distinguished this function in the mother country. The horses were not miserable, worn-out hacks, but young and alert mustangs; and the display of horsemanship by the picadors was not only wonderful, but secured an almost safety to horse and rider" (45). The narrator mentions only two bulls, the second of which, obviously a *manso* with a *querencia*, was "more sullen, uncertain, and discomposing to his butchers [for] he declined the challenge of whirling and insulting picadors [and] remained with his haunches backed against the barrier" (46). When a sudden gust of wind blows the young woman's sketch of the events into the bullring, Enriquez vaults the barrier, captures the piece of paper, bows to the bull (his actions cause it to charge), and quickly, gracefully, and safely exits the ring while the matador dispatches the bull. One of the story's several illustrations shows "Enriquez in the ring"; he is displaying the rescued piece of paper to the charging bull while the matador approaches calmly, sword and muleta in hand; two members of his *cuadrilla* lounge nonchalantly near the *barrera*, quite some distance away. Five large Mexican-style hats have been tossed into the arena, and a sixth is being added to them by a member of the audience (40).

Hartley, Catherine Gasquoine (Catherine Gallichan, Mrs. Walter M. Gallichan). *Spain Revisited: A Summer Holiday in Galicia*. London: S. Paul & Co., 1911; New York: E. P. Dutton & Co., 1911.

———. *Things Seen in Spain*. With fifty illustrations. London: Seeley, Service & Co., 1911, 1921, 1923, 1927; New York: E. P. Dutton & Co., 1911, 1912.

Hawkes, C. P. *Mauresques, with Some Basque & Spanish Cameos*. With twenty-one illustrations. Boston: Houghton Mifflin, 1926.

*Hay, John. *Castilian Days*. With illustrations by Joseph Pennell. Boston: Houghton Mifflin, 1871, 1903; London: William Heinemann, 1903.

Higgin, L. *Spanish Life in Town and Country*. London: George Newnes, Ltd., 1902; New York: G. P. Putnam's Sons, 1904.

Holdredge, William. *A Winter in Madeira and a Summer in Spain and Florence*. New York: W. Holdredge, 1850.

Honan, Michael B. *The Andalusian Annual for 1836*. London: John Macrone, 1836.

Hoskins, G. A. *Spain as It Is*. London: Colburn, 1851.

Howe, Maud (Maud Howe Elliot). *Sun and Shadow in Spain*. Boston: Little, Brown & Co., 1908.

Howells, William Dean. *Familiar Spanish Travels*. New York: Harper Bros., 1913. Howells wanted to go to a bullfight in order to walk out on it as a mark of his disapproval; he bought tickets for one bullfight but it was rained out; by the time he reached the southern cities, the taurine season was over and he never got to express his contempt.

Huddleston, Sisley. *Europe in Zigzags: Social, Artistic, Literary, and Political Affairs in the Continent*. With thirty-six illustrations. Philadelphia and London: J. B. Lippincott, 1929.

Hugh, James Rose. *Among the Spanish People*. 2 vols. London: n.p., 1877.

Hume, Martin Andrew Sharp. *Spain: 1479–1788*. London: Cambridge UP, 1901.

*———. *The Spanish People: Their Origin, Growth and Influence*. London: William Heinemann, 1901.

Huntington, Archer M. *A Note-Book in Northern Spain*. New York: G. P. Putnam's Sons, 1898.

Hutton, Edward. *The Cities of Spain*. New York: Macmillan, 1906; London: Methuen, 1907.

Ilchester, Earl of. *The Spanish Journal of Elizabeth, Lady Holland*. London: Longman's Green & Co., 1910.

Inglis, Henry D. *Spain*. London: Whittaker & Co., 1837.

*Irving, Washington. *Tales of the Alhambra: A Series of Sketches of the Moors and Spaniards*. Philadelphia: Carey Lea, 1832; London: H. Colburn, 1932.

Israels, Jozef. *Spain: The Story of a Journey*. London: John D. Nimmo, 1900.

Jacobs, William. *Travels in the South of Spain, in Letters Written AD 1809 and 1810*. London: J. Johnson & Co., 1811.

James, Will. *Sand*. New York: A. L. Burt Co., 1929.

James-Rose, Hugh. *Among the Spanish People*. 2 vols. London: n.p., 1877.

*Jones, Tom (Thomas Wallace Jones). *Bull Fighting Illustrated*. Cincinnati, OH: T. Jones, 1904.

Keatinge, Maurice. *Travels Through France and Spain to Morocco*. London: Henry Colburn & Co., 1817.

Kennedy, Bart. *A Tramp in Spain, from Andalusia to Andorra.* New York: Frederick Warne & Co., 1904; London: S. Low, Marston & Co., 1912.

Keyser, Arthur. *Trifles and Travels.* New York: E. P. Dutton & Co., 1923.

King, Georgiana Goddard. *The Way of Saint James.* New York: Macmillan Co., 1920. Discusses Spain's art and literature.

*Kipling, Rudyard. "The Bull That Thought." In *Animal Stories,* London: Macmillan & Co., Ltd., 1932; in *Debits and Credits,* New York: Doubleday & Co., Inc., 1926; in *The Humorous Tales of Rudyard Kipling,* New York: Doubleday Doran & Co., 1931.

Lanning, J. Frank. *The Pilgrimage.* Pittsburgh: Gallatin Co., 1931.

Lathrop, George P. *Spanish Vistas.* New York: Harper Bros., 1883, 1898.

Latrobe, Charles J. *The Rambler in Spain.* London: R. B. Selley and N. Burnside, 1736.

*Laughlin, Clara Elizabeth. *So You're Going to Spain! And if I Were Going with You These Are the Things I'd Invite You to Do.* Boston: Houghton Mifflin, 1931.

*Lawrence, D. H. *The Plumed Serpent.* New York: Alfred A. Knopf, Inc., 1926; London: Secker, 1926.

Lee, Sidney. *Bearbaiting, Bullbaiting and Cockfighting.* N.p.: n.p., 1916.

Lent, William Bement. *Across the Country of the Little King: A Trip Through Spain.* New York: Bonnell, Silver & Co., 1897.

Lewis, John F. *Spain and the Spanish Character.* London: F. G. Moon, 1834.

Lockhart, J. G. *Spanish Ballads.* London: George Routledge, 1823.

Lomas, John. *In Spain.* London: Adam and Charles Black, 1908.

———. *Sketches in Spain from Nature, Art, and Life.* Edinburgh: A. & C. Black, 1884; London: Longmans Green & Co., 1884.

———, ed. *O'Shea's Guide to Spain and Portugal.* London: Adam and Charles Black, 1895.

London, Jack. *The Night Born.* New York: The Century Co., 1913. Contains "The Madness of John Harned."

Longfellow, Henry Wadsworth. *Outre-Mer: A Pilgrimage Beyond the Sea.* Rev. ed. Philadelphia: David McKay, Publisher, 1893. Essays about his travels in France, Spain, and Italy, with about a third of the book devoted to each country.

Lowell, James Russell. *Impressions of Spain.* Boston: Houghton Mifflin Co., 1899. Very anti-bullfight: his first bullfight, which he did not see through to the end, was his last.

Luffman, C. Bogue. *Quiet Days in Spain.* New York: Scribner's, 1910.

———. *A Vagabond in Spain*. New York: Scribner's, 1895.

MacDonald, John. *Memoirs of an Eighteenth Century Footman*. London: G. Routledge & Sons, Ltd., 1778; New York: Harper Bros., 1927.

Mackenzie, Alexander Slidell. *Spain Revisited*. 2 vols. New York: Harper Brothers, 1836.

———. *Two Years in Spain, by a Young American*. London: R. Bentley, 1839.

———. *A Year in Spain, by a Young American*. Boston: Hilliard, Gray, Little and Wilkins, 1829; London: John Murray, 1831; New York: G. & C. & H. Carvill, 1830; New York: Harper & Brothers, 1836, 1847, 1857.

Mackie, J. M. *Cosas de España or Going to Madrid via Barcelona*. New York: J. S. Redfield, 1855.

Madariaga, Salvador de. *Englishmen, Frenchmen, Spaniards*. London: Oxford UP, 1928, 1929.

*———. *Spain*. New York: Scribner's, 1930: London: Benn, 1931.

Manning, Rev. Samuel. *Spanish Pictures*. London: Religious Tract Society, ca. 1890.

Marden, Philip S. *Travels in Spain*. Boston: Houghton Mifflin, 1910.

Marriot, Charles. *A Spanish Holiday*. London: Methuen & Co., 1908.

*Maugham, W. Somerset. *Andalucia: Sketches and Impressions*. New York: Alfred A. Knopf, 1923.

May, Stella Burke. *Men, Maidens, and Mantillas*. London: The Century Co., 1923; London: John Long Ltd., 1924.

*McBride, Robert Medill. *Spanish Towns and People*. With pictures by Edward C. Caswell. New York: Robert M. McBride & Co., 1925.

McIntyre, O. O. *Twenty-Five Selected Stories*. New York: Cosmopolitan Magazine, 1929, 1930, 1931. All three editions contain "Bravo the Bull."

M'Collester, Sullivan Holman. *After Thoughts of Foreign Travel in Historic Lands and Capital Cities*. Boston: Universalist Pub. House, 1891.

*Meier-Graefe, Julius. *The Spanish Journey*. Trans. from the German by J. Holroyd-Reece. London: Jonathan Cape, 1926; New York: Harcourt, Brace, 1927.

Mérimée, Prosper. *Carmen*. New York: A. L. Burt Co., 1915.

———. *Carmen and Letters from Spain*. New York: Milton Balch & Co., 1931. First Letter is "The Bullfights"; the second is called "Postcript"; they date from 1830 and 1842. Mérimée's First Letter repeats the usual justifications for the bullfight, but then adds his own explanation as to why it is irresistible even to foreigners: it speaks directly to the human passion for and fascination with combat and warfare. Mérimée attended bullfights as often as he could. He describes the various inner parts of the *plaza de toros,* the seating arrangements, the crowd, and the events of a generic bullfight, from the *despejo* (the clearing of the arena, to which the public was then admitted) through the bull's entrance, the performance of the picadors (not being English, he shows none of the usual horror at the disemboweling of the horses), of the banderilleros (he discusses regular banderillas, *banderillas de fuego*, and banderillas that held live birds that were released upon impact), and the matador. He recognizes not only the danger that faces each type of bullfighter, but also and even more admirably, the fact that each bull is different and needs to be treated according to its individual characteristics. He even discusses such details as the *querencia*, the *media-luna* (the crescent-shaped knife used to hamstring the bull, the only item he dislikes), the public, and various extraordinary events. The Second Letter, dated 1842, focuses on two bullfighters he admires: the recently deceased picador Francisco Sevilla, whom he had known personally; and the matador Francisco Montes (Paquiro), who was then still unknown in France. Mérimée's attention to detail gives vividness and immediacy to his well-informed discussion. Gautier, also a Frenchman, was equally well-informed.

Michael, A. C. *An Artist in Spain*. London: Hodder and Stoughton, 1914.

Middleman, Mrs. S. G. C. *Spanish Legendary Tales*. London: n.p., 1885.

Mills, L. E. *Glimpses of Southern France and Spain*. Cincinnati, OH: Clarke & Co., 1867.

*Montherland, Henri de. *Bullfighters*. Translated from the French. New York: Dial Press, 1927.

Moore, Thomas Ewing. *In the Heart of Spain*. New York: The Universal Knowledge Foundation, 1927. Contains "an excerpt from a French book published in 1700, describing a bullfight." This excerpt probably comes from Antoine de Brunel's *A Journey into Spain* (1670). Sections of Moore, including the excerpt, are reprinted in Smith's *Biography of the Bulls* (115–20).

Moran, Catherine. *Spain: Its Story Briefly Told*. Boston: The Stratford Co., 1930.

Moulton, Louise Chandler. *Lazy Tours of Spain and Elsewhere*. 1896. Boston: Roberts Bros., 1897.

Muirhead, Findley. *Northern Spain: Blue Guide*. London: Macmillan, 1930.

*Newbigin, Alice, M. S. *A Wayfarer in Spain*. Boston: Houghton Mifflin, 1927.

Newman, E. M. *Seeing Spain and Morocco*. New York: Funk & Wagnalls, 1930.

Nexo, Martin A. *Days in the Sun*. New York: Coward-McCann, Inc., 1929.

Nisbet, Hume. *The Matador and Other Recitative Pieces*. London: Hutchinson & Co., 1893. Limited edition of twelve copies.

Nixon-Roulet, Mary E. *The Spaniard at Home*. Chicago: A. C. McClurg, 1910.

Oakley, Amy. *Hill Towns of the Pyrenees*. New York: The Century Co., 1923.

Ober, Frederick A. *Knockabout Club in Spain*. Boston: Estes & Lauriat, 1889.

Obermaier, Hugo. *Fossil Man in Spain*. New Haven: Yale UP, 1924.

O'Reilly, Eliza Boyle. *Heroic Spain*. New York: Duffield & Co., 1910.

Orme, Edward. *Spanish Bull Fighting*. London: Edward Orme, 1813.

O'Shea, John Augustus. *Romantic Spain: A Record of Personal Experiences*. London: Ward and Downey, 1887.

Packard, J. F., ed. *Grant's Tour Around the World*. San Francisco: S. W. Dunn, 1880.

Pan American Airways. *Spain and Portugal*. 1922.

Patch, Olive. *Sunny Spain, Its People and Places, with Glimpses of Its History*. London, Paris, and New York: Cassell & Co., 1884.

Peck, Anne Marriman. *Roundabout Europe*. New York: Harper Bros., 1931.

———. *A Vagabond's Province*. New York: Dodd, Mead & Co., 1929.

Peek, Hedley, and Aflalo Peek. *The Encyclopedia of Sport and Games*. 4 vols. London: n.p., 1898. Contains entries on "Bullbaiting" and "Spanish Bullfights."

*Peers, Edgar Allison. *Spain: A Companion to Spanish Studies*. New York: Dodd, Mead & Co., 1929.

*———. *Spain: A Companion to Spanish Travel*. New York: Farrar & Rinehart, 1930.

Peixotto, Ernest. *Through Spain and Portugal*. New York: Scribner's, 1922.

Penfield, Edward. *Spanish Sketches*. New York: Scribner's, 1906, 1911; London: Bicket & Sons, 1911. Color illustrations by the author. One of the book's three chapters is dedicated to the bullfight; the author attends a bullfight in Madrid with a former matador, who explains some of the finer points and helps the author overcome his dismay over the horses. Penfield is knowledgeable and enthusiastic about the bullfight.

Pennell, Joseph, and Elizabeth Pennell. *Play in Provence*. New York: The Century Co., 1892.

Perkins, Charles. *The Phantom Bull*. Boston: Houghton Mifflin Co., 1932.

Phillips, Henry A. *Meet the Spaniards*. Philadelphia: J. B. Lippincott, 1931.

Phillips, Richard. *A Tour through the Principal Provinces of Spain and Portugal Performed in the Year 1803, with Cursory Observations on the Manners of the Inhabitants*. London: n.p., 1806.

Plummer, Mary W. *Contemporary Spain*. New York and London: Truslove, Hanson & Comba, 1899.

Pocomas. *Scenes and Adventures in Spain*. London: n.p., 1845.

———. *Scenes and Adventures in Spain from 1835 to 1840*. Philadelphia: J. W. Moore, 1846.

Poitou, Eugene. *Spain and Its People*. London: T. Nelson & Sons, 1873.

Pollard, Hugh B. *A Busy Time in Mexico*. London: Arnold Constable & Co., Ltd., 1913.

*Praz, Mario. *Unromantic Spain*. New York: Alfred A. Knopf, Inc., 1929.

Price, Lake. *Tauromachia or the Bullfights in Spain, Illustrated by Twenty-Six Plates*. London: J. Hogarth, 1852.

Prime, Samuel Irenaeus. *Alhambra and the Kremlin*. New York: Andson D. F. Randolph Co., 1873.

Prothero, Rowland E., ed. *The Letters of Richard Ford, 1797–1858*. London: John Murray, 1905.

Redfield, J. S. *Cosas de España*. New York: J. S. Redfield, 1855.

Reyles, Carlos. *Castanets*. Trans. by Jacques Le Clercq. London: Longmans, Green, 1929.

Riggs, Arthur. *The Spanish Pageant*. New York: Bobbs-Merrill, 1928.

Riley, C. D. *Skimming Spain in Five Weeks by Motor*. Los Angeles, CA: Saturday Night Pub. Co., 1931.

Robert, David. *Picturesque Sketches in Spain*. London: Hullmandel's Lithographic Estmt., 1837. Contains twenty-six plates of drawings.

Robert, Felix. *Scientific Bullfighting*. El Paso, TX: El Paso Printing Co., 1905.

Roberts, Richard. *An Autumn Tour in Spain in the Year 1859*. London: Saunders, Otley and Co., 1860.

Rolt-Wheeler, Francis. *A Toreador in Spain*. New York: George H. Doran Co., 1923.

Roscoe, Thomas. *The Jennings Landscape Manual (The Tourist in Spain)*. Illustrated from drawings by David Roberts. 5 vols. London: Robert Jennings & Co., 1836–39.

Rose, Fred W. *Notes of a Town in Spain*. London: n.p., 1885.

Salgado, James. *An Impartial and Brief Description of the Plaza or Sumptuous Market Place of Madrid and the Bull Baiting There, Together with the History of the Famous and much Admired Placidus. As also a Large Scheme, Being the Liverly [sic] Representation of the Order of Ornament of this Solemnity*. London: printed by Francis Clark for the Author, 1683.

Savage, Juanita. *The Spaniard*. New York: The H. K. Fly Co., 1924.

Sawtell, R. O., and Ida Treat. *Primitive Hearths in the Pyrenees*. New York: D. Appleton & Co., 1927.

Scott, S. P. *Through Spain*. Philadelphia: J. B. Lippincott, 1886.

*Sedgwick, Henry Dwight. *Spain: A Short History of Its Politics, Literature, and Art from Earliest Times to the Present*. London: George Harrap, 1925; Boston: Little Brown, 1926, 1929.

Shaw, Joseph T. *Spain of Today*. New York: Grafton Press, 1909.

Slater, Ernest (Paul Gwynne). *Along Spain's River of Romance (Guadalquivir)*. New York: McBride & Co., 1912; London: Constable, 1912.

———. *The Guadalquivir: Its Personality, Its People, and Its Associations*. London: Constable & Company., Ltd., 1912. Color illustrations, including one of a picador and another of a bullfighter. Contains a few remarks about bulls (225–28) and a humorous footnote: "I have no intention of inflicting an Andalucian bull-fight upon the reader. It has been worn to death; it has made a tableau in many a writer's works, including those of that unspeakable person Paul Gwynne, who seems to imagine that he put the finishing touch to it in *The Bandolero*" (228, n. 1).

Smith, Eleanor F. *Flamenco*. Indianapolis: Bobbs Merrill Co., 1931.

Smith, Horatio. *Festivals, Games and Amusements, Ancient and Modern*. London: Henry Colburn & Co., 1831.

*Stein, Gertrude. "I Must Try to Write the History of Belmonte." In her *Geography and Plays*. 1922. Madison: U of Wisconsin P, 1993. 69–74.

———. *The Life and Death of Juan Gris*. New York: Transition (Museum of Modern Art), 1927.

*Stewart, Alexander. *In Darkest Spain*. N.p.: n.p., n.d.

Stewart, George C. *Spanish Summer*. Milwaukee: Morehouse Pub. Co., 1928.

Stirling-Maxwell, William. *Sir William Stirling-Maxwell, 1818–1878*. London: Nimmo, 1891.

*Stoddard, Charles Augustus. *Spanish Cities, with Glimpses of Gibraltar and Tangier*. New York: Scribner's, 1892.

Stoddard, John L. *J. L. Stoddard's Lectures*. Boston: Balch Bros., 1898.

Stone, J. B. *A Tour with Cook Through Spain*. London: S. and Marstian Low and Scarle, 1873.

Storey, G. A. *Sketches from Memory*. London: Chatto & Windus, 1899.

Storm, Marian. *Prologue to Mexico: Echo of the Bullring*. New York: Alfred A. Knopf, Inc., 1931.

Stribling, T. S. *Red Sand*. New York: Harcourt, Brace & Co., 1924.

Sutton, Ranson. *The Passing of the Fourteen*. New York: A. Roman, 1914.

Swinburne, Henry. *Travels Through Spain in the Years 1775 and 1776*. London: Printed for P. Elmsly, 1779, 1787, 1813.

Sylvanus. *Pedestrian Reminiscences.* London: Brown, Green and Longman's, 1846.

Symons, Arthur. *Cities and Sea-Coasts and Islands.* New York: Brentano's, 1919.

Taylor, Susette M. *The Humor of Spain.* London: Sidney Kick, 1894.

Thicknesse, Philip. *A Year's Journey through France, and part of Spain.* Dublin: n.p., 1775; Bath: Printed by R. Cruttwell for the Author, 1777; London: W. Brown, 1778, 1789.

Thieblin, N. L. *Spain and the Spaniards.* London: Hurst and Blackett, Ltd., 1874.

Thirlmere, Rowland. *Letters from Catalonia and Other Parts of Spain.* London: Hutchinson & Co., Ltd., 1905.

Thornbury, Walter. *Life in Spain, Past and Present.* New York: Harper Bros., 1860.

Tiber, A. A. *Bullfights: Ninety-Six Sketches.* N.p.: n.p., 1886.

Ticknor, George T. "Amusements in Spain." *NAR* 21 (July 1825): 52–78.

———. *George Ticknor's Travels in Spain.* Ed. G. T. Northrup. Toronto: University of Toronto, 1913. Ticknor, who was Smith professor of modern languages at Harvard from 1819 to 1835, was among the first North American Hispanists, and author of the first history of Spanish literature in America. This is a posthumous publication of his account of his travels in Spain in 1818.

Tilden, Freeman. *The Spanish Prisoner.* New York: Doubleday, Doran & Co., 1928.

Tousey, Sinclair. *Papers from over the Water.* New York: British Book Centre, 1869.

Townsend, Joseph. *A Journey Through Spain in the Years 1786–1787.* 3 vols. London: C. Dilly, 1791, 1792.

Trend, John Brande. *Pictures of Modern Spain, Men and Music.* London: A. Constable & Co., Ltd., 1921.

———. *Spain from the South.* New York: Alfred A. Knopf, Inc., 1928.

Twiss, Richard. *Travels Through Portugal and Spain in 1772 and 1773.* London: Printed for the Author and sold by G. Robinson, T. Becket, and J. Robson, 1775. Also Dublin, 1775.

Tyler, Royall. *Spain: Her Life and Arts.* London: Grant Richards, Ltd., 1909.

*Unamuno y Jugo, Miguel de. *L'essence de l'Espagne: Cinq essais.* Trans. from Spanish by Marcel Bataillon. Paris: Plon, 1923.

Urquhart, David. *The Pillars of Hercules, or Travels in Spain & Morocco in 1848.* New York: Harper Bros., 1850.

Van Vechten, Carl. *The Music of Spain*. New York: Alfred A. Knopf, Inc., 1918; London: Kegan Paul, Trench, Trubner & Co., Ltd., 1920.

Villiers-Wardell, Janie. *Spain of the Spanish*. New York: Scribner's, 1909, 1910, 1912, 1914.

Wallis, Severn Teackle. *Glimpses of Spain; or, Notes of an Unfinished Tour in 1847*. By S. T. Wallis. New York: Harper & Brothers, 1849, 1854.

Walter, Ellery. *High Hats and Low Bows*. New York and London: G. P. Putnam's Sons, 1931.

Ward, G. H. B. *The Truth about Spain*. London: Cassel & Co., Ltd., 1911; 2nd ed., rev., 1913.

Warner, Charles Dudley. "The Bullfight." *The Century Magazine* 27.1 (1883): 3–13. This traveler's report focuses on two events, one in Seville and the second in Jerez. The first was a private "entertainment given by the gentlemen of Seville to their lady friends" (3) in *La Maestranza*, Seville's bullring. The well-informed first-person narrator assumes objectivity when he describes the bullring (3), but in general this is an opinionated, rather condescending account of Spanish women, Spanish men, the Spanish character, and the *fiesta nacional*. The author's sympathies are consistently with the animal, an attitude which he carries to its logical conclusion when, at the end of the essay, he desires the death of the human being. In the Seville episode, he sees two-year-old animals, which he mistakenly terms "bulls"; their horns have been shaved in deference to the fact that the men they face are not professional bullfighters. Warner, of course, objects to this. He denigrates the men as invariably clumsy, inept, and heartless "tormentors," while the animal is endowed with human feelings — he is "tired and bloody and hot, and has had enough of it"; he "bellows at the hurt" and is "astonished" by the sword thrust (7) — that invite the reader to identify with it. The afternoon's three animals are subjected to "prolonged and ceremonious torture" and although "[t]here is nothing very exciting about it, [. . .] the crowd apparently enjoy the torture of the animal" (7). The second half of the Seville event is a display of equine skill, the Spanish riders being unfavorably compared to "our Western and Indian horsemen" (8). The treatment of the equine games is not quite as scornful as the preceding discussion of the bullfight, which is the essay's primary concern. In the second half of the essay, the narrator speaks briefly and more generally about the social and financial success of top-notch bullfighters, the careful breeding of the bulls, the Spanish passion for the bullfight and their "unconquerable hatred of the animal" (8), and then moves to a bullfight in Jerez that starred Antonio Carmona (El Gordito) and Salvador Sánchez (Frascuelo), two top-notch performers. He details the first two bullfights of the afternoon, sits through the third, and then leaves the ring, commenting that "Perhaps I should have got used to the cruelty, the disgusting sight of the gored horses, and the cheap barbarity, if I had staid through the entire performance; but I could no longer endure the weariness and monotony of the show [. . .]. One's sympathy went always with the tormented bull [. . .]. There were times when it would have been a relief to see him dispatch one of his tormentors" (12–13). After delivering this murderous remark, and apparently unaware of its import, the narrator "sought refuge in an old church near by, to bathe our tired eyes and bruised nerves in its coolness and serenity" (12).

———. *A Roundabout Journey.* Boston: Houghton Mifflin, 1884, 1890.

*Wells, Herbert George. *The Outline of History.* 2 vols. New York: Garden City Pub. Co., 1920; 3rd ed., rev., New York: Mc-Graw Hill Co., 1921.

Wells, N. A. *The Picturesque Antiquities of Spain.* London: R. Bentley, 1846.

White, George. *The Heart and Songs of the Spanish Sierras.* London: n.p., 1894.

Wigram, Edgar T. A. *Northern Spain.* London: Adam and Charles Black, 1906.

Wilberforce, Archibald. *Nations of the World Salute Spain.* New York: Peter, Fenelon, Collier, 1898.

———. *Spain and Her Colonies.* New York: Peter, Fenelon, Collier, 1898.

Williams, E. Carleton. *The Lure of Castile.* London: Mills & Boon, Ltd., 1927.

Williams, Leonard. *The Land of the Dons.* London: Cassel & Co., Ltd., 1902.

———. *Toledo and Madrid.* London: Cassel & Co., Ltd., 1903.

Wolff, Henry Drummond. *Rambling Recollections.* 2 vols. London: Macmillan & Co., Ltd., 1908.

Wood, Ruth Kedzie. *The Tourist's Spain and Portugal.* London: Andrew Melrose, Ltd., 1914.

York, Duke of. *The Tour of His Royal Highness Edward Duke of York from England to London, Gibraltar, etc. etc. . . . also a Particular Account of a Bullfight.* London: Dixwell, 1764.

Zimmerman, Jeremiah. *Spain and Her People.* Philadelphia: G. Jacobs & Co., 1902.

# II: Hemingway's Reading on Spain and the Bullfight, Pre-1932

**Journals and Newspapers**

*ABC.* Spanish newspaper, founded as a weekly in 1903 and transformed into a daily paper in 1905. By the 1910s, the newspaper carried bullfighting reviews on a regular basis. Gregorio Corrochano, the eminent taurine critic and author of the famous phrase Hemingway quotes (*DIA,* 89), wrote for *ABC* from 1912 to 1936, when his political views forced him to leave Spain. Hemingway kept the *ABC* issues of 1 May 1924, 26 May 1925, and 6 August 1925 (JFK).

*El Clarín.* Established in Valencia, 1922. Hemingway read *El Clarín* in Spain and maintained a subscription when he returned to Key West. He echoes its negative opinion of Domingo Ortega, which was a minority opinion. Mentioned in *DIA* Glossary, s. v. *Revistas.*

*La corrida* (Barcelona). In the 1920s, the photographer Juan Pacheco, known as Vandel, was a correspondent photographer for this newspaper. Many of Vandel's excellent photographs appear in *Death in the Afternoon.* Hemingway saved several issues of June and July 1923 (JFK).

*El eco taurino.* Hemingway read it in Spain and subscribed to it in 1931 and 1932. The JFK holds the issues he saved from the years 1927, 1930, 1931, and 1932. Mentioned in *DIA* Glossary, s. v. *Periódicos* and *Revistas.*

*La fiesta brava: Semanario taurino.* Established in Barcelona in 1926. Hemingway read it in Spain, subscribed to it when he was in the States, and ordered back issues, several of which are in the JFK. Hemingway also saved the issue of 7 April 1933, which carried a glowing review of *DIA. La fiesta brava* is mentioned in *DIA* Glossary, s. v. *Periódicos* and *Revistas.*

*Fiestas de toros.* The JFK holds loose issues.

*Le Journal du Midi.* Hemingway saved the issue of 26 April 1924 (JFK).

*Kikiriki: España taurina.* Hemingway owned issues from 1918.

*Ledgers de toros.* 2 vols. (JFK)

*Libro de Gallito.* About José Gómez Ortega (Joselito), known as Gallito at the beginning of his career (JFK).

*La lidia: Revista taurina ilustrada.* Established in 1880 or 1881, in Madrid. It ceased publication at the turn of the century and resumed in the 1910s, as a weekly. Hemingway saved scattered issues from 1887, 1889, 1892, and 1920 (a special double issue commemorating Joselito), and several later issues. Mentioned in *DIA* Glossary, s. v. *Lidia* and *Revistas.*

*Sangre y arena* (Barcelona). Hemingway saved the issues of 23 April, 28 May, 25 June, and 9 July of 1924 (JFK).

*El sol.* The JFK holds the issue of 7 February 1927.

*Sol y sombra: Semanario taurino ilustrado.* Published in Madrid, 22 April 1897 to 1926 and again from 1941 to 1943. Hemingway owned fourteen vols. Mentioned in *DIA* Glossary, s. v. *Revistas.*

*Tauro* (Madrid). The JFK holds the issue of 5 July 1923.

*El toreo* (Madrid). The authoritative annual *Toros y toreros en 1924* identifies *El toreo* as Spain's oldest taurine periodical; it was established in 1874. Hemingway saved the issue of 30 July 1923 (JFK).

*Torerías: Semanario taurino bolcheviki.* Established in Madrid, in 1920. Hemingway saved several issues from 1925. Mentioned in *DIA* Glossary, s. v. *Revistas.*

*Le torero: Revue Taurine Française.* Established in 1891, it was published weekly during the taurine season and monthly in the winter. Hemingway saved several issues. This is probably the unnamed paper that Jake Barnes reads in *The Sun Also Rises* (30). JFK holds the issues of 27 April, 7 September, and 21 September 1924.

*Toreros y toros.* Established in Madrid, in 1918, it was published uninterruptedly all the years Hemingway visited Spain. Mentioned in *DIA* Glossary, s. v. *Revistas.* The JFK holds the issues of 3 and 10 June 1923, and 23 and 30 March 1924.

*Le toril: Revue Tauromachique Indépendante Illustrée.* Established March 1922, in Toulouse. In French, although a few articles are in Spanish or contain untranslated quotes from Spanish newspapers and journals. Hemingway subscribed to this taurine newspaper in 1925, 1926, and 1927 and saved about twenty issues from these years. Mentioned in *The Sun Also Rises* (30) and in *DIA* Glossary, s. v. *Revistas.* According to the French taurine writer Pierre Dupuy, Hemingway's subscription began in 1922.[6]

*El Universal* (newspaper, probably Mexican). Hemingway saved the issue of 7 February 1927, when there are no bullfights in Spain and many of the bullfighters he was interested in were in Mexico for that country's bullfight season (JFK).

*La voz de Navarra.* Hemingway saved the issues of 11 July 1923 and 4 July 1927, which contain material on the Pamplona fiestas of those years, both of which he attended (JFK).

*Zig-Zag: Tragicomedia taurina.* Published from May 1923 to November 1924, in Madrid. Hemingway saved several copies. Mentioned in *DIA* Glossary, s. v. *Revistas.*

**Books**

Alcázar, Federico M. *Sánchez Mejías: El torero y el hombre.* Foreword by Gregorio Corrochano. Madrid: Imprenta Juan Pueyo, 1922. A study of the life and art of the bullfighter (and writer) Ignacio Sánchez Mejías. With photographs and illustrations.

Alvarez, Marcelino (Marcelo). *Las competencias: Bomba-Gallo-Machaco-Pastor.* Madrid: Prudencio Pérez de Velasco, 1911.

Aulnoy, Madame d'. *Travels into Spain.* Ca. 1692; trans., London: George Routledge, 1930. Scholars have determined that this French noblewoman did not write the material that appeared under her name. According to Rex Smith, "her books on Spain were compilations of writings and items from the publication in Paris, *Gazette,* which had an official status and correspondents abroad" (120). She seems to have used other sources as well. Mariano Tomás gives the Spanish version of her full name, María Catalina Jumel de Berneville, condesa D'Aulnoy, and describes her as a novelist and writer of children's stories and fables. The bullfight she "describes" is dated 1679 and embellished with romantic interest: the bullfighter is fighting in honor of a young lady, the bulls are tempted to run from their pasture lands to Madrid by "mandarines" (cows), there is much flirting in the stands, and the account ends with a story about two lovers who are fatally gored by the same bull: they "begged the favour that they might be married" before dying, and were "buried together in one and the same grave" (qtd. in Smith, 130).

Baedeker, Karl. *Spain and Portugal: Handbook for Travelers.* Leipzig: Baedeker, 1913. Hemingway refers to Baedeker and his guidebooks repeatedly and mockingly, in *Across the River and into the Trees.*

Bagüés, Ventura (don Ventura). *Efemérides taurinas: Hoy hace años.* Barcelona: Lux (La Ibérica), n.d. (probably 1928). An account of landmark events in the bullfighting world. See also Orts-Ramos, Tomás.

Barriobero y Herrán, Eduardo. *El libro de la fiesta nacional: Preceptiva, cronistas, censores.* Madrid: Mundo Latino, 1931.

Becerra y Alvarez, José (Capotito). *El consultor taurino.* Sevilla: Santigosa y Rodríguez, 1916. A *consultor* is a professional directory, listing people, places, and organizations relevant to the bullfight; this one contains a chapter on bull-breeding ranches that offers a historical survey of each ranch.

Bell, Aubrey FitzGerald. *Spanish Galicia.* New York: Duffield & Co., 1923.

Bellsolá, Joaquín (Relance). *El toro de lidia.* Foreword by José de la Lorna (Don Modesto). Madrid: Marso, 1912. Book-length discussion of the bull, contains photographs.

Bergamín, José. *El arte de birlibirloque: Entendimiento del toreo.* Madrid: Plutarco, 1930.

Blasco Ibáñez, Vicente. *Blood and Sand.* Trans. from the Spanish by Mrs. W. A. Gillespie. New York: E. P. Dutton Co., 1919. There are other translations: by Douglas, 1911; by Campbell, 1911; by Cushing, 1921. For the influence of this novel, see Susan F. Beegel's "'The Undefeated' and *Sangre y Arena:* Hemingway's *Mano a Mano* with Blasco Ibáñez" (in *Hemingway Repossessed,* ed. Kenneth Rosen [Westport CT and London: Praeger, 1994], 71–85).

———. *La Corrida / The Bullfight.* Abridged bilingual edition. English translation by C. D. Campbell. Philadelphia: David Mackay, 1911, 1919. Hemingway owned the 1919 edition.

———. *Sangre y arena.* Valencia: n.p., 1908. Hemingway also owned a translation and a bilingual edition.

Bleu, F. (Félix Borrell Vidal). *Antes y después del Guerra: Medio siglo de toreo.* Madrid: Clásica Española, 1914. Writing in 1913, Bleu surveys the bullfight as he has seen it develop over the preceding half-century. He decries modern developments (the lessening of risk embodied in the smaller bull, the fact that the kill itself has lost primacy). Bleu begins with El Tato and Gordito, delights in Frascuelo and Lagartijo (whom he sees as representing the heroic age of bullfighting, when bulls were splendidly powerful and the kill was the high point), and then discusses Mazzantini and a few others. The second section focuses on Guerra himself, who imposed conditions — he demanded smaller bulls with shorter horns, refused to fight bulls he disapproved of, emphasized his skills with cape, banderillas, and *muleta* at the expense, writes Bleu, of the sword — and thus marked an "unhealthy" break with the past. The third and last section portrays later figures, starting with Antonio Fuentes and Emilio Torres and ending with Joselito and Belmonte. An important book, one of three studies of Guerra that Hemingway owned.

Borrow, George Henry. *The Bible in Spain*. 1843. London: Murray, 1923. In *For Whom the Bell Tolls,* Robert Jordan admires Borrow's books about Spain (248).

Byron, George Gordon, Lord. *Childe Harold's Pilgrimage*. Hemingway seems to have owned this poem in a separate edition (Brasch and Sigman do not give bibliographic details), as well as Byron's *Complete Poetical Works* (Boston: Houghton Mifflin, 1905), where the poem appears on pp. 1–83. In describing "the ungentle sport," Byron focuses on the presence of women, the richness of the clothes, and the injuries inflicted upon the horses and the bull (*Childe Harold's Pilgrimage,* Canto the First, LXXVII) — a vivid but not sympathetic treatment.

Calvo Martínez, Ricardo. *Resumen taurino de 1930*. Madrid: Sindicato Exportador del Libro Español, 1931. Facts and figures relevant to the 1930 season, which Hemingway did not witness.

Camisero. *See* Carmona, Angel.

Campbell, Roy. *Taurine Provence: The Philosophy, Technique and Religion of the Bullfight*. London: Desmond Harmsworth, 1932. Hemingway owned two copies.

Carmona, Angel (Camisero). *Consultor indicador taurino universal para profesionales y aficionados en general*. Madrid: Published for the Author by the Sindicato de Publicidad, 1924. Camisero was a bullfighter with a minor career. His *Consultor,* compiled and published after his retirement from the ring, is a professional directory that lists bullfighters of all ranks, journalists, managers, doctors, impresarios, and other personnel connected with the bullfighting world in all the countries where bullfights are held. The directory also lists establishments that cater to bullfighters and aficionados: hotels, restaurants, clubs, book shops, and so on. Train schedules, post offices, and other services are also detailed.

———. *Consultor indicador taurino universal para profesionales y aficionados en general*. Madrid: published by the author, 1932. With Foreword by Gregorio Corrochano. This is an updated version of his earlier *consultor*.

Carralero, José, and Gonzalo Borge. *Toros célebres.* Santoña: Imprenta de R. Meléndez, 1908, 1930. Hemingway's use of this book has been explored by Nancy Bredendick, in "*Toros célebres:* Its Meaning in *Death in the Afternoon*" (*The Hemingway Review* 17.2 [1998]: 64–73).

Carreras y Candi, Francesco, ed. *Folklore y costumbres de España.* 3 vols. Barcelona: Martín, 1931–34.

Carretero, José María (El caballero andaluz), and Juan Farragut. *Granero, el ídolo: Vida, amores y muerte del gladiador.* Madrid: G. Hernández y Galo Sáez, 1922. Published in the year of Manuel Granero's spectacular death.

Cervantes, Miguel de. *Don Quijote de la Mancha.* This book has been translated into English several times, but the translations Hemingway owned seem to postdate *DIA.* Still, it is highly likely that he read Cervantes' short account of how Don Quixote and Sancho Panza were trampled by a herd of bulls who were being run from their ranch to a nearby village where they were to be fought.

Chapman, Abel, and Walter J. Buck. *Unexplored Spain.* London: Edward Arnold, 1910.

———. *Wild Spain: Records of Sport with Rifle, Rod and Gun; Natural History and Exploration.* London: Gurney & Jackson, 1893.

Ciria y Nasarre, Higinio. *Los toros de Bonaparte.* Madrid: Ducazcal, 1903.

Clavo, Maximiliano (Corinto y Oro). *Charlas taurinas.* Madrid: Fernández Fé, 1924.

Colvil, Helen Hester. *In the Footsteps of a Saint and Other Sketches from Spain.* London: Burns, Otis & Washbourne, 1931.

Conde de las Navas. *See* López Valdemoro y de Quesada, Juan Gualberto.

Corinto y Oro. *See* Clavo, Maximiliano.

Díaz Arquer, Graciano. *Libros y folletos de toros: Bibliografía taurina, compuesta con vista de la biblioteca taurómaca de José Luis de Ybarra y López de la Calle.* Madrid: Pedro Vindel, 1931. Mentioned in the "Bibliographical Note" that closes *DIA*.

don Luis. *See* Uriarte, Luis.

don Parando. *See* Rivera, José.

don Pío. *See* Pérez Lugín, Alejandro.

don Ventura. *See* Bagüés, Ventura.

Dos Passos, John. *Rosinante to the Road Again.* New York: George H. Doran, 1922. A book of essays that explore Spain's landscape, literature, and the character of its people.

Dowsett, J. Morewood. *The Spanish Bullring, being Some Account of the Spanish Bull Fight from its Earliest History and To-day.* London: Bale, 1928. This fifty-one page pamphlet takes the historical view as it discusses the relationship of the monarchy and the church to the bullfight as well as various aspects of a bullfight afternoon (the dressing of the bullfighter, the trip to the bullring, the admiration of the crowd, the *paseo,* and the events of a contemporary corrida) more or less accurately but with palpable hostility. Dowsett dwells upon the treatment of the horses before and during the bullfight (39–47); the pain of the bull that is "tortured," "teased," "mocked," and "baited" by the bullfighters; and Spain's national penchant for "cruelty to animals" (47–49) — what Hemingway identifies as the "animalarian" attitude. Dowsett rejoices in the elimination of the *banderillas de fuego* [banned in 1928, as he reports, but reinstituted in 1930] and inaccurately and self-aggrandizingly takes credit for the introduction of the *peto,* which he applauds "as a first stage for the elimination of the horse from the ring"; he "look[s] forward to the day when, with the spread of education and modern ideas, so long delayed in the Iberian peninsula, bull-fighting will be abolished" and "Spain will seek some noble sport to replace what has been a national disgrace for many centuries" (50–51). The pamphlet contains a short Glossary which defines *maestro* and *verónica* incorrectly, and confuses *espada* with *alternativa*. The preface by R. B. Cunninghame Grahame applauds Dowsett's "righteous indignation" about "the stupid cruelty of introducing worn-out, blindfolded horses [. . .] into the ring" (v) but chides him for not having read basic materials and for failing "to trace the genesis of bull-fighting from Hillo and Romero [. . .] down to Belmonte, and poor Nacional II, slain not in the exercise of his art, but basely by a bottle thrown by an iconoclast" (vii–ix; Hemingway takes the hint and discusses this very incident, *DIA,* 77). The preface points out Dowsett's other failings: "he does not tell us" which bullfighters he saw (x) and "does not touch upon the danger the Espada has to face" (x). The preface in fact outlines the better book Dowsett should have written.

Ellis, Havelock. *The Soul of Spain*. Boston and New York: Houghton, Mifflin & Co., ca. 1908, 1923; New York: G. P. Putnam's Sons, 1923. Hemingway had a 1939 reprint, but he owned several other books by Ellis, which suggests an admiration for this author, so it seems likely that he read this book before writing *Death in the Afternoon*. Ellis focuses on the symbolism of the bullfight, seeing it as "an elaborate ritual" that is "sacred" and drenched in "solemnity," like the rituals of the Roman Catholic church (348–49). But Ellis shows his lack of sympathy and understanding for the bullfight when he calls it a sport and "an anachronism under the conditions of modern civilisation" (350). He holds himself aloof from "the Spaniard's easy familiarity with divine things," which "we people of northern race," who are given to "a tense and rigid virtue," do not share (353). Ellis finds that the Spaniard is hard and indifferent to pain, and therefore akin to the "savage": the Spanish "indifference to pain [. . .] is alien to the tenderness, fully as much egoistic as alrtuistic [*sic*], which marks civilisation" (41). Allying himself with "civilisation," Ellis refrains from observing or describing the bullfight, but still claims to understand the "essential Spain," which is "primitive and eternal" and "spiritual" (vii–viii).

Fernández Coello de Portugal, Antonio and José. *Belmonte en 1919.* Madrid: Impresa Artística de Sáez Hermanos, 1919. 246 pages, focuses on Joselito.

Fernández de Heredia, Antonio (Hache). *Doctrinal taurómaco de "Hache."* Madrid: Antonio Marzo, 1904. This rare, expensive book is a study of the bullring of Bilbao; it includes the *Reglamento* that governed that plaza.

Ford, Richard. *Gatherings from Spain.* London: John Murray, 1846, 1851, 1861; London: J. M. Dent, [1906]; New York: E. P. Dutton & Co., 1906, 1913, 1927. The book was also issued under the title *The Spaniards and Their Country:* London: n.p., 1847; New York: Wiley and Putnam, 1847; and New York: G. P. Putnam, 1848, 1850, 1852, 1854. Ford was an English lawyer, painter, and collector who lived many years in Spain; his work established him as an authority on many aspects of Spanish history and culture. Ford makes some untenable generalizations (e.g., that the Spaniard's "hostility to the horned beast is instinctive, and grows with their growth" [qtd. in Smith, *Biography of the Bulls,* 152), but on the whole his discussion of the bullfight is sensible and well-informed. He discusses the economic connection between the bullfight and the church, describes the pomp of royal corridas, offers a few anecdotes involving women, describes the *encierro* (bringing the bulls from the ranch to the bullring) and various breeders, and then describes a generic bullfight, in rather high style. His heart bleeds for the horse, but he recognizes that "It is poor and illogical philosophy to judge of foreign customs by our habits, prejudices, and conventional opinions" (qtd. in Smith, 169). Ford is mentioned approvingly both in *Death in the Afternoon* (53) and in *For Whom the Bell Tolls* (248).

Frank, Waldo. *Virgin Spain: Scenes from the Spiritual Drama of a Great People.* New York: Boni and Liveright, 1926. *Death in the Afternoon* rails against this book, but without mentioning its author. Frank's account of the bullfight has some errors (he mistakes the cape for the *muleta,* for example), but he is capable of reading the bullfight as something more significant than "sport." Frank differs from most writers in that he sees "The horse [as] the comedian of the drama" [232–33], an opinion which Hemingway repeats. For more detail on *Virgin Spain,* which is comprehensive and scholarly, even if the prose is occasionally purple, see Mandel, *Complete Annotations,* 458–60 (s. v. *Virgin Spain*).

Frazer, James George. *The Golden Bough: A Study in Magic and Religion.* New York: Macmillan, 1922. Frazer discusses the bull as divine, as a sacrificial animal, and as a disguise or incarnation of Dionysus, whose enemies then cut him (as a bull) to pieces with knives (swords); this event was reenacted biannually in Crete, in a ceremony in which a bull was ripped to pieces; and in Cynaetha, where a bull, which represented Dionysus, was taken to the sanctuary. In other, non-Dionysian rites, an ox or bull, representing the spirit of vegetation, was sacrificed every summer to prevent drought and thus ensure rich crops.

García Carrafa, Arturo. *Frases célebres de toreros*. Madrid: Sanz Calleja y Antonio Marzo, 1917–1919. A compendium of remarks and witticisms attributed to bullfighters and other taurine personalities through the ages.

García Rodrigo, Ramón (Resquemores, R. G. R.). *Anales taurinos*. Madrid: Avrial, 1900. This is a professional directory, listing bulls ranches, bull breeders, bullfighters, and other important people, places, organizations, and events of the bullfighting world. Most such *consultores* were hefty books; this one is 505 pages. *See also* Becerra y Alvarez, José; *and* Carmona, Angel.

Giles, Dorothy. *The Road Through Spain*. Philadelphia: Penn Pub. Co., 1929.

Gómez Hidalgo, Francisco. *Belmonte, el misterioso: Su vida y su arte*. Madrid: Libro Popular, 1913. Biography and analysis of Belmonte and his art; illustrated with photographs and drawings by Ricardo Marín.

Goya y Lucientes, Francisco José de. *Tauromaquia*. 2 vols. (43 drawings). N.p., n.d. Hemingway acquired these books in 1923.

Guerra, Rafael. *See* Vázquez y Rodríguez, Leopoldo; *see also* Bleu, F.; Peña y Goñi, Antonio; *and* Redondo y Zuñiga, Ladislao.

*La guía Michelin de España-Portugal*.

*Guía para los viajeros de los ferrocarriles de España, Francia y Portugal y de los servicios marítimos*. Madrid: Compañía de los Ferrocariles, ca. 1888.

Guides Bleus. *Espagne*. Paris: Hachette, 1927.

Gutiérrez de la Hacera, Pascual Ramón. *Descripción general de la Europa, y particular de sus estados, y cortes, especialmente de España, y Madrid, antiguo y moderno*. Madrid: Doblado, 1771.

Hay, John. *Castilian Days*. With one hundred and eleven illustrations by Joseph Pennell (black and white drawings). 1871. London: William Heinemann, 1903; Boston: Houghton Mifflin, 1903. In this wide-ranging, historically oriented book, Hay discusses Madrid, the Prado Museum, Spanish class systems, attitudes to family, work, play, religion, and so on, in an occasionally admiring, often condescending tone. His twenty-two page chapter on the bullfight extols its folkloristic elements (colorful crowd, dress, orange vendors) but is critical of the bullfight itself and particularly of the Spanish public, which is deemed to be bloodthirsty and unsympathetic to the pain of the animals (horses and bulls) and even to the matador or picador who shows weakness. Hay reviews statistics that indicate that agriculture is more profitable than bull breeding and ends the section on the bullfight by quoting an old aficionado who claims that the current bullfight [that is, before Joselito and Belmonte] is decadent, not as fine as the old days.

Hernández Girbal, F. *Julián Gayarre: Una vida triunfal*. Madrid: Atlántico, 1931. Pamplona's Teatro Gayarre, named after this tenor, is mentioned in *The Sun Also Rises* (153) and in *DIA* (273).

———. *Manuel Fernández y González: Una vida pintoresca*. Madrid: Atlántico, 1931. A biography of the writer Manuel Fernández y González, who wrote about Madrid and the bullfights.

Hume, Martin Andrew Sharp. *The Spanish People: Their Origin, Growth and Influence*. London: William Heinemann, 1901.

Irving, Washington. *Tales of the Alhambra: A Series of Sketches of the Moors and Spaniards*. Philadelphia: Carey Lea, 1832; London: H. Colburn, 1832. There were many subsequent editions, some with illustrations, some revised and expanded by Irving, some with introductions by other hands, and some with different or no subtitle. Hemingway owned an edition which included introduction and notes by Ricardo Villa-Real (Granada: Editorial Padre Suárez, 1953); he may have read an earlier edition.

Jerezano. *See* Vela, Carlos.

Jones, Tom (Thomas Wallace Jones). *Bull Fighting Illustrated*. Cincinnati, OH: T. Jones, 1904. Noel Fitch records that Hemingway borrowed this item from Sylvia Beach's bookstore on 30 January 1926. It is an interesting booklet of about thirty pages, shaped like a bull's head and neck, rather than having the normal rectangular shape of a book. It looks like a child's book, but in fact it is more sophisticated than most of what was being published at the time. Each page carries one or two illustrations, with excellent explanatory captions prepared by a well-informed Mexican aficionado. This organization, which emphasizes the visual, indicates that in order to understand the bullfight, one must look carefully, and not avert one's eyes at "difficult" moments, as another author recommends. An unusual and excellent booklet, marred only by a few errors in spelling and fact.

Kipling, Rudyard. *Animal Stories*. London: Macmillan & Co., Ltd., 1932. Contains story, "The Bull That Thought."

———. *Debits and Credits*. New York: Doubleday & Co., Inc., 1926. Contains story, "The Bull That Thought."

———. *The Humorous Tales of Rudyard Kipling*. New York: Doubleday Doran & Co., 1931. Contains story, "The Bull That Thought."

L. R. *See* Redondo y Zuñiga, Ladislao.

Laughlin, Clara Elizabeth. *So You're Going to Spain! And if I Were Going with You These Are the Things I'd Invite You to Do*. Boston: Houghton Mifflin, 1931.

Lawrence, D. H. *The Plumed Serpent*. New York: Alfred A. Knopf, Inc., 1926; London: Secker, 1926. In the novel's first chapter, the main character, Kate Leslie, and two male companions go to see the last bullfight of Mexico City's taurine season. The chapter seethes with social, sexual, national, and generational hostility, all of it apparent before the bullfight begins. Kate, an Irishwoman, doesn't particularly admire her companions, who are Americans, and she is appalled by the Mexican audience and by the bullfight itself. The bullfight is actually a *novillada*, as the costumes of the "toreadors" are "plastered with silver [not gold] embroidery," but neither the narrator nor the characters seems to be aware of this distinction. The description of the events is vivid but rather inaccurate (banderillas are placed between the first and second pic) and incomplete, as Kate leaves in horror and disgust during the pic-ing; hence the title of the chapter, "Beginnings of a Bull-Fight." Kate learns to respond more positively to Mexico as the book progresses, but she never attends another bullfight. Hemingway "admitted to having learned from [Lawrence's] writing a few tricks about describing landscape" (Baker, *Life Story,* 240), but this first chapter probably annoyed him.

López Valdemoro y de Quesada, Juan Gualberto (Conde de las Navas). *El espectáculo más nacional.* Madrid: Rivadeneyra, 1899. This is an oversized, historically oriented, wide-ranging account of the bullfight and its effect on Spanish culture. It contains many excerpts of works that deal with the bullfight in various ways (papal bulls, royal decrees, poetry, fiction, criticism, etc.), lists royal corridas held from the twelfth to the nineteenth centuries, lists promotions (*alternativas*) and other data; it also contains a fairly comprehensive, annotated list of authors and other figures associated with the bullfight, as well as indices of places and titles. It was published as a limited edition of 1,010 copies, ten to be given to important personalities, the rest to be sold; only one hundred or so copies are extant. This is an important and now rare reference work.

Madariaga, Salvador de. *Spain.* New York: Scribner's, 1930: London: Benn, 1931.

Marcelo. *See* Alvarez, Marcelino.

Maugham, W. Somerset. *Andalucia: Sketches and Impressions.* New York: Alfred A. Knopf, 1923. Two chapters are dedicated to the bullfight.

McBride, Robert Medill. *Spanish Towns and People.* With pictures by Edward C. Caswell. New York: Robert M. McBride & Co., 1925. McBride's chapter on the bullfight, "Modern Gladiators of Spain" (83–99), follows the usual formula: it describes the crowds going to the bullfight, compares the bullfight to some other sport, and then describes the *plaza de toros,* the clearing away of the crowd from the arena, the entrance of the matadors and other personnel, and the entrance of the bull — all of this with reasonable sympathy. As soon as the picadors come into play, however, all sympathy and interest devolve upon the horse, and the picador is inaccurately dismissed as "just a make-believe warrior, protected by armor concealed under his costume" (91). The matador is treated with some respect (93–94), but the author returns to the plight of the horse. The article concludes that bullfights in general are "excessively wearying" (97). McBride was a publisher who published several books on Spain, by himself and by other hands (see the entries for Flitch, Gordon, and Slater).

Meier-Graefe, Julius. *The Spanish Journey*. Trans. from the German by J. Holroyd-Reece. London: Jonathan Cape, 1926; New York: Harcourt, Brace, 1927. Hemingway borrowed the 1926 edition from Sylvia Beach's Shakespeare and Company; he owned the 1927 edition. He mentions Meier-Graefe in *Death in the Afternoon* (203); Comley and Scholes analyze that reference in *Hemingway's Genders* (115–16).

Millán, Pascual. *La escuela de tauromaquia de Sevilla y el toreo moderno*. Madrid: Romero, 1887. Details the history of the bullfighting academy of Seville, discusses its more prominent students, and evaluates its effect on the history and development of the bullfight. Although the school functioned for only two years, 1830–32 (most of that time under the direction of Pedro Romero), it had enormous influence.

———. *Los novillos: Estudio histórico*. Madrid: Moderna, 1892.

———. *Los toros en Madrid: Estudio histórico*. Madrid: Palacios, 1890. This book gives an early history of the spectacles which preceded the bullfight, a history of Madrid, the royal house, the colonization of Perú, and other matters, all through the prism of the bullfight. It contains a large, detailed fold-out floor plan of the Madrid bullring.

———. *Trilogia taurina*. Madrid: Ginés Carrión, 1905. Hemingway owned the first and third volumes of this trilogy.

Minguet y Calderón de la Barca, Enrique (Pensamientos). *Desde la grada: Anuario taurino de 1913*. Madrid: El Porvenir, Martínez de Velasco, 1914. Detailed summary of a single season, like those of Ricardo Calvo Martínez, Tomás Orts-Ramos, Luis Uriarte, and Carlos Vera. The calendars report dates of fights; names of performers, bull breeders, and plazas; and injuries, deaths, and other important events of the year.

———. *Desde la grada: Anuario taurino de 1918*. Madrid: n.p., 1918.

———. *Desde la grada: Anuario taurino de 1925*. Madrid: Núñez Samper, 1925.

———. *Desde la grada: Anuario taurino de 1928*. Madrid: n.p., 1928.

Montes, Francisco (Paquiro). *Tauromaquia completa, o sea el arte de torear en plaza*. Madrid: Imprenta José María Repullés, 1836. Montes' explanation of all aspects and logic of the art of the bullfight is an important book, frequently reissued. *Death in the Afternoon* quotes Montes (Glossary, s. v. *Ligereza* and *Maleante*); *The Dangerous Summer* misquotes him (51).

Montherland, Henri de. *Bullfighters*. English translation, New York: Dial Press, 1927. Hemingway owned this novel, *Les bestiaires: Roman*, in the original French edition (Paris: Grasset, 1926). He borrowed the 1927 translation from Sylvia Beach's Shakespeare and Company. The novel deals with bullfighters in Andalucía.

Muñoz Díaz, Eugenio (Eugenio Noel). *Las capeas.* Madrid: Helénica, 1915. Eugenio Noel lobbied for the abolition of the bullfight, considering it an anachronism in a modern country. In *Las capeas,* he focuses on the brutality of these village bullfights, citing examples from the many small towns throughout Spain where they were held.

Navas, Conde de las. *See* López Valdemoro y de Quesada, Juan Gualberto.

Newbigin, Alice. *A Wayfarer in Spain.* Boston: Houghton Mifflin, 1927.

Orts-Ramos, Tomás (Uno al Sesgo). *Los ases del toreo.* Barcelona: Lux, 1927. Biographical and professional details about leading bullfighters.

———, and Ventura Bagüés (don Ventura). *Toros y toreros en 1925: Resumen crítico-estadístico de la temporada taurina.* Barcelona: Lux, 1925. These annuals, like those of Minguet (Pensamientos), give detailed accounts, statistics, and reviews of the bull-breeding ranches and the bullfighters during one season. They have calendars of various sorts (of *novilladas,* corridas, comic bullfighting, injuries, and other important events), bibliographies, addresses, summary essays, and so on.

———, and Ventura Bagüés. *Toros y toreros en 1926: Resumen crítico-estadístico de la temporada taurina.* Barcelona: Lux, 1926.

———, and Ventura Bagüés. *Toros y toreros en 1927: Resumen crítico-estadístico de la temporada taurina.* Barcelona: Lux, 1927.

———, and Ventura Bagüés. *Toros y toreros en 1929: Resumen crítico-estadístico de la temporada taurina.* Barcelona: La Fiesta Brava, 1929.

———, and Ventura Bagüés. *Toros y toreros en 1930: Resumen crítico-estadístico de la temporada taurina.* Barcelona: La Fiesta Brava, 1930.

*Páginas taurómacas (por José Delgado [Pepe Hillo], condesa d'Aulnoy* [. . .] *Lord Byron* [and others]. Madrid: Caro Raggio, 1920.

Paquiro. *See* Montes, Francisco.

Parando, don Parando. *See* Rivera, José.

Peers, Edgar Allison. *Spain: A Companion to Spanish Studies.* New York: Dodd, Mead & Co., 1929.

———. *Spain: A Companion to Spanish Travel.* New York: Farrar & Rinehart, 1930.

Peña y Goñi, Antonio. *Guerrita.* Madrid: La viuda de J. Ducazcal, 1894. Authoritative biography of Rafael Guerra Bejarano (Guerrita) by a professional taurine critic, less critical of him than F. Bleu's book, *Antes y después del Guerra,* which Hemingway also owned.

———. *Lagartijo y Frascuelo y su tiempo.* Madrid: Palacios, 1887. Biography of two important bullfighters, discussion of their professional relationship and the historical moment in which they lived and performed.

Pensamientos. *See* Minguet y Calderón de la Barca, Enrique.

Perea, Daniel. *A los toros: Album compuesto de 28 acuarelas originales del reputado pintor de escenas taurinas, Daniel Perea, con la explicación de cada suerte en español, francés e inglés; conteniendo además la Marcha de la manolería de la zarzuela "Pan y toros."* Barcelona: Miralles, 1895.

Pérez Lugín, Alejandro (don Pío). *Currito de la cruz: Novela.* 2 vols. 1921. Madrid: Pueyo, 1929. Hemingway also owned Sidney Franklin's translation of this novel into English, published as *Shadows of the Sun* (New York: Scribner's, 1934). Hemingway may have mediated between Franklin and Charles Scribner.

———. *¡¡¡Ki ki ri ki!!! Los Gallos: Sus rivales y su prensa.* Madrid: Pueyo, 1919.

———. *El torero artista, Rafael Gómez (Gallito): Apuntes para la historia.* Madrid: Renacimiento, 1890.

Pío, don Pío. *See* Pérez Lugín, Alejandro.

Praz, Mario. *Unromantic Spain.* New York: Alfred A. Knopf, Inc., 1929.

Redondo y Zuñiga, Ladislao (L. R.). *Guerrita: Su tiempo y su retirada.* Madrid: Velasco, 1899. This is another study of Rafael Guerra (*see also* F. Bleu *and* Antonio Peña y Goñi). Guerra was a spectacular bullfighter who dominated the bullfight world after Lagartijo and Frascuelo, whose rivalry affected his own career. His early retirement at the age of thirty-nine was precipitated by taurine politics and the hostility of the Madrid public, including many of the more influential critics. He said that "Yo no me voy de los toros; me echan" (I am not leaving the bulls; I am being thrown [or forced] out). This book was written in the year of Guerra's retirement and shortly after Spain's loss of Cuba, Puerto Rico, Guam, and the Philippines.

Resquemores. *See* García Rodrigo, Ramón.

Rivera, José (don Parando). Coauthor with Carlos Vela (Jerezano). *Resumen pitonudo de 1929: Resumen crítico-estadístico de la temporada taurina.* Madrid: n.p., 1930.

Sáenz de Heredia, Cesáreo (El Bachiller Garrocha). *Las corridas de toros en la actualidad.* 2nd rev. ed. Madrid: Los hijos de Gómez Fuentenebro, 1914. Includes critical evaluations of Joselito and Belmonte.

Salabert y Arteaga, Andrés Avelino (Marqués de Torrecilla). *Indice de bibliografía hípica española y portuguesa catalogada alfabéticamente por orden de autores y por orden de títulos de las obras.* Madrid: Sucesores de Rivadeneyra, 1916–1921. This multi-volume bibliography probably contains material on equine bullfighting (*rejoneo*).

Sánchez Cantón, Francisco Javier. *L'Espagne.* Madrid: Gráficas Reunidas, n.d. (may predate *DIA*).

Sánchez Carrere, Adolfo. *Hablando con el Gallo de la Pasión: Informaciones cómicas por "El Coco" Repórter*. Foreword by J. Pérez Zúñiga. Madrid: Velasco, 1914.

Sánchez de Neira, José. *El toreo: Gran diccionario tauromáquico*. 2 vols. Madrid: Guijarro, 1879. Rev. and enlarged edition, Madrid: Velasco, 1896. Dictionary of taurine terms; Hemingway owned both editions of this excellent and rare book.

Sedgwick, Henry Dwight. *Spain: A Short History of Its Politics, Literature, and Art from Earliest Times to the Present*. London: George Harrap, 1925; Boston: Little Brown, 1926, 1929.

Stein, Gertrude. "I Must Try to Write the History of Belmonte." In her *Geography and Plays*. 1922. Madison: U of Wisconsin P, 1993, 69–74. The poem expresses Stein's admiration for Belmonte; Hemingway read it in typescript, probably before he saw his first bullfights.

Stewart, Alexander. *In Darkest Spain*. N.p.: n.p., n.d.

Stoddard, Charles Augustus. *Spanish Cities, with Glimpses of Gibraltar and Tangier*. New York: Scribner's, 1892.

Torrecilla, Marqués de. *See* Salabert y Arteaga, Andrés Avelino.

Unamuno y Jugo, Miguel de. *L'essence de l'Espagne: Cinq essais*. Trans. from Spanish by Marcel Bataillon. Paris: Plon, 1923.

Uno al Sesgo. *See* Orts-Ramos, Tomás.

Uriarte, Luis (don Luis). *Toros y toreros en 1920: Detalles y apreciaciones de la temporada*. Madrid: El Liberal, 1920. Hemingway did not go to the bullfights until 1923; Uriarte's books gave him details about earlier seasons.

———. *Toros y toreros en 1921: Detalles y apreciaciones de la temporada*. Madrid: La Mañana (or La Montaña), 1921. This volume details and evaluates the 1921 season, which Hemingway did not witness.

Vázquez y Rodríguez, Leopoldo, and Rafael Guerra, Luis Gandullo, and Leopoldo López de Saa. *La tauromaquia*. 2 vols. Madrid: Pedro Nuñez (or Mariano Nuñez Samper), n.d. (probably 1895 or 1897). An explanation and definition of all aspects of bullfighting, as understood and practiced by Rafael Guerra, a master of the art. Like Francisco Montes' *Tauromaquia*, this is a very important book.

Vela, Carlos (Jerezano), and José Rivera (don Parando). *Resumen pitonudo de 1929: Resumen crítico-estadístico de la temporada taurina*. Madrid: Sucesores de Rivadeneyra, 1930.

Velázquez y Sánchez, José. *Anales del toreo: Reseña histórica de la lidia de reses bravas y galería biográfica de los principales lidiadores*. Seville: Delgado, 1873. This illustrated, oversized book is an important reference work that surveys the history of the bullfight and offers biographies of important bullfighters.

Ventura, don Ventura. *See* Bagüés, Ventura; *see also* Orts-Ramos, Tomás.

Vindel, Pedro. *Estampas de toros: Reproducción y descripción de las más importantes publicadas en los siglos XVIII y XIX relativas a la fiesta nacional.* Introducción de Gregorio Corrochano. Madrid: Vindel, 1931.

Wells, Herbert George. *The Outline of History.* 2 vols. New York: Garden City Pub. Co., 1920; 3rd ed., rev., New York: Mc-Graw Hill Co., 1921. Hemingway owned the third edition.

# Notes

[1] Qtd. in John Hay, *Castilian Days,* 102.

[2] In 1933, Orts-Ramos wrote, "*Death in the Afternoon* es para mi gusto lo mejor, más documentado y tratado con mayor simpatía, de cuanto sobre toros han escrito los extranjeros. Una visión exacta, de buen aficionado, con respecto a la fiesta; un afán propagandista, que nunca podremos agradecerle bastante los españoles, pues no se limita al espectáculo, sino que se extiende a España entera de la que todo le agrada y satisface, hacen de este libro algo extraordinario, muy merecedor de los mayores encomios" (*Death in the Afternoon* is, in my opinion, the best, most thoroughly documented and sympathetic work on bullfighting ever written by a foreigner. [...] It does not limit itself to the bullfight, but deals with all of Spain, which it finds pleasant and satisfying; this is an extraordinary book, worthy of the highest praise; "Bibliografía taurina," 334). A longer review by the same critic expands upon this praise, qualifying it only by commenting on Hemingway's probable and detrimental adoption of Sidney Franklin's opinions ("Libros de toros," 2–3) and his failure to consult an important collection, housed in the United States (Bredendick identifies this as the collection of Luis Carmena Millán, acquired by the Hispanic Society in New York shortly after Carmena's death in 1904; email communication, 8 October 2003).

[3] *Death in the Afternoon* has been translated into French (by Rene Daumal, 1938), Italian (by Fernanda Pivano, 1947, 1962), German (by Annemarie Horschitz-Horst, 1957), Swedish (by Arne Häggqvist, 1958), Danish (by Michael Tejn, 1961), Finnish (by Tauno Tainio, 1962), Norwegian (by Nils Lie, 1963), and, belatedly, Spanish (by Lola Aguado, in magazine form in 1966 and as a book in 1968). Although the Spanish public was informed of the existence of the book in 1933, political considerations delayed the Spanish translation (see LaPrade).

[4] Shubert sidesteps Hemingway by quoting García Lorca's "Llanto por Ignacio Sánchez Mejías," whose refrain "a las cinco de la tarde, a las cinco en punto de la tarde" he quotes in translation "Five in the afternoon, It was five, sharp, in the afternoon" in his introduction.

[5] See the entries for F. Bleu, Antonio Peña y Goñi, and Ladislao Redondo y Zuñiga.

[6] Dupuy mentions that a correspondent for *Le Toril,* Auguste LaFront (Paco Tolosa), reported that Hemingway was one of the first subscribers, reading about the bullfight more than a year before he went to Spain to see one (Dupuy, *Hemingway et*

*l'Espagne* [n.p.: La Renaissance du Livre, 2001], 22–23; qtd. in Bredendick, email communication, 8 October 2003).

## Works Cited

Baker, Carlos. *Ernest Hemingway: A Life Story.* 1969. New York: Collier/Macmillan, 1988.

Brand, Anthony. Interviews, August–October 2003.

Brasch, James, and Joseph Sigman. *Hemingway's Library: A Composite Record.* New York: Garland, 1981.

Bredendick, Nancy. E-mail communication, 8 October 2003.

*La Busca.* Publication of Taurine Bibliophiles of America, vols. 9 (1973), 12 (1976), 16 (1980), 20 (1984), and 30 (1994).

*Catálogo Núm. 9: Catálogo de libros, folletos, revistas y carteles de asuntos taurinos.* Madrid: Librería Rodríguez, 2002.

Comley, Nancy R., and Robert Scholes. *Hemingway's Genders: Rereading the Hemingway Text.* New Haven: Yale UP, 1994.

Conrad, Barnaby. *Encyclopedia of Bullfighting.* Boston: Houghton Mifflin, 1961.

DeFazio, Albert John III. E-mail communications, September–October 2003.

Díaz Arquer, Graciano. *Libros y folletos de toros: Bibliografía taurina, compuesta con vista de la biblioteca taurómaca de José Luis de Ybarra y López de la Calle.* Madrid: Pedro Vindel, 1931.

*La Fiesta Nacional: Ensayo de bibliografía taurina.* Madrid: Biblioteca Nacional, 1973.

Fitch, Noel. "Ernest Hemingway — c/o Shakespeare and Company." *Fitzgerald-Hemingway Annual* (1977): 157–81.

Hay, John. *Castilian Days.* With Illustrations by Joseph Pennell. 1871. London: William Heinemann, 1903.

Hemingway, Ernest. "Bullfighting, Sport and Industry." *Fortune* (March 1930): 83–88, 139–146, 150.

———. *Death in the Afternoon.* New York: Scribner's, 1932.

LaPrade, Douglas E. *La censura de Hemingway en España.* Salamanca: Ediciones Universidad de Salamanca, 1991.

———. "The Reception of Hemingway in Spain." *The Hemingway Review* 12.2 (1992): 42–50.

Layman, Richard. "Hemingway's Library Cards at Shakespeare and Company." *Fitzgerald-Hemingway Annual* (1975): 191–207.

López Becerra, Aureliano (Desperdicios). *Los ingleses y los toros: El secreto de Uzcudun por Desperdicios y Asterisco*. 3rd ed. Bilbao: Editorial Vizcaína, 1926.

López Valdemoro y de Quesada, Juan Gualberto (Conde de las Navas). "Embollado. En beneficio de los extranjeros." In his *El Espectáculo más nacional*. Madrid: Rivadeneyra, 1899. 382.

McCormick, John, and Mario Sevilla Mascareñas. *The Complete Aficionado*. Cleveland: The World Publishing Company, 1967.

McNab, Angus. *The Bulls of Iberia*. London: William Heinemann Ltd., 1957.

*The National Union Catalogue Pre-1956 Imprints* and its *Supplements*. 754 vols. London: Mansell, 1971.

Orts-Ramos, Tomás (Uno al Sesgo). "Bibliografía taurina." In *Toros y toreros en 1933: Resumen crítico estadístico de la temporada taurina*. Eds. Tomás Orts-Ramos and Ventura Bagués (don Ventura). Barcelona: Talleres Gráficos Irández, 1933. 333–36.

———. "Libros de toros: Un rato a bibliografía." *La fiesta brava* (7 April 1933): 2–3.

Reynolds, Michael S. *Hemingway's Reading, 1910–1940: An Inventory*. Princeton: Princeton UP, 1981.

———. "A Supplement to *Hemingway's Reading: 1910–1940*." *Studies in American Fiction* 14.1 (1986): 99–108.

Shubert, Adrian. *Death and Money in the Afternoon: A History of the Spanish Bullfight*. New York and Oxford: Oxford UP, 1999.

Smith, Rex, ed. *Biography of the Bulls: An Anthology of Spanish Bullfighting*. New York and Toronto: Rinehart & Co., Inc., 1957.

Tomás, Mariano. *Los extranjeros en los toros*. Barcelona: Editorial Juventud, S.A., 1947.

Urquijo de Federico, Antonio, comp. *Catálogo de la biblioteca taurina de don Antonio Urquijo de Federico*. Madrid: n.p., 1956 (according to the title page) or 1957 (according to the colophon).

Wagner-Martin, Linda. "The Intertextual Hemingway." In *A Historical Guide to Ernest Hemingway*. Ed. Linda Wagner-Martin. New York: Oxford UP, 2000. 173–94.

#  Reading Texts, Paratexts, and Absence

# "The Real Thing"? Representing the Bullfight and Spain in *Death in the Afternoon*

*Peter Messent*

THE NOTION OF AUTHENTICITY, and the capturing of it by one means or another, was an important one to Hemingway throughout his artistic career. In *Death in the Afternoon,* he uses the phrase "the real thing" twice to describe, in turn, the two subjects, writing and bullfighting, which are linked in symbiotic connection throughout the book.[1] The best known of these occasions is early in the text, when he makes one of his most famous pronouncements on what he was aiming to achieve in his own writing: "the real thing, the sequence of motion and fact which made the emotion and which would be as valid in a year or in ten years or, with luck and if you stated it purely enough, always" (*DIA,* 2).[2] The second is when he is writing of the "ecstasy" produced by a "brilliant faena," the series of muleta passes made by the matador in the final third of the bullfight. Describing the "emotional and spiritual intensity and pure, classic beauty that can be produced by a man, an animal and a piece of scarlet serge draped over a stick," he then adds, "if you should ever see the real thing you would know it" (206–7). Throughout the book, this phrase is linked to words like "true," "pure," "honest," "sincere," "simple," "integral," and their derivatives.

But Hemingway does not give us "the real thing" when he describes bullfighting in *Death in the Afternoon.* Instead, we get his version of that reality. To view bullfighting in terms of ecstasy and emotional and spiritual intensity, and to see its climax in the death of the bull and the act of "killing beautifully" (252), "death uniting the two figures [man and bull] in the emotional, aesthetic and artistic climax of the fight" (247), is clearly to give a highly subjective version of what Hemingway sees not as a sport but as "a tragedy" (16) and a "sculptural art" (13). Most non-Spaniards, after all, present bullfighting from a quite different, and morally condemnatory, perspective. Hemingway in this respect is very much an exception to the norm, his view of bullfighting and its morality — "I know only that what is moral is what you feel good after" (4) — in strong contrast with the majority of foreign critics both before and after his time of writing. I hardly need to give examples here, but an earlier nineteenth-century example of bullfight writing by author and journalist, Charles Dudley Warner, stands as a perfect illustration of what Hemingway would see as the "animalarian" (see 5–6) tendency. The ironic opening of his November 1883 *Century* essay typifies Warner's complete lack of sympathy with the "barbaric" and "demoniac performance" (13) he witnesses:

> Let us begin tranquilly. We are going to kill a good many old horses [. . .] and we are going to torture them in their last hours on the way to the bone-yard; we are going to bait, and worry, and weaken by loss of blood, and finally slaughter a number of noble bulls; we are about to enter the region of chivalry, and engage in the pastime most characteristic of [. . .] the Spanish people; we promise gore and carnage enough farther on, and we may be pardoned for a gentle [. . .] introduction to the noble sport. (3)

A present-day British newspaper column takes those same cultural assumptions for granted: "with 10,000 licensed matadors in the country, it will be a few years yet before the Spanish join the rest of the human race and decide that torturing and killing animals for fun is no way to behave" (Wood, 14).

In other words, Hemingway's description of bullfighting, "what really happened in action" (2), conflicts with other versions of that "reality." Distancing himself from the first from "a modern moral point of view, that is, a Christian point of view" which makes "the whole bullfight [. . .] indefensible" (1), Hemingway is more a primitive than a barbarian, his view of "what really happened" dictated by this subject position. His remark that "Spain is the real old stuff" (*Selected Letters*, 131) is suggestive in this respect. We might indeed take Stanley Diamond's claim that "the sickness of [modern] civilization consists [. . .] in its failure [. . .] to incorporate [. . .] the primitive" (129) as a starting point for an analysis of Hemingway's treatment both of Spain and of the bullfighting that, for him, lay at the center of this foreign world. In a book that defies the boundaries of conventional literary taxonomy,[3] Hemingway operates as much as an anthropologist as anything else, explaining a pre-modern society and its rituals to his American audience. It is the nature of his role both as explicator and "translator" that concerns me in this essay.

Hemingway straddles cultural boundaries and barriers in *Death in the Afternoon*. Despite a degree of controversy, Spanish critics have generally agreed that, with his book, Hemingway proved his status as "the greatest of foreign aficionados of the Spanish bullfight" (Capellán, 154). His "commentaries and judgements have the ring of undeniable authenticity" (Hernández, qtd. in Capellán, 136). His knowledge of Spain, and of the bullfight, are considered the equivalent of that of any Spaniard, so Capellán writes, for instance, that "Hemingway got to know Pamplona as a native would know it" (30). In these quotations, the distance between foreign and native comes to be elided. Similarly, as Hemingway himself speaks and writes about Spain, we see instabilities as he negotiates the border area between these two identities.

Spain clearly served as an idyllic and "homelike" space in Hemingway's writing. If he found himself "a stranger in his own [American] home" after the First World War, he evidently thought of Spain differently: "This is my land. This is my country" (Capellán, 4, 10).[4] In July 1925, he wrote to Scott Fitzgerald about Spain: "God it has been wonderful country. [. . .] To me heaven would be a big bull ring with me holding two barrera seats and a trout stream outside" (*Selected Letters,* 165). During the Spanish Civil War, Hemingway both wrote the script for, and narrated *The Spanish Earth* (1937), the film Joris Ivens made to promote the Republican cause. Here, speaking of the village of Fuentedueña and the need to irrigate the land, Hemingway says: "For fifty years *we've* wanted to irrigate but *they* held us back" (my emphasis). Two decades later, Hemingway described his return to Spain — synonymous with a return to bullfighting — as a return from exile: "I had been away for fourteen years. A lot of that time [. . .] was like being in jail except that I was locked out; not locked in" (*The Dangerous Summer,* 46). He then proclaimed that "I loved this country in all seasons" (83).

The cultural identification Hemingway makes here — "we," "my country" — is, however, at odds with his actual status as a foreigner. In *Death in the Afternoon,* his position, as confirmed by the presence of the "Explanatory Glossary," is one of *translator*. And if he apparently comes to know bullfighting as a native does, he starts off his book in the role of foreigner, describing "the first bullfight I ever went to" in terms of his expectations as a cultural outsider who "expected to be horrified and perhaps sickened by what I had been told would happen to the horses" (1). Discussing the buying of tickets, too, he talks of the treatment "you" will receive "because you are a foreigner," and identifies himself with that treatment ("I have been lied to most in Galicia [. . .]," [35]). But it quickly becomes obvious that the end-result of his repeated attendance at bullfights has been that "they [have] come to mean something" to him: to mean in fact a great deal. Learning to "know what is good and what is bad" to the point that "nothing confuse[s] [his] standards" (162), Hemingway understands the very *essence* of the "art." His knowledge of it is analogous to his knowledge of Madrid, a place where there are no "local-colored place[s] for tourists" but where "the essence" of Spain itself can be found (51).

The assumption throughout the book is that Hemingway has found, and understood, this essence: both of bullfighting and of Spain. His status as tourist is displaced by his *afición,* the "love of bullfights" shared by "the most intelligent part" of the "bull ring public" (Glossary, s. v. *Afición*). Accordingly, he comes to present himself as an insider rather than an outsider, one who takes his sometime dialogic partner, the Old lady who becomes his pupil, to the Café Fornos, which is frequented *only by people connected with the bullfights* and by whores. There is smoke, hurrying of waiters, noise of glasses [...]. We can discuss the fights, if you wish [...]. There are bullfighters at every table and for all tastes. (64, my emphasis)

Similarly, when Hemingway writes about the Prado and the vague disappointment of "the tourist" over the way the pictures are hung (52), it is clear that he excepts himself from that category. But Hemingway *is* still a tourist, however much of an insider, and like a native, he becomes. For he is an outsider, too, judging between cultures: "I believe [...] the *vin ordinaire* in Spain [...] to be the best in Europe by far" (Glossary, s. v. *Vino*). And the experiences he describes — the bullfight as "the best two dollars' worth I have ever had" (234), Hadley and the bull's ear (270), "being pickpocketed in Spain" ("they do not destroy your [...] passports," Glossary, s. v. *Maleante*) — are necessarily part and parcel of his foreign identity.

So, as one who is both foreign but also in a certain way — in his understanding of Spanish life and rituals — native, Hemingway's dominant role in *Death in the Afternoon* is that of a mediator. He is not writing as a Spaniard or for a Spanish audience. The book, rather:

> is intended as an introduction to the modern Spanish bullfight and attempts to explain that spectacle both emotionally and practically. It was written because there was no book which did this in Spanish or in English. ("Bibliographical Note")

What he produces, then, is a "sor[t] of guide boo[k]" (63) for an Anglo-American readership. And if his book serves to translate the rituals of one culture for another, Hemingway is not oblivious to the slippages and arbitrary nature of this, and of any such act of translation. This is true of the individual word. Thus Hemingway writes that "suerte," from "suerte de varas, or the trial of the lances," means, according to the dictionary, "chance, hazard, lots, fortune, [...] doom, destiny, [...] mode, way, skillful manoeuvre; trick, feat, juggle, and piece of ground separated by landmark." As he concludes: "So the translation of trial or manoeuvre is quite arbitrary, *as any translation must be from the Spanish*" (96, my emphasis). The difficulty, even at times the impossibility, of translation operates at a larger level too. So when Hemingway speaks of the way in which a Spanish audience judges the killing of the horses in the bullring he says that it is the inability to share "this view-point [...] which has made the bullfight unexplainable to non-Spaniards" (404). This is of a piece with his earlier comment on the impossibility of making anything but a subjective account of bullfighting "come true on paper" (63). The text moves in contradictory directions as his own insistence on authenticity and on representing "the real thing" is necessarily, though briefly, undermined.[5]

Hemingway writes in *Death in the Afternoon* a type of anthropology. And the translation of one culture for the understanding of another can never be a neutral process. Marc Manganaro, in his edited book on *Modernist Anthropology,* comments on contemporary understandings of the discipline to say that "insights gained into the nature of representation and power relations have made impossible the comfortable assumption that other cultures can be grasped, categorized, and put on paper" (Manganaro, 3). This can be put another way by taking James Clifford's view of the ethnographer's activity, and adjusting the context to fit the case of Hemingway's book. For if Spain, and the bullfight ritual that stands in synecdochal relation to it, stand as a type of cultural "Other" for the American writer here, that Other "represents what the modernized individual, because of his 'sense of pervasive social fragmentation'" is searching for. And the object of that search is "a 'wholeness' that 'by definition becomes a thing of the past (rural, primitive [. . .]), accessible only as a fiction, grasped from a stance of incomplete involvement.' [. . .] This quite contrived fiction is wrought at the price of the presence of the Other" (Clifford, qtd. in Manganaro, 29).[6]

But Manganaro and Clifford are speaking here of accounts of the "vanishing 'primitive'" and that does not entirely fit the case of Hemingway and Spain. Moreover phrases like "incomplete involvement" and "contrived fiction" and even the notion of the "Other" may seem, at first glance, one-sided given the depths of Hemingway's involvement with Spanish culture and his immersion in its rituals and ways of life. But I do, nonetheless, see these words as offering significant insights into the nature of Hemingway's "anthropological" project in *Death in the Afternoon*.

To put things more bluntly: whenever we examine any text written about a "foreign" culture we need to be aware of the way in which the ideology of the author influences his representation of the cultural differences he or she portrays.[7] And Clifford's stress on the "social fragmentation" of the ethnographer's or anthropologist's own culture, and its influence, is certainly relevant in Hemingway's case, for he measures Spain ("the real old stuff") against America and its modernized culture throughout his book. This process of cultural comparison and contrast lies at the heart of his writing project and helps to explain the particular version of Spain that he gives.

Throughout *Death in the Afternoon,* Spain is described in terms of its similarity to and difference from America. This is often done in a neutral and non-evaluative way. So Bilbao, we read, "gets as hot as [. . .] St. Louis, Missouri" (38), and the peculiar climate in Spain means that a springtime train ride takes one "through country as bare and cold as the badlands in November" (47). More significant for my purposes are the examples of the way the Spanish culture Hemingway describes in his book becomes the healthy yardstick against which an absent and "diseased" America is measured. There is something paradoxical here in the association of his own sanitized country and culture with the unhealthy rather than the healthy. But what Hemingway is concerned with is what makes for the fullest response to life and its living. This helps explain the dismissive nature of his remarks about "the Y.M.C.A. and other institutions for clean living" (103). More crucially, when Hemingway describes those "modern comforts" which include "a bathtub in every American home," he is suggesting the poverty of a materialistic and therapeutic culture, and particularly the way it chooses to repress any knowledge of, or "intelligent interest in," the taboo subject of death (266). Americans here are compared to Spaniards, whose attitude is seen as healthily mature: "they are interested in death and do not spend their lives avoiding the thought of it and hoping it does not exist only to discover it when they come to die" (264).[8]

American modernity is, often implicitly but sometimes explicitly, unfavorably compared with Spanish traditionalism throughout the book. This opposition is not architectural or even necessarily demographic: Madrid is a modern urban center after all, but it is also "the most Spanish of all cities, the best to live in, [with] the finest people" (51). The "malady of specialization" (85) which affects bullfighting points the reader back to American culture just as surely as does the earlier reference to the "civilized" aspects of wine-drinking (10).[9] So, too, does the description of Juan Luis de la Rosa, a skillful bullfighter but one who — as a "perfectly manufactured product" — lacked "emotion or elation" (74).

The Spain that Hemingway constructs, then, acts as the desired Other, a contrast or corrective counterbalance to the modernized American world from which the author is in full retreat. Hemingway was trying "to present the bullfight integrally" (7). *Integral,* indeed, is a key word in a text that, in one sense, is all about the relationship of the part to the whole. Hemingway's description of bullfighting is the central component in his larger celebration of the Spain he "love[s] very much" (277). Throughout the text he gives the sense of a geography and culture that offer what America has lost; of a culture that is in itself "integral," focused round the ritual spectacle at its core.

This reading of the text is supported by looking at passages Hemingway cut from the final version of *Death in the Afternoon*. In these passages, Hemingway describes the geographical movements of his own life, tracing them back to the Michigan where he spent his summers as a boy. He recalls a simpler rural American world that has now been obliterated:[10]

> Michigan I loved very much when I lived in it, and when I was away from it, but as I grew up each time I returned to it it was changed. It was a country of forests, lakes and streams and small farms with hills and pastures, always with a background of woods. [. . .] They cut down the forests, the streams lost their water, the lakes had their levels low-

ered and raised by the taking or not taking of water to float sewerage from Chicago down the drainage canals; they built concrete roads across all the country and around the lakes, the motorists caught all the fish out of the streams [. . .], they abandoned the farms. [. . .] Now the second growth is coming back where the forests were slashed [. . .] and people seeing the second growth believe that they know what the forest was like. But it was not like that and you will never know what it was like if you did not see it. Nor will you know what the heart of a country was after it is gone. (Qtd. in Beegel, 52–53)

Unspoiled country in America has been despoiled, suburbanized, polluted by the effects of urban living, covered over by the signs of a commercial and faceless mass culture. So, elsewhere, Hemingway remembers the place where in boyhood he shot his first pheasant as now transformed: "there was a hot dog place and filling stations and the north prairie [. . .] was all a subdivision of mean houses" ("Remembering Shooting-Flying: A Key West Letter," 188).[11]

Hemingway's idyllic notion of America as sacred space, as true "home," belonged to his childhood. He saw the "heart of [the] country" as gone after that time, ripped out by modernization and its effects: a fragmentation that separated the author both from the land and from the citizens he saw contributing to its ruin. In the Spain of *Death in the Afternoon,* the sense of unspoiled country is still just present. In the final chapter of the book, he does focus on recent changes that, he says, have made the country "in the end [. . .] just like home except for yellow gorse on the high meadows and the thin rain" (274). But this is a retrospective note that jars with the book's general tendency, apparent even in that same last chapter, to describe Spain in terms of idyllic and predominantly rural space, and Spaniards in terms of their harmonic and pre-technological relationship with their land:

> If I could make [. . .] the smell of olive oil; the feel of leather; rope soled shoes; the loops of twisted garlics; earthen pots; [. . .] the pitchforks made of natural wood (the tines were branches); the early morning smells [. . .] then you would have a little of Navarra. But it's not in this book.
> There ought to be Astorga, Lugo, Orense [. . .] the chestnut woods on the high hills, the green country and the rivers, the red dust, the small shade beside the dry rivers and the white, baked clay hills. [. . .] (275)

The main thrust of the book is to describe Spain in terms of a "rural, primitive [. . .] wholeness" which, even if it may be disappearing,[12] can still in Hemingway's eyes be clearly identified and celebrated.

This version of Spain, then, is focused through the eyes of an author turning his back as far as that might be possible on modernity and its effects, and particularly on the experience of the First World War and the physical and psychological damage associated with it. For the effects of that war on the individual subject stand in Hemingway as a type of figure for the "sense of pervasive social fragmentation" associated with modernity on a larger and collective scale. So on the one hand in this book, we have a Spanish culture associated with ordered ritual (bullfighting) and coherence, all its various parts representing one attractive whole. On the other we have the war and the literal and figurative sense of fragmentation associated with it.[13]

This accounts for the presence of "A Natural History of the Dead" in *Death in the Afternoon*. For the sequence is not just "dropped in [...] as a way of closing out" a particularly uninspired section of the book (Weber, 53–54) but is, rather, crucial to the final structure and intention of Hemingway's text. Fragmentation is the precise subject of this story, where Hemingway rejects a "Humanist" version of the world — that is, the belief in man's innate nobility and in a universe proceeding according to a human-centered divine plan — in favor of his own "observations [as a] naturalist" (133–34). The narrative, which contains both the apparently unfocused prologue and the present-time dialogue between the author and the Old lady, describes various forms of the breaking of bodily wholes during the war. Such descriptions include the narrator's first-person tale of the collecting of "fragments" and "detached bits" of female corpses after "the explosion of a munition factory" near Milan. Of particular note here is the apparent detachment he (and the other observers) show in the pseudo-scientific manner of their conclusions:

> We agreed [...] that the picking up of the fragments had been an extraordinary business; it being amazing that the human body should be blown into pieces which exploded along no anatomical lines, but rather divided as capriciously as the fragmentation in the burst of a high explosive shell. (135–37)[14]

The narrator also gives details about the decaying bodies of the dead following the Austrian offensive of June 1918: "If left long enough in the heat the flesh comes to resemble coal-tar, especially where it has been broken or torn" (137). Some general remarks on the way men die in war ("like cats, a skull broken in and iron in the brain," 139) lead to the climaxing story of the badly wounded soldier "whose head was broken as a flower-pot may be broken" (141) and the argument between an artillery officer and a doctor over whether the man should be swiftly put out of his misery or left to die naturally.[15]

The random violence and grotesque forms of death that mark modern warfare are implicitly, then, measured against the risk, and form and function, of death within the major art form that Hemingway sees the bullfight to be. In much of his fiction, and especially in the Nick Adams stories,

Hemingway uses the First World War to allegorically signify a modern world where larger, dislocating, and uncontrollable force operates over and over again. "A Natural History of the Dead" is paradigmatic of this modernity, in which the individual is completely powerless, out of kilter with an impinging and threatening world. In this world, the human subject is metaphorically or literally (in the war itself) fragmented, unable to function in any "whole," autonomous, or socially significant way.

The bullfighter, on the other hand, *does* function in just that way: he remains physically and psychologically whole. In "A Natural History of the Dead" and in Hemingway's other First World War narratives, the individual is torn to fragments. Or, if he survives, like both Nick Adams and the narrator here, he is psychologically damaged by his experiences, unable to fully connect with the modern socio-historical world around him. The bullfighter, on the other hand, stands at the center of that ritual which lies, for Hemingway, at the heart of a Spanish cultural life that still remains untainted (or pre-modern), vibrant, and meaningful. *Death in the Afternoon,* then, is a text which always looks two ways. The version of bullfighting and Spain that Hemingway constructs is comprehensible only in terms of his own response to the First World War and in his paradigmatic reading of its damaging effects.

And this is where the ritualistic aspects of his book come in. First, there is the ritual killing of the bull and the role the bullfighter himself plays in it. In the First World War the notion of individual autonomy and heroism suffered, for Hemingway, a complete collapse: we are told of Catherine's fiancé right at the start of *A Farewell to Arms* that "They blew him all to bits" (20). The bullfighter is, in contrast, the active rather than the passive subject. He takes to himself "one of the Godlike attributes; that of giving [death]" (233) and is "an icon of essential masculinity,"[16] challenging the bull within the ring in a type of "mythical drama": "the Beast mastered, then killed, by the Hero" (Leiris, 64). If "abstract words such as glory, honor, [and] courage" have lost their meaning in the slaughterhouse world of the First World War (*A Farewell to Arms,* 185), in Spain and in the bullring "a sense of honour and a sense of glory" are present in the acts of "real killing" (232) still to be found there: "bullfighting is the only art in which the artist is in danger of death and in which the degree of brilliance in the performance is left to the fighter's honor" (91).[17] Honor or "pundonor," indeed, is right at the heart of bullfighting. The bullfighter deliberately risks his life in the ritualized contest with the bull, relies on his skill and art both to survive that encounter and to administer the killing that acts as its climax — and doing it, as Zurito does, "like a priest at benediction" (259). In contrast to the broken subjects and passive victims of a war-time world, the bullfighter at his best is a culture hero: a model of grace, power and supreme authority — killer, artist and magician all in one.[18]

The contest structuring the bullfight itself is for Hemingway, however, part of something larger: the way in which the bullfight stands as a ritual at the very heart of Spanish culture. Leiris's comment on "the coincidence of the great bullfights with local *fiestas*, which correspond to religious festivals" (66) is apposite here. For throughout Hemingway's text is the sense of Spain as offering what America has lost: an integral culture focused, in its case, round the ritual spectacle at its center — the bullfight as *fiesta nacional*. It may be useful at this point to consider Hemingway's attraction to Spain and to the bullfighting seen by others to symbolize the "backwardness" of its culture (Glossary, s. v. *Fiesta*) in the context of Mircea Eliade's work *The Sacred and the Profane*.[19] If Hemingway's sensibility was clearly secular, he can nonetheless be considered in the context of what Eliade calls "crypto-religious behaviour" (23). Eliade, in his discussion of the difference between the sacred and the secular, talks about religious man and his concept of "sacred [. . .] space," his opposition "between space that is sacred — the only *real* and *real-ly* existing space — and all other space, the formless expanse surrounding it" (20). And he claims that "even the most desacralised existence still preserves traces of a religious valorization of the world" (23). Associating "sacred space" with a "fixed point" that offers "orientation in the chaos of homogeneity," he says that "even for the most frankly non-religious man, all these [privileged] places [. . .] still retain an exceptional, a unique quality; they are the 'holy places' of his private universe" (24). Religious man's "desire to live *in the sacred*" is, he continues, "equivalent to his desire to take up his abode in objective reality, not to let himself be paralysed by the never-ceasing relativity of purely subjective experiences" (28).

One of Hemingway's most distinctive narrative techniques in his fiction is precisely the way he strands his reader between "purely subjective" ways of viewing reality, thus representing experience as both relativistic and indeterminate. He himself though, it seems, was able — and I again use Eliade's phrases — to "rediscover the sacred dimension of existence in the world" (51), the assertion of "being" in the face of a "terror of nothingness" (64), in the series of festivals (*fiestas*) that had the bullfight at their heart. To Eliade, it is "in the festival [that] the sacred dimension of life is recovered" (89). Eliade speaks of the "existential choice" modern non-religious man makes as he "desacralises himself and his world" and "refuses all appeal to transcendence" (203). But he also refers to modern man's position as an "inheritor," the way in which "profane man cannot help preserving some vestiges of the behaviour of religious man, though they are emptied of religious meaning" (204).

This is clearly just one reading of the relation between sacred and profane, primitive and modern, but it could almost have been written with Hemingway in mind. Hemingway sees the condition of modern man as locked in an existential battle, looking to live with dignity and courage in a naturalistic universe where, in the face of the constant presence and pressure of death, pain and violence, "winner takes nothing." But he is also deeply attracted to the notion of meaningful ritual, the desire to discover "privileged [. . .] 'holy places'" where "the sacred dimension of life" can be, at least temporarily, recovered. In *Death in the Afternoon,* Hemingway accordingly taps back into a source of primitive goodness and vitality, a simpler world than his modern American one, a restorative good country where a heroic masculine figure stars in a repeated ritual of "real" cultural value. This is a "fictional" version of Spain that is a product more of personal need than of objective reality,[20] a Spain that is marginal to the mainstream of modern history represented in the broken and senseless world of "A Natural History of the Dead." The version of Spain Hemingway has constructed is triggered by nostalgia; by a "crypto-religious" desire for an environment where nature is still a redemptive presence, where cultural practice is coherent and organic, centered round the primary ritual of the bullfight, and where individual autonomy and action are powerfully represented.

This Spain, then, acts as desired Other to a repellent modernized American world. And what is remarkable in *Death in the Afternoon* is the way Hemingway uses synecdoche, moves from parts or fragments — again "A Natural History of the Dead" comes to mind here — to wholes, uses his discussion of the "ritual of the [bull]fight" (9) as the jump-off point for a celebration of Spain and its culture as a whole. To know bullfighting in this book is to know Spain. The final chapter starts off with the words: "If I could have made this enough of a book it would have had everything in it" (270). And in its final paragraph Hemingway concludes: "Any part you make will represent the whole if it's made truly" (278). He continues to refer to bullfighting here but it comes to stand as a central subject that points in a far more comprehensive direction, toward the total celebration of the Spanish landscape and culture.[21] This is the book where Hemingway defines his "iceberg" theory of writing, and in his last chapter he gives the reader passages of considerable lyric intensity as a way of synecdochally suggesting what the book would contain "if it had Spain in it" (273): the places, the people, the sensual experiences. Underlying his writing project, he indicates, lies the idea of an impossible wholeness, the desire to get it all in — all of Spain and all of what it means to him. Spain still just is what America has long not been, a type of sacred space where individual subject, culture, and country come together in one harmonious whole:

> In the morning there we would have breakfast and then go out to swim in the Irati [. . .] the water clear as light [. . .] and the shade from the trees on the bank when the sun was hot, the ripe wheat in the wind up on the other side and sloping to the mountain [. . .]. And we lay naked on the short grass in the sun. (273)

To present bullfighting and Spain as coterminous is, however, questionable. In his fiction, where Hemingway often offers a more complicated and ambiguous picture of things, we can see not only the close identification between the rituals of the bullfight and the larger culture that contains it, but also the gaps that separate them. *The Sun Also Rises*, for example, foregrounds disparities between the bullfight code and the "everyday" fabric of community existence — it focuses on differences and tensions between the two areas, inside and outside the ring, that are almost never apparent in *Death in the Afternoon*. In the novel, the waiter's comment on the useless death of Vicente Girones, killed "All for sport. All for pleasure [. . .] All for fun" while running the bulls, leaving a wife and orphaned children behind him, taken together with his comment on bulls as just "Animals. Brute animals" (*The Sun Also Rises*, 197), opens up an alternative reading of bullfight culture. For the waiter, the bulls offer dangerous sport rather than cathartic art, and the "sport" is peripheral and, finally, damaging to the business of Spanish life. The waiter's reactions open the question of the relationship of this "sport" to Spanish life and to Spanish culture as a whole, a relationship that is unquestioned in *Death in the Afternoon* where the discussion of bullfighting is symbiotically linked to the discussion of Spain.[22] Only at one point in the later book does the whole house of cards momentarily threaten to collapse, as Hemingway starts one of his appendices with the recognition that "Most Spaniards do not go to bull fights" ("A Short Estimate").

There is, furthermore, little information in Hemingway's text about those aspects of Spain that would contradict the representation of the country as a rural and primitive cultural space, attractive in its non-American difference. There are occasional references to the problems of Spanish agriculture — "the central sore which radiated throughout the country" (Thomas, 50) — in *Death in the Afternoon*, but they are undeveloped and do not affect the main thrust of the book. And there is only brief mention in the final chapter of the political and social difficulties that were to explode in the Spanish Civil War, four years after the book's publication. Again, the way Hemingway "translates" Spanish culture speaks as much of his own psychic needs and his own particular American modernity as of the country and culture he describes.

Hemingway, as I have earlier shown, positions himself somewhere between native and tourist in this book. But the fact of his foreign status, and the impact that he and other foreigners were having on Spanish culture in the period, resonate significantly throughout the text. The notion of financial and cultural exchange — what one gets of Spain for one's money — and the tension between "buying into" and "being part of," may not be the main items on Hemingway's agenda as he writes *Death in the Afternoon*, but — throughout the book — they are difficult ones for the reader to ignore. In the Glossary, questions of cost and value for money are continually raised: paying "scalper's prices" for bullfight tickets (s. v. *Billetes*); the different prices of spectatorship and the advantage of certain kinds of seats "to any one who must watch expenditure closely" (s. v. *Sol y sombra*). It is clear Hemingway places himself in the latter category rather than that of "the wealthy curiosity trade from Biarritz" pushing barrera seats up to "a hundred pesetas apiece or over" at San Sebastian. He speaks of the rush for these last seats once the "well-fed, skull and bones-ed [. . .] Panama-hatted" people leave, "after the first bull," as belonging to "the good days of the free barreras." He also describes how, for that same money, one could buy a whole range of things, such as "good seats in the sun for two bullfights," food, and drink, "and still have something left to get his shoes shined with" (33–34).

That last detail, the shining of shoes at the fiesta, is a particularly telling one. It recurs in Hemingway's work, and the people who get their shoes shined or attended to in other ways — the writer among them — are by and large the tourists. In the Glossary (s. v. *Tacones*) he writes of the "racket" run by the "ambulatory vendors" who "come up to you while you are seated in the café," and who, before any realization occurs on the victim's part, cut off the heels of shoes with the special tool they carry for that purpose, to force the purchase of the rubber heels they sell. Hemingway's advice to those to whom this happens is succinct: "kick him in the belly or under the jaw" or, in the case of one particular "heel-selling bastard," put your shoes "inside your shirt" when you see him coming. If he then tries "to attach rubber heels to your bare feet, send for the American or British Consul." In *The Sun Also Rises,* Hemingway's bullfighting novel, the discourse of buying and selling is all-pervasive. The Pamplona merchants double their prices when the tourists arrive. Bill Gorton spends his money conspicuously, senselessly, and in a manner that demeans the local recipients, with the eleven shoe-shines he buys Mike at a single sitting. Only Jake Barnes, relatively sober and also more sensitive to the host culture than his compatriots, feels "a little uncomfortable about all this shoe-shining" (173).

Hemingway's own financial well-being as an expatriate in the postwar years, his ability to go to Spain and see the bullfights, depended on the strong value of the dollar. As Michael Reynolds notes: "Wherever Hemingway looked in 1925 [Spain, France, Austria], he saw dollar signs. Everything was for sale, its price clearly marked" (47).[23] So in June 1931, for instance, Hemingway writes to John Dos Passos from Madrid, saying "We live here damn well on 3.00 [three dollars] a day the two of us. Now is the time to buy anything if anybody had money" (*Selected Letters,* 342).

In other words, though Hemingway identifies with Spain "as a native," his very presence and everything he does there depends on his status as a tourist — with the American Consul as last resort if he is ripped off too badly by any "bastard" con-man or salesman.[24] In another (African) context,

Debra Moddelmog argues that we should "construct Hemingway" as both imperialist and anti-imperialist, sometimes clearly aware of the power relations involved in a colonialist situation, at other times "ignoring the ethics and effects of the colonizer-colonized relationship altogether" (129). And in *Death in the Afternoon,* and the fiction that connects to the bullfight, we see similarly uneasy and contradictory moves occurring between the identification with Spanish culture and values and the recognition of difference — a difference based on the relationships of power inherent in the financial and cultural transactions in which the tourist is necessarily involved.[25]

Tourists inevitably alter the territory they tread. Indeed, a number of passages in Hemingway's later bullfighting book, *The Dangerous Summer,* are highly suggestive of the way one culture affects the other in terms both of tourism and of the attendant consumer relations. So Hemingway describes banderillas in terms of an American shopping metaphor: "He put in four pairs of banderillas; not the very expensive kind he has placed in his first bull but good ones from Macy's" (*Dangerous Summer,* 117). Here we see two things: first that experience is automatically subject to change, to reconceptualization, once cultural translation occurs; and, second, that factors of economics and exchange are never far from the surface in that process. Both in *Death in the Afternoon* and in *The Dangerous Summer,* Hemingway tends to underestimate his foreign difference, describing himself as at one with the culture of which he tells. Thus, for instance, he joins the "brotherhood" (142) of bullfighting as a type of honorary member. Again, here, his status as tourist and the effect this has on the culture he visits is never fully recognized. So when he says that "I've written Pamplona once and for keeps. It is all there as it always was except forty thousand tourists have been added. There were not twenty tourists when I first went there nearly four decades ago" (136), his own status (as a tourist or not) remains ill-defined. And there certainly seems no recognition of the fact that it is he himself who bears major responsibility for the increase in numbers he so regrets. Spain is described in *Death in the Afternoon* as a place apart, resistant to foreign influence and culturally self-sufficient: "The bullfight is a Spanish institution; it has not existed because of the foreigners and tourists, but always in spite of them" (8). It was Hemingway, though, who in visiting Spain, and able to do so because of the strength of the dollar, helped to transform it to a tourist venue, catering to exactly that foreign influence which could earlier apparently be so easily contained. In his book, then, the particular version of Spain, and of the bullfight, Hemingway gives his readers is a construction of the modern American imagination. By the time of *The Dangerous Summer,* moreover, the Spain he describes is, in ever-increasing part, a product of the very tourist economy he represents.

What I indicate in this essay is the peculiarity of the process of cultural translation. Hemingway gives us an idealized version of Spain, the foreign culture he describes. He takes the part of Spanish culture he found so attractive and translates it for his audience to stand in oppositional relationship to what he saw as the empty modernity of his own America. His depiction of masculinity, of heroic individual action, and of an "integral" relationship between the land, the people, and the rituals by which they lived, are all finally a type of fiction constructed from a position of personal (and cultural) need. This recalls, to repeat, Clifford's view of the nostalgic and ideologically biased ethnographer and his search for a "wholeness" that "by definition becomes a thing of the past (rural, primitive [. . .]), accessible only as a fiction, grasped from a stance of incomplete involvement" (qtd. in Manganaro, 29). However intensely involved Hemingway did become with Spain, that involvement remained in some sense necessarily biased and incomplete. The version of "the real thing," the real Spain, real bullfighting, with which he presents us is often highly accurate in its details. In its larger outline, however — the manner in which it is described and the sometimes implicit, sometimes explicit cultural contrasts that are drawn — this must be judged, to some considerable degree, a fictional and subjective version of "reality."

# Notes

[1] See Thurston, more generally, on Hemingway's "compositional tic" in this book: his use of the word *and* to connect diverse subjects which "we are to read as somehow similar" (49).

[2] For a brief discussion of the utopian nature of Hemingway's apparent literary project to elide the gap between word and world, and so to make his writing into "the real thing" itself, see Messent, *Ernest Hemingway,* 164–70. Beegel speaks of Hemingway's recognition in *Death in the Afternoon* that "the artist's struggle to record life in its entirety was foredoomed to failure," adding that, nonetheless, "Hemingway valued that struggle as an end in itself" (63).

[3] Thurston calls the book "an anatomy, a logical dissection on the order of [. . .] Burton's *Anatomy of Melancholy.* [. . .] In its incorporation of various generic markers and discursive fragments, the book also resembles *Moby Dick,* the great American anatomy" (47–48).

[4] See too the tension throughout Hemingway between notions of "dwelling" and mere circulation.

[5] Stephen Plotkin suggests that we might see passages such as those identified here in the context of the strong concern with various forms of rhetoric in the book as a whole, and an overall awareness of the limits of rhetorical adequacy. Hemingway's position, in other words, may be more self-reflexively aware than my argument allows, as he projects his desired aesthetic and ethical mapping onto the Spanish cultural landscape. Plotkin's comments (in a letter to the author) are offered in a tentative and speculative manner. While I would hold to my present position, and would also argue for a difference between Hemingway's fiction and nonfiction in such forms

of awareness, this interpretation warrants further consideration. My thanks to Stephen Plotkin for his helpful response to the draft version of this essay.

[6] Neither Clifford nor Manganaro discuss Hemingway or Spain. I adjust their theoretical model to my own ends.

[7] I am aware of the slippage involved in the double move that can be identified here. *Any* act of representation necessarily lacks "authenticity," is shaped by the emotional and ideological positioning of the author. As Hemingway takes on the role of "anthropologist" and translator, explaining Spanish life for his American audience, a further gap opens up in the process of intercultural exchange involved. In this sense *Death in the Afternoon* may be seen as twice removed from "the real thing."

[8] See Brenner, 70–71, and Capellán, 162–77. The latter quotes Fernando Díaz Plaja on American attitudes to death: "Clearly this is a people for whom the mere mention of death is unpleasant. [. . .] For a nation dominated by comfort, to die is to lose it. [. . .] And if death does exist [. . .] one must try to make believe it does not" (163).

[9] See the story "Wine of Wyoming" where (American) Prohibition symbolically stands "as closure, as hypocrisy, as denial of communion" (Stoneback, 213). I borrow here, and at other points in this essay, from my earlier work on *Death in the Afternoon* (*Ernest Hemingway*, 125–63).

[10] See too the description of other nonfiction writing about America and the reading of the unfinished Nick Adams story, "The Last Good Country," in Messent, *Ernest Hemingway*, 126–28 and 130–33. Hemingway's fiction about the remembered past is never as straightforwardly nostalgic as his nonfiction.

[11] See Beegel on Hemingway's depiction of the relationship between writing and geography (53 ff.) and on the racial exclusivity of his version of an "American" identity (57–60).

[12] *Death in the Afternoon* is a text marked by a number of late revisions ("Since writing that about Gitanillo de Triana I saw him destroyed by a bull in Madrid on [. . .] May 31, 1931" [217]). It would be interesting to know the compositional date of the passage on the destruction of the landscape just mentioned.

[13] Fredric Jameson's work on modernist literary representations of subjectivity and the use of the romance form as, respectively, a "containment strategy" in, and "symbolic reaction" to, a "secularized and reified" modern world (*The Political Unconscious*, 221, 148, 135) is relevant here (I am thinking of *A Farewell to Arms* in particular). So too is his comment on what he sees as the "Hemingway cult of *machismo*" as an attempt "to come to terms with the great industrial transformation after World War I [. . .] it reconciles the deepest and most life-giving impulses toward wholeness with a status quo in which only sports allows you to feel alive and undamaged" (*Marxism and Form*, 412). Hemingway, of course, would have rejected any description of bullfighting as "only sports."

[14] See Eby (291), on Hemingway's actual part in this incident, and its possible traumatic effect.

[15] Brenner discusses the story in terms of the competing perspectives on how one "respond[s] humanely [. . .] when confronted with dying or dead human beings," saying that "Hemingway dares us to choose only one as the correct one" (75). This

connects with the general stress on epistemological indeterminacy throughout the author's work.

[16] I borrow here from the Davidsons' reading of Pedro Romero in *The Sun Also Rises* (97). I am aware here of three things of further relevance: the differences between Hemingway's fiction and nonfiction, the instability of the representation of gender in both types of text, and the implications of the "decadence" theme in *Death in the Afternoon*. See Comley and Scholes, among others, for commentary on the gender issue; Thurston on gender and "decadence."

[17] And see Jameson on Conrad for discussion of "the feudal ideology of honor" as a social value alien to the capitalist mode of production (*The Political Unconscious*, 217).

[18] Beegel makes the analogy with Hemingway's own authorship: his "existential pride in continuing to oppose his art to the unconquerable enemy, death" (64).

[19] See, too, Allen Joseph's reading of the bullfight, also based on Eliade, in "Toreo: The Moral Axis of *The Sun Also Rises*" (1986).

[20] See T. J. Jackson Lears on concepts of authenticity, grace, and antimodernism in late Victorian and early twentieth-century American culture. It is by no means incompatible to be aesthetically a modernist and by temperament antimodern. See T. S. Eliot, for instance.

[21] "The final published chapter [. . .] is an elegy for Spain, a farewell to her disappearing people and places. [. . .] Hemingway sets about capturing the vanishing heart of Spain in print" (Beegel, 62–63). I have not the space here to focus on the sense of change and loss represented within the book itself. The country he describes is changing for the worse, the bullfight is already a decadent art (though "paradoxically [. . .] [one] reaching its fullest flower" [Thurston, 55]). In "writing enduringly" (Beegel, 56–57) of Spain, Hemingway attempts to make the version of Spain he knows and loves endure. His sense of Spain as utopic haven would diminish as time passed. There is more to be said, too, about the various temporal and emotional shifts within the book's last chapter.

[22] Hemingway titles one section at the end of *Death in the Afternoon*, "Some Reactions [. . .] to the *Integral* Spanish Bullfight" (my emphasis).

[23] See too Messent, *New Readings of the American Novel*, 106–9.

[24] See too "The Friend of Spain: a Spanish Letter," where Hemingway's attempt to have a drink with an old friend in Madrid is first interrupted by the attentions of beggar, gypsy, and caricaturist (144), and is then adversely affected by the unnatural manner of the old friend himself. This turns out to be a result of the article, "Mister Hemingway, friend of Spain" (145), that the friend has written for a Spanish Sunday newspaper.

[25] That "necessarily" is important for I am in no way dismissing Hemingway's identification with Spain as "false." His position is similar to anyone from a richer and more "advanced" society who forms a strong emotional and cultural attachment to a less wealthy and more "primitive" one.

# Works Cited

Beegel, Susan. *Hemingway's Craft of Omission: Four Manuscript Examples.* Ann Arbor, MI: U of Michigan Research P, 1988.

Brenner, Gerry. *Concealments in Hemingway's Work.* Columbus: Ohio UP, 1983.

Capellán, Angel. *Hemingway and the Hispanic World.* Ann Arbor, MI: U Michigan Research P, 1977.

Comley, Nancy R., and Robert Scholes. *Hemingway's Genders: Rereading the Hemingway Text.* New Haven: Yale UP, 1994.

Davidson, Arnold E., and Cathy N. Davidson "Decoding the Hemingway Hero in *The Sun Also Rises.*" In *New Essays on "The Sun Also Rises."* Ed. Linda Wagner-Martin. Cambridge: Cambridge UP, 1987. 83–107.

Diamond, Stanley. *In Search of the Primitive: A Critique of Civilization.* 1974. New Brunswick, NJ: Transaction Books, 1987.

Eby, Carl P. *Hemingway's Fetishism: Psychoanalysis and the Mirror of Manhood.* Albany, NY: State U of New York P, 1999.

Eliade, Mircea. *The Sacred and the Profane: The Nature of Religion.* Trans. Willard R. Trask. 1957. New York: Harcourt, Brace and World, 1959.

Hemingway, Ernest. *The Dangerous Summer.* New York: Scribner's, 1985.

———. *Death in the Afternoon.* New York: Scribner's, 1932.

———. *Ernest Hemingway: Selected Letters, 1917–1961.* Ed. Carlos Baker. London: Granada, 1981.

———. *A Farewell to Arms.* 1929. New York: Scribner's, 1969.

———. "The Friend of Spain: A Spanish Letter." *Esquire* (January 1934); rpt. in *By Line: Ernest Hemingway, Selected Articles and Dispatches of Four Decades.* Ed. William White. New York: Scribner's, 1967. 144–52.

———. "Remembering Shooting-Flying: A Key West Letter." *Esquire* (February 1935); rpt. *By-Line, Ernest Hemingway, Selected Articles and Dispatches of Four Decades.* Ed. William White. New York: Scribner's, 1967. 186–91.

———. *The Sun Also Rises.* 1926. New York: Scribner's, 1970.

Jameson, Fredric. *Marxism and Form: Twentieth-Century Dialectical Theories of Literature.* Princeton, NJ: Princeton UP, 1971.

———. *The Political Unconscious: Narrative as a Socially Symbolic Act.* London: Methuen, 1981.

Josephs, Allen. "Toreo: The Moral Axis of *The Sun Also Rises*." In *Modern Critical Interpretations: Ernest Hemingway's "The Sun Also Rises."* Ed. Harold Bloom. New York: Chelsea House, 1987. 151–67.

Lears, T. J. Jackson. *No Place of Grace: Antimodernism and the Transformation of American Culture, 1880–1920*. New York: Pantheon, 1981.

Leiris, Michel. *Manhood*. Preceded by *The Autobiographer as Torero*. 1946. Trans. Richard Howard. London: Jonathan Cape, 1968.

Lewis, Robert W. "The Making of *Death in the Afternoon*." In *Ernest Hemingway: The Writer in Context*. Ed. James Nagel. Madison: U of Wisconsin P, 1984. 31–52.

Manganaro, Marc, ed. *Modernist Anthropology: From Fieldwork to Text*. Princeton, NJ: Princeton UP, 1990.

Messent, Peter. *Ernest Hemingway*. Houndmills, Basingstoke: Macmillan, 1992.

———. "Slippery Stuff: The Construction of Character in *The Sun Also Rises*." Chap. 3 in his *New Readings of the American Novel: Narrative Theory and its Application*. Houndmills, Basingstoke: Macmillan, 1990. 86–129.

Moddelmog, Debra A. "Re-Placing Africa in 'The Snows of Kilimanjaro': The Intersecting Economies of Capitalist-Imperialism and Hemingway Biography." In *New Essays on Hemingway's Short Fiction*. Ed. Paul Smith. Cambridge: Cambridge UP, 1998. 111–36.

Reynolds, Michael S. "*The Sun* in Its Time: Recovering the Historical Context." In *New Essays on "The Sun Also Rises."* Ed. Linda Wagner-Martin. Cambridge: Cambridge UP, 1987. 43–64.

Stoneback, H. R. "'Mais Je Reste Catholique': Communion, Betrayal, and Aridity in "Wine of Wyoming.'" In *Hemingway's Neglected Short Fiction: New Perspectives*. Ed. Susan F. Beegel. Ann Arbor, MI: U Michigan Research P, 1989. 209–24.

Thomas, Hugh. *The Spanish Civil War*. New York: Harper and Row, 1961.

Thurston, Michael. "Genre, Gender, and Truth in *Death in the Afternoon*." *The Hemingway Review* 17.2 (1998): 47–63.

Warner, Charles Dudley. "The Bull-Fight." *The Century Magazine* 27.1 (November 1883): 3–13.

Weber, Ronald. *Hemingway's Art of Non-fiction*. London: Macmillan, 1990.

Wood, Greg. "Blood, Sweat, Terror and a Whole Load of Macho Bull." *The Independent on Sunday,* "Sport," 6 August 2000, 14.

# "Very Sad but Very Fine": *Death in the Afternoon*'s Imagist Interpretation of the Bullfight-Text

Beatriz Penas Ibáñez

> *He gave emotion always and, finally, as he steadily improved his style, he was an artist.*
> *Death in the Afternoon, 79*

IN THE ACT OF WRITING *Death in the Afternoon* Hemingway was subtly announcing the completion of the first phase of his life and career as artist. He was telling his readers, present and future, how long and necessary this first learning phase is. Having overcome his initial difficulties, he tells us, the writer finally knows what he did not know before. He can now see beyond appearances, he sees meaning outside himself because he is now able to know himself. He has learned to differentiate between his own real feelings and the feelings he has been taught he is supposed to have; in other words, he has learned to disregard his white, Protestant, middle-class upbringing. His years abroad have given him the needed distance from his native America, enabling him to become himself. About ten years[1] have been necessary for him to write about things that he has slowly learned to understand and appreciate, things that he never knew before he came to Europe and saw the war and the bullfights.

To write about these matters, Hemingway employs a phenomenological approach which involves: (1) exposure to external action (watching, listening), (2) internalization (responding emotionally), (3) selective recall (isolating the elements in the external action that provoked the emotion), and (4) selective telling (stating purely). The process follows a movement from the outside to the inside and to the outside again: the transmutation of external action into internal experience and then the transmutation of that experience into text. In *Death in the Afternoon*, Hemingway indicates that his genuine interest in the bullfight was always subordinated to a higher interest, his interest in writing about the bullfight, or what is the same, his interest in literature.

Because the bullfight is radically foreign to the non-Spanish mind, the writer needs to make an extra effort both to understand it himself and to explain it to his readers. The bullfight is too complex to be readily acceptable or understandable: it is both an event and a sign, or symbolic representation of events; it is business, history, and art. The aspect of the bullfight which is most difficult to understand and most challenging to Hemingway is that it is a live performance that includes death as part of the spectacle.[2] Thus the last part of the bullfight, where either the bull or the bullfighter must be killed, is the one that receives most attention in *Death in the Afternoon*. The bull's death is difficult to understand and accept because the plaza is not a slaughter house, and the bullfighter's death is difficult to understand because the plaza is not a war front[3] — that is, violent death becomes questionable because it occurs outside the accepted, practical, or logical setting. In *Death in the Afternoon* Hemingway confronts what today might be called the political incorrectness of the bullfight; he gives his readers all the relevant and significant information about the bullfight and thus enables them to contextualize its most difficult aspect, the kill.

Both in words and with diagrams, Hemingway makes clear that the bullring is not built as a slaughterhouse but as an alternative world, a world of carnival, a fiesta world, a world of representation. He emphasizes its resemblance to an amphitheatre: the *plaza de toros* is a round high building formed by a series of concentric circles occupied by different people doing different things while the corrida lasts. The plaza contains the fiesta world of the bullfight, separating and isolating it from the everyday world outside. Walking in through the plaza doors means walking into a different conception of time and place, walking into suspended disbelief. It is like walking into a theater to see a carefully orchestrated spectacle, and not at all like walking into a slaughterhouse.

The architecture and organization of the plaza reveal its purpose. Its vertical design separates the spectators from the actors. The highest ranking spectator, the president, sits at the top, from whence he and his assistants can make sure that events proceed properly and that the law is obeyed. Below the president sit the paying spectators, whose seats become more expensive as they approach the inner circle. A wall separates the spectators from the *callejón*, where only bullfighters, their attendants, and other professional personnel are permitted. One more partition, the barrera, separates the *callejón* from the arena, the central point in the plaza, where only bulls and bullfighters are allowed and to which all gazes are attracted.

The plaza's orderly, hierarchical design allows all spectators to make visual contact with the action and, at the same time, separates them from the action. The barrera marks this essential partition between spectators and actors; neither the president nor the general public can cross this line. This partition points to a difference perceived as essential within Spanish culture: the difference between those who live dangerously and those who, from a position of safety, watch and judge them.

In this overall structure of watching versus fighting Hemingway perceives a similarity with the act of reading versus writing. In entering the plaza, spectators act like readers opening a book: they suspend disbelief and prepare themselves to watch a story which is retold with subtle variations. The bullfight's six *faenas* present a tragic story that locks its characters into conflict: it is a story about two people who, having nothing basically against each other, become trapped in an impossible situation from which the only escape is either to kill or to die. This conflict, performed by a man wearing a *traje de luces* (suit of lights) and a naked animal, is watched by Spanish spectators not only for what it is, but mainly for what it symbolizes,[4] for what it reveals and explains about their human life and behavior. At the inevitable moment of truth, when even a faker or coward must get very close to the bull in order to insert the sword, both the fighter and his craft will be judged by their audience, and the bullfighter will be judged not only for his craft but also for his character. In a culture where shame matters as much as honor, the bullfight exposes the social source of these emotions. For the writer, of course, the moment of truth also comes at the end, when his readers judge his work.

Like the Spanish public, Hemingway reads not only the man, but also the bull, as an allegory for human fate. The bull's three states — *levantado, parado, aplomado* (see these terms in the Glossary) — signify the human being's decay and eventual death. The bull's insistence on attacking, even at the last moment, represents world vision that does not shelter defeat: the brave bull may be tired, but he attacks till the very last moment — he dies while still attempting to kill. The same is expected of the bullfighter, who cannot give up whatever the circumstances. This world vision is woven into those of Hemingway's works that feature old men such as, to name a few, "Wine of Wyoming," "A Clean Well-Lighted Place," *The Old Man and the Sea,* and *True At First Light.*

Hemingway is not an "animalarian" (9) because what interests him in the bullfight is not the bull's fate but the human fate that the bull symbolizes. In this respect he, like Spanish aficionados, cannot rejoice in the bull's death, because it symbolizes their own death. But in the bullring, and in Hemingway's work, death is accepted because it is real, inescapable and true, the only truth in a world of appearances.[5]

The theatrical trappings of the bullfight emphasize its function as allegory, as a conflict to be read allegorically by spectators who recognize it as a ritual conflict in which fair play and the balance of forces are important factors. The bull's strength is pitted against the bullfighter's intelligence, training, and props. The two contestants are artificially made to resemble one another: the bull's most characteristic attributes, his horns and phallus, are mimed by the bullfighter's *montera* (a little black hat whose peculiar shape resembles the horn stands) and the sword (a penetrating instrument equivalent to the bull's horns). The bull's nakedness and the bullfighter's tight and sparkling *traje de luces* draw attention to their phalluses. On the other hand, the bull is dressed or decorated with colorful ribbons (the *divisa*) and banderillas which echo the bullfighter's suit. The humanization of the animal is also linguistically managed in the taurine jargon: the bull is said to "answer" or "fail to answer" the bullfighter's "invitation" to fight, the bull "knows" or "learns" how to take the cape, the bull is "noble," "brave," "insolent," and so on. Thus, in ways which are mainly visual and discursive but also factual, the bullfight substitutes the man and the bull for each other. The development and death of the humanized bull is like our own individual life and death; and the survival of the bullfighter, who has been attired to resemble the bull, bespeaks the survival of the human species as well as that of the bull. Another bull does, in fact, re-enter the arena minutes later. Survival and death, man and bull, are linked. And indeed, at the moment of truth, "man and bull form one figure [. . .], death uniting the two figures in the emotional, aesthetic, and artistic climax of the fight" (*DIA,* 247). For both man and animal, death is the end of the tragic, wordless story that they have told together and that others like them will tell again.

The bullfight can be read in social as well as individual terms. The bull's actions during the three phases of the fight show the gradual subjection of his natural power and instinctual freedom to the coercing maneuvers of an opposing force. This parallels human experience: the individual becomes progressively aware of social constraints until (usually quite late in life) he realizes that his freedom is limited. It is not only that he is not the center of the world, but that (even worse) he is decentered, losing control to cultural and economic pressures, and finally feeling himself to exist somewhere between subject and object. The bullfighter represents social forces: he enters the ring equipped with a well-defined system of taurine norms and conventions, which are part of and stand for the more general cultural order to which they belong. The bull's death (the bullfighter's victory) confirms the supremacy of the socialized man over the purely instinctive "natural" and therefore innocent or Edenic creature, the animal — or even of the Rousseauian natural man as represented by the bull. In the bullfight, as in people's lives, innocence and freedom do not last.

The bullfight insists that the bull's innocent natural wildness must succumb to the bullfighter's artifice, his schooling, his measured violence. The bullfighter's rationality is shown by his willing subjection to the constructed system of techniques, traditions, and rules, which enables him to dominate a creature that is much stronger than he is. Seeing this, the spectators understand the benefits of abiding by the law. The modern bullfight expresses the desirability of a legal system and a civil state that can guarantee the subjection of wild and unruly elements, no matter how powerful.

The years which produced *Death in the Afternoon* — Hemingway began writing it in 1930 and published it in 1932 — were critical in Spanish history. After centuries of monarchy, Spain was attempting republicanism: this turbulent, disordered period resulted in Franco's 1936 coup d'état and the ensuing three-year-long Spanish Civil War. As Miriam B. Mandel's *Complete Annotations* reveal, Hemingway's awareness of the contemporary sociopolitical unrest underlies chapter 20 of *Death in the Afternoon*, which, being about the Spanish bullfight, is also about Spain and, by refraction, about America.

The taurine ritual or text helps us understand not only the individual and social aspects of our existence, but also the historical and political history of the country that nurtured it. As an institution, bullfighting worked to reflect and legitimize the centralizing politics of the Spanish monarchy; the changes undergone by the Spanish monarchy are reflected in the changes evidenced in the bullfight, from the medieval period to the present. In medieval times, when bullfighting was an aristocratic peacetime occupation that enabled noblemen to exercise and display their horsemanship before the monarch, killing the bull was a menial task left to the nobleman's footmen. During the period of Spanish unification, when the various provincial monarchs both warred against each other and made short-lived alliances among themselves (against each other or against the Moors), the feudal bond between the landed gentry and the kings was weakened. As the monarch came to depend more heavily on paid or impressed warriors, the nobility was marginalized. In the bullring, the mounted aristocrats also lost ground, and bullfighting became paid work: professional bullfighters on foot killed the bull. The mounted bullfighter, the *rejoneador*, remained only as a marginalized decorative element within the event, reflecting the reduced power of the nobility when the king can depend on money lenders and a national army. Thus the fiesta changed radically, from being a high-culture display performed by nobility for an aristocratic audience, to a popular event, performed by the common man for a paying spectatorship of equals, the aficionados.

The Spanish bullfight reflected not only Spain's internal social changes as it moved towards unification, but also its politics and power ploys as it evolved from nation to empire. The unification of Spain was completed when Ferdinand, king of Aragón, and Isabella, queen of Castile and León, married and ruled jointly. Spain's Muslim, Jewish, and Roman-Visigothic ethnicities then came under the law of the Catholic monarchs and the law of the Church. Cultural diversity was sacrificed on the altar of national identity, as monarchs and church united to enforce the policy of conversion and assimilation. Spectacles of public torture and death — by *garrote vil* (a particularly cruel kind of garroting), hanging, or burning — were employed as punishment for offenses against the state or the Roman Catholic Church.

When the structure of the modern Spanish bullfight was codified, in the eighteenth century,[6] the Inquisition was still a strong presence in Spain. It is significant that the language describing the emerging modern bullfight reflected these public trials and executions.[7] The very term *lidia,* which comes from the Latin verb *litigare* (to quarrel or dispute through legal proceedings) indicates that the bullfight was perceived as a surrogate kind of *litigium* or trial in which the bull substitutes for the accused person. The bullfight was, unquestionably, a representation and a welcome replacement for the kind of spectacle then offered to the people. As unified Spain became an empire, it exported this policy to its colonies, although this process would take longer and would eventually overlap with other European, and eventually American, powers.

The bullfight, then, can be seen as a symbolic representation of both these processes of domination — the shifting power relations as the nation moved from feudalism to national unification, and the subsequent construction of a uniform national identity that was exported during the imperial conquest that engaged Spain between the fifteenth and eighteenth centuries. This makes the bullfight a valuable concept for Hemingway. The understanding he gained from studying the parallelism that joined the history of Spain and the bullfight worked to enhance his understanding of the forces at work in the formation of multi-ethnic empires like the United States at the end of the nineteenth century.[8] Realizing that the modern Spanish bullfight stages the process of cultural assimilation and appropriation of a naturally different creature for profit, Hemingway employs it in *Death in the Afternoon* to present analogous American issues.

By using the Spanish bullfight as a metaphor for the ideology and workings of power, Hemingway can omit redundant explanations about the process of formation of an American national identity and the development of the country from colony into empire. He approaches these developments quite explicitly in *Green Hills of Africa* (1935), where he discusses the relation between the streams of immigration to America and the stream of time,[9] and he joins this to the Spanish experience in *In Our Time* (1930), where he juxtaposes Spanish and American scenes in his vignettes and stories. In *Death in the Afternoon,* however, the American matter becomes practically invisible, the submerged portion of the iceberg-text which Hemingway has omitted from the linguistic surface. Only within the more visual section of his text, the photograph collection, does Hemingway use juxtaposition — rather than omission — as the mode of his indirect approach to the American scene. Here Hemingway not only offers two sets of contrasting images (the stud bull and the fighting bull, on the one hand, and the ox on the other), but uses the captions to focus our attention on the differences between them, identifying one group as admirable (the stud bull ensures the future of the corrida, the fighting bulls make its performance possible) and the other as pitiful (the ox is the object of economic exploitation that will be killed at the slaughter-house). The ox represents the exploited second-class citizen, the expendable, passive, unmourned piece of flesh that will be slaughtered at the war fronts or sacrificed to the factory or sweat shop.[10]

When seen from an American perspective, the bullfight can symbolize two analogous processes, the first occurring when the first white immigrants settled in America and embarked upon their Westward Expansion. These processes involved the conquest of the Native Americans,[11] who occupied the position of the fighting bull that is overpowered by a more centralized culture that comes armed with tools and weapons. But in the establishment's subsequent conflict with immigrant populations, the latter, in the guise of the immigrant factory worker, farm laborer, or soldier, take the position of the ox, as they would be sacrificed in civil or foreign wars, or exploited by big enterprises. Both the native American, associated with the fighting bull, and the immigrant American, associated with the ox, are present in the juxtaposition Hemingway presents as he presents American history through taurine lenses.

*Death in the Afternoon* reads the unpalatable facts about modern times through the same lenses, to indicate that powerful countries like Spain, Britain, and the United States, which have required the domestication and subjection of the individual to the higher authority of the State, are symbolically represented by the bullfighter in the bullfight. Hemingway's uncompromising clarity of vision, like Goya's, emerges from their knowledge of the modern Spanish bullfight. It seems understandable, then, that Hemingway considers the bullfight worth the enormous effort that produced *Death in the Afternoon*. This book, which is designed to initiate mainly American and English speaking readers in "the theory, practice and spectacle" (15) of the modern Spanish bullfight, can be read in national and historical terms that involve conquest, exploitation, and loss of natural power and autonomy. The modern national entity, represented by the cultural icon, the bullfighter, must perforce dominate, subjugate, and even exploit its citizens.

The bullfight can also be read as a representation of the war between the sexes. The bull quite naturally stands out as the most visible male in the couple formed by bull and bullfighter. The bullfighter, although usually a man, is typically young, slender, and delicate of movement, an adolescent dressed in fancy, tight-fitting gold-embroidered clothes that emphasize the line of leg, hip and waist. It is the gaze of the public (see Mulvey, 1975) that feminizes the bullfighter's body by his mere exhibition and also by contrast with the dark, muscular figure of the bull. When the bull enters the arena, he can be said to represent a man confronting a woman through an interplay of culture-bound roles which are social rather than natural in nature. The male emerges from a dark womb, seeks to penetrate the flesh of the other, and normally meets death, the final womb, at the end of the *faena*. The bull can either dominate or be dominated by the bullfighter, as a man might dominate or be dominated by women in his lifetime. The bullfight takes for granted that active and passive gender roles are always negotiated in the interaction rather than totally fixed by convention, the bull "being dominated if the bullfighter works him properly, and dominating the bullfighter if his work is deficient or cowardly" (*DIA*, 126–27).

In this sense the bullfight is close to Hemingway's preoccupation with shifting gender roles and androgyny. The idea that either of the sexes can choose to take on the masculine or the feminine roles in gender interaction is present in Hemingway stories like "The Sea Change," "The Short Happy Life of Francis Macomber," and most explicitly in *The Garden of Eden*. *Death in the Afternoon* further blurs sexual differences when it claims that the male and female of the species are similar in behavior, intelligence, and memory: "Either a bull calf or a cow calf, if passed a few times with cape or muleta, learns all about it [and] remembers" (106). Thus Hemingway disputes Virginia Woolf's assumptions about the "innate superior intelligence in the female" (106). Similarly, in the section entitled "Some Reactions of a Few Individuals to the Integral Spanish Bullfight" (495–501), no gender-biased pattern emerges: some men and women liked the bullfight, others did not.

The bullfight, then, addresses three fundamental questions: the existential problem (Why does one need to be born and why should one keep on living and fighting?), the sociopolitical question (Why should one freely accept social norms and a particular political system?), and the gender issue (Why should sexual conventions determine behavior?). All such questions make sense when they are asked within the horizon of mortality. Hemingway asks why there is so much aggression and violent death in our time when, as the Spanish people well know and others should know too, "death is the unescapable reality, the one thing any man may be sure of; the only security; [. . .] [L]ife is much shorter than death" (266).[12] Death, the ultimate issue addressed by the bullfight, is at the root of all the ethical questions which both the bullfight and Hemingway's writing raise.

Like the bullfight, Hemingway's fiction examines the sources of aggression and destructiveness in the life of the individual and of the group. In the bullfight aggression is partly the consequence of fear — the fear of someone dangerous who might kill us — and partly the consequence of confinement within a trapping circle, the arena. The bullfight shows that aggression is the best defense, and that domination is the obvious way to avoid being dominated. The Spanish bullfight exposes the causes and the consequences of the ideology of domination, thus making the spectators wiser and stronger. They are taught that conflict and violence exist necessarily and mainly as the result of the fear of domination and death. More importantly, they are also taught that no matter what differences separate the opposing creatures, there is an essential sameness between them that should cause them to seek peace and understanding rather than violence. All creatures are the same in that they are equally mortal, "death uniting the two figures" of bull and bullfighter.

The complexity of the bullfight necessarily addresses the spectators' rationality, a rationality that paradoxically questions the very spectacle that promotes it, a spectacle without teams and without winners. Usually, it is the bull who dies, but his death represents human death. The symbolic value of the bull's approaching death makes spectators feel at one with others, rather than against others. Hemingway insists that this feeling is both communal and cathartic, producing a feeling of transcendence in the spectators, who

> have the hope [. . .] of seeing the complete faena; the faena that takes a man out of himself and makes him feel immortal while it is proceeding, that gives him an ecstasy, that is, while momentary, as profound as any religious ecstasy; moving all the people in the ring together and increasing in emotional intensity as it proceeds, carrying the bullfighter with it, he playing on the crowd through the bull and being moved as it responds in a growing ecstasy of ordered, formal, passionate, increasing disregard for death that leaves you, when it is over [. . .] as empty, as changed and as sad as any major emotion will leave you. (206–7)

Like Hemingway, the spectators emerge from the ecstasy of a good corrida thinking that it was "very sad but very fine" (4).

The bullfight leads spectators, and Hemingway was one of the best possible spectators, to explore the tension that exists not only between rationality and irrationality but also in other conflicting tendencies in human nature. It acknowledges man's paradoxical "craving for freedom but also escape from responsibility [. . .] a need for creativity, but also powerful destructive drives; a readiness for self-sacrifice [. . .] but also a strong lust for personal power and domination; a need for love [. . .] [and] a need to inflict pain and suffering on both the hated and the beloved ones" (Marcoviç, 239). In situating a human being and an animal in an enclosed space, the bullfight unleashes the instinctual (natural) drives and the social (cultural) forces that trigger violence, and thus helps us study that phenomenon.

Hemingway's interest in the Spanish bullfight may reflect his dissatisfaction with mainstream explanations of human nature. Darwinian and Freudian approaches popular at the time explained human destructiveness and aggression as regressive impulses, as a descent to the animal instinct of survival. In a Marxist reading, aggressiveness is only a disposition produced by external stimuli, by specific historical and social conditions. The bullfight, old and wise, presents a more comprehensive theory of human violence. It acknowledges both the theory that violence is innate (innatism) and the Freudian / Marxist argument that violence is a learned or acquired answer to internal and external conditioning forces, the trap. But the bullfight finds these mainstream explanations to be limited, for neither can fully address the complexity of human behavior. They overlook, for example, those instances when men kill out of joy, a case which is of the utmost interest to Hemingway. When Hemingway says "it is [. . .] true enjoyment of killing which makes the great matador" (233), he is clearly associating killing and joy, but situating it against a specific background, the greatness of the matador. Hemingway insists that it is the great matador that feels the joy of killing, and if we are to understand him properly on this point we need to remember that for Hemingway the "great matador" is "a complete bullfighter who is at the same time an artist" (86). The feeling of joy that overcomes the artist when he is successfully immersed in the process of creation is, in the particular case of the bullfighter, the joy of performing the kill well; his artistic *faena* is inseparable from the process of destruction.[13] Hemingway understands the synthesis that the bullfighter makes of contradictory feelings rising from the tension between the destructive and constructive drives in him, the man and the artist. For Hemingway, the coexistence of sadness and elation in the bullfighter is correlative to the mixed feelings of the spectators, who emerge from the corrida thinking that they have seen something "very sad but very fine" (4).

Recognizing the sadness that the bullfighter and his spectators feel at the death of a brave, beautiful, living creature, Hemingway writes that "the tragedy is the death of the bull" (*By-Line*, 116). The bullfighter's creative joy is accompanied by pity and sadness for the diminution and destruction of the "transient wave of life," the wild bull, on the altar of art, and the emergence in its place of a quiet "fixed model,"[14] the slowed-down bull, or *toro parado*, that shows the "loss of the free, wild quality [the bull brings] with him into the ring" (98). In a good *faena* there is creation and destruction or, more precisely, there is creation within destruction, an idea that Hemingway synthesizes by calling it the matador's "joy of killing." Hemingway acknowledges the paradoxical nature of the bullfight as art, its necessary mixture of beauty and joy on the one hand and death and sadness on the other.

The creativity that is invested in the performance of a good *faena* operates, like all creativity, by transmuting raw everyday matter into meaningful pattern. What was formless and meaningless before the bull and bullfighter meet in the arena, develops into a structure addressing the essentially ethical issues of learning how to live and die. This is what the bullfight is about and what Hemingway considers moral about it, "the meaning and end of the whole thing" (8). But Hemingway is also interested in the "how," in the aesthetic way in which the structure of the bullfight and the personal style of a great bullfighter will transform a fight into art.

The bullfight obeys a theory of spectacle based on a very general theory of art that appeals to Hemingway for its truth and simplicity. In the bullfight Hemingway sees a living reminder that all creativity and all art rely on destruction in a more or less obvious manner. The bullfighter's art clearly "deals with death and death wipes it out" (99).[15] The bullfighter kills the bull to make art, and even though the bullring servants, the *monosabios* and the *areneros,* drag and sweep away all traces of the fight, the artistic effect remains in the memory of the spectator. In the case of literary writing, which is a permanent art, the association between art and destruction exists just as essentially, though perhaps less obviously. In *Death in the Afternoon,* Hemingway stresses the important role that the desire for permanence plays in literature and more specifically in his own writing. He alludes to the process that goes from the impermanence of experience to the permanence of the written record. The written record, the literary text, springs from the artist's memory of past emotion and depends on his ability to verbalize his reminiscence. Hemingway clearly associates the need to write with an awareness that the movement of time brings with it our own diminution and death. The desire to make experience (and therefore life) last, to make permanent what is impermanent by nature, is the trigger of art and of his own literature. But the question whether art can fully capture reality still remains. In chapter 20, Hemingway explores the workings of memory, desire, and literary imagination and reveals his awareness that he has both succeeded and failed to make *Death in the Afternoon* "enough of a book" (278).

There is no contradiction here. He is telling his readers that he is close to finishing a book that he only dared to write after he felt he was ready, a book he is proud of because he wrote it according to his own theory of art: "The great thing is to [. . .] see and hear and learn and understand; and write when there is something that you know; and not before; and not too damned much after" (278) — here Hemingway indicates the importance of experience, the process of internalizing that experience, and the timing of the act of writing. Experience and knowledge are essential: "A good writer should know as near everything as possible. [. . .] If a man is making a story up it will be true in proportion to the amount of knowledge of life he has and how conscientious he is, so that when he makes something up it is as it would truly be" (*DIA,* 191; *By-Line,* 215). And good writing requires the author not only to acquire a large reservoir of experience and knowledge, but to invest *all* of his knowledge and resources, be they technical or personal, in the writing: good writing "must be projected from the writer's assimilated experience, from his knowledge, from his head, from his heart and from all there is of him" (*DIA,* 191). *Death in the Afternoon* is artistic and "enough of a book" because it was written in accordance with these theoretical principles.

But *Death in the Afternoon* is also "not enough of a book" because, as Hemingway indicates in chapter 20, life is bigger than art. Hemingway, who is bigger than his theories, here acknowledges the limits of all theory, including his own. Chapter 20 contains his very explicit lament at the impossibility to "make it all come true again" (272) with writing.[16] For him the truth of art is inferior to experiential truth because art gives only a representation of reality, a translation of it into the written medium which lacks immediacy but which should *feel* like reality. This "effect of the real" is what Hemingway calls "true writing." But even his own true writing can only create an illusion of reality for the reader; reality itself is not only irreproducible, it is even destroyed or distorted by writing. Hemingway's is a disillusioned theory of literary truth: he is aware that although the artist must achieve self-expression by means of his writing, he must strive to communicate with his readers in spite of the writing. He is aware of the possibilities and also the limitations of his métier,[17] and he also knows that written language is his means of creation and his means of destruction. Writing, therefore, is creation that relies on destruction, for it destroys the transient wave of life by fixing it in a verbal textual model. This is a reason for sadness. But this disillusioned vision of his art does not prevent him from enjoying the fight to achieve the impossible, to invent new ways of telling and writing. Writing gives him plenty of reasons to feel both fine and sad.

Like Hemingway, who felt "very sad but very fine" (4) not only after watching the artistic bullfight, but also while practicing his own art, Hemingway's readers can feel both sad and fine after reading chapter 20. It is a poem in prose, an exceptional piece of writing that displaces bullfighting from the center of attention. It even displaces Hemingway's theory of art, removing it from our contemplation to let us contemplate love. Hemingway reverts to himself and to the residual feeling of nostalgia that comes from his being absent from places and faces he once loved and that are now gone. The movement of memory and writing makes present what is already past and brings Hemingway back in time, putting him in touch with a past version of himself, the man he had been years earlier, and the artist he had become then. In chapter 20, Hemingway is at a later moment — the moment of remembering and writing *Death in the Afternoon* — a moment when he was older, wiser, and finally able to write his book on bullfighting, a book which had been too difficult for him to write when first he came to Spain and saw a bullfight.

Chapter 20 is also exceptional for the change in tone and mood. The joyfulness that characterizes the great maestro while he is in the process of creation permeates the first nineteen chapters of the book. Here Hemingway tackles his *faena* confidently and openly, writing about all the relevant details of the bullfight and of his own art. But Hemingway changes his approach in the last chapter in the book. He lets chapter 20 be exceptional, as if it were an exceptionally brave bull whose rare perfection grants him reprieve (*indulto*) that enables him to come out of the plaza alive. Hemingway considers his experience of things and places in Spain too good to receive the same literary treatment as the rest of his book; he becomes less joyful, less explicit.

The artist wants to spare these experiences the destructiveness that writing necessarily brings; he does not want to create a "fixed model" but instead to leave them untouched in their "transient wave of life." And so Hemingway allows some of his Spanish memories to flit through the textual space. They are not totally a part of the book and they are not totally left out. They are insinuated and then omitted; they are considered for a moment and then transferred to the submerged part of the iceberg-text he called *Death in the Afternoon*. The submerged part is less visible and less readable but truer and more alive than the rest of the book. As Hemingway puts it, chapter 20 "is what the book is about but nobody seems to notice that. They think it is just a catalogue of things that were omitted" (*Selected Letters,* 378). Hemingway warns the reader that here he is not just making a list of omissions, but is actually summarizing the central concerns of *Death in the Afternoon:* impermanence, change, loss, the passing of time, and death. And because this chapter is about Hemingway, he personalizes these feelings: "Pamplona is changed, of course, but not as much as we are older. [. . .] I know things change now and I do not care. It's all been changed for me. Let it all change. We'll all be gone before it's changed too much. [. . .] We've seen it all go and we'll watch it go again" (278).

These changes produce sadness or melancholy, but the artist's creative answer to loss, his work and his ability to recreate or revive the past, at least for the little while that the reading lasts, brings joy. Sad but fine is the modernist writer's emotional, ambivalent answer to the paradoxical nature of art, which is creative and destructive. But paradox is not the main problem of the artist. His main problem is that not only life but art itself is ephemeral; time wears it out as it wears out a man. Fighting mortality by writing an immortal work is Hemingway's métier, his own version of a great *faena,* his language-fight, his fight with the tradition. In seeking to develop a new narrative style, Hemingway seeks to bury the past, to improve on the traditional narrative forms that were dead because with the passing of time they had become trite, worn-out formulae.

Hemingway worked hard on his narrative to differentiate it from nineteenth-century patterns. He followed Ezra Pound in using language sparingly, in "accepting the principles of good writing that had been contained in the early imagist document, and applying the stricture against superfluous words to his prose, polishing, repolishing, and eliminating" (Pound, 700). Hemingway agrees with Pound on the need for "making it new," but he places novelty in a moderate perspective: "the little new that each man gets from life is very costly and the only heritage he has to leave" (*DIA*, 192). He wanted to make his work memorable, to create a style that would last, if not forever, at least for a few generations. He expects that his artistic findings will survive in some form, "because in all arts all improvements and discoveries that are logical are carried on by some one else; so nothing is lost, really, except the man himself" (99). New art must of necessity reject earlier achievements, but it also continues, transmutes, and thus perpetuates them, only to be rejected in its turn.[18] Hemingway articulates a modernist version of the idea of tradition and fame. He wants to define his own place, to claim his literary position, in contradistinction to his predecessors and contemporaries. He needs to prove their standards obsolete, and to prove that his own, which are different, unfamiliar, and therefore vulnerable to rejection, are valid.

In *Death in the Afternoon* Hemingway defends not just the bullfight, he defends his own writing from misunderstanding. E. L. Doctorow speaks of the innovative and the confrontational aspects of Hemingway's craft: "when writing anything he would construct the sentences so as to produce an emotion not by claiming it but by rendering precisely the experience to cause it. What he made of all this was a rigorous art of compressive power. [. . .] His stuff was new. It moved. There was on every page of clear prose an implicit judgment of all other writing. The Hemingway voice hated pretense and cant and the rhetoric they rode in on" (1). Like Pound, Hemingway recommends the stripping away of inessentials, but Hemingway's statement on textual economy is more radical than Pound's, in that it stresses omission as well as compression: "If a writer of prose knows enough about what he is writing about he may omit things that he knows and the reader, if the writer is writing truly enough, will have a feeling of those things as strongly as though the writer had stated them" (192). Hemingway's famous iceberg theory suggests that as much as seven-eighths can be omitted.

In *Death in the Afternoon* Hemingway clarifies what he is trying to achieve in his innovative texts: he wants to bring his verbal narratives to a minimum of verbosity so that linguistic distortion is minimized. He assumes a sameness of experience and knowledge between reader and writer: "Nothing could happen to me that had not happened to all men before me" (qtd. in Baker, 39). If the interference of language is minimized, the reader will be able to recover the images lodged in Hemingway's memory and imagination more accurately. Intersubjectivity, the human bond, allows empathy, anticipation, and participation in the feelings and things that are not explicitly described but which the reader is able to recover inferentially from the pregnant gaps that the writer has carefully left in the text. In a way Hemingway is striving to bring his literature closer to the bullfight, which is a visual-image text and a wordless art. He is asking his readers to collaborate and accept a writing that challenges them to read between the lines, to rely less on the written word and more on the images of memory and imagination that experience imprints on the mind. From this perspective, Hemingway's iceberg theory casts a revolutionary perspective on reading and writing. It is a reconsideration of the centrality of words to literature, an art generally defined by its dependence on words. The theory entails a reconceptualization of literary narrative which I like to call Hemingway's fictional turn. The bullfighter tells a fictional story with materials that are not verbal, and Hemingway understands that he can do something similar by writing iceberg-texts in which the unsaid is as important as the said. The invisibility of the submerged seven-eighths of the iceberg parallels the unreadability of "most of the matter" not linguistically articulated on the surface of the text. The unsaid, the invisible, the part omitted from the linguistic surface of the text is truer to life than the actually said. In other words, unreadability, like invisibility, does not entail inexistence. The watcher's and the reader's imaginations, activated by an incomplete form, can infer the missing portions which, although invisible, exist and can be retrieved or inferred or reappropriated through personal interpretation. Hemingway's iceberg theory of writing is also a theory of reading, one that seeks to engage readers in a creative kind of reading that matches his own creativity as a writer.

Hemingway's iceberg metaphor exposes the illusory nature of widely accepted commonsensical notions about meaning. Hemingway affirms that both the said and the unsaid articulate a text's meaning. This view of meaning is not restricted to writing, reading, or even language. Hemingway sees meanings elsewhere — in the bullfight and in the world surrounding him — which are beyond the realm of the actually said. The iceberg is a powerful image not only for Hemingway's literary work but also for his native country. It is Hemingway's metaphor for the invisible meanings of his text as well as for the hidden, dark, invisible men and women of his country. As I see it, in *Death in the Afternoon* Hemingway was opening his readers' eyes to a modern world, a world that called into question old beliefs that overlooked or denied too many significant people and too many significant facts. They were beliefs deeply rooted in the ideology of domination, colonialization, subjugation. Paradoxically, he used an old Spanish institution, the bullfight — which is both an action of domination and a nonliteral representation of other domination processes — to enlighten his modern American-English readers.

In reading Hemingway's iceberg-texts we meet a wise man and artist whose ironic gaze is turned on his own native country as well as on his profession. *Death in the Afternoon* is a super iceberg-text. The visible tip, the bullfight, occupies the central textual space; it is exhaustively spoken about in the first nineteen chapters. That tip is supported by Spain, which just manages to appear briefly above the water-line in chapter 20. Spain's history and institutions, which are embedded in the meanings of the bullfight, are kept just below water-level in *Death in the Afternoon*. And totally submerged below Spain and the historical, social, and philosophical complexities of the bullfight, we can find America and the American literary scene, unvoiced and invisible but bearing most of the iceberg's weight.

The design of *Death in the Afternoon* reveals Hemingway's desire to stress the difference between other American writers and himself, rather than the difference between himself and the people of Spain. In *Death in the Afternoon* Hemingway makes clear that the radical difference between people is not a matter of national origin, ethnicity, or race, but rather a difference of quality or genius that makes an artist recognize another artist across all kinds of circumstantial barriers. In writing *Death in the Afternoon,* Hemingway establishes himself as an author and an authority in two fields, the art of bullfighting and literary art, and in two countries, his native America and Spain, a country that he "loved very much" (*DIA,* 277). The design of *Death in the Afternoon* allows the inattentive or literal-minded reader to overlook or disregard uncomfortable truths about modern America (modern American writing included) and modern Spain, and to concentrate instead on the spectacle of the modern bullfight. And conversely, the book's design pushes the more attentive or more daring readers into a more active role regarding the book they read and the life they live.

The combined application of a laconic style and the iceberg principle lends a quintessentially metonymic character to Hemingway's texts. As the last lines in chapter 20 of *Death in the Afternoon* tell us, "any part you make will represent the whole if it's made truly" (278). This all introduces a level of difficulty which in the particular case of *Death in the Afternoon* is high because in it Hemingway simultaneously states his theory and practices it in the form of his book. Michael Reynolds says that *Death in the Afternoon* is "a book before its time; unclassifiable, it was and remains largely ignored as a text by Hemingway critics but is pilfered freely for its pithy quotes" ("Brief Biography," 32). These "pithy quotes" are metaliterary comments on the writer's métier, on how to produce representations which strive to minimize the presence of language, how to reduce the distance between representation and the represented to a minimum, how to write well and truly.

Here lies the core of Hemingway's aesthetic, and fundamentally modernist, inquiry: the investigation of the status of the literary phenomenon regarding the real. For centuries this relationship has been contemplated by philosophy and literary aesthetics in relation to the issues of realism and the truth of mimetic representation. Modernism brings this contention to the fore not only in the work of theoreticians but within the creative writing of the modernist author. Hemingway the artist feels "very sad but very fine," an ambivalence between dissatisfaction and joy, the former resulting from knowing the powerlessness[19] of writing to eliminate the gulf between the living matter and its dead literary representations, and the latter, joy, emanating from the individual's power to invent new rules and thus increase the force of his art work: "It is because [the poet] realizes the inadequacy of the usual that he is obliged to invent" (Hulme, 167). In *Death in the Afternoon,* Hemingway dares to invade the territory of the theoretician, and he also dares to invent a style and invade the territory of the preceding literary tradition. He explains that words are not essential to the bullfight, a visual art, nor to literature, the so-called verbal art. For him verbosity is a liability and understatement an asset. He asks his readers to emulate him by behaving like aficionados to his texts, like involved interpreters daring to fill in the gaps left open in his narratives as well as in the narratives of their lives.

## Notes

[1] Between 1923 and 1932, Hemingway saw many bullfights, which was precisely what he needed before he could write *Death in the Afternoon*. In 1923 he had written "Bull Fighting a Tragedy," for *The Toronto Star Weekly* (20 October), but he was not happy with the result: "In writing for a newspaper you told what happened and, with one trick and another, you communicated the emotion [. . .]; but the real thing [. . .] was beyond me and I was working very hard to try to get it" (*DIA*, 2).

[2] What was so new and unacceptable in Hemingway's storytelling? Partly the exotic subject, bullfighting, and partly the taboo topic, death. Philip Young, for example, misunderstands *Death in the Afternoon* when he says "All of the author's tortured theories of art and tragedy and bulls — though not entirely silly — do very little to hide the fact [that it] is this fascination with highly stylized dying which primarily [counts]" (96). Of course dying is the fact that primarily counts, but for different reasons than those the critic suspects. In *The Denial of Death*, his study of violence and the nature of man, Becker stresses that "the idea of death, the fear of it, haunts the human animal like nothing else; it is a mainspring of human activity — activity designed largely to avoid the fatality of death, to overcome it by denying in some way that it is the final destiny of man" (ix). It is within this rational perspective on mortality as the basic problem of man that Hemingway focuses his work on killing and death in the afternoon. His awareness of death never was far from his awareness that, in the meantime, he should write.

[3] In *Death in the Afternoon*, war is an important though submerged part of the textual iceberg. Hemingway explicitly draws the connection between wars and bullfights and points out that his interest in the bullfight is derivative from his interest in war. Learning how to die through watching death in others is the essence of the Spanish corrida and of Hemingway's intellectual interest in it: "the only place where you could see life and death, i.e., violent death now that the wars were over, was in the bullring and I wanted very much to go to Spain where I could study it" (*DIA*, 2). From this quotation it is possible to learn not only of the already mentioned surrogate role the bullfight plays in relation to the war as the scenario of violent death, but also of the narrator's attitude, which is one of analytical interest in violence and violent death.

[4] In a similar way, Hemingway wants his readers to read the void in his text not for what a void is but for what it symbolizes. Reaching beyond the explicit and visible is what Hemingway recommends to his readers.

[5] "[The people of Spain] know death is the unescapable reality, the one thing any man may be sure of; the only security [. . .] life is much shorter than death" (266).

Hemingway is here alluding to a world vision typical of the Spanish Baroque. The great theater of the world as vanity fair in Calderón de la Barca's *El Gran Teatro del Mundo* can illustrate the point. These baroque ideas are pursued in *Death in the Afternoon* too, but in a new, unbaroque style because, as Hemingway ironically says, "the baroque is over" (191).

[6] In *Death in the Afternoon* Hemingway insists that he is explaining the *modern* Spanish bullfight. By modern he means the bullfight as it has been fought from the end of the eighteenth century onwards: "Ronda was one of the cradles of modern bullfighting. It was the birthplace of Pedro Romero, one of the first and greatest professional fighters and, in our times, of Niño de la Palma. [. . .] The bull ring at Ronda was built towards the end of the eighteenth century" (43).

Obviously there were bulls and bullfights before the eighteenth century, otherwise there would not have existed a precedent for Romero nor a need for building the plaza, but they were different in form and function. Hemingway mentions professionalism as one of the relevant differences.

[7] Hemingway calls the bullfight's three *tercios* "the trial," "the sentencing," and "the execution" (*DIA*, 98).

[8] Between 1870 and 1898, the United States experienced "the Gilded Age," which was characterized by an expanding economy and the emergence of plutocratic influences in government and social structures. In *Death in the Afternoon* Hemingway speaks of the bullfight's Golden Age (68–70), which he places between 1913 and 1920, the seven years of competition between José Gómez Ortega (Joselito) and Juan Belmonte. At this time, and for those great matadors and their new style, bull breeders reduced the size of the bulls and their horns. Hemingway criticizes this emphasis on specialization, "the decay of a complete art through a magnification of certain of its aspects" (70). What he says about the decadence of the bullfight in chapter 7 can be applied as well to the decadence of the ideals of the American Frontier precisely in the middle of the so called Gilded Age: "bullfighting for seven years had a golden age in spite of the fact that it was in the process of being destroyed" (69).

[9] "If you serve time for society, democracy, and the other things quite young, and declining any further enlistment make yourself responsible only to yourself, you exchange the pleasant, comforting stench of comrades for something you can never feel in any other way than by yourself. That something I cannot yet define completely but the feeling comes when you write well and truly [. . .] and when, on the sea, you are alone with it and know that this Gulf Stream you are living with, knowing, learning about, and loving, has moved, as it moves, since before man, and that it has gone by the shoreline of that long, beautiful, unhappy island since before Columbus sighted it and that the things that you find out about it, and those that have always lived in it are permanent and of value because that stream will flow, as it has flowed, after the Indians, after the Spaniards, after the British, after the Americans [. . .] are all gone" (*Green Hills of Africa*, 126–27).

[10] Wyndham Lewis's "The Dumb Ox" offers an excellent critical evaluation of the meaning of the ox in *Death in the Afternoon* and, more generally, within Hemingway's pattern of action, of the ox as the passive modern American to whom things are done. Nevertheless Lewis is partial when he forgets that the pattern is incomplete without the active bull, and becomes insulting when he compares Hemingway to the

ox for his lack of political commitment. Malcolm Cowley's more measured evaluation does not deprive *Death in the Afternoon* of its sociopolitical implications.

The caption to the photograph "the Ox" reads: "While here we have the ox built for beef and for service who might have been president with that face if he had started in some other line of work. He differs from the fighting bull in this, as well as in his general shape; [. . .] He may work hard all his life or he may be made into beef early in his career, but he will never kill a horse. Nor will he ever want to. Hail to the useful ox; a friend and contemporary of man" (282). Anthony Brand's essay, "Far from Simple," also discusses these images (pages 171–73 in this volume).

[11] Fiedler reminds us that, concerning Hemingway, "not everything is what it seems to a superficial scrutiny" (19). Looking hard at Hemingway's characters, Fiedler sees crypto-Indians in his Spanish peasants. The interesting factor is that in Fiedler's reading between the lines of the Hemingway text there results a homology between the Spanish folk and the Native American which contrasts with the late American scene.

[12] Hemingway's text reads: "As [the people of Spain] have common sense they are interested in death and do not spend their lives avoiding the thought of it and hoping it does not exist only to discover it when they come to die. [. . .] They know death is the unescapable reality, the one thing any man may be sure of; the only security; [. . .] life is much shorter than death" (264, 266). Here Hemingway sees the Spanish world vision as based on the idea that the impermanence of life contrasts with the permanence of death, which is an idea that recurs in Hemingway's vision of art as (deathly) artificial permanence imposed on the natural wave of life.

[13] Exposure to the dual nature of the bullfight experience — it is both painful and pleasurable — subordinates the a priori unacceptable cruelty of some parts of the corrida to the overall pattern where pain makes sense and death is articulated as functional and therefore necessary to life as well as to the narrative pattern of the bullfight: "There is no manoeuvre in the bullfight which has, as object, to inflict pain on the bull. The pain that is inflicted is incidental, not an end" (195).

[14] This is an allusion to T. E. Hulme, imagist, philosopher and ideologue of modernism, who acknowledges the influence of Bergson's theory of art on modernism when he writes: "The artist by making a fixed model of one of these transient waves enables you to isolate it out and to perceive it in yourself. In that sense art merely reveals, it never creates" (151–52).

[15] The quotation in full reads: "[Bullfighting] is an art that deals with death and death wipes it out. But it is never truly lost, you say, because in all arts all improvements and discoveries that are logical are carried on by some one else; so nothing is lost, really, except the man himself" (*DIA*, 99). In stating that bullfighting, even if minor, is an art like the others, especially in its forming part of tradition and inherited convention, Hemingway establishes a common ground between the lidia and literature: Hemingway's writing aspires to relative permanence. *Death in the Afternoon* explicitly associates art with death and with the desire to overcome impermanence.

[16] Hemingway discriminates between different kinds of facts and things, the important and the unimportant ones. When "the fact is of enough importance in itself [. . .] it is impossible to make [it] come true on paper [. . .] it being always an individual experience" (*DIA*, 63).

[17] Hotchner recalls a 1954 dinner conversation in which Hemingway, who had been drinking more wine than usual, "spoke steadily" (110) about books and writing and the past. There are recurring allusions to the métier triste, which is discussed in the context of war, death, and writing: "'You know what the French call war? Le métier triste. [. . .] You know the real métier triste?' he asked. 'Writing. There is a métier triste for you'" (115, 116).

In September 1929, Hemingway had used these words in a letter to Scott Fitzgerald. At the time, less than a year since his father's death, Hemingway was sad both for himself and for Fitzgerald. He was aware that Scott's depression, which he called "The Artist's Reward," was typically associated with the paralyzing fear of becoming barren as a creative writer (*Selected Letters*, 306).

[18] Hemingway rejected all of his immediate predecessors except Pound. Gertrude Stein, Sherwood Anderson, Scott Fitzgerald all were friends and then enemies. *Death in the Afternoon*'s list of derogated authors includes Waldo Frank, William Faulkner, T. S. Eliot, Jean Cocteau, Aldous Huxley, Oscar Wilde, and Walt Whitman. Others are only impersonally alluded to by mention of their schools: "all schools only serve to classify their members as failures" (100).

[19] T. E. Hulme, the theoretician of modernism, explained the root of this dissatisfaction: "Language, being a communal apparatus, only conveys over [*sic*] that part of the emotion which is common to all of us. If you are able to observe the actual individuality of the emotion you experience, you become dissatisfied with language" (162).

# Works Cited

Arendt, Hannah. *On Violence*. New York: Harcourt, Brace, 1969.

Baker, Carlos, ed. *Hemingway and His Critics: An International Anthology*. New York: Hill and Wang, 1961.

Becker, Ernest. *The Denial of Death*. New York: The Free Press, 1973.

Beegle, Susan F. "'That Always Absent Something Else': 'A Natural History of the Dead' and Its Discarded Coda." In *New Critical Approaches to the Short Stories of Ernest Hemingway*. Ed. Jackson Benson. Durham: Duke UP, 1990. 73–95.

Benson, Jackson. *Hemingway, The Writer's Art of Self-Defense*. Minneapolis: U of Minnesota P, 1969.

Cowley, Malcolm. "A Farewell to Spain." *New Republic* 73 (November 1932): 76–77. Rpt. in Meyers, 164–69.

Doctorow, E. L. "Braver Than We Thought." *The New York Times Book Review*, 18 May 1986, 1, 44–45.

Eliot, T. S. "Hamlet." 1919. In his *Selected Essays*. 3rd. ed. London: Faber and Faber, 1951. 141–46.

Fiedler, Leslie A. *The Return of the Vanishing American*. London: Granada-Paladin, 1972.

Foucault, Michel. *Surveiller et punir*. Paris: Gallimard, 1975.

Giger, Romeo. *The Creative Void: Hemingway's Iceberg Theory*. Bern: Francke Verlag, 1977.

Hemingway, Ernest. "Bull Fighting a Tragedy." *The Toronto Star Weekly* (20 October 1923). Rpt. in *By-Line: Ernest Hemingway. Selected Articles and Dispatches of Four Decades*. Ed. William White. London: Grafton / Collins, 1989. 111–18.

———. *Death in the Afternoon*. New York: Scribner's, 1932.

———. *Ernest Hemingway: Selected Letters, 1917–1961*. Ed. Carlos Baker. New York: Scribner's, 1981.

———. *Green Hills of Africa*. New York: Scribner's, 1935.

Hermann, Thomas. *"Quite a Little About Painters": Art and Artists in Hemingway's Life and Work*. Tübingen: Francke, 1987.

Hotchner, A. E. *Papa Hemingway: A Personal Memoir*. London: Weidenfeld and Nicolson, 1966.

Hulme, T. E. *Speculations: Essays on Humanism and the Philosophy of Art*. London: Routledge and Kegan Paul, 1987.

Levine, George, ed. *Realism and Representation*. Madison: U of Wisconsin P, 1993.

Lewis, Robert W. "The Making of *Death in the Afternoon*." In *Ernest Hemingway: The Writer in Context*. Ed. James Nagel. Madison: U of Wisconsin P, 1984. 31–52.

Lewis, Wyndham. "The Dumb Ox: A Study of Ernest Hemingway." In his *Men Without Art*. London: Cassel, 1934. 15–40. Rpt. in Meyers, 186–207.

Limon, John. *Writing After War: American War Fiction from Realism to Postmodernism*. Oxford: Oxford UP, 1994.

Lyotard, Jean-Francois. *The Postmodern Condition: A Report on Knowledge*. Minneapolis: U of Minnesota P, 1984.

Mandel, Miriam B. *Hemingway's "Death in the Afternoon": The Complete Annotations*. Lanham, MD: Scarecrow, 2002.

———. "Realidad, historia y poesía: el arte de Ernest Hemingway." Conference on Hemingway, "75 años de *Fiesta*," Universidad Pública de Navarra, Pamplona, Spain, July 2001.

Marcoviç, Mihailo. "Violence and Human Self-Realization." In *Violence and Aggression in the History of Ideas*. Eds. Philip P. Wiener and John Fisher. New Brunswick, New Jersey: Rutgers UP, 1974. 234–52.

McCarthy, E. Doyle. "The Sources of Human Destructiveness: Ernest Becker's Theory of Human Nature." *Thought* 56.220 (March 1981): 44–57.

Meyers, Jeffrey, ed. *Hemingway: The Critical Heritage*. London: Routledge and Kegan Paul, 1982.

Mulvey, Laura. "Visual Pleasure and Narrative Cinema." *Screen* 16.3 (1975): 6–18.

Penas Ibáñez, Beatriz. *Análisis semiótico de los aspectos taurinos de la obra de Ernest Hemingway*. Zaragoza: Prensas Universitarias de la Universidad de Zaragoza / Instituto de Estudios Riojanos, 1990. Microfiche.

———. "Looking Through The Garden's Mirrors: The Early Postmodernist Hemingway Text." *North Dakota Quarterly* 65.3 (1998): 91–104.

Pound, Ezra. "Small Magazines." *The English Journal* 19.9 (1930): 689–704.

Raeburn, John. *Fame Became of Him: Hemingway as Public Writer*. Bloomington: Indiana UP, 1984.

Reynolds, Michael. "Ernest Hemingway 1899–1961. A Brief Biography." In *A Historical Guide to Ernest Hemingway*. Ed. Linda Wagner-Martin. Oxford: Oxford UP, 2000. 15–50.

———. *Hemingway: The Paris Years*. New York: Blackwell, 1989.

———. *The Young Hemingway*. New York: Blackwell, 1986.

Scafella, Frank, ed. *Hemingway. Essays of Reassessment*. Oxford: Oxford UP, 1991.

Young, Philip. *Ernest Hemingway: A Reconsideration*. University Park: Pennsylvania State UP, 1966.

# "Far from Simple": The Published Photographs in *Death in the Afternoon*

*Anthony Brand*

> *I found the definite action; but the bullfight was so far from simple [...].*
> Death in the Afternoon, 3

> *While in principle all subjects are worthy pretexts for exercising the photographic way of seeing, the convention has arisen that photographic seeing is clearest in offbeat [...] subject matter[s]. [...] Because we are indifferent to them, they best show up the ability of the camera to "see."*       Susan Sontag, 136–37

FROM THE BEGINNING, Hemingway linked his writing about bullfighting with photographs. His first published essay on the subject, "Bull Fighting Is Not a Sport — It Is a Tragedy" (*Toronto Star Weekly*, 20 October 1923) featured three photographs and a drawing.[1] In 1925, writing to his editor, Maxwell Perkins, at Scribner's, he described the project which eventually became *Death in the Afternoon* as "a sort of Daughty's [*sic*] Arabia Deserta of the Bull Ring [...] a very big book with some wonderful pictures" (qtd. in Bruccoli, 34). Although Perkins made no comment, Hemingway brought up the project again about nine months later: "I will keep the bull fight book going [...]. It will have illustrations — drawings and photographs — and I think should have some colored reproductions" (qtd. in Bruccoli, 53) of works by Goya, Manet, Picasso, Juan Gris, Waldo Peirce, Roberto Domingo, Carlos Ruano Llopis, and Ricardo Marín.[2] And he collected photographs: as Robert W. Lewis comments, Hemingway went to Spain "Almost every summer [...] not only to see fights but also to gather information and photographs" (31) — about four hundred of them.

Hemingway's insistence on photographs is understandable: he recognized that recent advances in photography would enable him to present his subject more vividly than had previously been possible. Before the end of the nineteenth century, the nature of glass-plate emulsion photography and the short focal-length of the lenses (about fifty millimeters) made it difficult to capture the rapid action of the bullfight. We have, therefore, only a few memorable action shots of the great luminaries who fought at the turn of the century, stars like Manuel García (El Espartero, killed in 1894), Rafael Guerra (Guerrita, retired in 1899), or Luis Mazzantini (retired in 1904). By the 1910s, however, action photography was well developed: the depth of field and sharpness of focus were more precise, and longer focal-length lenses ensured a more reliable result. Modern German cameras such as the Ernemann "Klapp" model enabled the preservation of key moments in "an impermanent art" (*DIA,* 99) and, just as importantly, facilitated examination, discussion, and evaluation of these fleeting moments.[3] Spanish photojournalists such as Baldomero Fernández, Antonio Calvache, José Calvache (Walken), Manuel Vaquero, Aurelio Rodero, Juanito Vandel, Juan José Serrano, Manuel Cervera, and Manuel Mateo were using the new technology to capture crucial taurine details on film.[4] Their work appeared in several of the taurine newspapers and journals that Hemingway and other aficionados read so avidly,[5] and most of them are represented among the four hundred photographs that Hemingway collected for inclusion in *Death in the Afternoon.*[6]

As the reality of publication approached, however, Perkins insisted on cutting back on the photographs, to make the book affordable in the depressed economy.[7] By April 1932, Hemingway was noticeably upset by the dwindling numbers. He wrote Perkins, "I have something over a hundred pictures *necessary to make the book comprehensive* (my italics) having brought this number down from two hundred to, at present, one hundred and twelve. What was it gave you the idea of suggesting sixteen illustrations for the book [. . .]?" (qtd. in Bruccoli, 161). On 2 June he again wrote Perkins about the number: "I could not get them under 70 — without losing *the very necessary effect.* If that is an odd number to print can add two good ones and make 72 [. . .]" (qtd. in Bruccoli, 167, my italics). Hemingway was concerned not only about the number but also about the placement of the photographs. Although he had originally intended to intersperse them throughout the text and glossary, he liked Perkins's suggestion that they be grouped rather than scattered. He was insistent about their lay-out, cabling instructions to Perkins on 27 June: "DO NOT GROUP ONE AND TWO STOP GROUP TWENTY TWO AND TWENTY THREE INSTEAD STOP OTHER GROUPINGS OK IF GROUPINGS NECESSARY STOP WILL CORRECT ALL PROOFS IMMEDIATELY AND SEND FROM HERE BEFORE LEAVING [. . .]" (qtd. in Bruccoli, 170–71, capitals in the original).[8]

From 1925 to 1932, then, the photographs were a matter of intense and continuous interest to Hemingway, obviously an important part of his plan for *Death in the Afternoon.* Recognizing that photography would help him achieve his aims for this unusual new book, Hemingway spent considerable time, energy, and money — his own money, as he repeatedly and angrily pointed out to Perkins — in collecting visual materials and then in selecting, laying out, and captioning the eighty-one photographs that were finally included in the book. Their content and organization reveal the methods and principles Hemingway employed in producing this very personal photographic essay.

Although Hemingway claims that "the photograph does not give any sense of time" (*DIA,* 258), a careful reading of a taurine photograph can indicate the sequence, speed, or rhythm of the action. Blurry or swirling sand, for example, enables us to identify the direction and speed of the bull's charge, or of the bullfighter's action (how well he has stood his ground), or the presence of wind (which complicates the bullfighter's performance). A photograph can even reveal actions which preceded the photographed instant. In four images in *Death in the Afternoon,* for example, the bullfighters' torn costumes indicate that the men had been tossed, though not necessarily wounded, at some earlier point in that bullfight: we can see that Nicanor Villalta's trouser and jacket have been ripped (311), that Chicuelo wears someone's trousers over his damaged costume (361), and that two bullfighters were caught in the upper right abdomen, over the hipbone: Marcial Lalanda (381) and Luis Freg (393, center).[9]

Hemingway's photographs and their captions also reveal or comment on material not directly related to bullfighting, but relevant to the comprehensive portrait of Spain which *Death in the Afternoon* paints. Some of the photographs, for example, show the audience at a bullfight. The details of their dress express the regional and class distinctions that the text also comments upon, as well as each region's feeling for the bullfight. For taurine events in Pamplona, for example, people dressed informally: the Basque beret is much in evidence, and many fans in the stands wear the white or blue shirts and neckerchiefs typical for the festival of San Fermín (319). The photographs of the running of the bulls show men in suits and ties, indicating the participation of the local citizenry in contemporary everyday dress (385, 387). Photographs taken in Seville's bullrings[10] show a preponderance of elegant, high-topped wide-brimmed Cordoban hats (339, 341, 391) that express that city's pride in its more formal, even elitist traditions. In the Madrid bullring, we see men in the straw hats, fedoras, and bowlers that marked the fashion of the times, and in this cosmopolitan city, women are more visible and more elegantly dressed than in any other arena (289, 327, 347, 361). As Hemingway explains, Madrid "is modern rather than picturesque, no costumes, practically no Cordoban hats, except on the heads of phonies" (51). Looking at the people in the foreground or background of the photographs, the viewer can also recognize their level of sophistication, as evidenced by their self-consciousness in front of the camera and in the presence of such exotic celebrities as bullfighters (331, 363, 369).

Because Hemingway is so concerned to make us *see*, to look at details, he carefully controls *where* we look. Most of the photographs he chose for publication share the same camera angle: they were taken straight on, at eye level, not from below or from above or from far away. Not only the camera angle, but the setting of the photographs reveals an insistence on immediacy: many of the photographs were taken in areas which permit the photographer to stand close to his subjects: for example, in the plaza's *patio de caballos* (horse yard), where the bullfighters gather before entering the arena; at the barrera (the wooden fence surrounding the arena) or from the *callejón* (the passageway between the barrera and the stands — that is, from the positions which he himself preferred: close to the action. This is the ideal position for the viewer who is interested in *seeing* a bullfight. Even the photographs that were full-frame wide angle shots, like the one of Manolo Mejías (Bienvenida; 391 bottom) and of gorings (403), have been enlarged and cropped, because Hemingway wanted his readers to focus on a particular detail.

Hemingway's photographs not only encourage his readers to look carefully, they also force them to look at those bullfighters who elicited his strongest feelings. Hemingway had collected photographs of some sixty different matadors, but rather than even-handedly including one or two pictures per matador in his book (and thus introducing his readers to many matadors), Hemingway gives us pictures only of those artists who interested him personally, for whatever reason: ten of the published photographs show José Gómez Ortega (Joselito) and six show Juan Belmonte, the two most influential figures of the 1910s. There are four photographs each of Manuel García (Maera), Nicanor Villalta, Marcial Lalanda, and Rafael Gómez Ortega (El Gallo) — all of whom he admired — and four also of Manuel Jiménez (Chicuelo) — whom he disliked; and three apiece of Luis Freg and Manuel Varé (Varelito) — whom he admired — and of Joaquín Rodríguez (Cagancho), about whom he had reservations. Hemingway had expressed some of these biases earlier, in a variety of ways: by lionizing Maera in fiction (in an interchapter in *In Our Time* and in "The Undefeated"), by naming his first-born son after Villalta, and by attacking Chicuelo in a short story, "A Lack of Passion" (mentioned in *Death in the Afternoon* but not published until 1990). These biases are often cited by critics who are interested in proving or denying Hemingway's accuracy as a judge of taurine performance. Be that as it may, those opinions form an interesting personal subtext in the photographic essay.

Like the numbers, the content of the photographs reveals Hemingway's opinions: all the photos of Joselito, Maera, Varelito, Lalanda, Villalta, and Freg present them in a flattering or sympathetic light, whereas most of those of Chicuelo are used to ridicule him. Hemingway damns other bullfighters with the faintest of exposure: Ignacio Sánchez Mejías, a major figure of the period, is shown in only two photographs, both unflattering; and two rising stars are similarly disparaged: Manolo Mejías (Bienvenida) is seen twice, once simply marching into the ring, and once killing badly; and Domingo Ortega appears only once, as merely one of several bullfighters entering the arena. Cayetano Ordóñez (Niño de la Palma), to whom Hemingway responded intensely, both positively (he idealized him as Pedro Romero in *The Sun Also Rises*) and negatively (he attacked him repeatedly and sometimes unfairly in *Death in the Afternoon*, 43, 87–90, 167, 222, 250), suffers even more neglect: he is pointedly excluded from the photographic essay. This is not for lack of material: Hemingway had collected ten pictures of Ordóñez (most of them show him performing well). And Hemingway had, in addition to the unflattering ones he chose to publish, another nineteen photographs of Sánchez Mejías and five each of Ortega and Bienvenida. Hemingway's collection of photographs was comprehensive and wide-ranging; restricted to using only one-fifth of what he had collected, he chose to display those bullfighters about whom he had strong feelings. His choices, then, express his biases.[11] We might say that they reveal more than Hemingway expected or intended.

But above all, Hemingway's purpose in selecting his photographs was didactic: he wanted to teach the novice viewer how to recognize, understand, and feel the events he might witness at a corrida. Although his text had already explained everything from the virtues of any given *suerte* (maneuver) to the failure of the bullfighter to make an artistic statement, Hemingway now presents these matters in photographs "because a description in words cannot enable you to identify them before you have seen them as a photograph can" (176). It is no accident that the photographs appear immediately after the text. Recognizing that "[a] technical explanation is hard reading" (179), Hemingway gives us representative images of both good and bad bullfighting to support, illustrate, and expand his exposition. All this is consistent with Hemingway's intention: to teach his readers how to look. His book is not a guide on how to fight a bull; it is, rather, a guide on how to *look* at the bull and at the bullfighter who is fighting him.

For many reasons, then, the photographs in *Death in the Afternoon* reward careful study. Remarkably enough, this section — Hemingway's only excursion into photojournalism — has escaped critical attention. Of all the books and articles that discuss *Death in the Afternoon*, only one addresses this extended photo-essay, which comprises 128 pages of photographs and captions (279–407).[12] In *Hemingway and the Hispanic World*, Angel Capellán finds that

> the organization of the illustrations, an important element in a bullfighting book, is, to say the least, puzzling. The pictures should have followed the tight structure of the art of the bullfight, but Hem-

ingway's confused sequence made them loose a good deal of their impact. (142)

Capellán's puzzlement is justified, for Hemingway's organization is very unusual and complex. Although Hemingway does devote several photographs to each one of the bullfight's three *tercios,* or acts — the cape work and pic-ing; the banderillas; and the muleta and sword work — his photographs do not follow the order of the corrida: pictures of banderillas, for example, appear both before and after photos which illustrate muleta work. Bulls grazing on the ranch — that is, before they are even transported to the bullring — appear *after* we have been shown several pictures of the pic-ing and caping that occur *during* the bullfight. The photographic chapter on Joselito appears *after* we have seen several bullfighters who rose to fame *after* Joselito died in 1920. The ten photographs of Joselito are grouped together, but the focus on him is disturbed by a picture of Belmonte inserted into that essay; and the six photographs of Belmonte are scattered throughout the essay, and not grouped together in chronological order (i.e., the chronological order of events in the corrida), as they usually are in the many spectator guides which purport to help the viewer understand the corrida.[13]

Hemingway's interruptions and disjunctions are, I believe, purposefully orchestrated to disrupt standard expectations of organization (for example, by *tercio,* by *suerte,* by bullfighter, by chronology — the standard organizational principles adopted by Spanish tauromachic essays), to force the reader to contrast his own reading with that of the author, and thus to force the reader to look at the things *the author* wants us to look at: the bull, the bullfighter, and the interaction between them. Hemingway does show us the development of the bull, the three-act order of the bullfight, its history, and the individuals who excelled in it, but he uses his own organization, appropriate to his purpose: to present his own carefully orchestrated tour of the bullfight, aimed at an audience that needs instruction. To this end, Hemingway's photographic essay disrupts time, order, and thematic continuity, to teach the spectator how to look at and respond to a bullfight. He imposes his writer's instinct for contrast, drama, and unity upon his readers, by way of an extremely complex organization.

In August and September 1930, Hemingway had to interrupt work on *Death in the Afternoon* to prepare *In Our Time* for publication (Bruccoli, 144–49), and so he had the complex organization of that book in mind when he prepared his photo-essay. *In Our Time* alternates titled stories with numbered chapters, indicating that two separate methods or visions are working simultaneously and interdependently, to make a whole that is greater than its parts. In that modernist masterpiece, it is up to the reader to make the connections. In the photographic essay in *Death in the Afternoon,* Hemingway complicates the matter: we have three separate threads, and they simultaneously remain separate (by subject matter) and are closely interwoven (no formal signal, like a title or a chapter heading, separates one thread from the other). It is up to the reader to recognize the three different subject matters: the bull, the bullfighter, and the interaction between the two. And it is up to the reader to extract the organizing principles that govern the sequencing of the photographs and the interweaving of the three threads. No wonder Capellán was puzzled.

Most of the photographs (about sixty of the eighty-one) focus on the interaction between man and beast, emphasizing its drama and danger, its moments of ugliness, chaos, defeat, triumph, and transcendent beauty. But it is striking to note that seven photographs feature bulls unaccompanied by men; and that thirteen photographs feature bullfighters who are not interacting with bulls. These two sets of photographs focus our eyes on the individual, rather than the action; on the details, or the individual components, rather than the whole, because we can see and feel the whole more clearly if we understand its details. These two sets of photographs interrupt the main thread (the interaction that is the corrida) in order to help us see it and respond to it. As Hemingway wrote, "The [. . .] illustrations are [. . .] flashes designed to give some feeling of the fight."[14] Instead of following the standard organization of a spectator's guide or manual, Hemingway gives us his own, personal, carefully orchestrated tour of the bullfight and of taurine life and culture, aimed at an audience that needs both technical and emotional instruction.

### Photographs of Bulls

Hemingway begins his photographic essay with three photographs of the bull that serve as definition and introduction. He first shows a well-bred and handsome bull (he displays *trapío*), whose breeder has decided to use for stud. Quite appropriately, Hemingway shows this stud bull in the company of a cow (281), telling us that this is where it all begins. In the next photograph, we see the seed bull's opposite, the castrated ox.[15] Neither one of these bulls will be fought in a corrida; the two photographs define the *toro de lidia* (the fighting bull) by negation, and thus serve as an educational prelude, gradually leading us from the fields to the bullring.

The third photograph shows two *toros de lidia* already in the corrals of the Madrid bullring: they will certainly be fought. The caption of this photograph points out the raised *morrillo* (neck muscle) which indicates that a bull feels threatened and is ready to attack. The bull on the right, shown in full-body profile, displays the aroused *morrillo* clearly. In fact, this classic aggressive stance was used as a logo on the title page of *Death in the Afternoon*, to emphasize the book's focus on the fighting bull. He is handsome, powerful, and aggressive, and we admire him.

After this introduction, Hemingway takes us into the main thread, the interaction between bull and man. We see the bull interacting with the mounted bullfighter (a series of four photographs which emphasize the power of the bull) and with the bullfighter on foot (a series of seven photographs which emphasize the man's domination of the bull). Just as we begin to feel confident that the man is safe, however, Hemingway abruptly stops this thread to show us bulls without men (302–5). The photos are jarring in that they are anachronistic, taking us to the bull as he was *before* the fight, before the man began to dominate him. Both pictures emphasize the *toro de lidia*'s size and danger, as if to return this factor to the forefront of our consciousness. The first photograph shows two bulls "on the range" who lock horns aggressively, intent on goring and killing. Their size and the intensity of their encounter indicates that they have reached sexual maturity, although they are still on their breeder's ranch.[16] The next image presents five powerful, full-grown fighting bulls, descendants of the magnificent stud bull Diano.[17] They are in the bullring corral, only days or perhaps even hours away from the corrida.

After this intense interruption, which focuses us on the danger posed by the bull, the essay returns us to the interaction between bull and man. We see dangerous, deadly interaction between man and bull (306–72): sometimes the man is in control, but as the series progresses Hemingway often abandons the action photographs to show us frightening close ups — of Freg and Varelito suffering in the hospital (328–29, 372–73), of doctors struggling to save a man's life (362–63), and of Joselito and Granero dead (348–49, 368–69). We begin to understand that it is much better when things go as they should, and the bull is killed. To make this point, Hemingway shows us another bull by himself: the bull Chicuelo couldn't kill (374–75).[18] This bull represents the failure of the man, not because he killed the man, but because the man was unable to kill him. This close-up of the bull, coming at this point, encourages us to understand more fully the consequences of the interaction. Now when we see a bull by himself, we don't merely admire him and celebrate his beauty and strength, as we may have done earlier (285, 302–5); there, our awareness of danger was tinged with admiration of power. But now, we begin to see the necessity of the death of this animal. The picture of the bull Chicuelo couldn't kill is ominous.

That photograph was a proper prelude to the last picture of this series or thread: the dead bull we see towards the end of the photographic essay has the blood of a man on his horn. He has injured or perhaps killed someone; if he had not been killed, he would have injured and killed other people. It is proper that he lie dead before us: this thread has shown us that in a bullfight, it is improper, shocking, even irrational that a bull should survive. Except for the rare occasions when the bull is *indultado* (pardoned), the only acceptable outcome of any corrida is the death of the bull. This seven-photograph thread, then, has taught us to keep our eye on the bull, who offers mortal danger even when things go well; and to expect and even rejoice in his death, which reassures us that the human being is safe. We have moved from admiring the animal to requiring its death, and this is the proper emotional sequence for a spectator in a bullfight.

## Photographs of Men

In addition to the seven photographs that show us bulls who are not interacting with men, Hemingway included thirteen photographs of men who are not interacting with bulls. They do not follow the chronological order of the bullfight (both the first and last pictures show us the end of a performance, and the antepenultimate picture shows bullfighters entering the ring at the very *beginning* of an afternoon). They do not focus on any one particular performer, and they cover a short period of time, from 1912 (the group picture of the Gallo family, 330) to 1930 (the *paseíllo* of Bienvenida, Ortega, and Lalanda, 377). Two are group pictures which show bullfighters dressed in their *trajes de luces* but before they meet their bulls (330 and 337). Five show the aftereffects of a goring (329, 349, 363, 369, and 373). They are not in chronological order but are instead presented with increasing insistency: the picture of the suffering Freg (329) is the third in the series, the one of the dead Joselito is the fifth (349), and the other three close-ups of pain and death come in close succession, as the eighth, ninth, and tenth in this series (doctors operating on Rosario Olmos, 363;[19] Granero dead, 369; and a gaunt Varelito in his hospital bed, 373). Injury is an inescapable possibility in the bullring, and Hemingway's photographic essay makes no attempt to evade it. But the human spirit cannot be defeated, as Hemingway so famously said, and so this relentless look at pain is followed, in this series of human portraits, by the entry of a new set of matadors (the eleventh picture, 377), and by two photographs of Rafael Gómez Ortega (Gallo), the master survivor, who was promoted to matador de toros in 1902 and was still fighting occasionally in the 1930s, when he was more than fifty years old.

Four of the thirteen pictures show famous bullfighters — Maera, Belmonte, Chicuelo, and Gallo — performing the ceremony of the *brindis* that begins the final act of the bullfight. The *brindis* appears so often because, once the bullfight begins, it is the only moment when the audience focuses on the bullfighter, and not on his interaction with the bull.[20] Here also, Hemingway eschews chronology, but he draws attention to this intensely personal moment by presenting it often and by spacing it carefully. The *brindis* is seen at the beginning, middle, and end of this series: Maera's *brindis* is the second photograph (315), Belmonte's and Chicuelo's are the sixth and seventh (353, 354), and Gallo's is the penultimate (401).

Like the pictures of the bulls, these pictures force us look away from the motion and rhythm of the corrida in order to concentrate on one of its individual participants. The fact that there are almost twice as many pictures of men without bulls as there are of bulls without men shows us — in case we should tend to forget it — that the survival of the man is more important than the survival of the bull. As if to wear down the resistance of the viewer whose sympathies lie with the bull — the "animalarians" whom Hemingway scorns in the text — these thirteen pictures of men work to draw our sympathy to them (they show men who are suffering, injured, and dead) and to their capacity for friendship and optimism, as they dedicate their bulls in what they hope will be a memorable *faena* (muleta work). The first picture of this series comes surprisingly late: it is actually the twelfth picture of the photo-essay. But after that, pictures of men interrupt the corrida frequently, and even when the pictures show the interaction between man and bull, the captions often draw our attention to the individual man, by giving his name and explaining what he is doing.

The first photo of the sequence shows us a tired but successful Juan Belmonte, and thus looks forward to the last picture of the photographic essay, which shows us another master, Rafael el Gallo, with his dead bull in the background. Neither one of these older men looks joyful or triumphant: they simply look exhausted. But they have done what they had to do, and their faces and stances — and not the dead bulls in the background — ask for our attention. If the series on the bull was designed to wear down our admiration for him, and to accept and even desire his death, so the much longer but looser series on the men is designed to show them as individuals whose survival is important to us. And the caption of the last picture of the essay emphasizes the point: "The bull, as he should be, is dead. The man, as he should be, is alive and with a tendency to smile" (406). It could not be otherwise.

The series that focuses on the man, then, is carefully organized. Parts of it are balanced: the first and last photographs are related (they show the same moment, the matador after the successful completion of his work); and the second, middle, and penultimate pictures are related (they show the *brindis*). Danger appears early in the series (the third photograph) and intensifies as the series progresses. The series ends in triumph, with new men taking up the challenge (the twelfth picture) and an older man so full of technique, talent, and spirit that he can still vanquish a bull (the thirteenth picture).

**Photographs of the Corrida (Interaction between Bull and Man)**

The largest number of pictures show the bull and the man interacting with each other. The first four action photographs (288–93) are carefully ordered to emphasize the inescapable fact that the *toro de lidia* represents danger. In the first picture of this series, the bull, whose raised *morrillo* is powerful enough to lift the horse, is attacking Manuel de la Haba (Zurito), the great Cordoban picador. Zurito's expertise is evident both in the way he rides his mount and pics the bull:[21] the exemplary bull has charged an equally masterful picador. The next image shows the picador about to go down with his mount, both of them literally lifted off the ground by a bull that has thrown his full force at the horse and is not deterred from his purpose by the picador's lance. This picador, José Granados (Veneno)[22] uses his body weight to help push down on the pic, knowing the encounter with the bull will be brief and that he will soon find himself on the sand. Hemingway correctly points out that the bullfighters watching the action are ready to run to the rescue:[23] their tense figures emphasize the theme of this chapter, the power of the bull.

The next photograph also shows danger, but this time it comes from an unexpected source: the saddle girth has broken and the picador is suddenly plummeted on top of the bull's horns. He is still holding on to the reins, which indicates his horsemanship. The danger offered by the bull is complicated by mechanical failure, as it were. In the bullring, as elsewhere, accidents do occur. As in the previous image, the matadors are already moving in to take the bull away from their imperiled companion. And the last picture in this sequence is even more brutal. Danger is everywhere: the picador is down and, to make matters worse, the three matadors running to the rescue have to overcome the additional barrier of a dead horse in their path. This carefully ordered sequence, focused on the bull's power, builds up to and ends with an emotional climax. The admiration we felt for the *toro de lidia* when we first saw him (at the beginning of the photo-essay) has been modified by our knowledge of the danger he presents to horse and man.

At this point, following the chronology of the corrida, Hemingway turns our attention to the matador, the bullfighter on foot. The bull's power, which, as we have seen, can kill the horse, dismount the picador, cause general chaos, and threaten several lives, now comes under control. Here also Hemingway begins with an educational exposition. We see the fundamental pass with the cape, the verónica. Juan Belmonte faces the bull (*de frente*) and uses his marvelous arms and wrists to teach the bull to follow the cape, which is the purpose of the verónica. He will complete the pass by bringing the bull past his body and positioning it to receive the subsequent charge (294 top). Next, Hemingway presents one of the greatest *veroniqueadores*, Francisco Vega de los Reyes (Gitanillo de Triana, 296 bottom). While Belmonte took the bull on his left, Gitanillo passes the bull on his right side, and in the next photograph, Enrique Torres makes the bull pass to his left side (296 top). As the captions point out, we have seen a logical sequence (left, right, left) performed by three masters upon three different bulls. To finish the series on opening cape work, Belmonte is seen cape-ing the bull on his right side in a closing maneuver called the *media verónica,* a pass which forces the bull to turn sharply and fixes it in position for its encounter with the picadors.

If the corrida were being presented chronologically, we would next be introduced to banderillas, and then to the muleta and the sword. Instead, having shown us Belmonte in action, Hemingway skips all this, as if to focus our attention on this particular artist, whose importance to the development of the bullfight we have read about in the text. That is, the interaction is interrupted to present Belmonte with muleta and sword in hand. He is sharply in focus, while his fellow fighters are blurrily in the background and the dead bull is absent from the picture. Belmonte is visibly strained, the exhaustion in his face and figure bespeaking the danger he has survived. This human interest photograph draws our attention to the individual and balances the first photographs, which showed only bulls: man and bull are the main actors of the bullfight, and the power of the one and the exhaustion and isolation of the other define the strenuousness of their encounter.

The next two photographs take us back again, to the matador and his capework, as if to emphasize that chronology has been discarded. Joaquín Rodríguez (Cagancho) performs his *rebolera:* the bull is shown virtually stopped in its tracks, thus telling the reader the man is in control. In another eye-catching variation, the *gaonera,* the man holds the cape behind his back.[24] Having seen three superb verónicas, a *media verónica,* and these two artistic variations with the cape, we might expect to see another elegant moment in the bullfight's first *tercio,* or a move to the second *tercio.* Again, Hemingway subverts our expectations, this time to return our attention to the bull.

Hemingway offers two views of bulls: one of two bulls fighting each other, and one of five bulls waiting to be fought by men (302–5, discussed above). These two photographs flash back to the first chapter to remind us that, interesting as the cape is, we should, as the proverb instructs, keep our eyes constantly on the bull (*no quitarle el ojo al toro*).[25]

Hemingway's next group of action photographs, which return the focus to the bullfighter, flash forward to the last act of the bullfight. Whereas earlier sections were progressive (from less to more danger in the bull chapter; from basic to fancy in the cape section), here the internal principle will be contrast.

The action of the final act, the *tercio de muerte,* consists of the muleta work and the sword thrust. Hemingway shows one matador, Vicente Barrera, as he executes the same muleta pass in two different ways: he transmits emotion with his praiseworthy left-handed *pase de pecho* in Pamplona (307 top photograph) but looks awkward and unprofessional doing the same thing at the bullring at the Carretera de Aragón, Madrid (bottom photograph). These two versions of one pass are followed by two versions of another pass: Cagancho's magnificent *ayudado por alto* (309 top) and Nicanor Villalta's unaesthetic interpretation of the same pass (309 bottom). But the gracelessness of Villalta's work in this one instance contrasts sharply with the three photographs Hemingway presents next: Villalta's deadly accurate sword thrust (311) and his typically graceful right-handed *naturales* (313, top and bottom). These seven photographs give us a good look at three muleta passes, performed by three important bullfighters of the day; they contrast admirable and disreputable performances; and they end with a paean to Villalta. There is no doubt that the photographs were carefully chosen and purposefully organized.

Having shown us intimate interaction between man and bull, Hemingway again interrupts the action sequence, this time to focus on the man, by showing us a *brindis*. The dedication of the bull's death, of course, precedes the muleta work but, as we have already noticed, Hemingway is deliberately disregarding chronological order in order to focus on a particular detail, a particular bullfighter. Our first view of Manuel García (Maera), one of Hemingway's heroes, shows him alone, erect, proud, every inch a torero. The presence of a bull, with the inevitable suggestion of injury and death, would detract from this introductory photograph.

The next photograph returns us to the action, but not at the third act, where we left off. Instead, Hemingway flashes back to the second act, to show us Maera placing the banderillas, his specialty (317). The next photograph shows him taking suicidal risks as he cites a different bull for banderillas (319). The fourth and final photograph of Maera shows his personal interpretation of a *pase de pecho* (321), holding the muleta and sword in his right hand and his body in a way quite different from Barrera's more standard left-handed version of the same pass (307) — the principle of contrast again coming into play.

Contrast continues to dominate the organization of the action photographs, as does the focus on the individual and the disregard for chronological order. With Ignacio Sánchez Mejías (323, 325), Hemingway takes us back to the banderillas. But where we saw four photographs each of Villalta and Maera, Hemingway allots only two photographs to Sánchez Mejías, and they are not unambiguously flattering, as the caption suggests. Sánchez Mejías nails the sticks in technically praiseworthy fashion, but with the help of other bullfighters (Maera was shown by himself). There is, of course, nothing wrong with receiving such assistance, but the contrast exalts Maera and reiterates Hemingway's criticism that Sánchez Mejías exposed himself and those who worked for him to excessive danger (94, 322, and 324). Sánchez Mejías's self-aggrandizing exhibitionism seems to have displeased Hemingway; perhaps he needed to distance himself from a fellow artist whose creativity and experimentation resembled his own.[26] For whatever reason, his attitudes to Maera and Sánchez Mejías are quite different. But the main purpose of the photographs is not to express his subjective reactions: the focus continues to be on the interaction between man and the bull.

Banderillas are followed by the *brindis* and the muleta work, but Hemingway skips the former to show us the Mexican Luis Freg standing absolutely still as a large, powerful fighting bull leaps into the air, following the lure (327). In this photograph, the man masters danger.[27] The three toreros in the background are absorbed in Freg's performance; they are witnessing, not helping him. Freg's intensity turns everyone around him into audience. The next photograph shows the outcome: in the infirmary, Freg's face and posture reveal what the bull has done to him: he even has to be held up by the members of the surgical team for the obligatory photograph. The captions points to old as well as new wounds. Hemingway's didactic aim demands the inclusion of this painful photograph. Having exposed us to the bull, a variety of bullfighters, the basic *suertes* (maneuvers) poorly and expertly executed by a variety of bullfighters, Hemingway turns our attention away from the action and towards the man, who has come close to death.

The next photograph shows a new albeit anachronistic beginning: José Gómez Ortega (Joselito), the seventeen-year-old boy wonder, is at the Madrid bullring, ready to confirm his *alternativa* (promotion to the rank of matador de toros). To our left stands his oldest brother, Rafael (El Gallo), his sponsor, and at our far right, another brother, Fernando (whom Hemingway misidentifies as Paco Madrid). By including ten photographs of Joselito in this chapter, more than of any other bullfighter, Hemingway tells us the importance of this matador. Seven consecutive photographs show us a veritable tauromachy with sword and muleta. But, again, no sooner are we focused on the greatness of Joselito, when Hemingway interrupts the sequence with an image seemingly out of place: a photograph of Juan Belmonte.

Belmonte belongs in this chapter because he fought with Joselito, challenged him as no one else could, and finally stole the throne out from under the king. Joselito grew up in a taurine family, was physically gifted and a genius of bullfighting, but even he was forced to adopt the innovations of the minimally mentored, physically disadvantaged Belmonte. If the photographs were arranged chronologically, Belmonte would follow Joselito (Joselito's *alternativa* was 1912, Belmonte's 1913). If the point was to honor Belmonte, all the photos of him would appear together (as those of Maera and Joselito do). But Hemingway scatters the six photographs of Belmonte throughout the photo-essay to indicate both the length of his career and pervasive influence of this matador.

After the photograph of Belmonte's natural, Hemingway returns to Joselito, showing him performing the same pass (both on 347), and then shows us Joselito dead at Talavera de la Reina (349). Like the image of the wounded Luis Freg, this photograph insists on reminding us that danger is ever-present in the bullring. The death of Joselito marked the end not only of his career but of the *edad de oro* (golden age of bullfighting).

After this terrifying close-up of death, Hemingway returns us to the action by emphasizing the survival of the bullfighter: Belmonte defies a bull to do to him what another bull had done to Joselito (351). But he turns us away from the action again, to focus on Belmonte alone, as he dedicates the death of another bull (353). This *brindis* flashes back to the earlier one, of Maera (315), and connects to the next one, offered by Chicuelo (355), a star of the *edad de plata* (the silver age) which followed the reign of Joselito and Belmonte. Belmonte provides the transition from one era to the next, just as he here connects between the chapter on Joselito and subsequent generation, with particular emphasis on Chicuelo and, later in the chapter, Cagancho. The link is tight (Belmonte and Chicuelo strike the same pose) (353, 355), and the captions emphasize both the transition and the connection: "Last view of Juan Belmonte" (352) and "First view of Chicuelo" (354).[28]

The next three photographs of Chicuelo progress quickly from admiration to scorn. The first shows his artistic *pase natural*, the same pass we just saw Belmonte and Joselito performing (347). Here he follows Belmonte's *pase natural* (347), based on *temple* (slow movement) and wrist action, which ended with the bull positioned close by, ready to return. But whereas Belmonte would frequently follow such a *pase natural* with a *pase de pecho*, which would take advantage of the bull's readiness to return but did not require the rapid footwork of which he was incapable, Chicuelo took Belmonte's example one step further, obliging the bull to return into a series of *naturales*. These linked *naturales* marked an important innovation: they are the cornerstone of the modern *faena*. Chicuelo is on tiptoe, delicately grasping the lure by the tips of four fingers, his thumb elevated just above the muleta, the bull guided by the slow, measured movement of the cloth. In other words, the image praises Chicuelo's artistic delivery and shows him as Belmonte's stylistic heir.

But the next image shows a completely different Chicuelo. He is citing for the kill, at which he did not excel. Usually, a matador is alone when he prepares to kill his bull, but here Chicuelo's assistant stands close by, ready to help. And the last photograph is even worse: it shows Chicuelo in a disastrous performance, stabbing at the bull. Chicuelo seems overwhelmed by fear; his execution is deplorable, uncontrolled, graceless. The spectators, on their feet, are shouting their disapproval, thus expressing Hemingway's sentiments. It is the complete antithesis of the Chicuelo we saw only two photographs ago. Hemingway teaches us how the ever-present danger can produce art when it is controlled, chaos when it is not.

The subsequent pages catalogue the consequences Hemingway felt Chicuelo should not have avoided: the infirmary, the toss, the goring, death

(362–73). The pictures move us quickly from the infirmary to the arena and back to the infirmary. The relentless attack on Chicuelo ends outside the arena, with a close-up of a bull Chicuelo was unable to kill.[29] This is the bullfighter's nightmare, living evidence of his failure, and Hemingway castigates Chicuelo. In general, where Chicuelo is concerned, Hemingway is unforgiving. He insists that Chicuelo's fear of danger made him a failure (nine photographs) in spite of his artistry and stylistic innovation (one photograph). Hemingway forcefully finishes the series on Chicuelo by insisting on three points: the objective facts that the bullfight is always dangerous and the bull must always be killed, and the subjective and rather inaccurate insistence that Chicuelo is finished.[30]

Hemingway's next photograph offers another new, hopeful beginning: it presents a new crop of bullfighters ("These took his [Chicuelo's] place") as they perform the ceremonial entrance into the ring on 6 September 1930 (Aranjuez). The bullfighters are, from left to right, Manuel Mejías (Manolo Bienvenida), Domingo Ortega (the most junior), and Marcial Lalanda (the most senior). As the caption explains, Ortega was still a newcomer. Hemingway's suspicious disapproval of Ortega and Manolo Bienvenida led him into a misjudgment of these two undisputed masters[31] of *la edad de plata*. Again like the Chicuelo section, this one begins with praise (of Lalanda) and spirals into scorn (of Cagancho).

Hemingway shows Lalanda in a consistently positive light. In the text he described him as the "most scientific and able of present fighters" (382), and in the next three photographs he shows him in control of the bull (378–83). There is no disparaging Lalanda, who maintained a consistent standard of dependable performances. Although lacking in aesthetic qualities, he possessed a rounded knowledge and extensive repertoire, and this is exactly what Hemingway admires in him: he is not a specialist.

Hemingway contrasts the photographs of Lalanda with an all-out attack on Cagancho. Although Cagancho often killed well, Hemingway chose a photo which shows him killing badly (385), and then, to intensify his disdain, compares him unfavorably not only to provincial amateurs (four photographs, to drive the point home) but even to a foreigner, the American Sidney Franklin. Franklin is first shown killing with impeccable style, and then performing admirably with the cape, Cagancho's own forte (389).

Criticism of Cagancho and Chicuelo is the implied subtext of the prolonged exposition of the art of killing that follows. Hemingway shows Varelito, the master killer, performing a truly grand sword thrust (391 top). He connects Manolo Bienvenida to Chicuelo — he is one of "Those [who] took his place" (376) — and captions him as killing badly. (Hemingway seems not to have noticed that the bull has stopped short, probing with its horns and front legs; he offers such danger that Bienvenida's hasty sword thrust is justified.) The next images offer three interesting sword thrusts: the upper photo shows the effect of the faultlessly placed sword;[32] the middle image shows Luis Freg killing his adversary beautifully; and the bottom shows Manuel García (El Espartero) inserting the sword skillfully and effectively (Hemingway notes this matador's dexterity in the Glossary, s. v. *Cruz,* but fails to mention that Espartero was killed making the sword thrust Hemingway praises). These images unify the photo essay by referring back to bullfighters shown in earlier photographs (Freg and Varelito appeared on 327, 329, and 373). They also teach us to distinguish between good and bad killing, and they cast aspersions on bullfighters Hemingway disliked: Cagancho, Bienvenida, and Chicuelo.

After crowding seven photographs onto three pages, Hemingway closes this section with three emotional, full-page images. The first one emphasizes danger: even the master Varelito could be caught by a bull that did not follow the cloth (395). The second emphasizes art: it pays homage to Félix Rodríguez, one of "the finest artists [. . .] the ring has known" (296). In this memorable photograph by Aurelio Rodero, Rodríguez seems Christ-like.[33] The style is unorthodox but praiseworthy: the image is one of the most striking in *Death in the Afternoon.* And the third image shows brutality: the unscrupulous picador, probably acting at the order of his equally dishonorable matador, is destroying a bull. Although the moment is ugly, the photograph is artistic, contrasting light and shadow, foreground and background. Earlier, the action photographs were interrupted by glimpses of the man's pain or death (293, 329, 349): this one emphasizes the destruction of the bull.

The short last section, or coda, moves from tragedy to triumph. It is dedicated to the legendary Gypsy artist, Rafael Gómez Ortega (El Gallo). Two earlier pictures showed his professionalism (293) and provenance (331). The next four images show us, directly and indirectly, the facets of this extravagant, ingenuous, irrepressible character (401–8).

Gallo's *brindis,* the fourth such image, focuses on the man and his audience. Gallo is confident; his wit and charm can be deduced from the amused smile of his banderillero, Enrique Ortega (Almendro).[34] The next photographs show situations (bulls goring bullfighters) which, the caption tells us, "El Gallo avoided so assiduously" (402) — a phrase which is far more forgiving and sympathetic than the scathing "Afraid of This," which Hemingway attached to Chicuelo.

In the essay's penultimate image, Hemingway returns to the bull, dead in a field, its horn bloodied by an encounter. It leads to the next photograph, where another bull lies dead on the ground, in precisely the same position, shiny eyes wide open. But this last photograph focuses on the man, triumphantly alive, even smiling as Gallo is in the image. This closure is pleasant, appealing, and reassuring to the viewer, the appropriate ending for Hemingway's taurine photo-essay.

The sections of this photographic essay do not follow traditional organization. Although we are taught to look at cape work, banderillas, muleta work, and the sword thrust, the focus is not on the discrete *tercios* of the corrida. Although we see almost forty years of bullfighting, from the 1894 photo of El Espartero (393) to several photos taken in 1930, there is no consistent chronological order. What we have instead is Hemingway's vision and commentary on the bullfight. He wants us to look at details, to identify "what really happened in action; what the actual things were which produced the emotion" (2). These are, as the photographic essay shows us repeatedly — even interrupting itself twenty times to do so — the power and danger of the bull, and the actions and personalities of the men. Once we see that this is the thrust of the essay, and once we identify his techniques (contrast, progression, repetition, variation, foreshadowing and flashback, instructive exposition, and emotional endings), we understand that the material falls into three uneven sections: an introduction that focuses on the bull, a series of overlapping and frequently interrupted sections, and a coda that focuses on the man. The introductions themselves fall into two chapters, each of which tells its own story. It is a complex organization indeed, aimed at making us see and making us feel.

One last point: The element of humor, so visible in the other sections of *Death in the Afternoon,* is noticeably absent from the photo-essay. The bullfight is, of course, a serious matter. That is not to say that there are no light moments in the afternoon's events. The *brindis,* for example, may contain a pleasantry or an expression of the matador's friendship towards the person who receives the dedication. Sometimes, in the *tercio de banderillas,* an artist's grace and even joy can result in a short, swift dance which lightens the atmosphere. Or a bullfighter may, in the exuberance of a performance that is going well, treat himself to an *adorno,* an inspired or unexpected variant performed with the cape or muleta. The bandleader may contribute to the good feeling with an appropriate musical offering. But the bullfight is not funny: not to the bullfighters, and not to those members of the audience who understand what is at stake and at what risk life is maintained and art is created. When one looks intensely at such a serious matter, there is no room for jokes, or for showing off one's own wit and cleverness: attention is focused on the Other, on the bull and the bullfighter, and not on one's self or on one's audience. In teaching us, in the most effective and efficient medium at hand, how to look at the bullfight — its component parts, and the significance of the interaction of these parts — Hemingway did not make jokes. The photo-essay is perhaps the most intense, focused, and serious section of *Death in the Afternoon.*

## Notes

[1] Reproduced in Broer, 23.

[2] JFK, Item 30. Economic considerations scuttled this plan, and only two colored items actually appeared in the book: the dust jacket painting by Roberto Domingo and the frontispiece by Juan Gris. Hemingway's 1930 article, "Bull Fighting, Sport and Industry," did include several color reproductions of works by Goya and Ignacio Zuloaga.

[3] Durán Blázquez and Sánchez Vigil, I: 240.

[4] Padilla quotes Rodero's statement that he used a Nette [sic] camera with a state-of-the-art Zeiss 120 mm focal-length lens (289). Durán Blázquez and Sánchez Vigil correctly identify this type of camera, which Baldomero used as well, as a Nettel (I: 246).

[5] As Reynolds points out, in May 1930, early in the writing of *Death in the Afternoon*, Hemingway requested subscriptions to four illustrated journals (*El Clarín, Toreros y toros, El eco taurino,* and *La fiesta brava*) as well as bound back issues (going as far back as 1917) of three or four others, all of which he mentions in the Glossary, s. v. *Revistas*, with a remark about the "excellent photographs" in *La fiesta brava* and *El Clarín* (Reynolds, 323 n. 13).

[6] On page 408, Hemigway notes that some of the photographs of the photo-essay are by Vandel and others are by Rodero. The page numbers that he provides indicate that he is crediting Vandel with twenty-six photographs and Rodero with another fifty-two, for a total of seventy-eight photographs. Hemingway does not name a photographer for the remaining three photographs, which show Juan Belmonte (on page 299) and Sidney Franklin (two photos on page 389).

[7] For a detailed discussion of the publication history of *Death in the Afternoon*, including the haggling over the pictures, see the article by Robert Trogdon, pages 21–41 in this volume.

[8] Hemingway also sent Perkins a lay-out format page for some of these illustrations. The photos were published according to Hemingway's design.

[9] In the Scribner first edition of *Death in the Afternoon,* captions appear on the left-hand pages, which are numbered, and the photographs themselves appear on the unnumbered right-hand pages. Throughout, the page numbers I give for the photographs refer to these unnumbered pages. When I refer to a series of photographs, I give inclusive page numbers, even though some of the included pages offer captions, not photographs.

[10] The photographs of Joselito and Gallo (339, 341, 342, 407) were taken in Seville's Plaza Monumental, which was torn down before Hemingway ever visited Spain. Other photographs show Seville's Maestranza (351, 353, 389 top, 391 top).

[11] Looking at the captions, Weber came to the same conclusion: "The captions of the photographs are alive with personal reaction" (58).

[12] Those few critics who do address the illustrations generally pay more attention to the captions than to the illustrations themselves. Weber devotes one sentence to the

captions (58); Mandel indexed and annotated the material from the captions ("Index" and *Annotations,* passim); Fernández Salcedo simply remarks that he is proud that Hemingway included photographs of Diano and his grandsons (front matter); and Bredendick, who places the illustrations within the traditions of the bullfight manual, finds that, with their captions, they offer a historical survey of bullfighting in the early twentieth century, thus "exceed[ing] the traditional functions of illustrations" (page 222 in this volume). Because my own interest lies in discovering the logic of the photographs, I generally privilege the photographs over the captions.

[13] Hemingway's photographic essay begins like a traditional spectator guide, with a look at the bull, his interactions with the picador, and his first experience of the cape. But then, instead of moving on to the pic-ing, as a traditional spectator guide would, Hemingway presents a picture of Belmonte (299; the twelfth of the eighty-one pictures), thus clearly signaling that this is *not* a traditionally organized pictorial tour of the bullfight.

[14] Item 48, JFK. In another unpublished manuscript, he remarks that "If only 64 [pages of] illustrations — many [photographs] must go — cannot be comprehensive," then the illustrations must be presented as powerfully as possible. He insists that there "must be flashes," and comments that the paucity of pictures allowed him is a "god damned shame" (Item 30, JFK).

[15] These illustrations receive another reading in Beatriz Penas Ibáñez's essay (see pages 148–49 in this volume).

[16] They are clearly *toros de lidia* and not oxen (because they are not castrated) or seed bulls (because seed bulls are kept in a separate corral, and not in a herd with the *toros de lidia*).

[17] A similar photograph of Diano may be seen in Fernández Salcedo's biography of this bull (bottom photo facing 337), and the photograph of the five bulls also appears in that book (Fernández Salcedo, top photo facing 288). In discussing these five, Fernández Salcedo reports that they performed in San Sebastián in 1919, and that they were sired by a son of Diano. They are, therefore, Diano's grandsons, and not his sons, as Hemingway claims in the caption.

[18] As Mandel points out, Chicuelo fought and killed Vicente Martínez bulls on 10 June 1923. The bull he didn't kill was fought on 23 May 1923; it was a Matías Sánchez (formerly Trespalacios), and not a Vicente Martínez bull (Mandel, "Birth of Hemingway's *Afición*," 132, 143).

[19] Hemingway does not identify the patient as Rosario Olmos, but in fact it is Olmos who is being operated on in the infirmary of the Madrid plaza. He was badly gored in the right thigh, on 5 July 1925; Hemingway shows the goring itself, without identifying the victim, on page 403. Photographs of the goring and the infirmary appeared in *La Lidia,* with identifying captions. See also "Olmos Caballero (Rosario)," Cossío 3: 683.

[20] During the *brindis,* the bull is kept occupied at one end of the arena so that the matador can give his full attention to the president, the public, friend, or relative to whom he is dedicating its death. There is one other moment when the audience focuses on the bullfighter, and not on his interaction with the bull. That is the *alternativa,* when one bullfighter confers upon another the rank of *matador de toros*. This

ceremony occurs immediately before the *brindis,* but it does not, of course, occur in every corrida. Perhaps that is why, when Hemingway was required to cut down the number of photographs, he decided not to use the seven or so photographs of *alternativas* he had collected (JFK Collection).

[21] Indeed, one of the most often heard complaints about picadors is that they do not know how to ride or sit a horse and that they inflict excessive punishment, usually at the orders of unscrupulous matadors intent on minimizing the danger they face.

[22] Veneno was, as Hemingway writes in the caption, killed by a bull in the Madrid ring. Among the photographs Hemingway owned but did not include in *Death in the Afternoon,* was one of the bull which killed Veneno in 1921. Clearly, Hemingway never saw Veneno in action.

[23] Not all the men waiting to rescue Veneno are matadors. The photograph shows six men: two *monosabios* without capes, and four men with capes, of whom probably only the three in the foreground are matadors. The one closer to the fence is a banderillero. A close look also reveals a second mounted picador and a dead horse — a very complex picture.

[24] Hemingway identifies the bullfighter as Gaona, but *La Lidia,* which originally published the photo on 18 August 1919, correctly identifies him as Domingo González Mateos (Dominguín).

[25] These photographs, together with Hemingway's long discussion of the bull (chapters 11–13 and portions of 14) and several bull-related entries in the Glossary, invalidate McCormick's complaint that Hemingway is not *torista* enough — that is, that he pays insufficient attention to the bull (McCormick and Sevilla Mascareñas, 31, 237).

[26] Hemingway, who saw himself as an original, distanced himself (or attacked) any artist to whom he was or might be compared. Beegel argues that Hemingway attacked Chicuelo because he saw in him traits he feared existed in himself. His attack on Sánchez Mejías probably stems from the same cause. Hemingway and Sánchez Mejías had a great deal in common: both were the sons of doctors, both rejected parental expectations that they follow suit, both ran away from home as teenagers, both had unsuccessful marriages, both enjoyed literary success, and both were showy, aggressive performers who bridled at criticism.

[27] Freg was often called *Don Valor* (Mr. Bravery) because he, like Maera, scorned death and destruction.

[28] An additional connection is the fact that Chicuelo, like Joselito and Belmonte, was a Sevillian. Hemingway erred in identifying the bullfighter on p. 355 as Manuel Jiménez Moreno (Chicuelo); it is most likely a picture of his father, Manuel Jiménez Vera, also nicknamed Chicuelo (see Mandel, "Birth of Hemingway's *Afición,*" 129 n. 8). It is an understandable error. All the other photographs of Chicuelo do in fact show Manuel Jiménez Moreno.

[29] As Mandel points out, Chicuelo fought Vicente Martínez bulls on 10 June 1923. He killed them. The bull he didn't kill was fought on 23 May 1923; it was a Matías Sánchez (formerly Trespalacios), and not a Vicente Martínez (Mandel, "Birth of Hemingway's *Afición,*" 132, 143).

[30] As a matter of fact, Chicuelo was far from finished: he continued to fight, off and on, until 1951.

[31] Capellán remarks that "Two of [Hemingway's] greatest mistakes are his near silence on Antonio Márquez [. . .] and his estimate of Manuel Jiménez, 'Chicuelo II,' both considered by critics among the very best matadors of the decade" (146–47). The text's "near silence on Antonio Márquez" is reinforced by his absence from the photo-spread. Hemingway had collected photographs of Márquez — they are in the JFK — but did not use them.

[32] In the caption (392), the sword thrust is mistakenly attributed to Antonio de la Haba (Zurito). *La Lidia,* which originally published the photo on 12 May 1924, pp. 6–7, correctly identifies the bullfighter as José Roger (Valencia).

[33] Rodríguez has been praised by countless members of the fraternity of matadors, including Fermín Espinosa (Armillita Chico), Antonio Márquez, and the Bienvenida family, as one of the truly great artists in the ring. His reckless life-style — he refused to follow the prescribed treatment for his syphilis — cost him his career, family, fortune, and life.

[34] In the background, dressed in black, is Joselito, the ultimate torero. He is the only one of four bullfighters in the photograph who appears to be watching the bull, faithful to one of the canons of bullfighting: *no quitarle el ojo al toro* (never take your eye off the bull, be it yours or a companion's).

## Works Cited

Beegel, Susan F. "Ernest Hemingway's 'A Lack of Passion.'" In *Hemingway: Essays of Reassessment.* Ed. Frank Scafella. New York: Oxford UP, 1991. 62–78.

Broer, Lawrence R. *Hemingway's Spanish Tragedy.* University, Alabama: The U of Alabama P, 1973.

Bruccoli, Matthew J., ed., with the assistance of Robert W. Trogdon. *The Only Thing That Counts: The Ernest Hemingway / Maxwell Perkins Correspondence 1925–1947.* New York: Scribner's, 1996.

Capellán, Angel. *Hemingway and the Hispanic World.* Ann Arbor: UMI Research P, 1977, 1985.

Cossío, José María de. *Los toros: Tratado técnico e histórico.* 12 vols. to date. Vol. 3. Madrid: Espasa-Calpe, 1943.

Durán Blázquez, Manuel, and Juan Miguel Sánchez Vigil. *Historia de la fotografía taurina.* Vol. 1. Madrid: Espasa-Calpe, 1991.

Fernández Salcedo, Luis. *Diano (o el libro que quedó sin escribir).* Madrid: Librería Merced, 1959.

Hemingway, Ernest. "Bull Fighting, Sport and Industry." *Fortune* 1 (1930): 83–88, 139–46, 150.

———. *Death in the Afternoon.* New York: Scribner's, 1932.

———. "A Lack of Passion." *The Hemingway Review* 9.2 (1990): 57–93.

———. Manuscripts of *Death in the Afternoon.* Hemingway Collection, John F. Kennedy Library.

*La Lidia.* Madrid, 1914–1928.

Lewis, Robert W. "The Making of *Death in the Afternoon.*" In *Hemingway: The Writer in Context.* Ed. James Nagel. Madison: The U of Wisconsin P, 1984. 31–52.

Mandel, Miriam B. "The Birth of Hemingway's *Afición:* Madrid and 'The First Bullfight I Ever Saw.'" *Journal of Modern Literature* 23.1 (1999): 127–43.

———. *Hemingway's* Death in the Afternoon: *The Complete Annotations.* Lanham, MD: Scarecrow, 2002.

———. "Index to Ernest Hemingway's *Death in the Afternoon.*" *Resources for American Literary Study* 23.1 (1997): 86–132.

McCormick, John, and Mario Sevilla Mascareñas. *The Complete Aficionado.* Cleveland: The World Publishing Company, 1967.

Padilla, Guillermo Ernesto. *El maestro de Gaona.* Mexico City: Compañía Editorial Impresora y Distribuidora, S.A., 1987.

Reynolds, Michael. *Hemingway: The 1930s.* New York: W. W. Norton, 1997.

Sontag, Susan. *On Photography.* New York: Farrar, Straus and Giroux, 1977.

Weber, Ronald. *Hemingway's Art of Non-Fiction.* New York: St. Martin's Press, 1990.

# Deleted "Flashes": The Unpublished Photographs of *Death in the Afternoon*

*Anthony Brand*

IN HIS UNPUBLISHED INTRODUCTION to the photo-essay of *Death in the Afternoon*, Hemingway bemoans the fact that financial considerations made it impossible to publish all of the "four hundred photographs, drawings and paintings [that] were obtained or made to show the phases, technical and otherwise of the modern Spanish bull fight" ("Some four hundred photographs," Hemingway Collection, John F. Kennedy Library [Boston], Item 48). That large collection features about sixty matadors, most of whom I have been able to identify. When he was forced to lower his sights, Hemingway prepared a lightly annotated, five-page list or outline of the images he wanted: it specifies some one hundred and twenty items and names about forty-five different matadors. In a note at the top of this outline, Hemingway mourns that so "many must go — cannot be comprehensive — must be flashes — god damned shame" ("Necessary photographs," JFK, Item 30). And indeed, many went: when the book was finally published, it showed only eighty-one illustrations, foregrounding twenty-six matadors (some of whom also appear in the background of other photos). The winnowing was drastic — from "some four hundred" to one hundred and twenty to eighty-one photos, and from sixty to forty-five to twenty-six matadors. Clearly, Hemingway had many decisions to make.

Hemingway had a discerning eye, and most of the items he collected are really fine. A few are blurry, although Hemingway may have prized them for historical considerations. And it is interesting that the collection, large as it is (some three hundred and thirty items survive in the JFK), seems to be incomplete. Some of the images mentioned in Hemingway's list are missing. Hemingway indicates, for example, that he would like to include photos of "Armillitas I and II very Indian [Armillita]1 great banderillero — [Armillita] 2nd child wonder — cold, disillusioned" (Item 30). The John F. Kennedy Library holds several photographs of Fermín Espinosa, known as "Armillita chico" or "Armillita II," but none that I could identify as being of his older brother, Juan Espinosa (Armillita, that is, the older or first of the Armillita brothers). Hemingway also listed "Waldo Peirce — pile up in the encierro at Pamplona" (Item 30), but the JFK does not hold that painting or drawing.

A complete study of Hemingway's collection of taurine illustrations would require not only an indexing and cross-indexing of the items at the JFK, but also an attempt to locate and retrieve the materials included in Hemingway's list but absent from the collection.

In selecting a few of Hemingway's many unpublished photographs for this *Companion,* I consulted the Hemingway-Perkins correspondence related to the photographs, Hemingway's draft for an introduction to the illustrations (Item 48), his unpublished list (Item 30), and the text of *Death in the Afternoon.* Some of the "four hundred photographs" were closely related, showing the same detail (e.g., a cape pass, or the placing of the banderillas) as it was performed by different bullfighters in different bullrings, or by the same bullfighter on different occasions, or sometimes even showing a bullfighter at consecutive moments of the same performance. The first six of the thirteen photographs that follow are alternative possibilities to three of the photographs Hemingway finally did choose to publish. I include them because looking at what he discarded may help us understand why he chose as he did. And I present the other photographs because they are relevant either to the published text of *Death in the Afternoon* or to the list Hemingway prepared. That is, they seem to be photos Hemingway had at some stage planned to include.

Hemingway clearly understood that photographs are a valuable addition to *Death in the Afternoon,* which focuses, after all, on a highly visual art. The thirteen photographs that follow will give the *Companion*'s readers a flavor of the decisions Hemingway made and of the visual "flashes" he had hoped to provide.

Hemingway's sympathetic defense of the picador led to his collecting some thirty-five photos of this type of bullfighter in action. These two discarded photos show matadors moving in to rescue unseated picadors. In the first, Nicanor Villalta approaches a dangerous situation confidently, cape unfurled. The next photo shows an even more urgent moment: Chicuelo and Antonio Márquez, both just behind the bull, rush in to rescue the still-airborne picador. In both photographs, the picadors still hold the reins, which reveals their professionalism and horsemanship.

(Courtesy John F. Kennedy Library, Boston)

For the section "Chicuelo of the disasters," Hemingway published an unflattering photo that shows this matador *cuarteando* (encircling) a difficult bull without getting too close to it; the bull appears to have taken a *querencia* near the fence (361; Glossary, s. v. *Querencia* — "part of the ring [. . .] where [the bull] feels at home"). Here are two photographs Hemingway could have used but didn't: they present different moments of this same difficult situation. The first photo may have been discarded because it shows the audience's disapproval less clearly. In the second photo, Chicuelo, who has lost his *montera* (hat) by now, is coping: he has managed to draw the bull away from its *querencia* and to insert almost the entire sword in its withers. Hemingway may have discarded this photo because here Chicuelo is somewhat less of a disaster. (Courtesy John F. Kennedy Library, Boston)

The photo that Hemingway finally published shows Chicuelo in the least favorable light: more people are rushing in to help him, and the audience is clearly protesting his ineptness.

Hemingway had five photos of "Maera in his characteristic right-handed pass made in the manner of a pase de pecho" (*DIA*, 321). Here are two of the four he discarded: in the first, the bull is so small and squalid as to remove all seriousness from the performance. In the second, the bull is large and well-armed, lifting its head up into the muleta; the pass is well-executed and the photo is dramatic, but not as successful as the published one in communicating the balletic flow of bull and man. Because he admired Maera, Hemingway chose the most rhythmic and emotive photo for publication (321).

(Courtesy John F. Kennedy Library, Boston)

Hemingway collected ten photos of Cayetano Ordóñez (Niño de la Palma), but by 1932 he had become so disillusioned with him that he excluded him completely from the photo-essay. These two discarded photos document Ordóñez's beautiful form and control with both cape and muleta. In this photo, he is ending a series of passes with a beautifully timed artistic swirl, a *rebolera*. On the facing page, he performs a moving version of the *ayudado por alto:* here also he is in full control of the bull, making it pass his body and forcing it to leap into the air and thus tire itself.

(Courtesy John F. Kennedy Library, Boston)

Hemingway's notes indicate that he planned to use photos to show Saturio Torón's "bad technique" (JFK, Item 30), which is described in the published text (223). He collected three photos of Torón, but none was published. This one would have served Hemingway's purpose nicely: it shows Torón in Pamplona, failing to take advantage of a fine, large bull. The bull's hoof prints show it made a left turn as Torón approached it from the fence, which reveals that it has good vision, charges from a distance, and is properly fixed on the muleta. But Torón is actually stepping away from this ideal specimen, thus displaying his own self-doubt, lack of control, and poor technique. The photo also shows that his muleta is too large and awkwardly handled.

(Courtesy John F. Kennedy Library, Boston)

# The Unpublished Photographs of *Death in the Afternoon* ♦ 201

Hemingway's notes indicate he wanted to include photos of several Mexicans, among them Rodolfo Gaona, Luis Freg, and Juan Silveti. Hemingway's caption for one of his published photos (301) claims that it shows Gaona, but the identification is mistaken: the matador is actually Domingo González Mateos (Dominguín). This photo, the only identifiable one of Gaona in the Hemingway Collection, shows the Mexican master placing banderillas on a Veragua bull in Madrid.

(Courtesy John F. Kennedy Library, Boston)

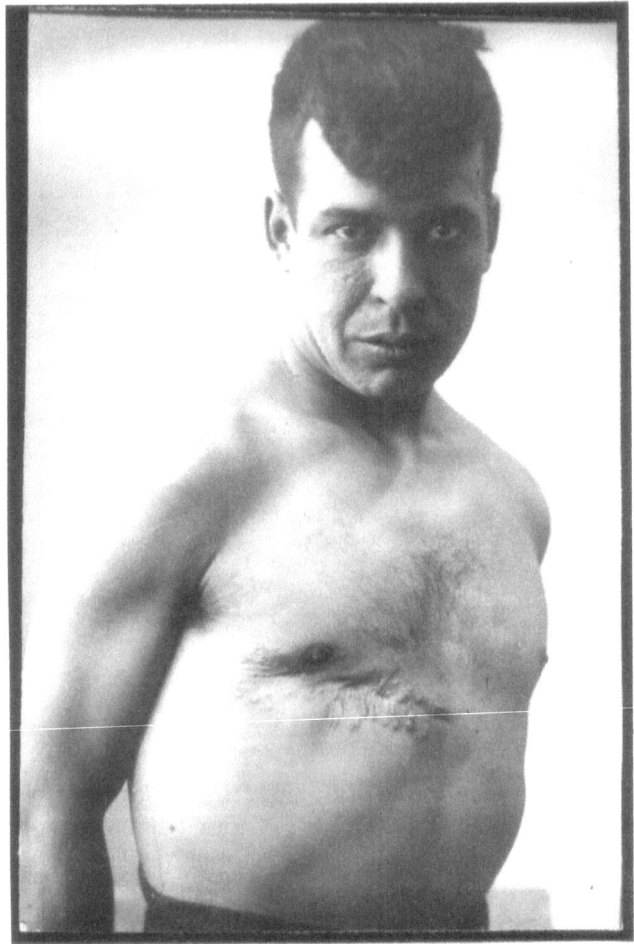

Hemingway's notes describe Freg and Silveti as exemplifying "Indian valor" (JFK, Item 30). But while Freg's bravery earned him a place in both the text and the photographs of *Death in the Afternoon,* Silveti is completely absent from both, probably because Hemingway saw him less often and because his life was not as intriguing as Freg's. Hemingway's description of Freg — "his chest and his abdomen are covered with scars of wounds that should have killed him" (*DIA,* 263; see also illustrations on 326, 328, 392) — applies to Silveti as well, as this photograph reveals.

(Courtesy John F. Kennedy Library, Boston)

Hemingway writes that Martín Agüero "was a secure and rapid killer. His estocadas always looked wonderful in photographs [. . .] crossing magnificently" (*DIA*, 258), just as we see here. Agüero's position is perfect: weight on the left leg, left arm guiding the bull past his body in a beautifully timed and executed pass, and the sword perfectly placed. The tear in Agüero's jacket tells us he had been tossed by one of his bulls.

(Courtesy John F. Kennedy Library, Boston)

Hemingway began and ended his published photo-essay with pictures of bulls, but here is one he decided not to include. It shows the bull's *nobleza*, or nobility, a prized characteristic which the text identifies as "the most extraordinary part of the whole business. The bull is a wild animal whose greatest pleasure is combat [. . .] yet the very best fighting bulls of all often recognize the [. . .] herder [. . .] and will even allow him to stroke and pat them. I have seen a bull which in the corrals allowed the herder to stroke its nose [. . .] and even mount on its back, go into the ring [. . .] and be, in the ring, vicious as a cobra and brave as a charging lioness" (113–14). Such noble bulls charge openly and cleanly, but not indiscriminately. They have the uncanny ability of differentiating between a bullfighter who is challenging them to battle and an unarmed man who poses no threat: a noble bull will not, for example, attack a bullfighter he has felled or unseated.

This photo shows Brujito, a fine specimen from the ranch of José García Aleas. Brujito was celebrated for his *nobleza*.

(Courtesy John F. Kennedy Library, Boston)

## "¿Qué tal, hombre, qué tal?": How Paratexts Narrow the Gap between Reader and Text in *Death in the Afternoon*

*Nancy Bredendick*

GERARD GENETTE DEVELOPED the concept of paratexts in his book, *Seuils* (1987; translated as *Paratexts: Thresholds of Interpretation*, 1997). As Genette defines the term, *paratexts* are any and all texts, inside and outside the covers of the book, that present, explain, situate, contextualize, illustrate, comment on, and classify the work for the reader. Genette distinguishes between two types of paratexts. *Epitexts* include any texts that are relevant to but not materially attached to the book: interviews, letters, diaries, and manuscripts containing authorial comment on the text. *Peritexts*, on the other hand, are those texts that are physically connected to the book (5). Genette maintains this distinction when discussing the relation between epitexts and peritexts — for example, when discussing what an author might say in his dedication (peritext) and in an interview (epitext). But in discussing the *function* of these texts and their relationship to the main text, Genette (and this essay in his wake[1]) prefer the broader term, *paratext*. Because he defines paratexts as author-authorized matter ("something is not a paratext unless the author or one of his associates accepts responsibility for it" [9]), discussions of paratexts generally adopt the date of a text's original edition as their point of reference (5).[2]

For Genette, all paratexts are subordinate to the main text. They occupy a threshold area filled with clues — some verbal, some iconic, some material, and some factual — whose function is to present the book to its readers. In short, they are devices and conventions that contain messages about how the book is to be received. Within this zone, both what is there and what is not there carry meaning. Literally or figuratively, verbally or visually, straightforwardly or obliquely, the presence or absence of matter on the cover and on the front and back pages has been calculated, as Genette explains, to influence the reader and to ensure that the text is properly read (2).

What *is* it, this text we are reading? And how — in what context, in what spirit — are we to read it? *Death in the Afternoon* has been variously identified and read as a personal memoir, an anatomy, a bullfight manual, a travel book, a dissertation on life and letters, and so on. Unsure of the book's genre, the reader is unsure about what literary conventions apply. In terms of structure, the book is also difficult for the reader to comprehend: what precisely constitutes this book that we are reading? Of *Death in the Afternoon*'s 518 numbered pages (in the Scribner's hardcover first edition), only 278, divided into twenty chapters of text, follow a conventional pattern. The remaining 239 pages — almost half of the book — are devoted to a series of individually titled sections placed after the main text. Sometimes called appendixes (although not designated as such in the headers or in the table of contents), one or another of these sections has on occasion been omitted in reprint editions and translations.³ Are these texts paratextual, in the way that the book jacket, the dedication, the table of contents, and the title page are paratextual? Or are they instead a kind of optional extension of points raised in the main body of the work, and therefore textual? In other words, just what is the relationship of these texts to each other and to the work as a whole?

Before proceeding to an analysis of how the paratexts relate to the text and how they mediate between book and reader, these generic and structural questions need to be addressed. In recognition of its complexity, I define *Death in the Afternoon* in terms that range from narrow to broad. Narrowly defined, *Death in the Afternoon* is a complete manual of bullfighting for the spectator. (The paratexts also offer various markers that set the book, for all its idiosyncrasies, within the conventions of taurine writing in Spanish.) More broadly defined, it is a work of criticism and art appreciation, in which the art of bullfighting is universalized to the point where its taurine dicta are congruent with dicta on the art of writing. And broadest of all, it is in itself a work of art, by a major artist, on a taurine theme — as is, for example, Juan Gris's painting *The Bullfighter,* the work of analytical cubism that Hemingway chose for his frontispiece. On the question of how to read the "appendixes" at the back of *Death in the Afternoon,* I find that only one, the "Bibliographical Note," is, strictly speaking, a paratext. Whereas the glossary, the illustrations and the other appendixes elaborate on discrete items and issues brought up in the main body of the text, only the "Bibliographical Note" (which in spite of its title is a kind of author's note or brief postface) characterizes and comments on the work as a whole and is therefore, like the title, the book jacket, and the table of contents, *outside the text* in a way that the other sections, although formally separate from each other and from the main body of the text, are not. I will return to this point in my discussion of the table of contents, but for now suffice it to say that hereafter when I refer to any of the sections at the back of *Death in the Afternoon,* the only one which I will define as a paratext is the "Bibliographical Note." Having clarified these points, I want to look at the paratexts of *Death in the Afternoon* — the title, the dust jacket, the frontispiece, the dedication, the table of contents, and the postface, or "Bibliographical Note" — to determine how the choices and decisions that Hemingway (and Scribner's) made about them affect our view of *Death in the Afternoon*, guide our expectations and control our experience of the text.

Authors generally provide paratexts in order to narrow the gap between reader and text. In the case of *Death in the Afternoon*, the gap is a large one, because, at the outset, there is so little context, so little common ground, shared by text and reader. Because *Death in the Afternoon* is at once a literary and a practical work — forms that are virtually mutually exclusive for the modern reader — its reader requires authorial mediation in order to read the text "properly." Because the book celebrates the art of bullfighting — an unusual and rather shocking phenomenon for its English-speaking audience — it is likely to alienate its reader. And because it is a manual, complete with explanatory glossary and photographs to illustrate difficult points, it undoubtedly disconcerts readers who expect a Hemingway volume to present fiction of some sort, a novel or a collection of short stories.

Because the gap between the reader and this particular text is such a large one, the paratexts assume greater significance. It comes as a surprise, then, to find that the signals emanating from the paratexts in *Death in the Afternoon* are decidedly mixed. Instead of presenting his intentions directly and unambiguously to his prospective reader, Hemingway adopts a complex paratextual style that might even be termed confusing or oblique in the sense that his paratexts point first in one direction and then another, generating in the reader conflicting feelings and ideas. But these mixed signals, which tend to blur the divisions between the literary and the factual, the aesthetic and the practical, the classic and the popular, the universal and the local, and even the inside and the outside of the text, are not mistakes or idle gestures. Instead they are functioning parts of the paratext that give us clues as to how Hemingway is going to mount his defense of bullfighting and frame his explanation of the art.

The obliqueness of Hemingway's paratextual style can be seen in his definitions and descriptions of the book. Peritextually, in his postface (the "Bibliographical Note"), Hemingway describes *Death in the Afternoon* as "an introduction to the modern Spanish bullfight" (517), and there is no doubt that instruction forms part of his definition of his work. On the front flap of the dust jacket, the definition is much broader: the book is described as containing "all that is important and interesting about bullfighting—the bravery and cowardice, the bull, the costume and theatre and personality and craftsmanship and history." And yet another aspect of the book — the otherness of its author — was emphasized epitextually in an unpublished section of the manuscript where Hemingway defines the book as "a manual and a guide to Modern Bullfighting written by a foreigner."[4]

Although incongruent in details, these paratextual definitions lead us to read *Death in the Afternoon* as a bullfight manual. And so it seems to have been read in Spain. In 1933, Rafael Hernández, bullfight critic at the Madrid daily, *La Libertad,* called it "un tratado completo de tauromaquia" (a complete tauromachia) (7), and Tomás Orts-Ramos (Uno al Sesgo), bullfight critic at the weekly magazine, *La Fiesta Brava,* and author of the highly recommended spectator guide, *El arte de ver los toros,* finds *Death in the Afternoon* to be well written, technically and historically complete, and only minimally marred by inaccurate descriptions of technique and errors in appreciation, although no more so than books written by homegrown experts.[5]

Nonetheless, other paratexts point the reader away from this definition of the book as a bullfight manual. The work's lyric title, its "man-of-letters" celebration of Hemingway in the jacket copy, and the push in a fine arts direction given by the Juan Gris painting used as its frontispiece prepare us for a literary work (perhaps in the form of a personal essay) designed to take a permanent place in American letters. Without entirely misrepresenting the instructive nature of the text, these three paratexts — the title, much of the jacket copy, and the frontispiece — encourage the reader to perceive the book as literary art. This paratextual discrepancy, which presents the work both as a real bullfight manual (instruction) and as a serious work of literature (fine arts), signals to the reader that these two opposing elements work together; that is, they communicate to us that *Death in the Afternoon* is intended to be read as not just one, and not just the other, but somehow simultaneously as both. What other signals emanate out of the work's major paratexts, and how do they mediate between author and reader?

### The Title

The title is one of the paratexts most crucial to the presentation of a book. To put *Death in the Afternoon* in context, let us look at the titles of what were, in the first decades of the century, the most highly recommended taurine manuals and spectator guides: *Catecismo taurino* (A Taurine Catechism, 1913), *Las corridas de toros en la actualidad* (The Bullfight Today, 1914), and *El arte de ver los toros: Guía del espectador* (The Art of Watching the Bullfight: A Spectator's Guide, 1929).[6] In striking contrast, Hemingway's title is oblique: instead of openly announcing the book's subject matter and didactic intent, as these titles do so clearly, Hemingway's title evokes its subject matter figuratively, suggesting it by evoking its culminating moment, when death is administered to the bull. Indeed, the title is so poetic and so indirect that, were it to be seen alone, it would not necessarily suggest a taurine theme. It is the accompanying visual imagery, and not the words of the title, which alerts us to the nature of the subject matter.[7] Images accompany the title both on the title page (the solid black silhouette of a fighting bull) and on the dust jacket (a colorful, action-filled painting of a hard-charging bull). These images indicate, as the title does not, that the death in question is that of the fighting bull. They function, as Genette claims a subtitle would, to give "a more literal indication of the theme that the title evokes symbolically or cryptically" (85), and are a kind of subtitle in visual form. Without the images, however, the title suggests that the book is a literary work. Its rhythm and the contrasting images of darkness (death) and light (afternoon) moved Arnold Gingrich to call it the greatest four-word poem in the language (see Stephens, 15). And Hemingway was certainly aware that it would work well as the title of a literary work: it was "a title jotted down [in 1931] with notes for a story he never wrote" (Reynolds, *The 1930s,* 83). Not surprising, then, that *Death in the Afternoon* is often taken for a novel in situations where it is identified by title and author alone.

It would be inaccurate, however, to conclude that with the choice of this title Hemingway is simply trading on his fame as a novelist in an effort to attract a wider audience. The title does in fact accurately define the text, which features death — and not just the death of the bull — as a major theme. In *Death in the Afternoon,* Hemingway looks hard at violent death to teach himself how to write (2–3); he examines the feeling of rebellion against death that is part of the enjoyment of killing (232–33); and he explores the horrors and the fear of death on a battlefield and elsewhere in a narrative called "A Natural History of the Dead" (133–44). Fear of death also surfaces in the brief account of his small son's somewhat morbid reaction to historical and fictional reports of death (227–28). He dramatically renders Gitanillo de Triana's goring and lingering death (219–20), and he discusses attitudes toward death as defining terms of national character (264–66). In addition to all this about "human living and dying" (to borrow a phrase from the front flap of the dust jacket), Hemingway looks hard at the violent death and goring of horses in the ring, first to analyze its effect on people (*DIA,* 6–10) and then to call for reforms: better horses, better trained picadors, a better pic, and no protective mattress (185–89). The book's title, then, is accurate: *Death in the Afternoon* looks at the death of bulls, horses, and human beings, and he explores the philosophical, emotional, and artistic implications of death.

Although he looks hard at death and the sometimes fatal accidents that occur in the ring, Hemingway always contemplates them from the position of one who defends the bullfight. This contrasts with the perspective adopted by other authors writing on the bullfight in English. Richard Ford, author of *Gatherings from Spain* (1846) and the most influential writer in English on the bullfight before Hemingway, focuses on death and cruelty in the bull ring not to defend it, but to explain it away, by suggesting that what is gruesome and repulsive in one culture may not be considered so in another (339). J. Morewood Dowsett, author of *The Spanish Bullring* (1928), focuses on the death and goring of horses in order to attack the spectacle, and provides ghastly images of horror as part of his abolition campaign (44–46). Both Dowsett and Ford, whose works Hemingway owned and presumably read,[8] position themselves outside of bullfighting culture. But Hemingway, who situates himself within bullfighting culture, focuses on violence and cruelty in order to take a first step toward reform. He argues that violence and cruelty, while part of taurine reality, are not the point of the bullfight, and thus he does not use these factors to condemn or explain the institution as a whole. Instead, he focuses on ways to correct what he sees as abuses so that, in practice, the art can come closer to its essence, and the ugliest parts of the spectacle can be avoided or transformed (164–65, 184–89, 404, and Glossary, s. v. *Pica*).

Given the degree to which Hemingway deals with the theme of death in the text, there is every justification for foregrounding the word in the title. But why did he suppress the words *guide* and *manual*, which also define the book? Why choose a title that generates feelings of fear, awe, and natural inevitability, rather than one that would attract an audience interested in specialized knowledge and information? Probably for two reasons. One is that the title's appeal to feeling and sensation prefigures Hemingway's promise to explain the spectacle "emotionally" as well as practically ("Bibliographical Note," 517). The other is that, cast in such terms, the title widens our horizon of expectations to the point that our "literary competence" is engaged; a word like "manual" would have narrowed our reading to a merely technical, information-seeking level. Both absence and presence, the words that are not in the title and those which are, work similarly to allow us to see *Death in the Afternoon* as a work of art with a bullfight manual imbedded in it or, as it has more frequently been described, as a bullfight manual into which Hemingway has deliberately projected various levels of "literariness."[9]

Hemingway's title exemplifies his sophisticated and oblique use of paratexts: it is both thematically specific and poetically suggestive, it works with omission as well as inclusion, and, while literary and verbal, it is consistently accompanied and refined by nonverbal subtitles to indicate that the text is specifically focused on the bullfight. The title itself, *Death in the Afternoon*, presents the book in the broadest way possible as a work that both discusses art and performs it. At the same time, the title and the subtitles mediate between the text and the reader, signaling to us that the text is a defense of bullfighting. Indirectly but unerringly, the title disassociates the death of the bull from feelings of horror and morbidity. Foreshadowing the same effort in the text, *Death in the Afternoon* is a particularly effective title for the defense of an art that deals with death.

## The Dust Jacket

Whatever definition of *Death in the Afternoon* one prefers (a manual, a work about art, a work of art), Hemingway's basic purpose is to make us feel good about watching the bullfight. In the main body of the text, he does his best to make the bullfight matter to all his readers: he strives to overcome the automatic hostility of those who are opposed to it, to advise and instruct the uninitiated, and to engage the initiated in sophisticated dialogue. Most notably, he attempts to replace ignorance and rejection with knowledge, appreciation, and the promise of pleasure. And he connects bullfighting with the craft of writing in order to make the foreign, unfamiliar art comprehensible to his readers.

The process starts on the dust jacket. Showing an awareness that for most readers watching the bullfight is going to be an acquired taste, the producers of the jacket offer an invitation issued in the widest possible terms. Furthermore (and this becomes apparent once one has read the book), by its very nature the invitation is in harmony with an approach based on the conviction that, in order to teach an appreciation of the art to a reader who has never seen good bullfighting, something more than a straightforward, factual account of taurine craftsmanship and history is needed. Accordingly, the copy on the front flap of the dust jacket promises excitement, emotion, "episodes of gorgeous comedy and satire," and, in the course of the discussion and description of bullfighting and bullfighters, "collateral information [. . .] about life and letters and what it takes to be an artist — a real one."

The most arresting feature of the dust jacket is the painting by Roberto Domingo (1883–1956). Under the word "TOROS," a powerful looking bull is pursuing a banderillero who trails a swirling cape of yellow and magenta, as he leaps over the barrera into the confetti-colored crowd. So close is the man's escape that he seems to be helped over the fence by the bull's approaching horns. The man, however, is not the protagonist of the scene. The center of attention is the charging bull — a splendid animal, with a dappled gray body and a handsome black head outlined against the red barrera. There is power in the broad back and in the hump of muscle that surges up from behind his horns, there is speed in the splayed legs and sinuous line of spine from neck to tail, and danger in the solid curves of the sharp horns.

*Toros* (1923) is an oil painting, one of eighteen painted by Domingo between 1915 and 1942, to advertise bullfight festivals in Valencia (Agustí Guerrero, 190–98).[10] As reproduced in an art book (190), the poster version presents, under the painting, the columns of big black type that announce the dates of the festival (July 25–31), the names of the breeders who supplied the bulls (among them Conde de la Corte, Pablo Romero, Eduardo Miura), and the performers: Rafael Gómez Ortega (El Gallo), Manuel Jímenez Moreno (Chicuelo), Marcial Lalanda, Rosario Olmos, Manuel García López (Maera), José García Carranza (Algabeño), and Juan Silveti. It is typical of the large colored posters that are, as Hemingway explains in the text (37–38), the chief means of advertising the spectacle and that are ubiquitous in Spain's cities.

Like other kinds of advertising, the bullfight poster was originally focused on text but slowly evolved to a point where image dominates words (Cossío, 2: 691–95). In the version of Domingo's painting that appears on the dust jacket of *Death in the Afternoon,* the text is gone and the image is all. Free of the words that tie it to a specific event in a particular time and place, the image becomes a timeless appeal to the imagination. No documentary detail dilutes its lyric force. The scene celebrates the bull at the beginning of the bullfight, at the moment of his greatest strength and glory: he is using his energy to remove his enemies from the ring. The image is exciting and exhilarating. Like much of Domingo's large body of work, it idealizes the bull and the bullfight, providing "más que una visión realista de la fiesta, [. . .] la visión que el público quiere ver en ella: sus toros, de enormes cabezas cornamentadas, y sus elegantes toreros, pintados bien cerca del peligro, [. . .] siempre en movimiento en un ruedo resplandeciente por la luz del sol" (instead of a realistic image of the fiesta [Domingo's paintings present] the image the public wants: his bulls sporting huge horned heads and his elegant toreros, positioned as close as possible to danger [are] always in movement, in a ring blazing with sunshine; Martínez-Novillo, 138).

With its play of color, light, and movement, the jacket illustration highlights images of pleasure that will be picked up in the main body of the text: the emotional highs provided by drinking wine, looking at paintings in the Prado, skiing, sexual intercourse, and wing-shooting (10–12, 51–52, 63). These profoundly pleasurable activities are implicitly linked in this text to the experience of watching the bullfight. Hemingway gets to the emotion of the bullfight through the senses, and he fills his text with imagery, not just to moisten arid patches of technical writing, but to put directly up to our understanding the feeling of seeing a great *faena*. It is a kind of sensory education, in which our aesthetic sense of bullfighting is informed through poetic means.

The texts on the dust-jacket flaps and on the dust jacket perform the characteristic functions of these paratexts, as Genette defines them: they describe the text (by means of summary or in some other way), they comment on the book's theme and author's technique, and they praise the work (107–8). The jacket copy offers guidance as to how *Death in the Afternoon* is to be read in that it forges a link between the subject of the book, the author of the book, and the craft of writing. It also defines this author as someone whose views on writing we really want to hear. The back cover lists the author's five major works in reverse chronological order, from *A Farewell to Arms* (1929) to *In Our Time* (1925), each title followed by press quotations extolling Hemingway's contributions to American literature. More than just a list of the author's published works, it is a vehicle for putting Hemingway's growing fame as a writer at the service of this new book. The last paragraph of the front flap tells us that the book presents "dicta about writing so honest and true they will very likely become common axioms, so vivid and sincere and convincing is their presentation." More than just a casual attention-getter, the dicta about writing are part of the description of the book. This is justified because, in the text, the connection between writing and bullfighting is a fully functional one. Early on, the text establishes that the art of bullfighting, like literature and other fine arts, has its history, its rules, its periodic changes in taste, and its criteria for the appreciation of a performance. Bullfighters, the book tells us, are artists just as writers are, and each performance is a successful or an unsuccessful work of art.

Furthermore, the dicta about writing train our judgment and form our taste as aspiring aficionados, and they do so by foregrounding the principles and values on which any artist's performance can be evaluated and reviewed. Delivered, for the most part, in comic and satiric tones, the dicta about writing offer axioms on the difficulties involved in the depiction of simple things (2–3); the dangers of erectile writing (53–54); the liberating effect of Faulkner's revolutionary breakthrough (173); and, for the benefit of critics like Huxley (for whom the presence of just the tip of high culture in literature is not enough), the virtues of an iceberg theory of writing, which involves leaving out much of what you know (190–92).

In general, the values emanating out of these dicta involve personal taste, the taste of the age, and a moral criterion on which a performance is to be judged. For writing as for bullfighting, the values are consistent: they consist of a preference for the classic over the baroque, a recognition of the merits of the modern or the new (although not at the expense of the integrity of the art), and an uncompromising commitment to honesty in the exercise of one's craft. In accordance with these principles, then, we are to prefer clear writing to the obfuscating kind (*DIA*, 54) and the execution of a pure suerte to one embellished with romantic flourishes (12). We are to censure artists, be they literary or taurine, who exploit new styles, modern tastes or current preferences, aiming for fashionable popularity rather than using the new to make art (84, 205, 68). And we should also reject any artist who fakes the risks attendant upon his craft, whether it be someone who fakes danger in bullfighting (214–15) or profundity in writing (54,192). As we absorb Hemingway's views on writing, we are, simultaneously, learning how to read *Death in the Afternoon* as an "arte de ver los toros," or the art of watching the bullfight.

Although a dust jacket is detachable and discardable, the matter on the jacket of *Death in the Afternoon* has achieved a degree of permanence. Domingo's painting survives, albeit in black and white, on the cover of the

Scribner's Library paperback, the most widely read edition of *Death in the Afternoon*. And, in a way, the text of the original jacket copy also survives, in that its definition of *Death in the Afternoon* as a book that articulates Hemingway's views on writing has entered the culture and continues to shape the way we read the book — so much so that, paradoxically in view of their intended function, Hemingway's views on writing have become our most important reason for reading this book.[11]

### The Frontispiece: Juan Gris's *The Bullfighter*

Hemingway bought two Gris paintings in the early 1930s: *The Guitarist* (1926; oil on canvas, 29 x 36 1/2 inches) and *The Bullfighter* (1913; oil on canvas; 36 1/4 x 24 5/8 inches).[12] He hung *The Guitarist* in his bedroom (Hermann, 44–45) and placed *The Bullfighter* at the front of his book. Unfortunately, after the first edition of *Death in the Afternoon*, Gris's *Bullfighter* usually gets left out, and so not all of the book's readers connect the text with the painting and all it stands for. This is unfortunate because, from its position outside the text, it functions on various levels to comment on what is inside.

For one thing, this modern, abstract, museum-worthy work prepares the reader for a book that presents bullfighting as a fine art (and commercial spectacle) that is sophisticated, modern, and secular, and not as a mythic or folkloristic rite that is picturesque, ancient, and obscure. The painting represents bullfighting as urban and civilized, and not as barbarous and primitive. At the same time, by fusing elements of high and low culture (one of the defining characteristics of cubist painting), *The Bullfighter* supports Hemingway's effort inside the text to universalize bullfighting without cutting it off from its roots in popular culture.

Hemingway's frontispiece both honors and departs from tradition in another way. Classic *tauromaquias* customarily feature, on the cover or in a frontispiece, a portrait of the matador-codifier, the master artist and rulemaker whose work, style, or philosophy the book records. Portraits of José Delgado (Pepe-Hillo), Francisco Montes (Paquiro), and Rafael Guerra (Guerrita) adorn the classic eighteenth- and nineteenth-century *tauromaquias* they inspired. By using the portrait of a bullfighter in the frontispiece of *Death in the Afternoon*, Hemingway is, in effect, similarly and formally recognizing at the beginning of his *tauromaquia* the knowledge, talent, discipline, and artistry associated with the figure of the matador-artist. He is also honoring the classic convention of beginning a taurine rulebook with a picture of a bullfighter. Although unconventional in that it offers us a generic and not an individual bullfighter (and does so in an abstract, fragmented style), the frontispiece is, nonetheless, one of the markers that set the book within the traditions of taurine writing in Spanish, indirectly conferring on *Death in the Afternoon* the backing and authority of master bullfighters throughout the ages.

One's first impression of *The Bullfighter* is of multicolored geometric shapes and spaces. Pink and gray bullfight posters form the background for a bullfighter's head, headgear, and a face made up of black, white, and red triangles and planes. At the center, there is a cartoonish juxtaposition of nostrils and a lighted Havana cigar. Around them, ears, eye, and a neck with a silk-covered pigtail button are drawn in black. It is a simultaneous right, left, and three-quarter view. The torso, more figuratively rendered than the head, cants off at an angle in a white strip of shirt, slim red tie, and a *traje de luces* (traditional sequined suit) the color of burnished gold brocade. Angling further, thin white lines suggest the shirt and tie will change direction, but they are not colored in. Here the portrait ends, discontinued, in a plane of bright blue.

For all its abstraction, this is recognizably a portrait of a bullfighter wearing typical dress and smoking a cigar, a figure familiar in old lithographic prints from the romantic era, when bullfighters first emerged as mass culture heroes and international superstars (Martínez-Novillo, 170). These prints, the most famous of which presented Francisco Montes (1805–1851), circulated everywhere in nineteenth-century Spain and even elsewhere in Europe (Martínez-Novillo, 86, 90). But Gris's bullfighter does not romanticize a particular bullfighter or even the bullfight itself: it is, rather, a sophisticated, twentieth-century analytical breakdown of a popular poster image that reflects Gris's typically cubist interest in bringing popular culture into high art.

Cubist painting, crafted with the materials, techniques, and discipline inherited from the great tradition, and shaped by the kind of experimentation signaled by the words *analytical* and *synthetic,* took the consumer-oriented, machine-made stuff of early twentieth-century mass culture for its subject matter (Rosenblum, 117). Cubist still lifes featured images of newspaper advertising, packing-crate lettering, movie bills, posters, cigarette wrappers, light bulbs, crossword puzzles, cereal boxes, and package labels. At once elite (cubism is "one of the highest moments [. . .] in the history of art for art's sake") and popular (cubist painting is "witty, topical" and a precursor of pop art), this kind of painting erases the boundaries between mass culture and fine art (Rosenblum, 117, 118).

Gris's cubist *Bullfighter* brings together two disparate worlds — the world of taurine superstars, posters, and mass entertainment on the one hand; and the world of refinement, intellect, and complete abstraction on the other. By choosing it for his frontispiece, Hemingway suggests that in *Death in the Afternoon* he is similarly attempting to fuse elements of mass and high culture, to redefine bullfighting positively for the reader as both mass entertainment and fine art.

While the basic cubist techniques of fragmentation, defamiliarization, and simultaneous multiple perspective appear in *Death in the Afternoon* (see Amy Vondrak's essay, pages 257–79 in this volume), the cubist technique that most strongly influenced Hemingway's attitudes and prose is, I think, its unsentimental embrace of the stuff of popular culture. We see it most clearly in *Death in the Afternoon,* where Hemingway suggests that the modern bullfight, like modern painting, finds its nourishment and vitality in high art as well as low, in serious art as well as commercial art, and that all art forms — whether performed in a ring or displayed in a museum — need not be opposed (to use a phrase from Varnedoe), "in their intentions, audiences, or nature of endeavor" (16).

For those readers who fear their sensibilities may be too fine to appreciate the art of bullfighting, or for those who disdain mass entertainment of any kind, Hemingway puts *The Bullfighter* at the front of his book. And in the text, he makes a concerted effort to establish that enjoyment of the bullfight crosses all boundaries; it is not limited by education, age, sex, nationality, or religion. Indeed, it is not limited to any particular *kind* of person as measured "by any standard of civilization or experience" (4–5). To prove this, Hemingway, adopting the role of scientist-observer, reports the impressions of fifteen people he has brought with him to the bullring ("Some Reactions of a Few Individuals to the Integral Spanish Bullfight"). These individuals, all non-Spaniards and identified only by their initials, vary in age (they range from four to forty years old), sex (nine males and six females), nationality (twelve Americans, two British, and one "internationally famous novelist [who writes] in Yiddish"), level of education (one is too young to be sent to school, one has finished kindergarten, three attended finishing school or convent school, one graduated from a military academy, and eight are college educated), and occupation (five are writers, one is a musician, one paints, another is a soldier-sportsman, and one is described as a "very good mother" (500).

The scientist-observer indicates that his subjects' inclinations and experiences vary widely. More than half have significant equestrian experience; two have strong appetites, including one adult described as "alcoholic nymphomaniac" and another whose amusements are "drinking, night life and gossip" (498, 496); a third of the adults (two men, two women) like games of chance; six individuals (including one child) are shocked by what happens to the horses in the ring; the majority enjoy music, literature, or painting (Mrs. E. R.'s "favorite author [is] Henry James" [497]); and seven enjoy sports. All of this, tabulated in relation to their reactions upon first seeing "the integral Spanish bullfight," yields the following tally: eight individuals (four women and four men) liked what they saw, seven (counting the two children) did not. Five of the college educated liked it, as did the alcoholic nymphomaniac (Mrs. S. T.), but the other drinker (X. Y.) did not. Both the internationally famous novelist (S. A.) and the keenest of the aesthetes (A. U.) liked it, but another keen aesthete (Mrs. M. W.) did not.[13] As one might expect, sports enthusiasts and risk lovers tended to like it, and those repulsed by what happens to the horses tended to dislike it, but only by statistically insignificant margins. This tally is mine, but the conclusion is that of the naturalist: "In these few reactions of individuals I have tried to be completely accurate as to their first and ultimate impressions of the bullfight. The only conclusion I draw from these reactions is that some people will like the fights and others will not" (500).

It is funny: six pages of absurdly precise detail in the service of inconclusion. But, inconclusive as they may seem, the case studies have a point: no matter how moral or degenerate you are, no matter how much, by birth or by training, you are in possession of finer sensibilities or, for whatever reason, at the mercy of coarser ones, none of these qualities "scientifically speaking" can accurately predict your reaction to the modern Spanish bullfight. Nor, to judge by the following, are other widely held notions on these matters upheld by "scientific observation."

On the margins of the study, there are two women, one English, one Spanish, whose crying and suffering during the bullfight was observed from a short distance but whose histories could not be systematically chronicled. While it is widely held that members of the fair sex are horrified by the bullfight, the natural scientist observes the opposite may be true: "These are, speaking absolutely truthfully, the only women I have seen cry at over three hundred bullfights. It is to be understood, of course, that at these fights I could only observe my very immediate neighbors" (501). With this observation, Hemingway challenges both the sexist notion that it may be unwomanly for a woman to enjoy the bullfight and also the ethnocentric notion that it may be un-Spanish for a Spanish woman to cry all through it.

In its fragmentation and abstraction, Hemingway's frontispiece departs strikingly from taurine convention but it does so, at least in part, to send a cubist-inspired message: the bullfight encompasses both "mass culture" and fine art, and its audience includes highbrow and lowbrow alike. Thus, *The Bullfighter* does more than perform the functions of a frontispiece. In effect, it also works as a nonverbal epigraph (Genette, 150), specifying Hemingway's perspective on the art and emphasizing his universalizing efforts on behalf of the bullfight in the text. Epigraphs are often puzzling, and their significance may "not be clear or confirmed until the whole book is read" (158). Such is the case with *The Bullfighter*. It is a puzzle that takes the reader the whole book to solve. Finally, however, we realize that the portrait offers guidance on the meaning of the work.

## Dedication

The dedication, which appears on the first right hand page after the title page, reads simply "To Pauline." While Hemingway does not specify any relationship, the dedicatee is Pauline Pfeiffer Hemingway (1895–1951), who became Hemingway's second wife in 1927. She is connected to *Death in the Afternoon* in various ways. Most importantly, she accompanied him while he researched and wrote his bullfight book. Since she often typed his manuscripts, she may have typed parts of this one as well (Lewis, 35). Her uncle, Gustavus Adolphus Pfeiffer, who had business contacts in Barcelona, expedited Hemingway's order of basic reference materials, including several of the *tauromaquias* cited in *Death in the Afternoon* (Glossary, s. v *Tauromachia* and *Ligereza*); bound volumes and single issues of important bullfight magazines like *Sol y Sombra, La Lidia,* and *Zig-Zag*; and subscriptions to *El Clarin, El Eco Taurino,* and *La Fiesta Brava* (s. v. *Revistas*).[14]

More directly, Pauline is connected to the book in that she appears in it twice. Like Hemingway's sons and like Hadley, Hemingway's first wife, she is one of the respondents in "Some Reactions," where she is listed under her initials, as "P. M." (Pauline Marie, see Mandel, "Index," 119), and is one of the women in favor of bullfights: she "came to understand fights and enjoyed them more than any spectacle. Has attended them steadily" (*DIA*, 499). She also appears in the text itself, as "my wife," who is reading out loud to her husband (his eyes were bad) and small son (also unnamed but identified as John Hadley Nicanor by Mandel ["Index," 111]), from Dashiell Hammett's *The Dain Curse*, "[his] bloodiest [book] to date" (228). In deference to the boy's worries about death and dying, "my wife" substituted the word "umpty-umped" for Hammett's words "killed, cut the throat of, blew the brains out of, spattered around the room, and so on" (228). Admittedly, this anecdote is about the son, and not about Pauline, but her inspired use of "umpty-ump," which successfully eased the child's fears about death, communicates to the reader that denial of death in any form — including, one suspects, enjoying the riskless violence of detective fiction — is childish. It is part of a book-long effort to communicate the idea that an adult can have "a common sense interest in death" (as do the people of Castile, who "do not spend their lives avoiding the thought of it and hoping it does not exist" [264]). The book rejects Henry Wadsworth Longfellow's attitude that "Life is real; life is earnest, and the grave is not its goal" [266]), just as it "rejects" the child's (or anyone else's) unreasoning or unreasonable fear of death (or its equally unproductive counterpart, a morbid fascination with death). The anecdote involving Pauline does not advocate embracing death, but it does communicate a healthy acceptance of it.

Although at the beginning of the anecdote Hemingway says that the fatal goring of Isidoro Todó is "too ugly [. . .] to justify writing about when it is not necessary" (227), ten pages later he does offer a highly graphic description of the bullfighter's bone-cracking death (239). The description is justified on two counts. First and most explicitly, it explains to the reader just how much damage a horn wound can cause, a danger that may determine how a matador chooses to kill. And secondly, it constitutes a protest against agents and promoters who push unseasoned, out-of-shape, or simply untalented bullfighters into the Madrid ring, where they face very large bulls. In discussing Todó's death, the Madrid newspaper *ABC* speculated that one of the contributing factors was probably the intense pressure by Todó's agents to present him in Madrid's prestigious plaza; for whatever reason, the plaza's impresarios gave in and contracted him. Brave but not ready for the big leagues, Todó was, according to the newspaper report, a tragedy waiting to happen ("Un novillo," 39). Hemingway calls the story "ugly" and "dull" (227), presumably because such avoidable tragedies all too often form part of a *matador de novillo*'s lot (164–65).

In the "umpty-ump" anecdote and in the "Reactions" in the appendix, Hemingway uses his wife and sons to disassociate coarseness and morbidity from our concept of the aficionado and to introduce material on recurring themes, but he does not identify these functions in the dedication. The dedication could have included some words about Pauline's contribution to the work, its process of creation, or its themes; this would have made it what Genette calls "a motivated dedication" (125–26). When Richard Ford, for example, dedicated *Gatherings from Spain* (1846; mentioned in *DIA*, 53) to "the Honourable Mrs. Ford," he wrote such "a motivated dedication," mentioning that his wife perused and approved the book and hoping that "other fair readers may follow her example." In effect, the dedication of *Gatherings from Spain* defines that book as congenial to feminine tastes.

Waldo Frank's *Virgin Spain: Scenes from the Spiritual Drama of a Great People* (1926; mentioned in *DIA*, 53) also carries "a motivated dedication":

> To / those brother Americans / whose tongues are Spanish and Portuguese / whose homes are between the Río Grande and the Tierra del Fuego / but whose America / like mine / stretches from the Arctic to the Horn.

Frank's dedication, together with his title and subtitle, presents his book as a celebration of the ideal America, one that blurs the difference between the northern and southern hemispheres.

Felicitously avoiding these tendentious possibilities, Hemingway's dedication in *Death in the Afternoon* simply sings. Free of explicit identification, justification, or explanation of any kind, "To Pauline" is a message that is universal and timeless: man to woman, Hemingway to Pauline. And it serves *Death in the Afternoon* precisely, one presumes, by *not* tying it to a specific readership or theme. Choosing to render his dedication in the most modern and simplest of forms (Genette, 125), Hemingway refuses here to narrow the gap between reader and text. Instead, his unmotivated dedication, like his symbolic title and postponed preface, is of a piece with a strategy that can best be defined as exceptional paratextual restraint.

## Table of Contents

The table of contents announces the divisions of *Death in the Afternoon* and reveals the articulation of the parts of the work as a whole. Headed simply "Contents," it lists the titles and beginning page numbers of each of the seven sections of the book. Set in the same size type, placed flush with the left margin, and equidistantly spaced and separated from each other, these seven internal titles are strictly parallel in arrangement, suggesting that all of the sections are equally important. However, the first section, "Chapters I–XX, Inclusive," is set off from the others by being the only section subdivided into chapters, by being the only one to include the word "inclusive," and by being the only one for which both beginning and end page numbers (1–278) are provided. The six remaining titles — "Illustrations," "An Explanatory Glossary," "Some Reactions of a Few Individuals to the Integral Spanish Bullfight," "A Short Estimate of the American, Sidney Franklin, as a Matador," "Dates on Which Bullfights Will Be Held in Spain, France, Mexico, and Central and South America," and "Bibliographical Note" — comprise the back matter, which is more or less equal to the first section in terms of length (238 pages in the Scribner's hardcover first edition).

All this makes for a rather odd table of contents. Not only does it blur rather than clarify the distinction between text and back matter, making it hard for the reader to distinguish between what is essential and what is optional, but also (and most unconventionally), the back matter occupies almost all the space on the page. The chapters of the main text, which one would expect to be the more prominent item, are presented in a mute (merely numbered) mode, displayed as a block, and relegated to one line. The back matter, with its individually and sometimes lengthily titled sections, occupies ten lines and dominates the display.

Odd as it is, the table of contents is a proper guide to *Death in the Afternoon* in that it invites us to read the book simultaneously for pleasure and for instruction. Keeping opaque the nature of each chapter's contents, Hemingway signals that, rather than looking to it for specific points of information and consulting it like a manual, we are to read the main text slowly and consecutively, page by page and chapter by chapter, as if it were a literary work. At the same time, the generic titles of the back matter (illustrations, glossary, note) suggest that these sections are going to have a specific, practical application. By simultaneously featuring the back matter and blurring the distinctions between it (the extra text) and the text proper, Hemingway suggests that in *Death in the Afternoon* the reference material, normally considered optional and subordinate, is as important, practically and aesthetically, as the main text.

The absence of chapter headings for the twenty chapters of the main text is one of the most notable absences among the paratexts of *Death in the Afternoon*. Like the lack of an index, the missing chapter headings effectively prevent the reader from using *Death in the Afternoon* as a manual or book of instruction. Until very recently, indexes have not been customary features of Spanish bullfight manuals, their function being performed by a detailed contents page with descriptive headings and subheadings. Traditionally, the material in these manuals has been organized into separate chapters or sections on the properties of the fighting bull, the capework and pic-ing, the placing of the banderillas, the work with the muleta, and the kill. The early drafts of chapters 11, 15, 16, and 18 carry the working titles of "The Bulls," "The Cape," "The Picador," and "The Muleta," indicating that Hemingway organized the material in *Death in the Afternoon* along fairly conventional lines. But he crossed these titles off on the typescript (JFK, Item 22), and the published version of *Death in the Afternoon* lacks these guides. So great is the reader's need for orientation when faced with the integrality and the impenetrability of the main text that in 1997 a complete index of names, places, and key terms was compiled by Miriam B. Mandel ("Index," 86–132). Several years earlier, the Spanish translation of the main text of *Death in the Afternoon* (as serialized in the Madrid weekly, *Gaceta Ilustrada*, in 1966) had added entertaining, humorous titles for each of Hemingway's twenty chapters.

While the *Gaceta Ilustrada* titles do little to communicate the work's real value as a manual, they do show clearly how *Death in the Afternoon* can be read for pleasure. The titles for chapters 11, 12, 15, and 16 are: "Historias de toros y relatos amorosos" (Bull Stories and Love Stories); "Las ganaderías y una extraña historia de muerte" (Bull Breeding Ranches and a Strange Story About Death); "La capa, el matador y una historia de homosexuales" (The Cape, the Matador and a Story about Homosexuals); and "La crueldad de los picadores y la expulsión de la vieja señora" (The Cruelty of the Picadors and the Expulsion of the Old Lady).[15] The jaunty air of these titles, together with the mention of the Old lady, alerts readers to another attraction: Hemingway's use of comic characters or character types like the eccentric Old lady, whose curiosity and ignorance allow the narrator to expound at length on the qualities of the bull and bullfighters. Just as important as the Old lady are the comic nonfiction characters that Hemingway fashions out of himself and the reader. Dramatizing his persona (whom he calls "I"), Hemingway adopts roles that range all the way from something indistinguishable from his real-life self to the larger-than-life, eccentric "young man" (64), "old Dr. Hemingstein" (53), genial storyteller (180), nonromantic "naturalist" (122, 133–39), and harried "author" of the very book that the Old lady and a dramatized reader called "you" are reading.

At one extreme, the dramatized reader is nothing more than the quasi-impersonal "you" whose presence is found in manuals of all kinds. But at the other extreme, this "reader" (sometimes in concert with, sometimes in opposition to, the eccentric Old lady) is given the chance to scoff, demur, demand clarification, beg for comic relief, and witness the eviction from the text of anyone whom the "author" considers hopelessly uneducable (63, 65, 190, 203). All of this points to an "authorial intention [as much] literary [as] communicative or informative,"[16] and justifies at least to some degree the use of mute chapter headings, which are associated primarily with serious fiction (Genette, 305–8).

The first two internal titles of the back matter, "Illustrations" and "An Explanatory Glossary," send a genre signal essential to the identity of *Death in the Afternoon* as a bullfight manual. Canonically, bullfight manuals for spectators have illustrations, usually stock images in the form of sketches or photographs, of the set moves involved in the capework and pic-ing, the placement of the banderillas, the passes with the muleta, and so on. They also have glossaries to define the technical terms used to describe the fighting bull and the bullfighters' basic maneuvers. So essential are these features to an appreciation of the art that a spectator guide without them is incomplete. These two features, prominently placed on the Contents page, clearly place *Death in the Afternoon* within this genre.

The book's eighty-one photographs, taken from the archives of leading taurine photojournalists, illustrate the basic maneuvers as performed by the most significant figures of the golden and silver ages of bullfighting (Hernández, 7). Together with the image of the famous seed bull, Diano,[17] these photographs and their captions, which contain detailed instruction leavened by anecdote and irony, also provide a full chronicle of a legendary epoch. They exceed the traditional functions of illustrations in bullfight manuals and spectator guides.[18]

Nor is the "Explanatory Glossary" a typical guidebook vocabulary. Containing almost six hundred terms, the definitions for which are occasionally long and highly technical (e.g., *Kilos, Pica, Terreno, Veronica*), it looks more like a complete taurine dictionary than the usual brief listing of basic technical or professional vocabulary. Furthermore, it contains terms that relate the bullfight to its larger context (*Multa, Oreja, Rondeño, Mojiganga, Huevos,* and *Tapas*), and every so often, as with the entry *Tal . . . Qué tal?* it becomes a sort of mini-Spanish phrasebook or cultural guide that is a pleasure to read.

Equally interesting, each for its own sake, are the sections "Some Reactions," "A Short Estimate," and "Dates of Bullfights." Although none of them is essential to the work's identity as a bullfight manual, each is closely associated with a particular kind of popular taurine writing or theme. "A

Short Estimate," the critique of Sidney Franklin, a professional bullfighter who was Hemingway's friend and advisor, is cast as a *biografía,* or biographical sketch. A staple in historical works and encyclopedias, the *biografía* also exists, in a more flamboyant version, in publications like Tomás Orts-Ramos's popular series *Los ases del toreo* (The Aces of Bullfighting), which promote the fiesta by focusing on the lives and careers of star performers. In what can be read as a device to make the bullfighter less foreign or alien to his American readers, Hemingway features Franklin, "the son of a Brooklyn policeman" (196), in a *biografía* whose congenial tone falls midway between the restraint of historical record (like, for example, Cossío's entry for "Francklin" [*sic*], 3: 288–89) and the popular romanticized accounts aimed at fans.

Similarly, Hemingway's "Dates of Bullfights," a nine-page list of regularly scheduled performances held annually in cities all over Spain and abroad, would also be immediately recognized by readers of standard Spanish taurine literature. Such listings are staple features of taurine information almanacs. Almost totally faithful to the spare, telegraphic style of calendars such as the one in the *Vademécum taurino* (*Sol y Sombra,* 255–59), Hemingway departs from it slightly, by injecting pieces of friendly travel advice into the list: "If you go [to the minor rings of Madrid] be careful not to have your pocket picked" (508), and "Palencia — usually good fights — intelligent public. Nice Castillian town with good beer and excellent quail shooting" (512).

Even the serio-comic "Some Reactions of a Few Individuals to the Integral Spanish Bullfight" recalls a typical feature of taurine writing: the panorama of perspectives on the fiesta, gleaned from writings published in French, Portuguese, Italian, and English, as well as in Spanish. Foreigners' responses are detailed, for example, in the highly respected *El espectáculo más nacional* (López Valdemoro, 382) and in *Los ingleses y los toros* (1926) by the popular humorist Aurelio López Becerra (Desperdicios).

With his incursions into the minor taurine genres of *biografía,* calendar writing, and spectator reactions, Hemingway not only delivers the extra material promised, implicitly or explicitly, in the main body of text (about Franklin, 169, 196; about dates of bullfights, 37; and about spectator reactions, 4), but he does so in a highly literary and truly cosmopolitan way. Rather than presenting the material in a standardized series of appendixes familiar to his English-speaking audience, Hemingway sometimes mimics and sometimes improvises upon various forms of popular Spanish taurine literature, thereby giving us a direct experience of bullfight writing and culture. This gives his work a more authentic air.

Furthermore, in these five sections or appendixes, Hemingway uses the same tone, the same fusion of the literary and the practical, of the comic and the serious, that consistently characterized the twenty chapters of the main text. In contrast, the "Bibliographical Note" introduces what Genette calls "a break in the enunciative regime."[19] Gone are the layered combinations, the mix of genres, the tonal variations. Gone too are the role-playing and the I–you dialogue between a dramatized "author" and "reader," which also link the main body of the text with the rest of the book. In place of these congenial, speech-oriented signs, the "Bibliographical Note" presents a formal, neutral tone in which both reader and writer are referred to in the third person: "the reader who wishes to make a study of the history of [. . .]" and "the writer asks the indulgence of [. . .]" (517).

Moreover, when we see the note is signed "E. H.," we know that the author has dropped all masks. Undramatized, he is just Ernest Hemingway. In this sense, then, the "Bibliographical Note" is closer in register to the title, dedication, and table of contents at the front of the book than to anything in between. In the book's front matter, the sender of the paratextual messages is, of course, the real writer Hemingway, talking "over the head" or "behind the back" of the text, so to speak, in order to communicate his writerly decisions or intentions to the prospective reader through the attitudes embedded in the title, dedication, and table of contents (the book's organization). In the book's back matter, the "Bibliographical Note," Hemingway completes this direct commentary on the work, by telling the reader how he defines it. These two areas of paratextual commentary differ from the text (the twenty chapters and the five subsequent sections) very clearly: the text itself offers a set of dualities, indicating the binary of real-life / fiction, while the paratexts that frame it (the front matter and the "Bibliographical Note") work on a single level (real-life only).

This distinction is useful because it throws into relief the purposeful literariness of the text. It draws our attention to the extent to which creations like the Old lady may be meaningful rather than simply expedient, and the extent to which the Hemingway persona may be a rhetorical device rather than a self-portrait — all of which opens the way to an analysis of these characters as tools of persuasion rather than mere vehicles of self-indulgence and self-exhibition. The distinction also reveals the extent to which *Death in the Afternoon* is self-reflexive: a book about writing a book. From the first chapter, where the writer talks about the book's genesis, to the last one, where he talks about it as a work achieved, the text is studded with (mostly comic) references to the difficulties of its making (53, 101, 120, 135, 190) — so much so, that the "story" of *Death in the Afternoon*, insofar as it has one, is not so much "Hemingway and the bullfight" as it is "Hemingway and his bullfight book."

### The "Bibliographical Note"

Hemingway owned an impressive private taurine library. In addition to the several *tauromaquias* and taurine magazines and journals named in *Death in the Afternoon,* it included many other scholarly books such as José Sánchez de Neira's classic *Gran diccionario taurómaco* (1896); Pascual Millán's two important historical studies, *Los toros en Madrid* (1890) and *Los novillos* (1892); and Antonio Fernández de Heredia's *Doctrinal taurómaco* (1904), a proposal for reforming the then current legislation governing the bullfight in Spain. Also part of his library were *¡¡¡Ki ki ri ki!!! Los 'Gallos': sus rivales y su prensa* by Alejandro Pérez Lugín (1919), which is inscribed "Ernest Hemingway, Madrid 1923"; and *Anales del toreo* by José Velázquez Sánchez (1873), which is inscribed "Ernest Hemingway Madrid 1919" [*sic*].[20] These, together with *El espectáculo más nacional* by Juan Gualberto López Valdemoro y de Quesada, Conde de las Navas (1899), which Hemingway acquired sometime in the 1930s, are basic reference works that form the core of any good taurine collection.[21]

While it is generally accepted that all serious writing on a subject partakes of what has been written before, *Death in the Afternoon* does not — and especially not in its paratexts, where one would expect this to be done — acknowledge all of its sources. Perhaps to strengthen its claim to originality as a literary work, or perhaps to adhere to conventions of Spanish-language taurine writing, which, for the most part, eschewed systematic documentation, Hemingway failed to provide *Death in the Afternoon* with any of the usual means of validating an expository text: precise citation, full reference, and itemized bibliography.[22] In spite of its title and its placement at the back of the book, the "Bibliographical Note" does not offer an alphabetized list of sources. Instead, the authority of *Death in the Afternoon* lies in Hemingway's adherence to (and manipulation of) the established conventions of Spanish-language taurine writing, and manifests itself in certain features of the book that signal his reading and research on the subject, and his familiarity with the genre's conventions. These features — the eye-catching jacket illustration, the portrait of a bullfighter in the frontispiece, the photographs illustrating basic moves, the glossary, the biographical sketch, the calendar — testify to his familiarity with publications on the subject by echoing, replicating, or adapting features that are staples in the tradition of taurine literature. The outstanding quality of the material chosen (the jacket illustration is by Roberto Domingo, most of the photographs are by leading photojournalists Aurelio Rodero and Juan Vandel [408], and the taurine bibliography, discussed below, is by the highly respected Graciano Díaz Arquer) sends a signal of high taurine culture, and communicates the writer's conviction that such prestigious filiations are qualitatively and tonally appropriate in a work that itself represents the best of contemporary writing on the bullfight. Editions and translations that omit some or, as in the case of the Spanish translation *Muerte en la tarde* (1968), *all* of the front and back matter, deprive the reader not only of a full experience of the book, but also of its purposeful references to traditions out of which, implicitly, authority on its primary subject matter flows.

In the rare instances when *Death in the Afternoon* acknowledges its sources, it does so in the text, and not, as it pretends, in the "Bibliographical Note." It is in the text that Hemingway demonstrates that he was capable of doing serious research in Spanish, and that he was familiar with primary sources. At one point, for example, Hemingway, in the voice of his persona, reads from a book called *Toros célebres,* translating for his readers as he goes along (110–11). Although the ostensible reason for the two-page citation is to illustrate certain undesirable qualities in fighting bulls, it also works to signal to the reader that the author can read and translate professional literature written in Spanish.[23] Other quotations from Spanish — a well-known line from Francisco Montes's *Tauromaquia completa* (Glossary, s. v. *Ligereza*), the title of Gregorio Corrochano's famous review of Niño de la Palma (*DIA,* 89) — also signal Hemingway's familiarity with important critical and theoretical treatises, just as his repetition of taurine adages (calves so educated they talk Greek and Latin [107], bulls so brave they charge a locomotive [109], polygamous bulls that turn monogamous [121]) signals his familiarity with popular writing on the fighting bull. And in his five-page historical summary of former bullfight greats, he conjugates through time the notion that "the past was always better," and in doing so catches, in parody, the echo of a taurine traditionalist's characteristic refrain (239–44).

In view of this, it is no surprise that the "Bibliographical Note" actually functions like a postface, announcing the book's literary antecedents, defining its scope and limitations, justifying its existence, and, not incidentally, establishing its author's authority. In the first paragraph, Hemingway simply refers the reader to the "2077 books and pamphlets in Spanish dealing with or touching on tauromaquia" provided in Díaz Arquer's *Libros y folletos de toros* (517). The phrase "2077 books and pamphlets in Spanish" gives an idea of the impressive dimensions of the taurine tradition, and the implication is that the author, although an American, had access to them and that the document just read is firmly rooted in Spain's taurine literary tradition — a claim that the text amply satisfies.

Listing works dating from the sixteenth century up to 1931, *Libros y folletos de toros* was the most complete bibliography available when Hemingway was writing *Death in the Afternoon.* Only periodicals, musical compositions, and manuscripts are excluded from its listings (Díaz Arquer, vi). About five hundred items are from before the eighteenth century, published in the period prior to the development of the modern bullfight and well outside the scope of Hemingway's study.[24] Most of the works listed are in Spanish, but there are works in other languages as well, mainly in Portuguese, French, and English. Along with the dictionaries, rulebooks, histories, biographies of bullfighters, books on bulls and bull breeders, and issues of government regulations, it lists volumes of poetry, novels, and plays on taurine themes (122 in this latter genre alone). An illustrated bibliography, it reproduces important and interesting book covers, title pages, and even illustrations contained in some of the items it mentions. Simply by mentioning this bibliography — it is doubtful he consulted more than a fraction of its total listings — Hemingway acknowledges his debt to a large body of knowledge that had built up over four hundred years.

At the same time, Hemingway justifies his own book, explaining what makes it a novelty and how it fits into or contributes to the tradition: it serves "as an introduction to the modern Spanish bullfight and attempts to explain that spectacle both emotionally and practically." His claim to originality — "there was no book which did this in Spanish or English" (517) — is not as audacious as it may seem. As late as 1914, when Sáenz de Heredia (El Bachiller Garrocha) published *Las corridas de toros en la actualidad,* there were few proper introductions, even in Spanish. Sáenz de Heredia points out that although there were good reference books, a great deal of biography, several classic *tauromaquias,* and some polemical literature, there was no well-written, comprehensive introduction that would authoritatively explain the *suertes* (basic or set moves) or the define the qualities of a fighting bull, of a creditable torero, and of a satisfying performance (67–68). In 1929, Uno al Sesgo published his fine *El arte de ver los toros: Guía del espectador.* Apart from that, however, there was still little of distinction in the field when *Death in the Afternoon* appeared in 1932 (Cossío 2: 72).

But what is really original about *Death in the Afternoon* is its method. According to Hemingway, no book in Spanish or in English has attempted to "explain the spectacle both emotionally and practically" (*DIA,* 517). His claim may be accurate. The existing recommended spectator guides were purely practical, normative, and factual. *Death in the Afternoon,* an infinitely more ambitious and complex work, is a synthesis of the normative, the factual, and the figurative at the service of instruction. It seeks at once to define, in accessible prose, the methods of the craft, and to convey, through poetic means, the range of feelings a performance can provide. Having two completely disparate aims makes Hemingway's book unique among modern spectator guides.[25]

The "Bibliographical Note" ends by asking the indulgence of "competent aficionados" for the book's technical explanations: "When a volume of controversy may be written on the execution of a single suerte one man's arbitrary explanation is certain to be unacceptable to many" (517). What first strikes one about this request is that it presupposes Hemingway's competence as an aficionado. It constitutes a ready-made assessment of the author and his explanations, bestowing credibility on the former and enhancing the value of the latter. In bullfight books, these functions are performed by a foreword or preface written by an expert whose reputation and praise enhance the author's authority. Since the paratexts of *Death in the Afternoon* do not provide any such external voice, Hemingway himself assumes it.

*Death in the Afternoon* lacks a formal "Acknowledgments" section. Instead, Hemingway acknowledges the support he received from taurine experts in the last chapter of the text itself. He acknowledges an authoritative aficionado, Juanito Quintana, by "speaking" affectionately to him — "¿Qué tal, hombre, qué tal?" (274) — and also evokes and thus tacitly acknowledges the help of three taurine professionals: the matador Sidney Franklin, the critic Rafael Hernández, and the painter Roberto Domingo, who is "so polite always, so gentle and such a good friend" (271, 272, 276–77).[26] But no declarations of indebtedness to these or other authorities appear in the paratexts, and Hemingway continues to avoid the issue of his credibility and indebtedness by not raising it anywhere outside the text, except indirectly, in the "Bibliographical Note." In short, he lets his book speak for itself.

The second thing that strikes one about this plea for "the indulgence of competent aficionados" is that, by anticipating disagreement or criticism, it attempts to neutralize them by relegating them to the realm of taste. Referring to his own (competent) evaluations and explanations as "one man's arbitrary opinion," he suggests that — among competent aficionados — it is all a matter of individual judgment or conviction. Altogether, then, the request for indulgence constitutes a three-pronged message aimed at placing himself and his treatment of the bullfight in the best possible light for the reader.

In the space of two short paragraphs in the "Bibliographical Note," Hemingway defines his book, specifies what is original about it, and mounts a pre-emptive response to critics. Had this "Note" been placed at the front of *Death in the Afternoon,* it would orient a prospective reader. But placed at the end of the book and addressed, presumably, to the reader who has finished the book, it seems "curative" rather than "monitory" in nature (Genette, 238–39). Brief and non-cautionary, Hemingway's note is the most discreet of vehicles for an author's personal remarks.

This discussion has not commented upon all of the paratexts of *Death in the Afternoon.* There is other front matter, such as the cover, the "Books By" page, the name of the author, and the notice of copyright at the front. There are the photograph credits page at the back (408). In between, there are the running heads in the upper margins of the text and the appendixes, and there are three footnotes, which are textual in so far as they are discursive, and paratextual in so far as they may offer a guide to the organization of the text (6, 55, 184). Given the unmapped cultural and literary space *Death in the Afternoon* inhabits, however, the paratextual elements in the title, jacket, frontispiece, dedication, table of contents, and bibliographical note — the locations I have dealt with — are the ones that work hardest to bring us closer to an understanding of the work. Oblique, iconic, postponed, and restrained as they are, these paratexts contain a great many meaningfully integrated signs that cohere with others inside the text. They are highly effective in presenting, focusing, and defining Hemingway's view of his book for the reader. Of course, as Genette acknowledges, nothing obliges us to subscribe to the view of a work transmitted by an author's paratextual choices, but it is also true, as he quickly reminds us, that once exposed to a title, or a jacket illustration, or a frontispiece, or an author's note, we may find it almost impossible to entirely disregard them, elude their influence, and read the work as if we were ignorant of their existence (408–9).

# Notes

[1] This essay grew out of my work in an ongoing research project on "Threshold and Text," supported by a grant from the Spanish Ministry of Science and Technology (Dirección General de Investigación Científica y Técnica). A preliminary version of this essay was presented at the II International Seminar on Liminality and Text, Spring 2001, Universidad Autónoma de Madrid.

[2] For *Death in the Afternoon,* this would be the first edition published in hardcover by Scribner in 1932. Hemingway was actively involved in the decisions about language and graphic art for this edition. He gave his editor, Maxwell Perkins, explicit instructions on how to present the appendixes, the photographs, the jacket illustration, and the frontispiece (*Selected Letters,* 361–62, 364). He approved the copy on the blurbs, dictated the dedication (Bruccoli, 176), and chose the paintings for the dust jacket and the frontispiece; both paintings came from his own collection (Hermann, 44).

[3] For a complete list of the front and back matter of the first edition, see Hanneman, 31–32. See also "A Note on the Text" (xvii–xix in this volume).

[4] Hemingway Collection, John F. Kennedy Library, Item 24, unnumbered page 26.

[5] Hernández, "Míster Ernest Hemingway, el amigo de España," *La Libertad,* 23 September 1933. Tomás Orts-Ramos (Uno al Sesgo) reviewed *Death in the Afternoon* at length in *"Libros de toros II"* (2–3) and briefly in *Toros y toreros en 1933* (333–34). These Spanish reviews were based on the 1932 Scribner's edition of *Death in the Afternoon;* the book was not translated into Spanish until the 1960s (LaPrade, 20–21).

[6] All three are recommended by Cossío, although he singles out Tomás Orts-Ramos's *El arte de ver los toros* as the best (2: 72). Hemingway owned *Las corridas de toros en la actualidad* by Cesáreo Sáenz de Heredia (Brasch and Sigman, 323). *Catecismo taurino* is by Manuel Serrano García-Vaõ. Unless otherwise indicated, all translations from Spanish to English are mine.

[7] Another kind of connection between the title and the fighting bull lies in the possibility that Hemingway took his title from something he wrote himself. If so, it is an echo from "Pamplona in July," one of his earliest articles on the bullfight, and it ties the death in question unmistakably to the bull. Talking of the *encierro,* Hemingway describes how the bulls are run through the main streets in the morning to the ring, and how, once there, in the pens, they "will not leave until they come out into the glare of the arena *to die in the afternoon*" (*By-Line,* 103, my emphasis).

[8] See Brasch and Sigman, 106, 129.

[9] Both "literary competence" and "literariness" are Scholes's terms (19–21).

[10] Roberto Domingo, a postimpressionist painter with an important body of work on taurine and nontaurine themes to his credit, was also one of the leading bullfight poster painters and taurine illustrators in Spain. From 1910 through the 1940s, bullfight impresarios bought up his work because as advertising it was so effective (Agustí Guerrero, 75–76). Rex Smith offers a brief introduction to Domingo and reproduces seventeen of his taurine drawings (280–89). A black and white reproduction of *Toros* appears in Agustí Guerrero, 74–75.

[11] Thurston offers an extended analysis of the linkage between bullfight and writing. While I agree that such a linkage exists, I do not agree with Thurston's conclusion that Hemingway believes all modern writing, like modern bullfighting, to be bad: "Hemingway seems to despise all modern writing, which like modern bullfighting [. . .] suffers from enervating excesses" (48). By themselves, modernity and its accompanying degeneracy do not, for Hemingway, guarantee bad art. Proof of this is that he confers on Juan Belmonte, the modern revolutionary torero (and, by implication, on William Faulkner, Belmonte's revolutionary counterpart in the field of American letters) the status of genius (*DIA,* 68–69, 173).

[12] The paintings are described in Watts, 99, and Rosenblum, Figure 132. Juan Gris (1887–1927) was not an aficionado. *The Bullfighter* seems to be Gris's only known work on a taurine theme (Martínez-Novillo, 170). A color reproduction of the painting appears in Kahnweiler, 71.

[13] The respondents' full names, listed under their initials, as well as their correct ages, are found in Mandel's "Index."

[14] Incoming Correspondence, Pfeiffer, Hemingway Collection, John F. Kennedy Library. Reynolds also lists these titles, with the notation, "GP ordered for EH" (*Hemingway's Reading*).

[15] The complete list of chapter headings is in the "Indice de capítulos" (Table of Contents) in "Muerte en la tarde. Indices" (*Gaceta Ilustrada* 517 [3 September 1966]: 37). The translations of the titles are mine.

[16] I have taken these terms from Winterowd (52), whose discussion of reading for information versus reading for pleasure (21–22) informs my own discussion of this point.

[17] On the photograph of "Diano" that appears in *Death in the Afternoon,* see Luis Fernández Salcedo's note at the beginning of his book on Hemingway's references to this famous bull.

[18] For a fuller discussion of the photographs published in *Death in the Afternoon,* see Anthony Brand's essay, "Far from Simple" (pages 165–87 in this volume).

[19] The distinctions I draw between text (the twenty chapters and the five subsequent sections) and paratext (the "Bibliographical Note") are based on Genette's study of the form and function of endnotes in discursive texts and in texts of fiction (325–28, 332–36).

[20] There is no record of a Hemingway visit to Madrid in 1919.

[21] For a list of the works that form the core of a good collection, see Sánchez del Arco (Giraldillo). Information about Hemingway's library was obtained from several sources: Incoming Correspondence, Pfeiffer, JFK; the JFK *Catalogue;* Brasch and Sigman, xxxvi; and Reynolds, *Hemingway's Reading,* Item 1340. Many of these books are now very rare and valuable. For more detail on Hemingway's library of Spanish and taurine subjects, see Mandel, *Annotations,* 96–97 (s. v. *El Clarín*); 124–25 (s. v. *Díaz Arquer*); 242–43 (s. v. *La Lidia*); 407 (s. v. *Sol y Sombra*); 427 (s. v. *Toreros y toros*); and others of her entries, as well as her bibliographic essay, on pages 79–119 in this volume.

[22] In the 1950s, Álvarez de Miranda, who read extensively in preparation for his scholarly study on the origins of the bullfight, also noted that insufficient documentation was the rule: "Parece que muchos escritores, con el tema de los toros, se han colocado como Adán frente al mundo, como si nadie les hubiera precedido" (It would seem that many writers, when the subject is the bullfight, pretend to be Adam facing the world, as if no one had preceded them; Alvarez de Miranda, 30; my translation).

[23] Bredendick discusses Hemingway's translations from *Toros célebres* (73–77) and identifies his references to bullfight writing (64; 71 n.3).

[24] My discussion of Díaz Arquer's bibliography is heavily indebted to Mandel, *Annotations,* 124–25 (s. v. *Díaz Arquer, Graciano*).

[25] While spectator guides are purely practical, other taurine rulebooks *do* mix literary and factual discourse. For example, chapters 48 to 51 of the first volume of *La tauromaquia* [. . .] *del* [. . .] *diestro* [. . .] *Guerrita* (1896) contain a novel to relieve the "terrible aridity" of the discourse (Vázquez et al., 1: 740–823). But in *Guerrita* the literary discourse is not integrated into the philosophical or didactic sections, as it is in the text of *Death in the Afternoon.*

[26] For more information on these and other figures mentioned in chapter 20, see the corresponding individual entries in Mandel, *Annotations.*

# Works Cited

Agustí Guerrero, María Dolores. *Roberto Domingo: Arte y trapío.* Madrid: Agualarga, 1998.

Álvarez de Miranda, Ángel. *Ritos y juegos del toro.* Madrid: Biblioteca Nueva, 1998.

Brasch, James D., and Joseph Sigman. *Hemingway's Library: A Composite Record.* New York: Garland, 1981.

Bredendick, Nancy. "*Toros célebres:* Its Meaning in *Death in the Afternoon.*" *The Hemingway Review* 17.2 (1998): 64–77.

Bruccoli, Matthew J., ed., with the assistance of Robert W. Trogdon. *The Only Thing That Counts: The Ernest Hemingway–Maxwell Perkins Correspondence 1925–1947.* New York: Scribner's, 1996.

Cossío, José María de. *Los toros: Tratado técnico e histórico*. 12 vols. to date. Madrid: Espasa-Calpe, 1943–1997.

Delgado, José (Pepe-Hillo). *Tauromaquia o arte de torear*. 1796. Madrid: Turner, 1988.

Díaz Arquer, Graciano. *Libros y folletos de toros: bibliografía taurina compuesta con vista de la biblioteca taurómaca de D. José Luis de Ybarra y López de la Calle*. Madrid: Vindel, 1931.

Dowsett, J. Morewood. *The Spanish Bullring*. London: Bale, 1928.

Fernández Salcedo, Luis. *"Diano" (o el libro que quedó sin escribir)*. Madrid: Librería Merced, 1959.

Ford, Richard. *Gatherings from Spain*. 1846. London: J. M. Dent, [1906].

Frank, Waldo. *Virgin Spain: Scenes from the Spiritual Drama of a Great People*. New York: Boni and Liveright, 1926.

Genette, Gerard. *Paratexts: Thresholds of Interpretation*. Trans. Jane E. Lewin. Cambridge: Cambridge UP, 1997. Trans. of *Seuils*. Paris: Seuil, 1987.

Hanneman, Audre. *Ernest Hemingway: A Comprehensive Bibliography*. Princeton: Princeton UP, 1967.

Hemingway, Ernest. *Death in the Afternoon*. New York: Scribner's, 1932.

———. *Death in the Afternoon*. The Scribner Library of Contemporary Classics. New York: Scribner's, 1960.

———. *Ernest Hemingway. Selected Letters 1917–1961*. Ed. Carlos Baker. New York: Scribner's, 1981.

———. *Muerte en la tarde*. Trans. of *Death in the Afternoon* by Lola Aguado. Barcelona: Planeta, 1968.

———. "Muerte en la tarde." Trans. Lola Aguado. Photos Manuel Cervera. Illus. Pablo Picasso. *Gaceta Ilustrada* 506–17 (18 June–3 September 1966). In 12 installments. 188 pages, continuous pagination.

———. "Pamplona in July." *By-Line: Ernest Hemingway*. Ed. William White. New York: Scribner's, 1967. 99–108.

———. Unpublished manuscripts, The Ernest Hemingway Collection, John F. Kennedy Library: Item 22, folders 1–4; Item 24; Item 54.

Hermann, Thomas. *"Quite a Little about Painters": Art and Artists in Hemingway's Life and Work*. Tübingen, Basel: Francke, 1997.

Hernández, Rafael (RAFAEL). "Mr. Ernest Hemingway, el amigo de España." *La Libertad* (24 September 1933): 7.

John F. Kennedy Library. "Velázquez y Sánchez, José" in "Books." *Catalogue of the Ernest Hemingway Collection*. 2 vols. Boston: G. K. Hall, 1982. 2: 704.

Kahnweiler, Daniel-Henry. *Juan Gris: vida y pintura*. Trans. Concepción Falcón Rodríguez. Madrid: Patronato Nacional de Museos, D. L., 1971. Trans. of *Juan Gris. Sa vie, son oeuvre, ses ècrits*. Paris, Gallimard, 1946.

LaPrade, Douglas. *La censura de Hemingway en España*. Salamanca: Universidad de Salamanca, 1991.

Lewis, Robert W. "The Making of *Death in the Afternoon*." In *Ernest Hemingway: The Writer in Context*. Ed. James Nagel. Madison: U of Wisconsin P, 1984. 31–52.

López Becerra, Aureliano (Desperdicios). *Los ingleses y los toros. El secreto de Uzcudun por Desperdicios y Asterisco*. 3rd ed. Bilbao: Editorial Vizcaína, 1926.

López Valdemoro y de Quesada, Juan Gualberto (Conde de las Navas). "Embollado. En beneficio de los extranjeros." *El espectáculo más nacional*. Madrid: Rivadeneyra, 1899.

Mandel, Miriam B. *Hemingway's "Death in the Afternoon": The Complete Annotations*. Lanham, MD: Scarecrow Press, 2002.

———. "Index to Ernest Hemingway's *Death in the Afternoon*." *Resources for American Literary Study* 23.1 (1997): 86–132.

Martínez-Novillo, Alvaro. *El pintor y la tauromaquia*. Madrid: Turner, 1988.

Montes, Francisco. "Paquiro." *Tauromaquia completa*. 1836. Madrid: Turner, 1983.

Orts-Ramos, Tomás (Uno al Sesgo). *El arte de ver los toros: Guía del espectador*. Barcelona: Fiesta Brava, [1929].

———. "Bibliografía taurina." A listing of *Death in the Afternoon (La muerte en la tarde)* by Ernest Hemingway. *Toros y toreros en 1933*. Barcelona: Fiesta Brava, 1933. 333–34.

———. "Libros de toros: Un rato a bibliografía, II." Rev. of *Death in the Afternoon (La muerte en la tarde)* by Ernest Hemingway. *La Fiesta Brava* (7 April 1933): 2–3.

———. *Los ases del toreo: Estudio crítico biográfico de los primeros diestros de la actualidad*. 48 pamphlets. Barcelona: Ediciones Lux, 1920–1931.

Reynolds, Michael. *Hemingway: The 1930s*. New York: Norton, 1997.

———. *Hemingway's Reading, 1910–1940: An Inventory*. Princeton, Princeton UP, 1981.

Rosenblum, Robert. "Cubism as Pop Art." In *Modern Art and Popular Culture: Readings in High and Low*. Eds. Kirk Varnedoe and Adam Gropnik. New York: Harry N. Abrams, 1990. 116–32.

Sáenz de Heredia, Cesáreo (El Bachiller Garrocha). *Las corridas de toros en la actualidad*. 2nd ed. Madrid: Impresa Hijos de Gómez Fuentenebro, 1914.

Sánchez del Arco, Manuel (Giraldillo). "Informaciones taurinas: 'Los Toros' de José María Izquierdo a José María de Cossío." *ABC* (1 March 1944): 16.

Scholes, Robert. *Semiotics and Interpretation.* New Haven: Yale UP, 1982.

Serrano García-Vaõ, Manuel (Dulzuras). *Catecismo taurino: Breve compendio de conocimientos útiles a los aficionados a los toros.* Rev. ed. Madrid: Hijos de R. Álvarez, 1913.

Smith, Rex, comp. "The Album of Roberto Domingo." In *Biography of the Bulls: An Anthology of Spanish Bullfighting.* Ed. Rex Smith. New York: Rinehart, 1957. 280–89.

*Sol y Sombra.* "Días en que se celebran generalmente corridas de toros propiamente dichas en los principales circos taurinos de España. Francia y Portugal." *Vademécum taurino por la redacción de Sol y Sombra.* Madrid: Ginés Carrión, 1909. 255–59.

Stephens, Robert O. *Hemingway's Non-fiction: The Public Voice.* Chapel Hill: U of North Carolina P, 1968.

Thurston, Michael. "Genre, Gender, and Truth in *Death in the Afternoon*." *The Hemingway Review* 17.2 (1998): 47–63.

"Un novillo de Conradi mata al diestro Alcalareño II." *ABC* (25 August 1931): 39.

Uno as Sesgo. *See* Orts-Ramos, Tomás.

Varnedoe, Kirk, and Adam Gopnik. *High and Low: Modern Art and Popular Culture.* Exhibition Catalogue, Museum of Modern Art, New York, 1990–1991. New York: Harry N. Abrams, 1990.

Vázquez, Leopoldo, et al. *La tauromaquia escrita por D. Leopoldo Vázquez, D. Luis Gandullo y D. Leopoldo López de Sáa bajo la dirección técnica del célebre diestro cordobés Rafael Guerra, "Guerrita."* 2 vols. Madrid, 1896.

Watts, Emily Stipes. *Ernest Hemingway and the Arts.* Urbana: U of Illinois P, 1971.

Winterowd, W. Ross. *The Rhetoric of the "Other" Literature.* Carbondale: Southern Illinois UP, 1990.

On Authorship and Art

# "Prejudiced through Experience": *Death in the Afternoon* and the Problem of Authorship

*Hilary K. Justice*

> *All art is only done by the individual.*
> Death in the Afternoon, 99
>
> *[I]t is always a mistake to know an author.*
> Death in the Afternoon, 144
>
> *The critic, out on a limb, is more fun to see than a mountain lion.*
> Ernest Hemingway, "Interview," 58

IN *DEATH IN THE AFTERNOON*, Ernest Hemingway locates public, or published, art within a discursive matrix that is at once individual, artistic, aesthetic, professional, social and cultural. He insists that "All art is only done by the individual" (99), but admits the matrix as a necessity without which art cannot reach its publics. On nearly every page he critiques this matrix for the decadent compromises it works on art and its participants. In *Death in the Afternoon*, Hemingway metacritically argues that bullfighting — and, by analogy, any published art form — comprises a symbiotic dialogue between an artist and the public. This dialogue consists of the exchange of fiscal, cultural, and critical capital; the nature of the exchange inevitably, Hemingway insists, introduces mutations to the art form and to the artist. Against such mutations he proposes knowledge: specifically, an educated public.

*Death in the Afternoon*'s Author / Old lady dialogues are central to Hemingway's metacritical and pedagogical agendas. In these dialogues, Hemingway deconstructs the discursive exchange between an artist and art's publics to illustrate the dangers intrinsic to that exchange. He first illustrates how his narrator, a writer, becomes additionally a character named "Author" through interaction with a lowest-common-denominator public (personified by another character, the Old lady). He then instructs his readers to judge the Author's product as lacking in quality when compared to that of the narrator. Within Hemingway's logic, writer and author are necessarily connected but not synonymous: the writer is the individual artist, someone who *does,* whereas authorship is a professional role, distinguishable from the writer by being no less a product of writing than are the characters that the writer creates.¹ When Hemingway began writing *Death in the Afternoon,* he was already aware of the extent to which he was becoming a brand name author (a condition he would both court and resist for the rest of his career), and he had begun to glimpse how potentially detrimental the interest created by his public persona might be to his private writerly self, to his writing, and to his readers' experience of that writing.

*Death in the Afternoon*'s Author / Old lady dialogues were designed, in part, to alleviate a problem that the book as a whole was destined to exacerbate: the inescapable and multivalent problem of being "Ernest Hemingway, author." Hemingway's growing disdain for the mechanisms of art production, and, consequently, for his own implication in them, manifests itself in the text in three related ways: first, in his analogies between bullfighting and writing, or more precisely, in the conflicts between art and business that both bullfighting and writing share; second, in his distinctions between the quality of artistic endeavor and the decay to which it is inevitably susceptible within the processes of art publication; and, finally, in his somewhat idealistic faith in education (of the audience, by the artist) as the means by which to check the decadent trends in art perpetuated by the economic mechanisms of art production, in bullfighting, in writing, and, by implication, in all published or public art forms.

Hemingway understood the problem of authorship (or, as he first called it, "professional writing") from two angles. By the time he began writing *Death in the Afternoon,* the success of his first two novels and his quasi-autobiographical tone had begun to shift the focus of "Hemingway" criticism from product to person. The second angle, which complicates the first, is the linguistic convention that obfuscates the distinction between product and person — the tendency to use a writer's name either to reference the person or to metonymously signify the writing.² A further complication, the one around which the metacriticism implicit in the Author / Old lady dialogues coalesces, lies in common and sometimes critical usage of the word *author,* a word which may refer to the private man, the creative writer, and / or to the intrinsically public roles the man / writer plays in relation to his work. Thus criticism of "Hemingway" (his writing) may morph into criticism of "Hemingway" (the person) without any linguistic cues to alert the reader — and sometimes the critic — that the critical terrain has shifted. And although the terms *Hemingway* and *criticism* remain the same, the connotations and the stakes change dramatically as the shift occurs, especially for Ernest Hemingway. His role as a professional writer (someone who is implicated within, and dependent upon, the mechanisms of art production and their related receptive discourses) forms the subtext of the Author / Old lady dialogues, perhaps the least understood formal element of *Death in the Afternoon.*

The ambiguity of the term *author* (and, by implication, *Hemingway*) accounts for much of the difficulty of *Death in the Afternoon*. Hemingway used the book as an opportunity to address this ambiguity and to underscore the dangers he locates therein. He provides two important signposts to indicate that these dangers are his subjects. First, he creates an abstract character called "Author," and secondly, he changes genres when that character appears. By using the labeling conventions of drama (in which a character's name precedes each line) to differentiate the Author / Old lady dialogues from the rest of the text, Hemingway underscores that this Author is as much an "artificially constructed character" as the Old lady. Much that is "odd" in *Death in the Afternoon* begins to come clear once one realizes that authorship and publication are as central to the book as bullfighting is, and as applicable to bullfighting as to writing.

Hemingway's metacritical project, subtly present in *Death in the Afternoon*, resides in the complex analogy between the art and business of bullfighting and the art and business of writing. Hemingway's generic term for bullfighters and writers is *artists;* his generic term for what they do is *art*. Bullfighters and writers are artists, honing and developing their art; *picador, banderillero, matador,* and *author* are professional titles, referring to the roles these artists play in bringing their art to a public. Hemingway's is a modernist allegory; he achieves it through form (by juxtaposition) and through genre (by switching from expository prose to dramatic dialogue to short fiction), without warning or explanation.

The Author / Old lady dialogues are presented as a play in which the Author, initially indistinguishable from the narrator, is easily mistaken for the author of the book. As the dialogues develop, Hemingway separates the Author from the narrator, thus revealing the Author as a character. The Author is not so much unmasked as revealed to be a mask worn by Hemingway, the mask superimposed on his writerly identity by public — especially critical — perception. By naming this masking character *Author,* Hemingway aimed for several ends: 1. to distinguish between "writer" and "author" (a difficult task); 2. to remind his reviewers that their business was to address his writing, not his image (a consummation devoutly to be wished); 3. to reveal his reviewers' inadequacies where warranted (a plan that backfired); and 4. to argue that what should matter most — to himself, to his reviewers, to his readers — is the quality of his writing, not his public persona.

The apostrophic nature of these characters (their burlesque personification of single character traits) further refines Hemingway's generic distinction and clarifies his project: the dialogues are not merely a dramatic script, but comprise a morality play, one in which Hemingway demonstrates and delivers his sermon on the mount against the dangers of professional authorship. Because *Death in the Afternoon*'s metacritical morality play comprises Hemingway's response to specific extratextual circumstances, an explication of the embedded play's structure and internal logic best begins, likewise, outside the text, with a reconstruction of the conditions that crystallized Hemingway's awareness of the problem and that catalyzed his response.

Hemingway first identified the negative effects of authorship after having undergone the process of publishing *A Farewell to Arms*, although he had begun to suspect them years earlier. In a letter to his editor, Max Perkins, Hemingway complained about the changes he was asked to make in order to see that novel into print. Although these concessions were relatively minor (replacing profanity with dashes and softening certain anatomical references), Hemingway objected on principle, concluding that "I have become a Professional Writer [. . .] — Than which there isn't anything lower" (qtd. in Bruccoli, 119).

Necessary concessions, however galling, did not provide Hemingway's only impetus toward a pedagogical crusade for artist / audience solidarity against the decadent effects of art production on art and artist. By the late 1920s, he had begun to receive invitations to write celebrity articles for magazines (invitations he would soon begin to accept). One such invitation came from Henry Goddard Leach, the editor of *The Forum* magazine. Leach wrote Hemingway two letters that bracketed the 1929 publication of *A Farewell to Arms*. The first addresses a him as a creative writer, the second as a public figure, an author. Leach's letters irritated Hemingway so thoroughly that in response he wrote or modified three short texts, all related to *Death in the Afternoon*. The first letter resulted in the short story "The Sea Change" and in two unpublished pieces — one on bullfighting (KL / EH file 681A), and one on a soldier's death in the First World War (KL / EH file 734–35), topically related to "A Natural History of the Dead" (Smith, 223). Both the timing and the wording of Leach's second letter suggest that it may have inspired the creation of the Author / Old lady dialogues; at the very least, it contributed directly to the Author's introduction to "A Natural History of the Dead," the short story he tells the Old lady in chapter 12.[3]

In his first letter, dated 28 June 1929 (and thus prior to the publication of *A Farewell to Arms*), Leach requested a short story "of about two thousand words in length" and gave instructions as to its form:

> As the FORUM reaches not only trained readers but the general public the story must contain narrative or at least plot. In other words it must not be merely a sketch. (KL / EH, Leach Correspondence)[4]

Paul Smith notes that "in some forty words the editor managed to raise Hemingway's ire with misconceptions of the reading public, narrative or plot, and what is 'merely' a sketch" (223). Worse, he implicitly challenged Hemingway's artistic judgment by presuming to tell Hemingway how to write.

Hemingway predictably turned combative. His first response to Leach introduces an (unpublished) series entitled "Unsuited to Our Needs," stating, as Smith notes, "'Let us see what we can do in twelve hundred and sixty-two words' — the word count on his fair copy of 'The Sea Change'" (Smith, 223; KL / EH files 680 and 681). In this story, a woman is leaving her male lover for a woman; the narrative obliquely suggests that her reasons and the man's reaction may have something to do with writing and publication. The word count links "The Sea Change" to Leach's letter, thus supporting Robert Fleming's argument that the male lover, Phil, whose profession is never mentioned, is a writer who holds nothing sacred but is compelled to publish intimacies that for most people remain private. Fleming's argument is based on the woman's remark that "We're made up of all sorts of things. You've known that. You've used it well enough" (Fleming, 216; Hemingway, "Sea Change," 400). How Phil has "used" this knowledge is less important to understanding "The Sea Change" than to understanding how the compulsion to write and to publish were beginning to erode Hemingway's personal privacy in the early 1930s.

Hemingway used everything in his writing, and he bridled at attempts to censor or shape his material or his style. He did not need — and clearly did not like — to be told how to write. How he wrote was still a private matter, and, if "Sea Change" is any indication, a sensitive one. It was not (yet, to him) an object for direct public consumption.

Leach's second letter, dated 2 May 1930, was written after the publication of *A Farewell to Arms* and its reviews; by then, Hemingway had started to write *Death in the Afternoon*.[5] This letter touched an even more sensitive nerve. In it, Leach does not presume to tell the author of *A Farewell to Arms* how to write; instead, and, to Hemingway, more intrusively, he tells him what to write:

> I am writing to place before you a suggestion which I hope and believe will be worthy of your serious consideration.
>
> As editor of The FORUM magazine, I have been publishing each month [. . .] an article by some well known scientist, philosopher, or author in which each of these people has attempted to set forth his intimate beliefs. [. . .] Among those who have contributed [are] Theodore Dreiser, Irving Babbitt, John Dewey, Sir Arthur Keith, James Truslow Adams, H. L. Mencken, and Dr. Albert Einstein. You will see by this list that most of these contributors are elderly men. [. . .]
>
> To put it briefly, what we want from you is a statement of your personal credo, your convictions and beliefs concerning the nature of the world and of man. It would necessarily be suggestive since it would have to touch intimately on your own hopes and fears, the mainspring of your faith or the promptings of your despair.

> For such an article [...] The FORUM offers you $500. [...] (Leach Correspondence, JFK).

Even ignoring the closing insult (that Hemingway would be willing to bare his soul for $500), this letter was grating. Hemingway disliked Mencken, who, as coeditor for *The American Mercury,* had rejected several of his early stories (Reynolds, *Paris Years,* 234–35). Leach's use of titles and honorifics was pretentious; his pointing out the uniform age of the eminent personages, condescending. And with its name-dropping, Leach's letter panders to Hemingway's new status as a public figure, to the detriment of his status as writer. Why should Ernest Hemingway's intimate feelings matter more to readers than his fiction writing?

Leach's requests and instructions provide the sounding board from which *Death in the Afternoon*'s Author / Old lady dialogues echo. His request for a "personal credo," to address "the nature of the world and of man," and to reveal "the mainspring of [his] faith or the promptings of [his] despair," are reflected in the Author's anticipation of the Old lady's criticism (specifically, in chapter 12, *DIA,* 132) and by his anticipation of her desire for a different kind of story with different content:

> [Author:] What would you like to have? More major truths about the passions of the race? [...] A few bright thoughts on death and dissolution? Or would you care to hear about the author's experience with a porcupine during his earliest years [...]?
>
> [Old lady:] Please, sir, no more about animals to-day.
>
> What do you say to one of those homilies on life and death that delight an author to write?
>
> I cannot truly say I want that either. (*DIA,* 132–33)

In this exchange, Hemingway turns the tables on Leach (and others of similar ilk) who would pre-empt his creative agency: the Author does just that to the Old lady's agency, granting her only enough room to protest his suggestions weakly before he steamrolls her with even more outrageous ones, culminating in his "giving" her "A Natural History of the Dead" — a story she is guaranteed not to like, despite the fact that it meets her criteria of having "conversation" and being something "of a sort I've never read, amusing, yet instructive" (133). Although her criteria differ from Leach's "general reader's," she, like Leach, gives writing instructions: Leach's demand for "narrative or at least plot" has become her request for "conversation," or at least novelty.

Despite the fact that the Old lady interrupts the narrative of "A Natural History of the Dead" by complaining that it is "not amusing" (137) and by wondering, halfway through it, when it will start (140), she persists in asking for something she will like. Her request recalls Leach's second letter in that she, too, tells the Author what to write, and she, too, asks not for fiction but memoir. Having learned her lesson about the Author's fiction with "A Natural History of the Dead," she asks instead for stories that the Author "knows" about the "unfortunate people" (by which she means homosexuals) in the Paris cafés — like Leach (in his second letter), she wants titillation, not art.

The Author complies and delivers an anecdote, but only after he has warned her that it will "lack drama as do all tales of abnormality since no one can predict what will happen in the abnormal while all tales of the normal end much the same" (180). Undaunted, she insists, and, quite predictably, she dislikes this story, finding the content boring and the craft weak, because it lacks the obvious "wow" with which "stories" ended "in her youth" (182). She is unsatisfiable: she asks for a story and is disappointed that it is not an anecdote; she insists on an anecdote and, having been warned that it is not a story, is still disappointed that it is not a story. Her final judgment is that the Author is no good, and his final judgment is to throw her out of the book (190).

When she exits, the Author also disappears, revealing that his existence depended on hers. The voice that delivers news of this ejection may seem to be his own, but since the first person plural is employed, the narrative identity is changing: "Where is the Old lady? She's gone. *We* threw her out of the book, finally" (190; emphasis added). This "we" may merely continue the pompous tone of the Author, yet both Author and narrator were, previously, "I." The plural refers to the momentary hybridity of the narrative voices — Author and writer. After this brief passage, the plural disappears, because the reader has seen the last of the Author.

Halfway through the book, then, one is finally given enough information to understand why one has been reading a play in the middle of an encyclopedia about bullfighting. Only retrospectively can the Author / Old lady dialogues' internal logic and their function within the larger text become clear. Initially, they recreate for the reader the transitional moment at which a writer, represented by the narrator, assumes an additional role, the discursive nexus represented by the character of the Author. Subsequently, the dialogues deliver Hemingway's consequent judgment on the relative value of these two roles within the process of art production.

Hemingway opens the bullfighting discussion in *Death in the Afternoon* with a lesson for the novice spectator regarding the mutating compromises that an uneducated public can unwittingly force on an art form. In chapter 1, he illustrates the dangers of spectator ignorance in terms of the horses in the bullring whose disemboweling was then the object of public concern. He reports that

> These visceral accidents, as I write this, are no longer a part of the Spanish bullfight, as under the government of Primo de Rivera it was decided to protect the abdomens of the horses with a sort of quilted mattress designed in the terms of the decree "to avoid those horrible sights which so disgust foreigners and tourists." (7)

But, he notes, although the "sights" are avoided, the mattresses

> in no way decrease the pain suffered by the horses; they take away much of the bravery from the bull, [. . .] and they are the first step toward the suppression of the bullfight. The bullfight is a Spanish institution; it has not existed because of the foreigners and tourists, but always in spite of them and any step to modify it to secure their approval, which it will never have, is a step towards its complete suppression. (8)

Hemingway is clearly subscribing to the "well-wrought urn" definition of art (that no single element constitutes the whole, but all affect it):

> If [the audience senses] the meaning and end of the whole thing even when they know nothing about it; feel that this thing they do not understand is going on, the business of the horses is no more than an incident. If they get no feeling of the whole tragedy naturally they will react emotionally to the most picturesque incident [. . .] The aficionado [. . .] may be said, broadly, then, to be one who has this sense of the tragedy and ritual of the fight so that the minor aspects are not important except as they relate to the whole. (8–9)

The lesson for the novice spectator is clear. It is not "You must love bullfighting," but, rather, "If you cannot judge the whole, do not base your judgment of the whole on parts whose connections you do not see." And, more urgently, "Do not demand the removal or modification of those parts you do not understand or which, for reasons unrelated to the whole, you disapprove of." In the economy of art, such partial judgments can lead to changes to the whole that will detract from the experience of those who understand and appreciate the work of art in its entirety.

Hemingway's concerns over the damages wrought by a financially powerful but artistically uninformed audience applied not only to bullfighting but to his own art as well, given his experience publishing *A Farewell to Arms* that prompted his "Professional Writer" complaint to Perkins. Scribner's had objected to his use of the word "fucking" in that text on legal and moral grounds, but Hemingway was quick to perceive the financial reality that at best coexisted with these grounds and at worst constituted the truth behind them. The analogy between literary censorship (an effort not to alienate squeamish book buyers) and the padding of the horses (to placate squeamish foreigners) is clear: both changes pandered to an audience whose power lay in its pocketbook.

By 1930, Hemingway was fairly free of such pressure. On the basis of his previous successes (*The Sun Also Rises* and *A Farewell to Arms*), and with the financial backing of his wealthy uncle-in-law Gus Pfeiffer, he could finally write the book he had planned for years, without worrying about critical or popular success. For the first time in his career, he believed that he could enact his own authority with little concern for the consequences.

Hemingway begins his discussion of his writing by introducing his project and illustrating his technique (a kind of *novillada* for literature). He announces that he will try "only to tell honestly the things I have found true [. . .] to be altogether frank, or to try to be." He expects that his critics and his readers will judge him, rather than his work: "if those who read this decide with disgust that it is written by some one who lacks their, the readers', fineness of feeling I can only plead that this may be true" (1). Anticipating this personal judgment, which he dismisses as irrelevant, he presents the only criterion that he considers valid: a reader "can only truly make such a judgment when he, or she, has seen the things that are spoken of and knows truly what their reactions to them would be" (1). At the outset, Hemingway acknowledges the widening gap between his writerly goals and his professional image, a gap created by the fact that his critics were paying too much attention to his public persona and not enough to his writing.

Hemingway was setting a trap. "If you pay the right kind of attention as you read this book," he implies, "you will understand my writing. But if you bring to it only preconceptions (as people are wont to do with bullfighting, and as critics are wont to do with my work), not only will you miss the point, but you will miss a point I have made so obvious that you will be proven the fool."

Because this presumably nonfiction text begins in first person singular narration, readers may assume that the narrator's voice and Ernest Hemingway's are one and the same. Soon, however, Hemingway begins to draw a subtle, practical distinction between "the author" and "I":

> This that has been written [. . .] is not put in because of a desire of the author to write about himself and his own reactions, considering them as important and taking delight in them because they are his, but rather to establish the fact that the reactions were instant and unexpected.

and

> I did not become indifferent to the fate of the horses through [. . .] callousness. (8)

In these adjacent sentences, "the author" and "I" both seem to refer to Hemingway. But the awkwardness of the passive construction in the first sentence ("this that has been written [. . .] is not put in") contrasts so sharply with the active directness of the second ("I did not become indifferent") that the two sentences command the reader's close attention. The first anticipates criticism that the passive author will receive (that is, that he has an ego problem); the second asserts agency. Hemingway will clarify this distinction (the "author" as a passive, receptive role vs. "I" as an active force) as the book progresses, according to the following system: "I" experience, "the writer" writes, and "the author" is a public, professional role, a one-dimensional mask that may be mistaken for the writer and the man behind it.

Before the narrative voice splits into the two distinct writer / Author voices, it describes with careful precision the process whereby experience becomes writing. The narrator states that "the problem was one of depiction" (the writer's task), and, to illustrate the point, he recounts "what it was" that was "important" about Domingo Hernandorena's goring:

> waking in the night I tried to remember what it was that seemed just out of my remembering and that was the thing that I had really seen and, finally, remembering all around it, I got it. When he stood up, his face white and dirty and the silk of his breeches opened from waist to knee, it was the dirtiness of the rented breeches, the dirtiness of his slit underwear and the clean, clean, unbearably clean whiteness of the thigh bone that I had seen. (20)

This is clearly a writer's voice, finding and focusing on the detail that enables him to transform experience into writing. This voice will change with the appearance of the Old lady in chapter 7, and it will eventually give way to a caricature named "Author," from which one learns little about writing, the writer, or bullfighting (or, finally, anything but his scorn for the Old lady).

The inclusion of the Old lady — her ignorance, her preconceptions, and her judgments — enables Hemingway to represent the medium of exchange between artist and public, an interactive but usually inarticulate medium that necessarily changes the artist, and not for the better. Like the introduction of the padding on the horses, these interactions represent a mutation of form. Textually, they occur within a mutation of form (a Bunyanesque interplay of prose and drama); they inherently present a mutation of form (in which the narrator becomes the Author); and they address a mutation of form (in the Old lady's criticism of "The Natural History of the Dead" and the anecdote about homosexuals in Paris).

In the nine Author / Old lady dialogues, several things happen:

1. The narrative voice gradually splits into two, one retaining its original tone and purpose (to discuss bullfighting), and the other becoming, by chapter 9, an abstract character named "Author."

2. This character introduces the Old lady to several things about professional bullfighting, professional writing, and their attendant dangers.
3. The Old lady character becomes a literary critic, then a personal one, and confuses the two. Meanwhile the Author character becomes abrasive, smug, and condescending.
4. The Author and the Old lady are thrown out of the book by the original narrator.

The first-person narration of the first six chapters slides invisibly into the lines of the Author (63). Later, however, Hemingway sets the Author's lines apart from the rest of the text as he does with the Old lady's throughout (the Author is first labeled on page 93). The deliberate invisibility of this transition emphasizes Hemingway's point — that the narrator / writer has invisibly (and inevitably) "become" the Author through his interaction with this conservative public, represented by the Old lady. He further underscores this transition, topically, in the Author's second labeled line, which addresses a similar professional transition: "[the restaurant] is full of politicians who are becoming statesmen as one watches them" (93). "Politicians" is their métier; the "statesmen" label is their professional role, here endowed by the gaze of their public (the "watching" audience). Only in retrospect is it obvious that the narrator / writer has similarly "become" the Author as — and because — one has been watching "him."

The Old lady remains static; the narrator-cum-writer devolves. He eventually becomes "the Author" through his engagement with her as "his" public, literally performing Hemingway's thesis that economic pressures and publication endanger art and the artist, making them both susceptible to "decadence" (in the sense of "decay"), a word that, like authorship, has "from loose using lost [its] edge" (71).

In the earliest Author / Old lady dialogues, the narrative voice is nearly indistinguishable from that of previous chapters. It delivers much the same information as the narrator, listing the matadors of the day (70) and (appropriately, if pompously) alluding to the dual connotations of the word "decadence" (71). The same voice will caution the Old lady against starting "your writer to talking of words" and alerting her to the dangers of linguistic ambiguity, since terms "cannot mean the same to all" (71). It is crucial that the identity of the voice also be ambiguous in this early dialogue in order that the distinction may be seen as a process of mutation and decay. By transforming this unnamed didactic voice — what the critics would name "the author" — into the Author character, Hemingway underscores that the word *author*, like the apt word *decadence*, is itself susceptible to multiple meanings, depending on one's perspective.

As the dialogue continues, the Old lady's presence proves that, like "A bullfighter," an Author "will not be better than his audience very long" (163). The Old lady soon begins to ask stupid questions ("But surely the horse could not permanently replace those [lost internal] organs with sawdust?" [92]), and to deliver insipid observations ("I find it [that replacement] very cleanly, that is if the sawdust be pure and sweet" — in other words, she opines that sawdust is clean if it is clean [92]). At this point, the narrator begins to lose patience. Within a page, this exasperation is given its own voice, labeled "Author." The narrator will co-exist with this newly named voice; which one "speaks" depends on the presence of the Old lady. From now on, the value of the Old lady's questions determines the tone of the Author's response. When she asks serious questions about bullfighters and bulls, she is answered seriously; when she critiques the narrator or the content of his replies, she is answered, increasingly caustically, by the Author:

> *Author:* Madame, rarely will you meet a more prejudiced man nor one who tells himself he keeps his mind more open. But cannot that be because one part of our mind, that which we act with, becomes prejudiced through experience and still we keep another part completely open to observe and judge with?
> *Old lady:* Sir, I do not know.
> *Author:* Madame, neither do I and it may well be that we are talking horseshit. (95)

Within this particular dialogue (92–95), the narrator becomes prejudiced through his experience of the Old lady — and becomes the Author in the process. As the narrator responds to her limited perspective "his" tone changes from humorous to irascible to sarcastic. Hemingway thus articulates the split between the Author, who has become "prejudiced through experience," and the writer, whose mind remains "completely open."

The power of the Old lady's limited perception determines the identity of the Author. Once the Old lady's attention turns entirely away from the bullfights to treat the narrator as an authority not on bullfighting or words, but rather on "the gentleman smoking the cigar," "those things he is eating," and where to dine (93), the Author is given his label. The formal presentation of the dialogue now has two labeled parts, "Author" and "Old lady"; it has become a script for a play. This Author responds to the Old lady's attention by toying with her, thus isolating "another part" of the now disjunct narrative voice in order that it may remain "completely open to observe and judge."

When delivering information about bullfighting and writing, the Author is indistinguishable from the original first-person narrator. When the Old lady asks stupid, random questions, Hemingway labels the Author's lines, thus distinguishing between "I" as narrator and "I" as abstract character, one aspect of whose identity (authority) has been magnified to the elision of the rest. This dialogue ends with the Old lady's dramatically ironic line "I must learn to use these terms correctly" (95); the term she least understands is *Author*.

Immediately after discarding the Author and the Old lady, the narrator (now back in the first person) turns his attention to the critics. He quotes and replies to a critical piece by Aldous Huxley, "Foreheads Villainous Low," in which Huxley accused Hemingway of "feign[ing] stupidity":

> In [naming a book by this writer] Mr. H. ventures, once, to name an Old Master. There is a phrase, quite admirably expressive [here Mr. Huxley inserts a compliment], a single phrase, no more, about "the bitter nail-holes" of Mantegna's Christs; then quickly, quickly, appalled by his own temerity, the author passes on (as Mrs. Gaskell might hastily have passed on, if she had somehow been betrayed into mentioning a water-closet), passes on, shamefacedly, to speak once more of Lower Things.
>
> "There was a time, not so long ago, when the stupid and uneducated aspired to be thought intelligent and cultured. The current of aspiration has changed its direction. It is not at all uncommon now to find intelligent and cultured people doing their best to feign stupidity and to conceal the fact that they have received an education" — and more; more in Mr. Huxley's best educated vein which is a highly educated vein indeed.
>
> What about that, you say? Mr. Huxley scores there, all right, all right. What have you to say to that? (190)

The narrator proceeds "to answer truly" (190). He insists that authorship is but a performance, a seeming, and that writing is what matters. He begins,

> I believe it is more than a question of simulation or avoidance of the appearance of culture. When writing a novel a writer should create living people; people not characters. A *character* is a caricature. (191)

As are the "Author" and "Old lady."

> If a writer can make people live there may be no great characters in his book, but it is possible that his book will remain as a whole; as an entity; as a novel. If the people the writer is making talk of old masters; of music; of modern painting; of letters; or of science then they should talk of those subjects in the novel. If they do not talk of those subjects and the writer makes them talk of them he is a faker, and if he talks about them himself to show how much he knows then he is showing off. (191)

As has the "Author."

> No matter how good a phrase or a simile he may have if he puts it in where it is not absolutely necessary and irreplaceable he is spoiling his work for egotism. (191).

As did the "Author."

> People in a novel, not skillfully constructed *characters,* must be projected from the writer's assimilated experience, from his knowledge, from his heart and from all there is of him. If he ever has luck as well as seriousness and gets them out entire they will have more than one dimension and they will last a long time. (191)

Neither the "Author" nor the "Old lady" has more than one dimension; having just been thrown out of the book by the narrator, they will not last — nor, by this logic, should they.

> If a writer of prose knows enough about what he is writing about he may omit things that he knows and the reader, if the writer is writing truly enough, will have a feeling of those things as strongly as though the writer had stated them. The dignity of movement of an ice-berg is due to only one-eighth of it being above water. (192)

There has been nothing "dignified" about the Author / Old lady dialogues; here that is revealed as deliberate.

> A writer who omits things because he does not know them only makes hollow places in his writing. A writer who appreciates the seriousness of writing so little that he is anxious to make people see he is formally educated, cultured or well-bred is merely a popinjay. (192)

As was the "Author," the guise assumed by Hemingway in the construction of the dialogues.

Given the choice between "the simulation or avoidance of the appearance of culture" and "writing," Hemingway chooses writing. Grammatically, *simulation* and *appearance* are distanced from their verbal actions by nominalization and doubly distanced by their combination: the "simulation of appearance" is effectively "seeming to seem." Even the literal actions that these words signify (*simulate* and *appear*) are static, snapshots of performances (for an implied audience) rather than real actions. Huxley's performative criticism of Hemingway is thus turned back on itself. Through Hemingway's response, Huxley is revealed as the performative author as we watch, and Hemingway emerges as the writer.

The difference that the narrative voice underscores in Hemingway's "true answer" is precisely the difference between "seems to seem" (or authorship) versus "does" (writing). In these two-and-a-half pages, Hemingway uses the words *writing* and *writer* twenty-two times, proposing the act of writing as an antidote to Authorial poison. Hemingway is not Author; the Author is but an apostrophic caricature, an abstraction of "the decay of a complete art through a magnification of certain of its aspects" (70). The Author's existence is entirely discursive and dependent on the presence of his public, the Old lady (who is more obviously a caricature, one of the "general reader" assumed for Hemingway by the editors, publishers, and critics who policed his language and his subject matter). With the disappearance of the Author, the inclusion of an author / critic (Huxley), and the linguistically insistent resurgence of the writer, Hemingway makes clear the meaning of the Author / Old lady dialogues. Writing subtly and well was Hemingway's antidote to seeming, and his best revenge against those who would have him seem.

Initial critical response to *Death in the Afternoon* confirmed and exacerbated the problem of being "Ernest Hemingway, author" by identifying two audiences for the book: readers interested in bullfighting and readers interested in Hemingway (Coates, 115; Hicks, 163; Duffus, noting the book's certain appeal to "Hemingway addicts," 113). Despite wondering why Hemingway had written a book on bullfighting (Cowley, 120), critics universally accepted him as an authority on that subject. They also accepted him, somewhat grudgingly, as an authority on his own writing, but most seemed baffled as to why he had to muddy an otherwise perfectly good book on bullfighting by talking about himself (one critic, Patterson, noted that "the semi-autobiographical details" made him "faintly sick" [118]). Cowley and Hicks, at least, realized that Hemingway was deliberately structuring his chapters to underscore the similarities he perceived between the two art forms. But generally, critics who were sharp enough to realize that the book was "something more" than a tauromachic guide nonetheless floundered in their efforts to identify what that "something more" was. Granville Hicks, like many others (for example, Duffus, 113; Coates, 115; Patterson, 118; Cowley, 121; Mencken, 123) concluded it was about the author. When Hicks reviewed *Death in the Afternoon* for *The Nation* in 1932, he wrote that "more people will read the book because they are interested in Hemingway than will . . . because they are interested in bullfighting." He continued:

> Fortunately, the author, fully aware of the interest in his personality, has made a vigorous effort to put as much of himself as possible into his book. As a rule, these intimate revelations are placed, for the convenience of the author . . . as well as for the convenience of the reader, at the end of each chapter. At first they take the form of dialogues between the author and an old lady. [. . .] Later on [. . .] the old lady disappears, and the author speaks directly to his readers. (163)

Although Hicks noticed the structural and tonal differences between the sections on writing and the Author / Old lady dialogues, he missed Hemingway's important distinction. The end-of-chapter dialogues are with the "Author" character, and not with the author, Hemingway. The author, fully aware of the interest in his personality, had provided a burlesque Hemingway, a windmill for his critics' jousting practice, and he placed them at the end of the chapters because they were a different genre entirely. Distracted by the sweeping red cape of authorship, critics mistook the caricature for the writer behind it.

That distinction is central to Hemingway's project; that distinction is what unifies the book's seemingly disparate genres — the "Baedeker of bulls" (Cowley, 121), the essays on writing, the dramatic Author / Old lady dialogues, and the short story called "A Natural History of the Dead." One reviewer, confused by the generic shifts, described his reading experience as feeling "like a chameleon on a patchwork quilt" (Duffus, 113). Like his colleagues, he did not see that the parts cohered into a unified pedagogical and metacritical project.

The critic whom Hemingway manipulated most effectively with *Death in the Afternoon* was H. L. Mencken, whose review in *The American Mercury* applauds the writing in the bullfighting sections even as it misses the pointed institutional critique in the Author / Old lady dialogues. Mencken identifies the Old lady not as a representation of institutional assumptions regarding readership but as Hemingway's own idea of his readers, as Hemingway's perception of some "common denominator of all the Ladies' Aid Societies of his native Oak Park, Ill" (123). Although Hemingway clearly had the "Ladies' Aid" type in mind when he created the Old lady,[6] and although he was never averse to slighting the "broad lawns and narrow minds" of Oak Park, his motives were more complex. His object was not merely to taunt that element of his readership, but to reveal that they were a construction of the publishing industry, of discourses in which critics like Mencken participated. Thus when Mencken missed Hemingway's critique of this assumption, he implicated himself in that very critique. In his conclusion that Hemingway's graphic description of groin-goring would "give the Oak Park W.C.T.U. [Women's Christian Temperance Union] another conniption fit" and "[t]hat the Hemingway boy is really a case" (124), Mencken committed a spectacular rhetorical error, unwittingly revealing his own implication with the system under Hemingway's scrutiny, committing the very crime Hemingway accused it of.

Neither the Old lady nor the Author is real; they are abstractions, burlesques of assumptions made by those forces that irresponsibly enact their own authority over art production. *Death in the Afternoon* thus presents, in microcosm, Hemingway's lover's quarrel with his profession. Hemingway chose as the object of his point those purported experts ("authorities") who, although they derived benefit (indeed, their professional existence) from the economic matrix of art production, were nonetheless blind to its intrinsic dangers. He used the book as an opportunity not only to consider "critics and their shortcomings," but to provide these critics with the opportunity either to overcome or prove these shortcomings, each according to his abilities. Like a skilled matador with a bull, Hemingway metaphorically forced his worst critics to "turn in less than their turning radius," using their own momentum and limitations to bring them to their knees. Coming off the popular success of *A Farewell to Arms,* Hemingway did not feel he needed redemption. Only his detractors — certain critics — would have argued that redemption was necessary. They, least of all, would be inclined to see *Death in the Afternoon* as redemptive; they, least of all, would take its point. His manipulation of his critics was, however, too subtle. Hemingway had seriously miscalculated his own authority; his reputation, at least, would require more redemption after *Death in the Afternoon* than before it.

His antagonism for his critics was his public response to the problem of being "Ernest Hemingway, author."Knowing that they would comment on the author of *Death in the Afternoon,* he readied for them a straw man, one designed to illustrate and emphasize that an author — like the Author — is a social construct, an economically and discursively defined entity. In *Death in the Afternoon,* Hemingway thus warns his readers not to confuse the author with the man, and, most emphatically, not to trust the judgment of any critic who cannot tell the difference. So warns the Author, in response to Old lady's "criticism," "I like you less and less the more I know you": "Madame, it is always a mistake to know an author" (144).

Despite the fact that the Author deserves her negative judgment just as thoroughly as she deserves his, it is tempting to assume that Hemingway's sympathies lie entirely with his Author. To do so is to fall into the trap. They lie with neither Author nor Old lady, but with the writer, lying awake at night, trying to remember the "clean, clean, unbearably clean whiteness" of Domingo Hernandorena's thigh bone and its contrast to his dirty underwear. Hemingway's sympathies lie with the writer, with himself-as-writer, whose unbearably clean prose would, for the rest of his life, be confused with its author's dirty linen. The problem of being "Ernest Hemingway, author," was inescapable and insoluble as long as the writer was also an author, as much a product of the writer writing as the writing itself. Authorship may have been hell, but it was, for Hemingway, a necessary danger.

# Notes

[1] This essay is informed by an extension of Jerome McGann's social theory of textual transmission. In his 1983 volume, *A Critique of Modern Textual Criticism,* McGann

argues that literary authority is result of complex interactions among individuals, institutions, society, and culture. McGann's theory contests the Romantic notion of authority, which holds that literary works are produced in isolation. He rejects the idea that an individual can "author" a work, identifying authorship not as person but as process, one in which the figure commonly identified as "the author" is but one node in a network of textual creation that includes editors, publishers, reviewers, etc. "Authority," McGann insists, "is a social nexus" (48). His insistence upon the intrinsically social quality of authorship and authority would have made sense to Ernest Hemingway. Hemingway's metacritical stance in *Death in the Afternoon* differs from McGann's later argument in two ways. First, Hemingway draws a distinction McGann does not: between writer and author. (In this he anticipates by some sixty years Sean Burke's theoretical call for a "situated embodied authorial subjectivity" [ix] in discourses of authorship.) Further, Hemingway makes a judgment value which McGann does not espouse: that the contextual network required to bring a work of art to its public is intrinsically destructive to the art and to the artist.

[2] Michel Foucault isolates the challenge of the author's name as a catalyst for incomprehension in discourses of authorship, noting that "the links between the proper name and the individual named and between the author's name and what it names are not isomorphic and do not function in the same way." Unlike a proper name, the author's name "performs a certain role with regard to narrative discourse, assuring a classificatory function" (227). *Death in the Afternoon* thus anticipates Foucault's work by several decades, in that it implicitly asks and answers the question, "What is an author?"

[3] Biographer Carlos Baker notes that the Old lady was added relatively late in the writing of the book (214).

[4] In *A Moveable Feast* Hemingway responds to the phrase "mere sketch," using it scathingly, verbatim, from the perspective of a Nobel Prize-winning writer.

[5] Hemingway began working on *Death in the Afternoon* in March of 1930 (Reynolds, *Chronology,* 61; see also the essay by Robert Trogdon, pages 21–41 in this volume).

[6] For a different view of the Old lady figure, see Linda Wagner-Martin's essay on the Gertrude Stein subtext in *Death in the Afternoon,* pages 59–77 in this volume.

# Works Cited

Baker, Carlos. *Ernest Hemingway: A Life Story.* New York: Collier, 1969.

Burke, Sean. *The Death and Return of the Author.* 2nd ed. Edinburgh: Edinburgh UP, 1998.

Bruccoli, Matthew J., ed., with the assistance of Robert W. Trogdon. *The Only Thing that Counts: The Ernest Hemingway–Maxwell Perkins Correspondence 1925–1947.* New York: Scribner's, 1996.

Coates, Robert M. "Bullfighters." *The New Yorker* 8 (1 October 1932): 61–63. Rpt. in *Ernest Hemingway: The Critical Heritage.* Ed. Jeffrey Meyers. London: Routledge, 1982. 160–62.

Cowley, Malcolm. "A Farewell to Spain." *New Republic* 73 (30 November 1932): 76–77. Rpt. in *Ernest Hemingway: The Critical Heritage.* Ed. Jeffrey Meyers. London: Routledge, 1982. 164–69.

Duffus, R. L. "Hemingway Now Writes of Bull-fighting As an Art." *New York Times Book Review* (25 September 1932): 5, 17. Rpt. in *Ernest Hemingway: The Critical Reception.* Ed. Robert O. Stephens. N.p.: Burt Franklin & Co., 1977. 112–13.

Fleming, Robert E. "Perversion and the Writer in 'The Sea Change.'" *Studies in American Fiction* 14 (1986): 215–20.

Foucault, Michel. "What is an Author?" Rpt. in *The Book History Reader.* Eds. David Finkelstein and Alistair McCleery. London: Routledge, 2002. 225–30.

Hemingway, Ernest. *Death in the Afternoon.* New York: Scribner's, 1932.

———. *A Moveable Feast.* New York: Scribner's, 1964.

———. "The Sea Change." 1933. *The Short Stories of Ernest Hemingway.* New York: Scribner's, 1938. 397–401.

———. "The Sea Change" Drafts. Files 222, 679, 680, 681, Hemingway Collection, John F. Kennedy Library, Boston.

———. "Success, It's Wonderful!" Interview with Harvey Breit, *New York Times Book Review* (3 December 1950): 58.

———. "Then It Was Early June." Unpublished manuscript. Files 734, 734a, 735, 735a, Hemingway Collection, John F. Kennedy Library, Boston.

———. Unpublished, untitled bullfighting fragment. File 681A, Hemingway Collection, John F. Kennedy Library, Boston.

Hicks, Granville. "Bulls and Bottles." *The Nation* 135 (9 November 1932): 461. Rpt. in *Ernest Hemingway: The Critical Heritage.* Ed. Jeffrey Meyers. London: Routledge, 1982. 162–64.

Leach, Henry Goddard. Letters to Ernest Hemingway, 28 June 1929 and 2 May 1930. Incoming Correspondence, Hemingway Collection, John F. Kennedy Library, Boston.

*Los Sitios Cubanos de Ernest Hemingway.* Videocassette. Cuba: N.p., n.d.

McGann, Jerome J. *A Critique of Modern Textual Criticism.* 1983. Charlottesville: U of Virginia P, 1992.

Mencken, H. L. "The Spanish Idea of a Good Time." *The American Mercury* 27 (December 1932): 506–7. Rpt. in *Ernest Hemingway: The Critical Heritage.* Ed. Jeffrey Meyers. London: Routledge, 1982. 170–72.

Patterson, Curtis. "The Ancients are Ancients —." *Town & Country* 87 (15 October 1932): 50. Rpt. in *Ernest Hemingway: The Critical Reception.* Ed. Robert O. Stephens. New York: Burt Franklin & Co., 1977. 118–19.

Reynolds, Michael S. *Hemingway: An Annotated Chronology*. Detroit: Omnigraphics, 1991.

———. *Hemingway: The Paris Years*. Oxford: Basil Blackwell, 1989.

Smith, Paul. *A Reader's Guide to the Short Fiction of Ernest Hemingway*. Boston: G. K. Hall, 1989.

# "The Sequence of Motion and Fact": Cubist Collage and Filmic Montage in *Death in the Afternoon*[1]

## Amy Vondrak

ALTHOUGH HEMINGWAY COMMENTED to Max Perkins that he did not go to movies,[2] his statement is inaccurate, and in fact the impact of film is quite apparent in his writing.[3] One of the most lyrical passages in *Death in the Afternoon* creates its effect by juxtaposing images that are not narratively or chronologically connected, as if it were a film montage. It appears in the last chapter of *Death in the Afternoon*:

> The Prado, looking like some big American college building, with sprinklers watering the grass early in the bright Madrid summer morning; the bare white mud hills looking across toward Carabanchel; days on the train in August with the blinds pulled down on the side against the sun and the wind blowing them; chaff blown against the car in the wind from the hard earthen threshing floors; the odor of grain and the stone windmills. (270)

Like the filmic montages that Hemingway saw in D. W. Griffith's *Birth of a Nation* (1915), this passage builds to a powerful emotional climax by piling up disparate images that mix sense impressions (the brightness of the sun, the warmth of summer, the dryness of chaff, the odor of grain), connote motion (of sprinklers, of a train, of the wind), and thus build to an emotional whole that is more than the sum of its parts. This "sequence of motion and fact" (*DIA*, 2) puts "everything in," not by leaving something out, but by combining fragments of experience into a new, larger whole.

This new whole poses new questions: How do we unravel the condensation of time, place, and space in this dense conglomerate? How do we read this new kind of map? One key lies in understanding the workings of montage, particularly filmic montage, in *Death in the Afternoon*. The deliberate juxtapositions of montage work to alter or disrupt conventional relations between time, space, and the audience, to alter the way we read history. *Death in the Afternoon* is, among other things, a history of bullfighting — not a complete history, but a recounting of the state of the art — between approximately 1900 and 1932,[4] a moment in time when history seemed to be very out of joint. By 1932, Hemingway had already wrestled with the problem of making the short story and novel represent the reality of the Lost Generation. Now he had to figure out how to write history, or the history of an art, or the description of an art that was strongly colored by history. He found a solution in the then-new technique of filmic montage, which works precisely to reshape time in order to show the disjointed relationship between past and present that characterizes late modernity and modernism. The problem of the relation of past to present is particularly pressing when one examines an impermanent art that "deals with death and death wipes it out" (*DIA*, 99). The montage structure of *Death in the Afternoon* allows Hemingway to produce a multidimensional history that includes the past as well as the present, a history that death cannot wipe out.

In addition to fragmenting and jumbling time, *Death in the Afternoon* also tangles genres. In a kind of literary montage, the book pastes together "journalism [. . .] short story [. . .] dramatic sketch, travel writing, parody, humor [. . .] biography, autobiography, lexicography, history, prophecy, criticism, scientific description, folklore study, translation, and, in the beautiful Chapter Twenty, an extended prose poem" (Mandel, 88).5 This literary montage supplements the book's deformations of time. Rather than a line moving in one direction, past to present, history and time in *Death in the Afternoon* step out of line, and finally, in the last chapter, they converge with space.

### Origins and Definitions

Montage, which transgresses boundaries of time, space, and genre, is closely related to collage, which transgresses boundaries of materials. Both have their origins in American and European folk art, and were widely used in nineteenth-century mass culture publications such as illustrated weekly newspapers and postcards. Andrew Clearfield argues that montage and collage, though originally not clearly distinguished, are two distinct mediums. Montage does not import materials, either plastic or formal, from outside the medium or the work; that is, a literary montage might mix literary forms, or play with typography and spacing, but it does not use nonliterary elements. But collage — for example, Picasso's *Still-Life with Chair-Caning*, in which the chair caning is represented by a piece of wicker-patterned wallpaper pasted onto the canvas — does import external elements. Montage uproots sequence and chronology, while collage disturbs the symmetry and geometry of the artistic medium itself. That is, montage "is ultimately founded upon mental processes, and the phenomena of integrating disparate and distracting elements over time," while collage "is rooted in the icon, itself an artistic product" (9–11, 14). The boundaries of these definitions, like most generic classifications of art, are permeable, and perhaps less important than their cultural relevance.

Montage and collage emerged as common artistic practice in response to the increasing industrialization and urbanization (in part in reaction to the First World War) in the first decades of the twentieth century. According to Christopher Phillips,

> this was a period of heightened awareness of being caught up in an epoch of accelerated transformation. This period marked the culmination of a series of irreversible passages: the passage from the seasonal rhythms of rural society to the frenzied tempo of an urban culture; the passage from national economies based on the land and on the artisanal occupations to industrial economies driven by machine technology; the passage from a social life rooted in traditional family life and local communities to the larger, more impersonal aggregations of mass society. [. . .] Montage, then, is examined for its power to register something of the shock of these transitions. (28–31)

Much of Hemingway's writing, as we know, is an attempt to capture the way of life he saw withering in the heat of industrialization. From the burned landscape of Northern Michigan in "Big Two-Hearted River" to the changed Spain in chapter 20 of *Death in the Afternoon* to the notion that even the weather "was insane now [. . .] it had not been normal since the war" (*Garden of Eden*, 94), Hemingway is deeply concerned with the paving over of paradise and the loss of community and tradition that accompanies that macadam.[6] As Miriam B. Mandel and Allen Josephs point out, *Death in the Afternoon* uses the bullfight as a mechanism for encapsulating as much of traditional Spanish culture as Hemingway can squeeze into one volume. *Death in the Afternoon* is, then, an act of preservation, a resistance to the changes and distortions introduced by modern urbanization and by modern war. The First World War had interrupted the sense of simple historical continuity that Hemingway and his contemporaries had known in their childhoods. The "lostness" of Hemingway and his generation was, in part, a loss of history. No longer was it possible to believe in the nineteenth-century model of progressive history in which science and reason carry humanity ever forward. The pastoral past was gone, reason had failed, and science had created mustard gas. *Death in the Afternoon* incorporates these ruptures into its montage.

The book begins by situating its narrator as having recently returned from the war-torn Near East. Initially the reference seems to contrast the pointless mistreatment of horses (the Greeks of Smyrna breaking the legs of their pack animals and pushing them into shallow water to drown) with the ritualized mistreatment of the horses in the bullfight, suggesting that the "animalarians" who decry the bullfight ought more properly to direct their outrage at the horrors perpetrated at Smyrna. If the bullfight is, "from a modern moral point of view [. . .] indefensible" (1), how then do we justify the greater cruelties of war? Compared to the war scenes depicted in the short story, "On the Quai at Smyrna," the bullfight seems not only civilized, but an absolute relief, a hope that killing and death can be controlled. The allusion to the story, then, suggests that the ordered, ritual killing of the bullfight makes far more sense than the random, senseless killing, of both people and animals, that characterizes war — although "animalarians" or humanists who object to the former often condone, and even patriotically participate in, the latter.

"A Natural History of the Dead" further warns the postwar reader against nineteenth-century humanism, which linked God with science and nature. The mocking, exaggeratedly scientific tone of "A Natural History of the Dead" announces that *Death in the Afternoon* is breaking from a defunct tradition of naturalist observation. The narrator's critique of *Virgin Spain*'s pretentious, "erectile" writing similarly enjoins us to seek something sharper, more informed, less trusting or innocent — something, that is, bearing the marks of recent events. It is no longer possible to believe in God, as Mungo Park did with such trusting abandon; it sounds silly to describe oneself as being, "Courtesy of God, *everywhere* and *everywhen*," as Waldo Frank did in *Virgin Spain* (53, italics in original). If the limits of time are to be transcended, it is not through faith or mysticism, but through art and knowledge.

Although Hemingway is "driven by nostalgia" and anxious to "capture the evanescent art of bullfighting" and the essence of a country that was about to be changed by war (Mandel, 89), he is also aware of the futility of that nostalgia. After having complained throughout the book that bullfighting has grown decadent, Hemingway writes that "bullfighting has *always* been considered to be in a period of decadence" (240, my italics). He recognizes that historians, always convinced that their own time is in decay, yearn for a past "golden age," which, to its own critics, was also ripe with decadence, and incomparable to the previous "golden age." The comment of four-year-old "P. H." ("Quand j'étais jeune la course de taureaux n'était pas comme ça" [495]) demonstrates the childish self-deception of nostalgia — including Hemingway's own.

*Death in the Afternoon* must also manage another systemic shock borne by the first decades of the twentieth century: Einstein's scientific revolution. After Einstein, time is no longer a linear constant. Time and place are traditional literary fixatives, a grid locating the story: July, Madrid; or winter, Switzerland, 1932.[7] However, in Hemingway's short story "Homage to Switzerland" (composed as he was finishing *Death in the Afternoon*), both time and place are variable. As Michael Reynolds points out, the settings of the three panels of the triptych, although they are all on the itinerary of the Simplon-Orient Express, are not presented in their correct geographic order. Internal clues that might place the story at a particular moment in time also conflict; nor do we know what to make of three travelers, waiting at three different stations for the same train and being told, apparently simultaneously, that the train will arrive in an hour ("Einstein's Train"). Time, like space, is dislocated, and the dislocation is emphasized by the story's confusing, because improbable, repetition of dialogue and scene. Similarity shattered by unexpected but significant difference renders the future uncertain and thus further destabilizes time. Such dissonances, the story suggests, characterize modern life.[8] *Death in the Afternoon* tries to find a similarly dissonant balance between repetition and difference. Its use of montage and collage — techniques employed by visual artists to depict the modern understanding of time and space — suggests that Hemingway had internalized the consequences of Einsteinian physics as much as those of the First World War. Old styles, like old verities, no longer sufficed.

Elements of montage and collage were so clearly apparent in Hemingway's earliest work (the 1924 Three Mountains Press edition of *in our time*) that the publishers decided to emphasize this feature in creating the book's cover. This cover overlaps newspaper clippings in Greek, English (both American and British), and French with a strangely compressed map of the Mediterranean and Tyrrhenian Seas and the surrounding bits of Spain, France, Italy, and Tunisia. The newspaper clippings include news articles, fashion reporting, and advertisements. This style reflects the use of photomontage in advertising and picture postcards that was common throughout Europe and America (Phillips, 26). It also registers the impact on the art world of the work of Picasso and Braque, who began experimenting with collage in 1912 (26). The later version of *In Our Time* (1925), with its splicing together of stories and interchapters, more clearly reflects the spread of montage from visual to literary art. The *In Our Time* interchapters are themselves generically unclassifiable, clearly different from the short stories they precede and follow. Do we call them sketches, prose poems, five-finger exercises? Any of these available classifications, not surprisingly, borrows from an art form different from the short story. Inserting these interchapters may simply have been a practical way for Hemingway to ensure reissue of his early work, but it also works to distinguish *In Our Time* from Anderson's *Winesburg, Ohio* and Joyce's *Dubliners*, with which it shares its structure of interconnected short stories. In any case, the insertions succeeded in heightening the thematic unity of the book through a fragmenting of its form, an effect typical of both collage and montage.

Like *in our time*, the first edition of *Death in the Afternoon* also calls attention to collage through its dust jacket, which features a visual medium, painting, to introduce a literary work. The visual element continues with the frontispiece, Juan Gris's beautiful painting, *The Bullfighter*, and with the photographs. These visual elements themselves come from different genres: the dust jacket reproduces a traditional scene designed to be used as a *cartel*, or bullfight poster, to be pasted on walls; Gris's painting, oil on canvas, was designed to hang more formally on a wall; and the photographs, representing a more modern medium, were, as Hemingway's letters and the text of the book indicate, to be interspersed with the text of the book (rather than gathered together into a separate section immediately following the text, as finally happened).[9] The photographs are themselves quite varied, including both action shots and pictures of one or two stationary figures, some human, some animal, and often the two together. Such a mixture of painting, photograph, and written text is characteristic of collage.

Hemingway's frontispiece, *The Bullfighter* (a painting Hemingway owned), is particularly interesting in that it itself simulates elements of collage. The bullfighter's costume is painted to show the different textures of the fabric, which contrast with the smoothness of the face pieces; in a fan around the face are cut-up pieces of bullfight posters. While it does not use actual fabric and paper, the painting's simulated textures work to the same effect.

The painting also uses the technique of montage: its geometric fragmentation is typical of the cubist works of Gris, Braque, and Picasso that Hemingway knew and liked. The depicted bullfighter is shattered into pieces that have only slight respect for "anatomical lines."[10] Although the painting carries the name of its subject, "Chicuelo," the destruction of the figure's face shatters and thus erases a crucial marker of identity, personhood, and wholeness. His face thus exploded, the bullfighter has no identity, no personhood. Only one element, his tie, remains whole and intact, as if to emphasize the general fragmentation of the subject. While this fragmentation shows the effects of modernity on a traditional figure, the painting also makes sense of fragmentation, in that its effect is perhaps more true and more real than a "realistic" representation.[11] The painting is then typically cubist in both its content and form.

**Literary Montage**

Critics tend to describe *Death in the Afternoon* with lists, such as Mandel's description of its various styles, or Donald Junkins's similar approach, which calls the book "a commentary on writing, an essay on honor, a discussion of art and the individual, a study of death, a lesson in writing style, a definition of terms, a primer of sentences, a psychology of the creative process, and a meditation on bravery" (196).[12] Many critics use lists because they are the only way to begin to encompass the book's large and complicated array of themes and techniques. I'm most interested, for the moment, in its techniques. Literary montage, which juxtaposes different literary styles, is the technique Hemingway uses most extensively in this book.

It is important not to confuse montage with chaos. Hemingway's use of montage is coherent and specific; it makes order out of chaos, especially the chaos of violence and war. The corrida lends order to death itself, which is otherwise all too random. The order of the bullfight redraws violent death as art.[13] This is demonstrated in the story of Maera killing with a right wrist dislocated by the rebound of the sword when it hit bone on his first attempt to kill:

> He went in twice more and hit bone both times. [. . .] His honor demanded that he kill him high up between the shoulders, going in as a man should, over the horn, following the sword with his body. And on the sixth time he went in this way and the sword went in too. He came out from the encounter, the horn just clearing his belly as he shrugged over it as he passed and then stood, tall and sunken eyed, his face wet with sweat, his hair down on his forehead, watching the bull as he swung, lost his feet and rolled over. He pulled the sword out with his right hand, as punishment for it I suppose, but shifted it to his left, and carrying it point down, walked over to the barrera. His rage was all over. (81)

The well-ordered corrida and honorable kill controls rage, orders narrative, and makes a sculpture out of the encounter of bull and man.[14] In contrast is "amateur or group killing" one finds in a provincial *capea:*

> Sometimes the bull is killed if the town has the money to afford it, or if the populace gets out of control; everyone swarming on him at once with knives, daggers, butcher knives and rocks; a man perhaps between his horns, being swung up and down, another flying through the air, surely several holding his tail, a swarm of choppers, thrusters and stabbers pushing into him, laying on him or cutting up at him until he sways and goes down. All amateur or group killing is a very barbarous, messy, though exciting business and is a long way from the ritual of the formal bullfight. (24)

While the ritual of the bullfight creates tragic order, when the ritual collapses, chaos returns. Hemingway's description of the capea scene resembles a filmic montage, its fragments joined, or separated, with semi-colons: the man between the horns, the men holding the tail, a swarm of choppers. This picture lacks a single or focal point, as the bull, which ordinarily might occupy the center of the picture, is obscured. Instead the eye must organize a mass of figures in a "flattened" plane.[15] Hemingway's technique, like the cubist paintings of Braque, Picasso, and Gris, splits the scene into shards, meaningless when separate, but forming a coherent whole. Montage reflects and orders the chaos of amateur killing. We also might suspect that "all amateur or group killing" includes war, or at least some aspects of it. A failed, disordered bullfight might be compared to the battle of Passchendaele: simple, ugly butchery (*DIA,* 154).[16] Such comparisons join *Death in the After-*

*noon* with its historical context and show its need to manage the effects of the First World War.

Chapter 7 begins by stressing the multiplicity of experience. Although bullfights always follow the same basic structure, each one is unique, and to explain every possible variation would make the book "interminable," the narrator tells us. The bullfight is a thing that "is impossible to make come true on paper, or at least impossible to attempt to make more than one version of at a time on paper, it always being an individual experience" (63). By inserting anecdotes and descriptions of many different bullfights Hemingway does, however, over the course of the book, take us to several bullfights. More fundamental than the immediate problem of bullfight variations, however, is the suggestion that experience itself is essentially multiple, repetitive, but repeating always with a difference. A man who could spend whole summers going to bullfight after bullfight, or spend months at a time on the Pilar fishing for marlin must have had not only an enormous capacity for repetition, but also a strong sensitivity to difference. His penchant for repetition is evident throughout *Death in the Afternoon*, which tirelessly assesses the strength and courage of many bulls and bullfighters.[17] The narrator of *Death in the Afternoon*, when he kindly consents to tell a story, seems aware that perhaps not all readers are as tolerant of taurine detail as he is, a sentiment echoed by Hemingway's caustic claim to Max Perkins that he added "all that stuff" (anecdotes, dialogues, short story, and so on) so that readers would feel they had gotten their money's worth (*Selected Letters*, 362). But the repetitions in *Death in the Afternoon* — like the repetition of scene and dialogue in "Homage to Switzerland," the repetition of geometric forms in a cubist painting, and the repetition of the rituals of the corrida — highlight difference, the difference which is experience.

In chapter 7 we first meet the Old lady, who appears suddenly and is startling, even confusing. We expect to be able to dismiss her as prudish, merely a foil for the astute, sophisticated narrator. However, she likes seeing the bulls hit the horses; it seems to her "sort of homey." Further, in keeping with one of Hemingway's personal rules, she "never discusses things she has enjoyed even with her most intimate friends" (65). She therefore has a certain respectability. She also often prods the narrator, keeping him in line, so he doesn't "go on until you are wearied and wish he would show more skill in using [words] and preach less of their significance" (71). She seems simply a framing device, a figure who gives the narrator an excuse to talk. However, she intrudes too deeply into the narrative; she breaks the frame, she shows the seams of the text, which, as Clearfield states, "are always more interesting than whatever is on either side of them" (10).

In the integration of "A Natural History of the Dead," for example, the Old lady's interruptions call attention to the blurring of two usually disparate elements, speech and writing. The author and Old lady are presented as if they are in conversation: their exchange begins in what seems to be a lecture hall, they then go to a café to talk; their dialogue is set off from the rest of the text and their lines are identified by speaker. The Old lady consents to read "A Natural History of the Dead," but only if there is conversation, which she has been deprived of, at the end of it — an odd stipulation for a written text. In addition, she interjects conversational comments into the written narrative, when she chides the author for writing again about animals. He responds, "Be patient, can't you? It's very hard to write like this," further calling attention to the fact that this is supposed to be a written, rather than a spoken text, although the Old lady seems to be speaking to the author. She interrupts twice more, once to remind the author that he is returning to Smyrna, which he has already "written" about, and to complain that the story is "not amusing." Both times the author asks her to "stop interrupting," as if she were breaking in while he was speaking (135–37). In an anticipatory moment that poststructuralist theorists might applaud, the Old lady's interruptions deconstruct a speech / writing binary, poking holes in the fabric of the text.[18]

But in spite of the interesting Old lady, the center of chapter 7 is its discussion of the corrida, the stabilizing structure that recurs throughout the book. The chapter expounds upon the narrator's concern with decadence, defined as "the decay of a complete art through a magnification of certain of its aspects" (70). The modern bullfight, perhaps like modern art, is decadent "in every way and like most decadent things it reaches its fullest flower at its rottenest point, which is the present" (68). The narrator is nervous about the word *decadent,* however, because its meanings are slippery. It may be simply "a term of abuse applied by critics to anything they do not yet understand" (71), a barb that seems applicable to the critical reception of postimpressionism in England and the United States. This concept of decadence derails any standpoint that might ground a critique of art. Decadence may be immediate, it may be "the present"; it also may make art incomprehensible to the present; it is also already dead (like the late Raymond Radiguet, whose demise is repeatedly referred to). It may simply be perversion, or a perverse reversal (such as the homosexual Radiguet sleeping with a female model).[19] Hemingway himself was often criticized for his decadence, and certainly writing a book about bullfighting during the depression was not likely to impress his readers with his asceticism. Hemingway's discussion of decadence, then, is perhaps another caution. Just as he has warns us not to look for humanist optimism, he also warns us against drawing easy conclusions about his work. His introduction of "other stuff" is not merely frivolous. Indeed, it is in the careful assemblage of anecdotes, dialogue, stories, and so on, that reality is most accurately reflected through the different voices (of the narrator, the Old lady, various bullfighters), places (Paris, Austria, the various regions of Spain), and moments that it splices together.

Most crucially, Hemingway's use of montage breaks up the grid of time and place which normally stabilize both prose and history, a rupture already discussed in terms of "Homage to Switzerland." The descriptions of the performances of José Gómez Ortega (Joselito) and of Juan Belmonte unbalance our temporal orientation by disordering the linear sequence of past to present. The narrator speaks as if he had witnessed their performances, jointly and separately; as if he had seen Joselito, "for whom everything in bullfighting was easy, who lived for bullfighting, and seemed to have been made and bred almost to the measurement of what a great bullfighter should be"; and even as if he had heard him speak: "he used to say, 'They say that he, Belmonte, works closer to the bull. It looks as though he does. But that isn't true. I really work closer. But it is more natural so it doesn't have to look so close'" (69). This recounting is similar to the narrator's report that he heard Diego Mazquiarán (Fortuna, 1895–1940) say to his picador, "Come on. Come on. Hurry it up. I'm bored in here" (260). The narrator, who is coextensive with Hemingway, could have actually seen and heard Fortuna. But as Joselito was killed in the ring on 16 May 1920, three years before Hemingway saw his first corrida, the apparent first-person report of his speech must be false. The narrator's representation of himself as there with Joselito and Belmonte disturbs our sense of before and after, our sense of sequence. This suggests a change to the shape of history, or suggests that a writer can change the shape of history and the fixity of sequence. Hemingway's montage shrugs off a model of time in which memory is two dimensional, and history is a line connecting past to present.

Later this crack in time will become three-dimensional. In chapter 20 the narrator laments that the past is over, never to return: "nor will there be that week of what happened in the night in that July in Madrid" (278). This phrase leaves the reader hanging: not only do we not know what happened "that night,"[20] the apparent specificity of the grid of July / Madrid (the traditional literary markers of time and place, or what we call setting) is skewed by the vague phrase: we don't know which night, or which July "that night" was. This seemingly solid location is shaky. This montage is playing with time, bringing the work into a fourth dimension.

### Filmic Montage

Although the artistic impact of films on this highly visual writer has not been assessed,[21] it would be perverse to argue that Hemingway was unaffected by the flourishing of cinema. Like any other artist in the 1920s and 1930s, Hemingway was surrounded by film and by both art and advertising photography, which frequently used montage. He could hardly have missed the importance of filmmakers like Charlie Chaplin, or of other writers' forays into film, such as the work of H. D. [Hilda Doolittle] on Kenneth MacPherson's film *Borderline,* or the crossovers between writing and film in the novels of his friend John Dos Passos. Kenneth Lynn notes that Hemingway saw *Birth of a Nation* (74), and in *The Torrents of Spring* (1926), Hemingway's character Yogi Johnson complains that "the last part" of Willa Cather's popular war novel, *One of Ours,* was stolen from that film (57; see also Baker, 119). In a 1925 letter, Hemingway reviewed several British, French, and German First World War films for Archibald MacLeish (*Selected Letters,* 178). As a journalist he probably saw newsreels frequently, and as an aficionado, he saw films of bullfights.[22] Nick Adams may have disapproved of movies — "God how that Da Veiga kid [a *rejoneador,* or mounted bullfighter] could ride. That was riding. It didn't show well in the movies. The movies ruined everything" (*Nick Adams Stories,* 237) — but Hemingway himself experimented with film one year in Pamplona.[23]

Most significant in Hemingway's exposure to montage techniques, however, was the work of John Dos Passos. Dos Passos's *Manhattan Transfer* and his *U.S.A.* trilogy clearly draw on both photo and filmic montage, especially in the latter's Newsreel and Camera Eye sections. Hemingway admired Dos Passos's work enormously,[24] perhaps in part because he suspected that Dos Passos was enlarging on the technique he had successfully used in *In Our Time.* He might also have realized that, innovating and captivating as it was, Dos Passos's highly topical work was not likely to have a long shelf-life.[25] Its references to popular songs, celebrities, and headlines fade before readers who lack an intimate familiarity with the mass culture of the 1920s and 1930s. Hemingway, who meant his work to last for generations,[26] developed his own versions of the technique.

In *A Farewell to Arms* (1926), Hemingway uses filmic montage to compress a year's time into two pages of prose. The book begins with the much-quoted sequence,

> In the last summer of that year we lived in a house in a village that looked across the river and the plain to the mountains. In the bed of the river there were pebbles and boulders, dry and white in the sun, and the water was clear and swiftly moving and blue in the channels. Troops went by the house and down the road and the dust they raised powdered the leaves of the trees. The trunks of the trees too were dusty and the leaves fell early that year and we saw the troops marching along the road and the dust rising and leaves, stirred by the breeze, falling and the soldiers marching and afterward the road bare and white except for the leaves.

Like *Death in the Afternoon*'s description of the Prado and Madrid (quoted above), this earlier sequence splices together disconnected visual fragments: a house, a flowing river, a road, marching soldiers, falling leaves, and again, a bare white road. Without saying "time passed," the sequence moves through time by juxtaposing, or pressing together, disparate moments. Montage allows pieces of time to be left out. Instead of following a line of time, montage drops out the middle of the time line and brings the ends together. Thus, showing us only the points on the line, and leaving out the line itself, Hemingway makes time flexible, relative to experience and memory, which tend to fragment.

The theory of filmic montage was developed largely in the films and writing of Russian filmmaker Sergei Eisenstein, who credits D. W. Griffith as its innovator (Eisenstein, *Film Sense,* xiv). Although it was part of his artistic milieu, we don't know if Hemingway saw or read Eisenstein's work.[27] Their theoretical similarities however, suggest a productive, if perhaps unexpected, conjunction. Most simply, filmic montage fragments narrative through the juxtaposing of disparate shots. Eisenstein and his colleagues saw enormous artistic and political potential in this technique,[28] since the resultant fragmented narrative generates "a maximum of emotion and stimulating power" (*Film Sense,* 4). Further, the juxtaposition of two shots, either shots that are clearly narratively related, or shots that seem to have no immediately apparent connection, produces "a third something," an effect which is more than the sum of its parts (10). This "third something," that is left out of the film and that the spectator fills in, sounds like the missing seven-eighths of Hemingway's famous iceberg. In an early articulation of this concept, Eisenstein explains that cinema creates audience response through

> the juxtaposition and accumulation, in the audience's psyche, of associations that the film's purpose requires, associations that are aroused by the separate elements of the stated (in practical terms, "montage fragments") fact, associations that produce, albeit tangentially, a similar (and often stronger) effect only when taken as a whole. Let us take that same murder as an example; a throat is gripped, eyes bulge, a knife is brandished, the victim closes his eyes, blood is spattered on a wall, the victim falls to the floor, a hand wipes off the knife — each fragment is chosen to "provoke" associations. ("Montage," 36)

The "thing left out," is, of course, the murder itself. Eisenstein's articulation of this roundabout way of creating audience response recalls Hemingway's "cushion shot": "I always try to do the thing by three cushion shots rather than by words or direct statement," Hemingway wrote to Owen Wister in 1929 (*Selected Letters,* 301). Slightly different from other explanations of the iceberg theory of omission, the "cushion shot" specifies a pattern of shooting around the center, looking at everything but the thing itself, a structure similar to Eisenstein's.[29]

Eisenstein's unexpected theoretical similarity to Hemingway continues: "the strength of montage resides in this," Eisenstein writes,

> that it involves the creative process, the emotions and mind of the spectator. The spectator is compelled to proceed along that self-

same creative path that the author traveled in creating the image (idea). The spectator not only sees the represented elements of the finished work, but also experiences the dynamic process of the emergence and assembly of the image (idea) just as it was experienced by the author. ("Montage," 32)

The work that Eisenstein's spectator must perform is similar to that demanded of Hemingway's readers. To get the full depth of Hemingway's work, readers must uncover the submerged, or invisible, seven-eighths of the iceberg, and in so doing, follow Hemingway's "creative path": they must acquire the same knowledge Hemingway states a writer must have to effectively omit important details.[30] In fact, in the anecdote about the unfortunate Hernandorena, who could not control his nervousness and was gored in a novillada, *Death in the Afternoon* takes the reader through the writer's creative path. Novilladas, we are told, are important for spectators interested in learning about the bullfight because they are good places to study technique, which is "always most visible in its imperfection" (17). When the deeply imperfect Hernandorena is gored, the narrator describes the result: "the heavy, soiled gray silk of his rented trousers open cleanly and deeply to show the thigh bone from hip almost to the knee" (19). A page later, as the narrator explains how that night he lay awake trying to remember what was important about that scene, we are told, "finally, remembering all around it, I got it. When he stood up, his face white and dirty and the silk of his breeches opened from waist to knee, it was the dirtiness of the rented breeches, the dirtiness of his slit underwear and the clean, clean, unbearable clean whiteness of the thigh bone that I had seen, and it was that which was important" (20). The young writer, increasing the "knowledge and science" which are essential to his craft, learns the important thing so that he can leave it out (21). For readers, this is a moment of clarity, a map of the writer's technique, a moment of insight into, even integration with, the writer's process. I suspect, however, that Hemingway would not have so fully revealed himself if he were not concealing something else, some other special technical invention. We find a clue to that invention in a seemingly unlikely place: Einstein's theory of relativity.

Hemingway and Eisenstein shared a train of thought that was both frightening and liberating: the impact of Einsteinian physics. As Erwin Schrödinger wrote, the Theory of Relativity meant

> the dethronement of time as a rigid tyrant imposed on us from the outside, a liberation from the unbreakable rule of "before and after." For indeed time is our most severe master by ostensibly restricting the existence of each of us to narrow limits — seventy or eighty years, as the Pentateuch has it. To be allowed to play about with such a master's programme believed to be unassailable until then, to play about with it

albeit in a small way, seems to be a great relief, it seems to encourage the thought that the whole "timetable" is probably not quite as serious as it appears at first sight. (Qtd. in Clark, 249)

This flexibility of time enables sequence to be altered, as we've seen in "Homage to Switzerland" and *Death in the Afternoon*. Einstein's theory also may have fed Hemingway's creative strainings at the limits of history, time, and mortality. In *Death in the Afternoon,* however, the relativity of time crucially changes the shape of memory and history. Writing that can access the fluidity of time can defeat the "rule of 'before and after'" making memory and history immediate, rather than remote and removed.

For Eisenstein in a similar way, Einsteinian physics, along with the invention of sound film, opened the way to a "filmic fourth dimension." Time becomes an essential element of film when sound and visual montage are synchronized. Eisenstein reasons that both music and film use "overtone," a resonant combination of elements produced only in performance (not visible on the score or editing table), which unaccountably affects the spectator. This overtone might be understood as a kind of third dimension. In the synchronizing of film and sound these two separate third dimensions combine to create a fourth dimension, one of pure feeling. Eisenstein writes: "For the musical overtone (a throb) it is not strictly fitting to say: 'I hear.' Nor for the visual overtone: 'I see.' For both, a new uniform formula must enter our vocabulary: 'I feel'" (*Film Form,* 69–71). Eisenstein hoped this holistic experience might spark social change through the powerful critical emotion it could produce.[31]

Hemingway's montage is distinctly less political. His "real thing, the sequence of motion and fact which made the emotion and which would be as valid in a year or in ten years or, with luck and if you stated it purely enough, always" (*DIA,* 2) is a revolution in realism, not politics. This is the revolution that Hemingway describes himself as seeking. Eisenstein's theory also resonates with Hemingway's project to produce works that would enable readers not merely to learn about a place (Spain, for example), but to feel as if they had actually experienced it. Of "Homage to Switzerland," he says that "anyone will have been there [Switzerland] once they have read the Homage" (*Selected Letters,* 367). *Death in the Afternoon* was similarly meant to make Spain real for its readers. Hemingway acknowledges the difficulty of this project in *Green Hills of Africa,* in which his narrator alter-ego says that there is a "fourth and fifth dimension that can be gotten," but that many writers avoid trying to do so because, "too many factors must combine to make it possible" (26–27). For both Hemingway and Eisenstein, it was worth trying to combine those many factors not merely to represent experience, but to create a new reality.

Although Hemingway uses montage description in a scattered way throughout *Death in the Afternoon,* the most clearly filmic section is chapter 20. In this chapter he combines the many factors that must come together if one is to produce multidimensional writing. The essence of the chapter is this: breaking the linear sequence of time, Hemingway opens a door from the past to the present. With the juxtaposition of disparate sensations, people, and places, he creates such an intense feeling of a place and time that the reader is (ideally) not merely informed of Spain, but made to feel it: Hemingway's memory becomes the reader's reality. Combining sensory association, Hemingway forges his multidimensional work.

Temporal specifics are largely stricken from chapter 20. There is "July, Madrid," there is "such a year," but we don't know what year it is, and "July" becomes an idea as much as a moment in time. By 1932, when Hemingway finished *Death in the Afternoon,* he had made several trips to Spain; but even with biographical information, we cannot untangle the mesh of memories in this chapter. Instead of historical specifics, we languish in colors, tastes, smells, views, sensations. Time is submerged in an overflow of sense.

Much of chapter 20, like the passage from it quoted at the start of this essay, offers chains of disconnected images without sequence or chronology:

> It should, if it were enough of a book, have the forced smile of Lagartito; it was once a real smile, and the unsuccessful matadors swimming with the cheap whores out on the Manzanares along the Pardo road; beggars can't be choosers, Luis said; playing ball on the grass by the stream where the fairy marquis came out in his car with the boxer; where we made the paellas, and walked home in the dark with the cars coming fast along the road; and with the electric lights through the green leaves and the dew settling the dust, in the cool at night; cider in Bombilla and the road to Pontevedra from Santiago de Campostella with the high turn in the pines and blackberries beside the road; Algabeno [*sic*] the worst faker of them all; and Maera up in the room at Quintana's changing clothes with the priest the one year everyone drank so much and no one was nasty. There really was such a year, but this is not enough of a book. (271)

This passage gives little sense of the passage of time. Time is compressed into what might be a single day of swimming, playing ball, and making paella, or expanded into a whole summer, or a series of summers. Less important than time are the sensations, the associations. The sequence piles up images, some of which are probably familiar to many readers (playing ball, cars going fast along a road, swimming), others of which are probably obscure (Spanish roads, Bombilla, Algabeño the faker). Mixing the unfamiliar with the familiar, the passage augments the reader's knowledge with Hemingway's. The sensory impact of the passage is then real and immediate.

Unfortunately, it is, by definition, impossible to fully untangle the many "factors" of this book without making a multidimensional prose linear. If I tell you that in chapter 20 Hemingway layers descriptions of the country, the food, the beer and wine, the weather, the people, smells, sights, "cool walking under palms," "long hot days of summer," evening, night, morning, "yellow gorse on the high meadows and the thin rain," I have only strung along a line what expands beyond two dimensions. If I try to describe time in that chapter — short moments ("Maera up in the room [. . .] changing outfits with the priest"); long moments ("that year"); telescoping into the past ("the beer place on the cool side of the street [. . .] is a citroen [*sic*] show room now"); deeper into the past and into Hemingway's own fiction ("the same cornada that killed El Espartero");[32] memory that projects into the future ("And if you ride and if your memory is good you may ride still through the forest of the Irati with the trees like drawings in a child's fairy book") — I have only taken disparate moments built in careful architecture and knocked them down. Instead let there be the drinking of the wine, "the wine of that year and the year before and the great four years before that and the other years that I lost track of while the long arms of the mechanical fly chaser that wound by clock work went round and round and we talked French. We all knew Spanish better" (276). Time, finally, is artificial, a clockwork fly chaser that measures nothing. Experience is measured not by the moments scratched into the face of the clock, but in the accumulation of events and sensations, the "sequence of motion and fact" that describes our experience of a material world. Each moment is defined not by its relations to the moments that came before and after it, but by its relation to the place it happened: "July, Madrid." Chapter 20 describes Spain not in a chronology of events, but in a blending of time into space in which "when" and "where" are more real in the montage of memory, and the montage of art, than in the linearity of conventional history. Although change is inevitable, and art is insufficient to capture the whole of any experience, true art, good work, can make the reader experience a place and time as if it were their own. "Pamplona is changed, of course. [. . .] I know things change now and I do not care. [. . .] We've seen it all go and we'll watch it go again. The great thing is to last and get your work done and see and hear and learn and understand; and write when there is something that you know; and not before; and not too damned much after. Let those who want to save the world if you can get to see it clear and as a whole. Then any part you make will represent the whole if it's made truly. The thing to do is work and learn to make it" (278).

# Notes

[1] My thanks to the Hemingway Society for their generous Paul Smith Fellowship, and to the John F. Kennedy Library for an equally generous Hemingway Research Fellowship, both of which supported this essay.

[2] Discussing the possible film adaptation of *The Sun Also Rises,* Hemingway wrote to Perkins, "As for movie rights please get the best you can i.e. the most money — I do not go to the movies and would not care what changes they made" (*Selected Letters,* 236). As all the royalties from *The Sun Also Rises* went to his first wife Hadley, this was merely a nice gesture. Later, when discussing royalties that would come to him, he was less cavalier about changes Hollywood made to his books. Reynolds reports his sarcastic responses to Hollywood's decisions to allow Catherine Barkley and Harry to survive in the movies of *A Farewell to Arms* and "The Snows of Kilimanjaro" (*The 1930's,* 103–4, 188; *Final Years,* 198, 289–90). According to Reynolds, Hemingway was "stung time and again by Hollywood's treatment of his works" (*Final Years,* 260).

[3] As Comley and Scholes (and others) have argued, Hemingway often disguised or denied sources and influences. Miriam B. Mandel, Nancy Bredendick, and Linda Wagner-Martin make this point, the former two arguing that Hemingway covered up his Spanish sources (see pages 83 and 224–27 in this volume), and the latter that he denied the influence of Henry James and Gertrude Stein (see pages 62–64 and 69–73); see also the article by Lisa Tyler (pages 43–58 in this volume).

[4] I choose 1900 as a starting point that incorporates the apprenticeships of Belmonte and Joselito, which are mentioned in the book, but not dated. Although the book dips back as far as Pedro Romero's 1771–79 career, it concentrates mainly on the "golden age" of Joselito and Belmonte (which ended with Joselito's death in the ring on 16 May 1920), and the bullfighters that followed them, up until shortly before the book's publication in 1932. I do not suggest that *Death in the Afternoon* is simply or only a history of bullfighting. As is typical, Hemingway contradicts himself on this point even within the pages of the book. He writes that "no history of bullfighting that is ever written can be complete unless it gives [Sidney Franklin] the space he is entitled to" (506), thus suggesting that his own book, which includes a whole appendix on Franklin, is such a complete history. But later he states that "*Death in the Afternoon* is not intended to be either historical or exhaustive" (517). A good reader enjoys such ambiguity.

[5] Allen Josephs and Michael Thurston also discuss the problems of generically classifying *Death in the Afternoon.* Josephs allows the book to remain unclassified; Thurston concludes that its incorporative structure makes it most like an anatomy, "a logical dissection on the order of Nash's *Anatomy of Absurdity* or Burton's *Anatomy of Melancholy*" (47). I find "logical dissection" a bit too clinical for this playful book, and prefer montage and collage as generic classifiers.

[6] One of the oddest recognitions of the downside of urbanization is Hemingway's lament in *Death in the Afternoon* that the disappearance of the paving stone has greatly inhibited the populace's ability to resist oppressive governments: "The disappearance of cobble and paving stones has been more of a deterrent to the overthrow-

ing of governments than machine guns, tear bombs and automatic pistols. [. . .] Régimes are kept in with the club and the blackjack, not the machine gun or bayonet, and while there were paving stones there was never an unarmed mob to club" (112).

[7] In examining why many American photographers avoided montage, staying instead with a grid structure, i.e., a composition organized by vertical and horizontal lines, Sally Stein writes that "the form of the grid helped impose a rational, modern order on heterogeneous graphic elements; but it also resonated as a figure of republican spatial organization that had shaped the basic development of both country and city in America. By the twentieth century, the two-dimensional matrix could barely indicate the dense vertical development of metropolitan centers — one reason why Europeans frequently adopted montage to signify urbanism. But in a country where physical expansiveness still serves as an enduring source of national pride — where, consequently, the plight of destitute farmers was far more common a visual symbol of national crisis than the plight of industrial workers — the unaltered, 'natural' rectilinear photography presented in and set off by the orderly structure of the grid graphically articulated the space and strength of liberal individualism" (189). In breaking with the grid, Hemingway shows his distance from conservative art, a distance that is frequently underestimated.

[8] As Reynolds points out, there is something very odd in this exchange. Dr. Wyer's apparent shift of interest from Mr. Harris to T. E. Lawrence, who was gay, and whose writing resounds with homoeroticism, supports a possible homosexual reading. I also wonder, though I have little evidence for it other than the pressure of the other two vignettes, if, in an echo of "The Sea Change" (which was written shortly before "Homage"), Mr. Johnson's wife is perhaps leaving him for another woman. My thanks to Hilary Justice for her generous fact-check on the composition history of "The Sea Change."

[9] Folders K22.1–K23 at the Hemingway Collection in the John F. Kennedy library include the typescript of *Death in the Afternoon* and show marginal notes in Hemingway's handwriting indicating the intended placement of illustrations. For more on the inclusion of illustrations, see the essays by Robert Trogdon and Anthony Brand both in this volume; see also Bruccoli, 161–68 and 185–86.

[10] Cf. "A Natural History of the Dead": "it [is] amazing that the human body should be blown into pieces which exploded along no anatomical lines, but rather divided as capriciously as the fragmentation in the burst of a high explosive shell" (*DIA*, 137).

[11] In "A Paris-Strasbourg Flight" Hemingway remarks that, seeing the landscape from above, where its divisions are apparent (a familiar phenomena to anyone who has ever flown over the American Midwest), he begins to understand cubism, suggesting an immediacy between cubist technique and the world it represented (*Toronto Star Dispatches*, 206). Gertrude Stein expresses a similar sentiment in *The Autobiography of Alice B. Toklas*, 90.

[12] Thurston and Josephs use similar lists to describe the book.

[13] Further, the spectator new to the bullfight can, because of the careful order and ritual of the bullfight, understand it as a whole if without grasping each of the parts

(*DIA*, 8–9). The early chapters of *Death in the Afternoon* give the readers instructions for properly seeing, i.e., visually comprehending, the bullfight.

[14] "I know of no modern sculpture, except Brancusi's, that is in any way the equal of the sculptural art of modern bullfighting" (*DIA*, 99). Interestingly enough, "sculpture" is also often used to describe Catherine Bourne's tonsorial art in *The Garden of Eden*, suggesting a comparison between her impermanent arts (of storytelling and body sculpture) and the bullfighter's.

[15] In "Hemingway's *In Our Time:* A Cubist Anatomy," Jacqueline Vaught Brogan describes the "flattening" effect of Hemingway's structural parataxis. The different parts of *In Our Time,* she argues, the interchapters and stories, cannot be read in "a hierarchy of foreground and background" (35). Hemingway's scene of amateur killing similarly puts each fragment of the picture in the same plane.

[16] For a compelling description and analysis of Passchendaele and its effects see Paul Fussell, *The Great War and Modern Memory,* 3–35, esp. 16–18.

[17] As Michael Thurston points out, many of the chapters follow a regular structure: the *corrida* is analyzed in the past and present; the discussion shifts to language; finally, according to Thurston, gender or sexuality appears at the end of the chapter (56). While Thurston's description is clearly accurate for chapters 7, 9, 11, and 15, it is inadequate to summarize the whole of the book. The chapters do, however, tend to follow a rhythm of alternating "hard," "factual" information about the corrida and its past and present, with anecdotes, conversation with the Old lady, or, in chapter 12, a substantial short story.

[18] For a somewhat different view of the "author" and the "Old lady" see Hilary Justice's essay, pages 237–56 in this volume.

[19] For Hemingway, perversion is, however, central to art. See Nancy Comley and Robert Scholes' *Hemingway's Genders,* Carl Eby's *Hemingway's Fetishism,* and Debra Moddelmog's *Reading Desire* for analyses of the creative exchange between art and perversion in Hemingway's work.

[20] *The Garden of Eden,* which draws on Hemingway's life between 1924–32, the years during which *Death in the Afternoon* was conceived and written, suggests that Madrid seems to have special sexual significance for Hemingway. It is there that Catherine's gender transgression becomes most urgent, and later, when Marita repeats Catherine's experiments, she tells David that she understands what he and Catherine did in Madrid because she's "the same way" he is. She stresses her understanding of the Madrid by asking David if he would like her to "do her [Catherine's] things" which she knows and can do (*GE*, 185).

[21] The influence of painting on Hemingway, famously declared in Nick Adams' comment that he "wanted to write like Cezanne [sic] painted" (*NAS*, 239) has been pursued by critics such as Emily Stipes Watts, Raymond Nelson, Alfred Kazin, Erik Nakjavani, and Jacqueline Vaught Brogan. Books such as Gene D. Phillips' *Hemingway and Film,* Leonard J. Leff's *Hemingway and his Conspirators,* and Charles M. Oliver's collection *A Moving Picture Feast* chiefly attend to the transmutation of Hemingway's fiction into film, and the impact of those films on his career. Exceptions to this tendency include Eugene Kenjo's "Hemingway's Cinematic Style" and

Stanley Corkin's "Hemingway, Film, and U.S. Culture," both in Charles M. Oliver's collection.

[22] My thanks to Anthony Brand for reminding me of this, and for suggesting that Hemingway saw bullfight films.

[23] In 1924, Hemingway wrote to Gertrude Stein and Alice B. Toklas, "Our Movie [*sic*] of Pamplona Man Ray says is one of the best movies he's ever seen. [. . .] Now I have a bullfight every night" (*Selected Letters,* 121). In 1926 he described this movie to Max Perkins as having "the rush of people coming into the ring, coming faster and faster and then finally falling all over themselves and the bulls jamming over them and right into the camera. It was a wonderful thing but so short that it wasn't of any commercial value" (*Selected Letters,* 236). It is unlikely that this short film, which sounds like little more than a home movie, benefited from the editing that montage requires. However, Hemingway's description of the piling up of images recalls the effect that montage creates, and the passage from *Death in the Afternoon* quoted at the start of this essay. Further, his lament that the film had "no commercial value" suggests that he did consider it a potentially serious work.

[24] For Hemingway's positive comments on Dos Passos's work see *Selected Letters,* 288 and 354–55.

[25] Hemingway may have been thinking of this shortcoming of Dos Passos's work when he contrasted his goals for his fiction with journalism, in which, "with one trick and another, you communicated the emotion aided by the element of timelines which gives a certain emotion to any account of something that has happened on that day" (*DIA,* 2).

[26] Malcolm Cowley records Hemingway explaining, "You can do it or not do it in that league I am speaking of. And you only have to do it once to get remembered by some people. But if you can do it year after year after year quite a lot of people remember and they tell their children, and their children, and their grandchildren remember, and if it's books they can read them. And if it's good enough it lasts forever" (qtd. in Reynolds, *The 1930s,* 170).

[27] Dos Passos, however, did report in his *Paris Review* interview that he admired the work of both D. W. Griffiths and Eisenstein, especially the latter's 1925 film *The Battleship Potemkin* (qtd. in Foster, 186).

[28] Although Hemingway adapted montage techniques to writing, he seems, like D. W. Griffith, to have exploited little of the political potential.

[29] The "cushion shot," with its connotation of repetition, also may be an early suggestion of the "double-wall rebound" in jai-alai, or *remate,* which Hemingway would develop more fully in *A Moveable Feast* (Baker, 540). Rose Marie Burwell further associates the *remate* technique with the "twinning, cloning, and splitting of painters and writers in *Islands* and *Eden*" (54). Such continuity indicates a connected development in Hemingway's work, a kind of progression he is rarely credited with.

[30] Explaining his iceberg theory, Hemingway writes in *Death in the Afternoon,* "If a writer of prose knows enough about what he is writing about he may omit things that he knows and the reader, if the writer is writing truly enough, will have a feeling of those things as strongly as if the writer had stated them" (192).

[31] Montage, for Eisenstein, was not only a potentially revolutionary form, but one that was a specifically Marxist dialectical synthesis of opposing images. He argued that "revolutionary form would derive from revolutionary ideology" ("The Problem of the Materialist Approach to Form," 57). For Eisenstein, form is crucial to art as praxis: "The decisive factor 'for art in general and revolutionary art in particular' was 'the maximum intensification of the emotional seizure of the audience' and 'a formal approach that is correctly conducted in Marxist terms [and that] results in an ideologically valuable and socially useful product'" (Qtd. in Taylor, 6).

[32] Susan Beegel argues convincingly that the Manuel García of the short story "The Undefeated" was based on a Manuel García (El Espartero), who was killed in the Madrid bullring on 27 May 1894. Hemingway references El Espartero in a section of the *Death in the Afternoon* manuscript that was deleted from the final version, lamenting that he never saw him fight, but only read "accounts" of his performances (Beegel, 12).

## Works Cited

Baker, Carlos. *Ernest Hemingway: A Life Story*. New York: Macmillan, 1969.

Beegel, Susan. "The Death of El Espartero: An Historic Matador Links 'The Undefeated' and *Death in the Afternoon*." *The Hemingway Review* 5.2 (1986): 12–23.

Brogan, Jacqueline Vaught. "Hemingway's *In Our Time:* A Cubist Anatomy." *The Hemingway Review* 17.2 (1998): 31–46.

Bruccoli, Matthew J., ed., with the assistance of Robert W. Trogdon. *The Only Thing that Counts: The Ernest Hemingway–Maxwell Perkins Correspondence 1925–1947*. New York: Scribner's, 1996.

Burwell, Rose Marie. *Hemingway: The Postwar Years and the Posthumous Novels*. New York: Cambridge UP, 1996.

Clark, Ronald. *Einstein, the Life and Times*. New York: World Publishing, 1971.

Clearfield, Andrew. *These Fragments Have I Shared: Collage and Montage in Early Modernist Poetry*. Ann Arbor: U of Michigan Research P, 1984.

Comley, Nancy, and Robert Scholes. *Hemingway's Genders*. New Haven: Yale UP, 1994.

Eby, Carl. *Hemingway's Fetishism*. Albany: State U of New York P, 1999.

Eisenstein, Sergei. *Film Form*. Trans. Jay Leyda. New York: Harcourt, Brace and Company, 1949.

———. *The Film Sense*. Trans. Jay Leyda. New York: Harcourt, Brace and Company, 1942.

———. "The Montage of Film Attractions." In *The Eisenstein Reader*. Ed. Richard Taylor. Trans. Richard Taylor and William Powell. London: British Film Institute Publishing, 1998. 35–52.

———. "The Problem of the Materialist Approach to Form." In *The Eisenstein Reader*. Ed. Richard Taylor. Trans. Richards Taylor and William Powell. London: British Film Institute Publishing, 1998. 56–64.

Foster, Gretchen. "John Dos Passos' Use of Film Technique in *Manhattan Transfer* and *The 42nd Parallel*." *Literature / Film Quarterly* 14.3 (1986): 186–94.

Fussell, Paul. *The Great War and Modern Memory*. New York: Oxford UP, 1975.

Hemingway, Ernest. *The Complete Short Stories of Ernest Hemingway*. Finca Vigía Ed. New York: Scribner's, 1987.

———. *Dateline: Toronto: Hemingway's Complete Dispatches for "The Toronto Star," 1920–1924*. Ed. William White. New York: Scribner's, 1985.

———. *Death in the Afternoon*. New York: Scribner's, 1932.

———. *Death in the Afternoon* typescript. Hemingway Collection, John F. Kennedy Library, Boston.

———. *A Farewell to Arms*. New York: Scribner's, 1929.

———. *The Garden of Eden*. New York: Scribner's, 1986.

———. *Green Hills of Africa*. New York: Scribner's, 1935.

———. *in our time*. Paris: Three Mountains Press, 1924.

———. *The Nick Adams Stories*. Ed. Phillip Young. New York: Scribner's, 1972.

———. *Selected Letters 1917–1961*. Ed. Carlos Baker. New York: Scribner's, 1981.

———. *The Torrents of Spring*. New York: Scribner's, 1926.

Josephs, Allen. "*Death in the Afternoon:* A Reconsideration." *The Hemingway Review* 5.2 (1986): 2–16.

Junkins, Donald. "Hemingway's Old Lady and the Aesthetics of Pundonor." *North Dakota Quarterly* 62.2 (1994–95): 195–204.

Lynn, Kenneth. *Hemingway*. New York: Fawcett Columbine, 1987.

Maine, Barry. *Dos Passos: The Critical Heritage*. New York: Routledge, 1988.

Mandel, Miriam B. "Index to Ernest Hemingway's *Death in the Afternoon*." *Resources for American Literary Study* 23.1 (1997): 86–132.

Moddelmog, Debra. *Reading Desire*. Ithaca: Cornell UP, 1999.

Phillips, Christopher. "Introduction." *Montage and Modern Life 1919–1942*. Ed. Matthew Teitelbaum. Cambridge: MIT Press, 1992. 20–35.

Reynolds, Michael. *Hemingway: The Final Years*. New York: Norton, 1999.

———. *Hemingway: The 1930s*. New York: Norton, 1997.

———. "'Homage to Switzerland': Einstein's Train Stops at Hemingway's Station." In *Hemingway's Neglected Short Fiction: New Perspectives*. Ed. Susan F. Beegel. Tuscaloosa: U of Alabama P, 1989. 255–62.

———. *The Young Hemingway*. New York: Basil Blackwell, 1986.

Stein, Gertrude. *The Autobiography of Alice. B. Toklas*. New York: Vintage, 1933.

Stein, Sally. "Good fences make good neighbors": American Resistance to Photomontage between the Wars." In *Montage and Modern Life 1919–1942*. Ed. Matthew Teitelbaum. Cambridge: MIT Press, 1992. 128–89.

Taylor, Richard. "Eisenstein: A Soviet Artist." In *The Eisenstein Reader*. Ed. Richard Taylor. Trans. Richard Taylor and William Powell. London: British Film Institute Publishing, 1998. 1–28.

Thurston, Michael. "Gender, Genre and Truth in *Death in the Afternoon*." *The Hemingway Review* 17.2 (1998): 47–63.

# And What Came After

# The Legacy of *Death in the Afternoon:*
# Norman Mailer and Barnaby Conrad

*Keneth Kinnamon*

ALL MODERN AMERICAN TAURINE WRITING comes from one book by Ernest Hemingway called *Death in the Afternoon*. There was almost nothing before. There has been nothing as good since. But there has been a great deal. The thirty-fifth anniversary edition of *La Busca,* a bibliography of books in English concerning bullfighting through 1999, contains approximately two thousand items (Phelps, Brody, and Tuttle). This is quantitatively impressive, even if one discounts items that deal with the subject only in a chapter or two or those that appeared before 1932.[1]

Any effort to survey more than a fraction of these works, even if limited to those directly indebted to *Death in the Afternoon,* is bound to be superficial. Instead, this essay will consider only two writers, Norman Mailer and Barnaby Conrad, one a major figure in American literature of the last half century, the other a freelance writer who has written more on the bulls than any other American or British author. Both write under the clearly discernible shadow of Ernest Hemingway in general and of *Death in the Afternoon* in particular.

Of all American writers of importance, Norman Mailer has been the most fascinated by Hemingway's life and personality. Indeed, his carefully cultivated macho image has often seemed a comic parody of his model. As a freshman at Harvard he read Hemingway and such other "tough" writers as John Dos Passos, John Steinbeck, and James T. Farrell. In a creative writing class with Robert Gorham Davis he wrote "a Hemingwayesque exercise about a bellhop with a bloody ending" that met the approval of Davis but induced only laughter from his classmates, anti-Semitic or not, because it seemed so incongruous coming from a sixteen-year-old Jewish boy from Crown Heights (Dearborn, 27). This was the first of many literary efforts during Mailer's long career in which Hemingway's literary influence was apparent.

We do not know precisely when Mailer read *Death in the Afternoon,* but he surely read it before, during, or shortly after his summer trips to Mexico in 1954 and 1955, when he saw many bullfights, befriended bullfighters who explained the finer points to him, and even planned, with some friends, to rent a small ring and have a novillada of their own — a plan that was never realized.

*The Deer Park* (1955) is Mailer's third novel but the first to deal with bullfighting. Near the end of the novel, the narrator, Sergius O'Shaughnessey, leaves the sexual and political intrigues of Southern California for art school in Mexico City, where he becomes an aficionado, learning the elements of *toreo* from a *novillero* while becoming involved with the man's mistress. When his efforts to become "the first great and recognized American matador" come to nothing, however, he goes to New York, rents a loft in which he sets up an improbable taurine school, and tries to write a novel about *toreo,* informing the reader that "it was not very good. It was inevitably imitative of that excellently exiguous mathematician, Mr. Ernest Hemingway, and I was learning that it is not creatively satisfying to repeat the work of a good writer" (353). If unsuccessful as a taurine novelist or matador, O'Shaughnessey is quite proficient with the women of Greenwich Village, as he narrates in "The Time of Her Time," an excerpt from an unfinished novel published in Mailer's *Advertisements for Myself.*

At this stage of his career, Mailer adopted not only Hemingway's style and subject matter, but also his truculence towards critics and fellow writers, a truculence easily visible in *Death in the Afternoon*. Unfavorable responses to *The Deer Park* led Mailer to send an inscribed copy of the book to Hemingway in Cuba, hoping that his opinion might be more favorable than those of the critics. As an apt pupil of the master, he avoided any appearance of deference: "but if you do not answer, or if you answer with the kind of crap you use to answer unprofessional writers, sycophants, brown-nosers, etc., then fuck you, and I will never attempt to communicate with you again" (qtd. in Dearborn, 109). The package was returned unopened to sender, but Hemingway did express an opinion to Wallace Meyer of Scribner's: "In *The Deer Park* Mailer really blows the whistle on himself" (*Selected Letters,* 852).

A dozen years later, Mailer published *The Bullfight: A Photographic Narrative* (1967), with text by Mailer, who with his daughter Susan also provided a translation of some lines from Federico García Lorca's lament on the death of the bullfighter Ignacio Sánchez Mejías. The ninety-one photographs (one to a page) are chronologically arranged, starting with the crowd entering the plaza on a Sunday afternoon, continuing with the bullfighters' processional entry (the *paseíllo*), the bullfight's three acts (*tercios*), the triumphant bullfighter's turn around the ring (the *vuelta*), and the dead bull being dragged out of the ring (the *arrastre*). The photographic essay presents many bullfighters, including such luminaries as Luis Miguel Dominguín, Antonio Ordóñez, and Manuel Benítez (El Cordobés), but Mailer, who followed the bulls for only two summers, never saw any of the depicted toreros in performance.

Most of Mailer's narrative concerns a wildly uneven novillero named Amado Ramírez, who made his debut as a novillero in Plaza Mexico in 1954. José María de Cossío's biographical essay reports that

> En junio de 1954 se presenta en la plaza "Mexico" en una novillada [. . .] sin conseguir que el público lo tome en serio [. . .]. El domingo siguiente realiza algunas cosas aceptables, demostrando no carecer de personalidad. En los catorce festejos que torea durante dicha temporada da muestras de una gran desigualdad. El 20 de noviembre de 1954 toma una alternativa [. . . .] En dicha ocasión [. . .] el novel matador vió volver vivos a los corrales a todos sus enemigos. Después de semejante fracaso cayó en el olvido. Renunció el doctorado en 1957.
>
> [In June of 1954 he appeared in the Plaza Mexico in a *novillada* [. . .] without getting the public to take him seriously. [. . .] On the following Sunday he did some acceptable things, showing that he was not lacking in personality. In the fourteen performances of this season he showed signs of great unevenness. On 20 November 1954 he took the *alternativa* [promotion to the rank of matador de toros]. On this occasion the new matador had to have both his bulls returned alive to the corrals. After such a failure he was cast into oblivion and renounced his *alternativa* in 1957.] (4: 500)

Mailer follows Ramírez, whom he repeatedly calls "Beloved Remington," through the ups and downs of several performances and concludes his narrative with an occasionally inaccurate account of his protagonist's best afternoon. He attempts to extract transcendent meaning from this mediocre bullfighter:

> Because he never had the ability most bullfighters, like most artists, possess to be false with their art, tasty yet phony, he taught something about life with every move he made, including the paradox that courage can be found in men whose conflict is caught between their ambition and their cowardice. He even taught me how to look for form in other places. Do you see the curve of a beautiful breast? It is not necessarily the gift of God — it may be the record life left on a lady of the balance of forces between her desire, her modesty, her ambition, her timidity, her maternity, and her sense of an impulse which cannot be denied. So go through the pictures which follow. If we were wise enough, bold enough, and scholars, from head to motorcyclist's boot, we could extract the real history of Europe from forms elucidated between man and beast in the sequences soon to be glimpsed beneath your head, *torero de salon!* (*Bullfight*, 23)

With uncharacteristic modesty Mailer calls his narrative "Footnote to *Death in the Afternoon*," and although he avers that "it would be memorable not to sound like Hemingway" (1), he often does. Speaking of himself in the third person, Mailer insists that "for a great bullfight he would give up just about any other athletic or religious spectacle — the World Series in a minute, a pro football championship, a mass at the Vatican, perhaps even a great heavyweight championship — which, kids, is really saying it" (7). However intense, though, his *afición* was of short duration, for none of his biographers records that he has seen as much as a *novillada* since 1956.

Other problems with *The Bullfight* should not go unremarked. As in much of Mailer's work, the subject is not "the real thing, the sequence of motion and fact which made the emotion" (*DIA*, 2), but instead whatever extravagant hyperbole may serve to shift the focus to hasty generalizations or preposterous inferences. As Hemingway confessed, the bullfight was much more complicated than he expected, not to mention the complexities of Spanish culture of which it is an intrinsic part. Mailer waited more than ten years after his first bullfights (in 1954 and 1955) to write about *toreo*, but with no apparent gain in understanding. And his wild generalizations about Mexicans are absurd and at times even racist. It may be true, as Hilary Mills states, that "marijuana became Mailer's spiritual refuge in Mexico" (150). When he tried unsuccessfully to persuade the attorney Hank López to try pot, he accused him of being "a fucking false Mexican. I've never heard of a Mexican who doesn't smoke pot" (Mills, 150). Mailer additionally generalizes that "every Mexican is gloomy until the instant he becomes happy, and then he is a maniac. He howls, he whistles, smoke of murder passes off his pores, he bullies, he beseeches friendship, he is a clown, a brigand, a tragic figure suddenly merry" (*Bullfight*, 2). *The Bullfight* reveals that like his character Sergius O'Shaughnessey, Mailer planned to write *the* novel about bullfighting. It is just as well that it remains in his "Bureau of Abandoned Projects" (*Bullfight*, 6).

The most important and surely the most productive writer in English on the bulls is Barnaby Conrad. Like Hemingway, his life competes with his work for the reader's interest. By 1941, having graduated from Yale University, read *Death in the Afternoon*, and seen two mediocre novilladas in Mexico, Conrad jumped into El Toreo, Mexico City's huge bullring, as an *espontáneo*. The few passes he managed to perform impressed Felix Guzmán, a promising novillero who subsequently subjected him to the rigorous regimen of bullfighting. Conrad also had the good fortune to meet Ruano Llopis, the exiled Spanish taurine painter, who not only gave him his watercolor paintings of Fermín Espinosa (Armillita) but introduced him to the great matador: "I looked upon his brown chinless face with something akin to reverence. He was mentioned in *Death in the Afternoon*, and he signed the book graciously with a big toothy smile" (*Fun*, 49). Conrad seemed about to make a career choice, but then his mentor was gored and he himself was badly banged up by a bull. Conrad returned to Yale for another degree, worked as a code clerk at the State Department, and was then appointed to a vice-consulship in Spain. In Madrid he looked up Sidney Franklin, who gossiped about Hemingway, and he met several great bullfighters, among them Joaquín Rodríguez (Cagancho) and Juan Belmonte, who had been featured in *Death in Afternoon*. Two later bullfighters, Manuel Rodríguez (Manolete) and Carlos Arruza, featured prominently in Conrad's life and work: he wrote two books about the former and translated the autobiography of the latter.

Conrad's writing career has been productive and unusually varied. In addition to fiction, he has brought out books on San Francisco and Tahiti, translated two novels and the aforementioned autobiography from the Spanish, published two autobiographical volumes, compiled *Famous Last Words*, produced three books designed to help apprentice writers, written a juvenile on a pet fox, and researched a famous murder case involving his own family history, among other writing projects. The concern here, of course, is Conrad's taurine writing. Like John Fulton and Sidney Franklin, Conrad writes with the experiential authority of one who has studied, fought, and been injured by bulls.

*The Innocent Villa* (1948) is autobiographical fiction: Conrad's own taurine and amorous adventures in Andalusia are ascribed to the protagonist, Lance Peters, a name neatly combining bullfighting and venery. Although the setting is Cordoba, not Seville, the other main character, Luis Escobar, is clearly the counterpart of Juan Belmonte: "The shadows made Escobar's great jaw seem even greater as it reached up for his curving nose; he looked even uglier than the photographs Lance had seen of him. He was incontestably the ugliest man he had ever seen; he was so ugly he was beautiful" (90). Escobar has two sons, Domingo and Luisín, who are bullfighters. In the corridas that unfold in the last four chapters of *The Innocent Villa*, the brothers compete with the Mexican Cañitas (the nickname of a real Mexican bullfighter, Carlos Vera) for the top honors of the feria in Cordoba: Luisín wins with a superlative performance. Echoing *Death in the Afternoon*, "Lance found it incredible that such emotion and artistry could be produced by just a cape and a man and a wild animal" (235). Political passions add to the dramatic encounter between the native sons of the local hero and the foreign bullfighter, and Franco himself views the decisive corrida from the royal box, eliciting cries of support and disdain from the more and less expensive seats in the ring: "the *sol* [the cheaper seats] [. . .] is always leftist [. . .]. This was a contest between a rich young friend of aristocratic, fascist Spain and a poor Indian from the democratic country that was generously sheltering Republican Spain's exiled leaders" (201–2).

Conrad writes knowledgeably and well about both the action in the ring and the larger culture of *toreo*. His style is fluent and readable, but superficial. Because of this, and because the book fails to integrate its two story lines, the one involving the Aguilar family and the other the romantic adventures of Peters, *The Innocent Villa* is finally not a good novel.

The tightly structured and sharply focused short story "Cayetano the Perfect" (1949) is a better work. Ray B. West, Jr. compared it to Hemingway's "The Undefeated," mistakenly claiming that "it comes very close to plagiarism." Herschel Brickell, rejecting West's claim, asserted that Conrad "as a bullfighter [. . .] is incomparably superior to Ernest Hemingway" (as if Hemingway were a bullfighter!) and then gratuitously claims that Tom Lea's "*The Brave Bulls* [. . .] is so far superior to anything Mr. Hemingway has written as to make the author of *Death in the Afternoon* look like a rank amateur of the art he so much admires, but does not understand" (xviii).

In Conrad's story, the aging Cayetano competes with a much younger matador, both in the ring and, as he thinks, for his woman. During his career he has received three serious horn wounds, all resulting from the wind. On the day of the crucial corrida, he looks out of his hotel room and is reassured by "the red and yellow flag curled lifelessly around the pole" (110), for on this afternoon he hopes to impress his woman, achieve financial security, and regain his self-respect. He begins well, but when the wind starts up he loses his nerve and is gored. As the bull is about to gore him again, this time fatally, a fortunate gust of wind moves the muleta (out of reach on the sand), diverting the animal's charge. Consequently, Cayetano renews his courage, performs a magnificent *faena*, and kills perfectly and spectacularly, using his handkerchief instead of the muleta. The wind, his old enemy, has become his friend, and it "felt good on his sweaty face" (122) as the story ends.

"Cayetano the Perfect" has its strong points: it develops both the seedy setting and the love triangle economically, and it skillfully subordinates and connects these elements to the central struggle of Cayetano with his emotions and his bulls. The wind motif may be slightly slick, but to this reader it seems quite effective.

Conrad's most accomplished work of fiction is clearly *Matador* (1952), a tightly structured novel about the last day in the life of Manuel Rodríguez (Manolete) from the time he wakes up on the morning of his farewell corrida through visits by his manager, the members of his *cuadrilla*, and an intrusive American journalist; a trip to the plaza for the sorting of the bulls; a chat with Juan Belmonte; lunch in his hotel room; a visit from his mistress; efforts by his manager to sober him up; the short drive to the Maestranza; and finally fear, triumph, and tragedy in the ring and death in the infirmary. The main characters are thinly veiled historical figures: the protagonist, Francisco Torres y Nuñez (Pacote), is clearly based on Manolete; Pacote's manager, José Chaves, is based on Manolete's manager, José Camará; the woman, Socorro, is Manolete's lover, Antonia Bronchalo; and his rival, Tano Ruiz, is Luis Miguel Dominguín. Any possible doubt about these identifications is erased by Conrad himself in an essay on "The Writing of Matador," included in a recent edition of the novel: "Pacote was Manolete, as accurate a portrait of that magnetic man as I could draw with words on paper" (218). And in an epilogue Conrad comments on the subsequent lives of Bronchalo, Camará, and Domingín.

Nevertheless, *Matador* is a fully realized novel, not merely a factual report or even a nonfiction novel. "The Writing of *Matador*" is a revealing account of the outpouring of creative energy that produced the work in a mere two months in 1951, though the idea had come to him four years earlier, when he first heard that "a multimillionaire and a bull killed each other in Linares, Spain, and plunged a nation into deep mourning" (215). Conrad's essay also invites the reader to "see where fact and fiction part company" (219). Such a comparison enhances our appreciation of Conrad's treatment of his material.

An important change moves the setting from Linares, a small town in Jaen with a small *plaza de toros*, to Seville and its Maestranza, "the spiritual capital of bullfighting," a much more suitable stage for the unfolding of the tragic drama. The early chapters, especially, insist on the Sevillian setting, reflecting Conrad's thorough familiarity with the city. No other setting would serve as well for the development of the multiple conflicts of Pacote's ordeal. Conrad also deviates from fact with Pacote's drunkenness: although Manolete was drinking whisky in his final year, accounts of his last afternoon do not indicate that he was drunk either before or during his final corrida, as Pacote was. Conrad is exercising fictional license to enhance dramatic effect, as he does also in introducing the man who jumps into the ring (the *espontáneo*) and the substitute bull, neither of which appeared in the plaza at Linares.

The most obvious conflict is the rivalry between the prematurely aging matador, top-ranked in the taurine world, and the younger man who aspires to that position. But Pacote's love life is also conflicted: one reason he agrees to share the afternoon with the aggressively ambitious Ruiz is because the Ruiz challenge was made in Socorro's presence. He wants Socorro but is not sure he can hold her. If she is not quite the "five-peseta whore" (210) that Chaves calls her, she is certainly an unfaithful, mercenary refugee from "the poor country, the dirty country, the drab country" (79) who is intoxicated by urban excitements, heedless of Pacote's needs, and very averse to raising a family and sharing the pastoral future he envisions for them.

But Pacote's greatest conflict is with himself, with "the fear organ right [. . .] below his heart, a great hunk of fear" (8). This is not merely the usual fear before a corrida, not even the special fear that Miuras induce, but the fear of a nervous, demoralized matador who has turned to drink. He knows that the taurine critics are right to want more than the perfunctory "farewell exhibition" that Chaves advocates and that he plans to give. He is also pressured by Cayetano Montoya (Niño de Ronda), a character based on Cayetano Ordóñez (Niño de la Palma), who appears here as a ruined shell of a man asking to serve as Pacote's banderillero this afternoon. Pacote "remembered the book by the American where Cayetano — only the author called him Pedro Romero — went off with an English lady [. . .] 'the best-looking boy I have ever seen.' Well, [. . .] at forty-five he looked sixty" (15) — just as at twenty-nine Pacote looks forty. Against his manager's advice, Cayetano is hired.

All these pressures, conflicts, and characters converge in the dramatic farewell corrida. Tano Ruiz has a successful afternoon, and Pacote, weakened by his encounters with whiskey, with Socorro, and with fear, performs poorly. Whacked on the chest by the bull, he ends up in the infirmary, but returns to the ring for his last bull, which he fights very safely. Finally, however, personal and professional pride (*pundonor*) overcome fear and prudence. Pacote buys the substitute bull, brings the crowd back into the ring, performs all manner of wonders, and is mortally gored when he goes in for the kill. The bull dies; Pacote is taken to the infirmary and speaks Manolete's last words when he dies. Thus, Conrad resolves Pacote's inner conflict: courage and artistry triumph over fear, prudence, and the temptation to betray his artistic calling.

Bullfighting being intimately related to Roman Catholicism, the final scene of the novel resonates not only with the religious mystery of life through death, but also with a Catholic sense of charity. Leaving the infirmary, the grieving manager, Chaves, encounters a beggar without legs asking for "charity for the love of God." Emulating Pacote's generosity, and recognizing that his own career is over, the money-loving Chaves empties out his pockets, giving the beggar a whole collection of symbolic items: "all of his coins and the gold money clip [. . .] and a medallion [religious?] and the keys attached to his lucky monkey's head and his wallet and his cigars and his address book and the comb he carried for Pacote to use in the ring and his wig — all of it he showered down over the half-man," who calls down Heaven's blessing on him (213).

The success of *Matador* made possible the six nonfiction taurine books that followed. First of these was *La Fiesta Brava: The Art of the Bull Ring* (1953), profusely illustrated with 235 photographs as well as some historical illustrations and sketches by the author.[2] The text begins with a moving account of the life and death of Manolete (always the touchstone of Conrad's *afición*) as "the embodiment of la fiesta brava." A very brief discussion of the origins of bullfighting follows, then a longer explanation of the fighting bull, its breeding, its life on the ranch, the testing, transportation to the bullring, and the sorting into lots. Here as elsewhere Conrad and other taurine writers after 1932 confront a problem. Chapter 11 of *Death in the Afternoon* can hardly be improved upon in its description of the characteristics of the *toro bravo,* but one wants to avoid plagiarism. Hemingway's unforgettable first sentence is: "The fighting bull is to the domestic bull as the wolf is to the dog" (105). Conrad's variation is longer and less effective: "The savage toro bravo and the placid toro manso are as different as a cobra and a gopher snake" (14). Hemingway's "From a standing start a fighting bull will outrun a horse for twenty-five yards [. . . and] can turn on his feet much faster than a polo pony" (109) becomes Conrad's "Faster than race horses for the first few hundred feet, they can turn more quickly than polo ponies" (16). The discussion of the bulls is followed by an account of the bullfighters and their preparation for a corrida, enhanced by Conrad's excellent drawings. The plaza itself comes next, then the *paseíllo* (Conrad noting in the glossary that toreros call it "the only easy thing in bullfighting" [180]). Then the trumpets announce the beginning of the corrida, which occupies most of the book (42–249).[3] The text is fuller than the corresponding parts of *Death in the Afternoon,* and the photographs and drawings complement it quite well. The anecdotes, asides, digressions, meditations, literary and artistic pronouncements, philosophical ruminations, and other extratuarine material make Hemingway's book richer and better than *La Fiesta Brava,* of course, but as an orderly instructional guide to the corrida from opening trumpet (*clarín*) to the triumphant bullfighter's turn around the ring (*vuelta*), Conrad's book is superior. And it does no harm that the two decades separating the two works allow Conrad to include photographs of Manolete, Arruza, and Dominguín, as well as Joselito and Belmonte.

*La Fiesta Brava* ends with biographical profiles and photographs of Rafael Gómez Ortega (El Gallo), Belmonte, Manolete, Dominguín, Arruza, and Conchita Cintrón (these last four worked in the years following the publication of *Death in the Afternoon*), as well as with briefer references to bullfighters Hemingway discussed: Rodolfo Gaona, Fermín Espinosa (Armillita), Joaquín Rodríguez (Cagancho), Domingo Ortega, and others. It also adds suggestions on "Where and When to See Them," emphasizing Pamplona; terms for color and horn-shape with English translations; and a glossary of 347 other taurine terms. Hemingway's "Explanatory Glossary" is much longer, and many of its items comprise mini-essays. On the other hand, Conrad explains items in the text that Hemingway relegates to the glossary.

No English-speaking writer on bullfighting could fail to have been influenced by Hemingway, and it is clear that *La Fiesta Brava* was written with *Death in the Afternoon* very much in mind. Conrad mentions "Hemingway's Little Old Lady" [*sic*] and quotes him on the horses (64, 70). When he says that a matador "may swing a capote like Gitanillo de Triana, place banderillas like Maera, and kill like Fuentes Bejarano, but if he does not have a feeling for the small red flannel flag he will never rise to the top" (95), Conrad is probably thinking of Hemingway, for he came to Spain too late to see the first two. But *La Fiesta Brava* takes care to distinguish itself from *Death in the Afternoon*. Quoting Hemingway on Cagancho, Conrad notes pointedly that *Death in the Afternoon* "is still the finest philosophical approach to bullfighting written in English" (47). Philosophical or practical? Hemingway does say practical things, but he also philosophizes on any number of topics: death, the Spanish character, writing, painting, sexuality, and so on. Not at all philosophical, Conrad sticks to *toreo*. As a practical introduction to its subject, *La Fiesta Brava* has few if any peers.

Conrad's second nonfictional treatment of the bullfight assumes an audience possessed of the basic knowledge that *La Fiesta Brava* imparts. His introduction to *Gates of Fear* (1957) explores the nature of fear and courage, and the subsequent nineteen chapters, each carrying the name of a city or country, offer a mix of anecdote, statistics, quotations, translation, and original writing. Most of them focus on important events associated with a particular bullring. With disarming candor, Conrad admits that "the format is just a framework [. . .] for the author to tell his favorite stories about his favorite subject and to quote from other authors whose writings on the bulls he has admired over the years" (3). Since he is such a skilled raconteur with an excellent ear for the telling anecdote, the device works superbly.

A good example is the second chapter, "Talavera de la Reina," which begins with a personal anecdote (Conrad's long trip in an antique taxi with a deaf driver) and then focuses on the familiar story of Joselito, killed in the bullring of Talavera de la Reina. Conrad traces Joselito's phenomenal career from the triumph in the 1910 season when he was only fifteen through the Golden Age of his rivalry with Belmonte (the earlier rivalry with Bombita is not mentioned, however), his trip to Peru, the inexplicable turn of public opinion against him, and the final afternoon of 16 May 1920 with the bull Bailador. Enhancing Conrad's moving narration are a fine full-length portrait, quotations from newspaper files (not from Cossío), photographs, and a quotation from *The Sun Also Rises*. One could hardly ask for a better short treatment of this great bullfighter, born well over a century ago.

The chapter titled "Manzanares" tells another familiar story: the death of Ignacio Sánchez Mejías in that city's bullring. This chapter begins with long quotations from José María de Cossío and Nestor Luján, adding a partial text of Federico García Lorca's "Llanto por Ignacio Sánchez Mejías" in the original and in English translation. This chapter is followed by "Valladolid," which deals not with fact, but with Pilar's recollection in *For Whom the Bell Tolls* of the unfortunate party for Finito in that city, followed by a parody of that novel by Cornelia Otis Skinner, which leads to comments on taurine humor, *charlotadas,* and Kenneth Tynan on gushy writing on *toreo*. Conrad has lost focus here. And most of the text in these two chapters is devoted to quotation, that from Tynan's *Bull Fever* comprising half of "Valladolid."

"Madrid," on the other hand, begins as a historical survey, with comments on early figures (Pedro Romero, Pepe-Illo, Paquiro, Espartero, Guerrita, Mazzantini, Bombita, Machaquito, El Gallo, and Gaona, all of them mentioned in *Death in the Afternoon*), a list of 133 of the principal matadors since bullfighting began, with forty-one asterisks indicating those killed by a bull; and references to more recent matadors, up to César Girón. After this somewhat dry account, Conrad shifts from the ring to the streets of Madrid with the gripping story of a bull that escaped its herders at Carabanchel into the crowded city. Quoting Hemingway on the dangers of the *toro bravo*, Conrad recounts this animal's attacks on a cyclist, a taxi, a woman returning from market (she was killed), and a messenger boy. In the center of town, it encountered the matador Diego Mazquiarán (Fortuna), who engaged it with his coat and umbrella and, when his sword was brought to him, dispatched it with one thrust. A grateful public cut two ears and carried Fortuna around the Gran Vía for an hour.

Another chapter, "Puerto de Santa María," tells about a less familiar figure, Manuel Domínguez (Desperdicios), whom Conrad appropriately places in the context of Pedro Romero's School of Tauromachy (with a gloss from *Death in the Afternoon*), Jerez de la Frontera, and the taurine tradition of Puerto de Santa María. Conrad also devotes two chapters to his own exploits. "Barcelona" describes his performance (and injury) at an Andalusian festival while he was serving in the U.S. consulate in Barcelona. When he returns to Barcelona, the consul, who had prohibited him from entering a bull ring, tolerantly ignores the episode. Although not about Barcelona or events in that city's plaza, La Monumental, this chapter is well done and amusing. In "Castillo de las Guardas," Conrad narrates the "the happiest moment of my life" (192) in "one of the most unimportant plazas de toros in Spain" (177). He remembers "thinking throughout the whole day that it seemed as though everyone had read Hemingway and was trying to talk and act like it" (187). Conrad describes his animal, which was difficult at the beginning, and his own muleta and sword work, which were excellent: he received both ears and an approving phrase from Belmonte (192).

Based on Conrad's first trip to Navarra in 1945, the chapter on "Pamplona" focuses on a friend's adventures in that city's fiesta. This chapter is, unfortunately, a mélange of prejudice and inaccuracy. The absurd opening statement, for example, claims that the running of the bulls demonstrates that Pamplona is "the only city in the world whose entire male populace is made up of psychopaths" (165), a remark which not only ignores the fact that several other cities in Spain, and not a few in Mexico, also have a public running of the bulls, but also disdains that activity, a decidedly minority opinion among aficionados of bulls and of bullfighting. Conrad's friend, Jim, spent a wild night with young Spaniards — "for what wild nights can have I refer you to that splendid novel, *The Sun Also Rises*" (166) — before running the next morning, thus revealing himself a highly amateurish runner. Conrad places Jim on Santo Domingo in a sprinter's crouch and the bulls "a good hundred yards behind him." Jim does not "look back at the bulls pawing and bellowing restlessly in the enclosure back of him" (167). But to look back would have been pointless, for the corral is out of sight at the bottom of Santo Domingo at right angles to the street. Conrad incorrectly calls the rocket signaling the release of the herd a pistol shot. He then states that at Mercadores [*sic*], the bulls "picked up momentum" (167), but in fact the bulls are actually fastest when going up the incline of Santo Domingo. Despite falling down while "wave over wave" (167) of runners passed over his prostrate form, when Jim managed to get up, he was still ten feet ahead of the lead bull and entered the bullring still ahead of the bulls! Either Jim was the world's fastest runner or this *encierro* was the slowest in Pamplona history. Conrad made no corrections when he used the same material twelve years later in *Fun While It Lasted*, even though some of the errors should have been apparent to him while reading the excerpt from Dominique Aubier's *Fiesta in Pamplona*, with which he fills out this chapter.

In such a book as *Gates of Fear*, the chapter on "Sevilla" is crucial, for if Andalusia is the cradle and center of bullfighting, then Seville is its epicenter. Conrad rises to his subject here. A long quotation from Havelock Ellis's *The Soul of Spain* links Holy Week and the April feria, the sacred and the secular. The narratives focus on Belmonte and on two lesser figures from the succeeding generation: Belmonte's son and Joselito's nephew. First Conrad gives us the legendary life of Juan Belmonte, rising from the poverty of Triana to fame and riches by revolutionizing bullfighting, by taking incredible risks and suffering the consequences. For Belmonte, as Conrad powerfully shows, *toreo* was not a means to an end or even a way of life; it was life itself. Coming out of retirement again and again, Belmonte recognized his grand obsession: "The truth of the matter is that I shall probably never retire. When I can't handle bulls, I shall take on calves, and after that I shall probably swing my cape on goats, and then, perhaps, once again bicycles — but I am a torero, and fight I must" (qtd. in *Gates of Fear*, 216). The analogy with Hemingway, for whom life was writing, is unavoidable. When news of Hemingway's suicide reached Seville, Belmonte's comment was terse: "Well done" (qtd. in Michener, 498). One year later, in 1962, no longer able to fight, Belmonte killed himself.

Belmonte's son, Juan Belmonte y Campoy, was an accomplished bullfighter who lacked the strong will of his father. He became a *matador de toros* in 1938 and performed creditably for twenty years, but never met the unreasonably high expectations of the public or, perhaps, his father. After retirement he became a businessman. Even less able to meet the expectations raised by his forebears was José Gómez, nephew of the legendary brothers, Joselito and Rafael el Gallo, and regarded by his family as potentially the reincarnation of the great rival of Belmonte. In first appearance in Seville's Plaza de la Maestranza, he played his first novillo (a difficult one) cautiously, and his second one (an ideal, straight-charging animal) disgracefully. The grace and elegance he had displayed at tientas vanished as he confronted this second animal: he could not work close to it, could not control his feet, could not achieve grace under pressure. He had to be escorted from the Maestranza, scene of so many of his uncles' triumphs, by eight armed policemen and Civil Guards to protect him from the furiously hostile spectators whom he had so deeply disappointed. Returning home to the house that had belonged to Joselito, he took all the pictures of his uncle from the walls and destroyed them (227).

Most of the remaining Spanish chapters of *Gates of Fear* rely heavily on reprinted material. In "Málaga," Conrad calls Arruza's performance there on 27 August 1945 "unquestionably the greatest corrida I've ever witnessed," then reprints his account of it, which he had early published in his translation of Arruza's *My Life as a Matador*. Except for the first five sentences, "Huelva" consists entirely of Kenneth Tynan on Litri in *Bull Fever*. After the first three paragraphs, "Valencia" reprints Arruza's account of his relations with Manolete, first distant and cold, then close and friendly. "Linares," of course, centers on Manolete, reprinting much of the "Introduction" to *La Fiesta Brava* and quoting from Arruza, Tynan, and a long letter from "El Chino" to Antonio de la Villa in Mexico.

Six chapters deal with bullfighting outside of Spain. The two that focus on European countries are personal and opinionated. "Portugal" explains *rejoneo* and *forcados*, but purist that he is, Conrad thinks that *rejoneo*, however beautiful, should not be on the program with formal corridas, and that the performance of *forcados* (men who wrestle with a bull barehanded) is an "atavistic abomination" (232) rather than the exciting and light-hearted show that many spectators, including professional bullfighters and serious aficionados, consider it. In this chapter Conrad also quotes from Tynan and *Death in the Afternoon* on Carnicerito de Mexico; he also reprints six pages from *My Life as a Matador* on the huge success of the brothers Arruza in Lisbon.

The chapter on "France" engages the inevitable question: How can one justify a spectacle that is intrinsically cruel? Conrad quotes writers on both sides of the question, including E. V. Curling, Leslie Charteris, Washington Irving, and Hemingway, who justify it; and two long pieces which attack it: D. H. Lawrence's "choleric, emotional" outburst in *The Plumed Serpent*, and a thoughtful article entitled "The Only Beast: Reflections on Not Attending the Bullfights" by Lysander Kemp, a long-time resident of Mexico and experienced translator who conscientiously refrained from ever seeing a corrida. Instead, he had visited a taurine museum containing memento mori including a ghastly wax statue of Manolete dead in the hospital. Conrad himself states that he intends to "enjoy the nobler aspects [of the bullfight] and [. . .] put up with the less noble ones" but then says, strangely, "that if elimination of all bullfighting from this world depended on a single vote of mine, I would unhesitatingly cast that vote." He quickly adds that he would also ban all other forms of cruelty to animals (244).

*Gates of Fear* also includes four Central and South American chapters, but they contain very little original material. The long chapter on "Mexico" is a miscellany. Conrad identifies Antonio Ordóñez's 1956 performance in Mexico City's El Toreo as the greatest he ever saw in that bullring, but he does not describe it. The best he saw in the Plaza Mexico was Luis Procuna's on 15 February 1953, but instead of describing it he reprints True Bowen's account in the *Mexico City Daily News*. Mexico's northern bullrings, from Matamoros to Tijuana, are treated briefly and condescendingly by Conrad and in a downright silly way by his friend Herb Caen, the late San Francisco columnist. Much more valuable are Conrad's remarks on two American bullfighters who performed often in Mexico, Harper Lee and, especially, his friend Sidney Franklin (whom Conrad never saw in a formal corrida). Conrad's personal comments, supplemented by brief quotes from taurine authorities, support Hemingway's assessment of Franklin in *Death in the Afternoon*.

Most of "Peru" is a long letter from a Peruvian sociologist, César Graña, a surname long associated with bulls in that country. It contains much of interest on black and Italian toreros in Lima, bulls in Greek religion, and memorable work in La Plaza de Acho by El Gallo, Chicuelo, and the colorful Mexican Juan Silveti (El Tigre de Guanajuato). "Venezuela" reprints an essay on a *mano a mano* between César Girón and Domínguín in Maracay, and "Colombia" offers yet another selection from Arruza's autobiography, this one about a bad horn wound he suffered in Bogotá and the subsequent impromptu operation, performed under less than ideal circumstances.

Fear and courage, together with artistry, are the essence of *toreo* and the overall theme of *Gates of Fear*. It is a varied and uneven book, too much an anthology at times, but at its best — in the chapters on "Talavera de la Reina," "Linares," "Castillo de las Guardas," and "Sevilla" — it is better than any nonfiction taurine writing in English since *Death in the Afternoon*.

Appearing six years after *Matador, The Death of Manolete* (1961) has a somewhat misleading title, for it deals not merely with the fatal day in Linares, but with Manolete's family and his early life in Cordoba. As a boy, Manuel Rodríguez showed little interest in the bulls, preferring to stay at home with his mother even though his father and other relatives were toreros. But a few years after his father died, he turned to bullfighting, and at sixteen he was touring small rings. When José Camará saw his potential and began to tutor and promote him, he moved quickly up the ranks, becoming a national hero.

The last two thirds of *The Death of Manolete* focus on the meeting between Manolete and the bull Islero, whose pedigree and history are summarized. Texts and photographs describe Manolete as he dons the suit of lights, arrives at the plaza, and waits for the bullfight to begin. The corrida itself is described and depicted in detail, showing Manolete performing brilliantly at various stages of the fight and then being gored as he goes in over the horns for the kill. Not all the photographs of Manolete and Dominguín, his fellow performer that day, were actually taken in Linares, but the sequence of the sword thrust, the goring, and the removal of the mortally wounded matador are genuine — and genuinely chilling — as are the deathbed photographs. The enormous shock of his death to Spain is noted in word and picture. *The Death of Manolete* ends with a list of his appearances in Spanish rings from 1939 to 1947, but his fifty-three performances in Latin America are only mentioned, without dates or details.

The introduction to Conrad's useful and amply illustrated *Encyclopedia of Bullfighting* (1961) briefly reviews the fiction and nonfiction on the subject, paying the mandatory tribute to José María Cossío's massive *Los Toros: tratado técnico e histórico*. But, as Conrad points out, Cossío's history ends at 1938 while his own book comes right down to the year of publication.[4] In addition to the hundreds of individual entries on toreros and good explanations of taurine terminology, all arranged alphabetically, the *Encyclopedia of Bullfighting* contains a chronological chart of Spanish and Mexican matadors of the twentieth century with the places and dates of birth, *alternativa*, confirmation of *alternativa*, death or retirement, and other details. Separate charts provide similar information about those still active in 1960 and for foreigners (three Venezuelans, two Americans, two Portuguese, one Peruvian, and one Puerto Rican) — all this under the entry for *Matador*. Several entries focus on bulls and bull breeding: the entry for *Toros Célebres* runs for more than four pages, with illustrations; and the one for *Ganaderías* for more than eight, with drawings of brands, or *hierros*. The book ends with the first English translation of the *Reglamento Taurino* of 1930; and two bibliographies, a short one for nonfiction books in Spanish, English, and French, and an even shorter one for novels. Hemingway appears in both bibliographies, and the *Encyclopedia* itself mentions Hemingway several times and describes *Death in the Afternoon* as "still splendid" (xii). No aficionado should be without Cossío's *Los Toros,* Hemingway's *Death in the Afternoon,* and Conrad's *Encyclopedia of Bullfighting.*

The first third of *How to Fight a Bull* (1968) is in the most literal sense a how-to treatise. Through text, photographs, and his own drawings, Conrad takes the tyro through the basic cape and muleta passes, beginning with the stationary *de la muerte* and continuing through the *derechazo*, the *por alto*, the *natural,* and then the *verónica* and *media verónica* with the *capote*. The next two chapters concern the use of tools that the tourist will do well to avoid: the banderillas and the sword. In the latter part of *How to Fight a Bull* Conrad turns to what he does so well: tell a taurine story. The reader familiar with all of the author's previous books will know most of these stories almost by heart, but they are worth hearing again. A wonderful new one, though, is "Bravery in the Ring: Maera," which complements and extends Hemingway's account of this bullfighter in *Death in the Afternoon*.

The ideal coffee-table book for anyone interested in Hemingway, the bulls, and Spain is Conrad's *Hemingway's Spain* (1989) with superb photographs by *Life* magazine photographer Loomis Dean, forty in black and white and seventy-four in color. Several are views of rural Spain: horsemen on the ranch, Belmonte on his own spread, a peasant with his two-pronged pitchfork, a cloudy evening on the Castilian plain, a river below a castle on the edge of a cliff, a young woman lying in a wheat field with the towers of Segovia in the background, olive groves in Andalusia, a rugged mountain road with wild flowers in bloom. Spanish politics and religion are not ignored: bemedaled military brass chatting with a cardinal, a crowd scene with all right arms upraised in the fascist salute, with the following two-pager showing Franco and his henchmen (cleverly captioned "Franco and his Cuadrilla").

But the heart of Hemingway's Spain was the bullfight, and most of Conrad's attractive book rightly focuses on this subject. On the front dust jacket is a village *capea*, and the back jacket shows Hemingway and Ordóñez watching the action in the ring. Between these we find the old caretaker of the Linares bullring showing where Manolete and Islero killed each other, as well as action shots of Dominguín, Ordóñez, Manuel Benítez (El Cordobés), and others. The running of the bulls at Pamplona is amply presented, along with the revelry of that week-long festival. Conrad also includes pictures of flamenco and of Seville's April fair.

Conrad provided many of the captions, but drew on writers like Charles Wertenbaker, Angel Ganivet, Salvador de Madariaga, Gerald Brennan, James Morris, Allen Josephs, Julian Gray, V. S. Pritchett, John Steinbeck, and John McCormick for others. Wisely, Conrad selects more captions from Hemingway than from anyone else, and these come not only from *Death in the Afternoon* but from *For Whom the Bell Tolls*, *The Dangerous Summer*, *The Sun Also Rises*, dispatches to *The Toronto Star Weekly*, "The Capital of the World," and his correspondence. *Hemingway's Spain* is a beautiful and satisfying book.

Norman Mailer and Barnaby Conrad have much in common. Born a few months apart, they were educated at the two best Ivy League institutions, they were fascinated by Hemingway as man and writer, and their response to *toreo* was emotionally intense. Mailer's interest in the corrida was of brief duration; Conrad's was a lifelong passion. But Conrad is far from being Mailer's literary equal. Whereas Mailer's achievement is broad and various,

Conrad's is quite narrow, for his nontaurine books are the potboilers of a free-lance writer who makes no pretense of literary depth.

But if Conrad's niche in serious American literature is small, his position in taurine writing in English is enormous. Even allowing for his habit of recycling material from one book to another, often in similar or even the same language, he has written more on the bulls than any other writer in English, and only Hemingway has written better. The only possible rival of *Matador* as the best taurine novel is Tom Lea's *The Brave Bulls,* but Lea's perspective is much more parochial than Conrad's. As long as there are aficionados in English-speaking countries, Conrad will be read.

In his "Introduction" to *Hemingway's Spain,* Conrad recalls that "long before I ever went there, I fell in love with Spain through Hemingway's writings; *Death in the Afternoon* changed my life, shaped my life, and almost cost me my life." Except for the last phrase, Conrad speaks here for the writer of this essay, for many of its readers, and for English-speaking aficionados everywhere. This is the legacy of *Death in the Afternoon.*

# Notes

[1] For a survey and discussion of taurine literature before 1932, see Miriam B. Mandel's article, "Subject and Author: The Literary Backgrounds of *Death in the Afternoon,* pages 79–119 in this volume, and specifically 84–102.

[2] Each reader (or viewer) of *La Fiesta Brava* will choose his or her own favorites among the photographs, but some of the very best are surely the frontispiece of a dedication to "Bernabito," the herd (21), the Gómez Ortega brothers, Rafael and José (34), an arrogant (or annoyed?) Dominguín (41), four beautiful *reboleras* (54), a dull jet black bull (*negro zaino*) landing gracefully in the passageway between the ring and the first row of seats (57), the chilling face-off between a bull and a picador (65), a horizontal goring (75), an incredible pass performed on his knees by Arruza (79), Belmonte alone in the ring (107), Manolete dedicating a bull (121), Procuna's own famous pass, the *procunesa* (99), Silverio Pérez with the great Pastejé bull Tanguito (136–37), Manolete with an enormous Miura (168), Belmonte preparing to kill (179–80) and taking a triumphant turn around the ring (149), a seated Manolete (161), a standing Dominguín (164), and a pile-up in Pamplona (233–34).

[3] Dispensing with the usual *tercios* framework, Conrad employs a seven-act structure: Act I, The Doubling; Act II, The Matador's First Capework; Act III, The Pic-ing; Act IV, The Quites; Act V, The Banderillas; Act VI, The Faena; and Act VII, The Kill.

[4] Cossío's first three volumes, dealing with pre-Civil War events, were published in the 1940s; the fourth volume, which deals with postwar events, appeared in 1961; eight additional volumes have been published since.

# Works Cited

Brickell, Herschel. "Introduction." *Prize Stories of 1949: The O. Henry Awards.* Ed. Herschel Brickell. Garden City: Doubleday, 1949. ix–xxiv.

Conrad, Barnaby. "Cayetano the Perfect." *Prize Stories of 1949: The O. Henry Awards.* Ed. Herschel Brickell. Garden City: Doubleday, 1949. 110–22.

———. *The Death of Manolete.* Boston: Houghton Mifflin, 1961.

———. *Encyclopedia of Bullfighting.* Boston: Houghton Mifflin, 1961.

———. *La Fiesta Brava: The Art of the Bull Ring.* Boston: Houghton Mifflin, 1953.

———. *Fun While It Lasted.* New York: Random House, 1969.

———. *Gates of Fear.* New York: Crowell, 1957.

———. *Hemingway's Spain.* San Francisco: Chronicle Books, 1989.

———. *How to Fight a Bull.* Garden City: Doubleday, 1968.

———. *The Innocent Villa.* New York: Random House, 1948.

———. *Matador.* 1952. Santa Barbara: Capra Press, 1988.

———, comp. *Famous Last Words.* Garden City, NY: Doubleday, 1961.

———, trans. *My Life as a Matador,* by Carlos Arruza. Boston: Houghton Mifflin, 1956.

Cossío, José María de. *Los toros: Tratado técnico e histórico.* 12 vols. to date. Vol. 4. Madrid: Espasa-Calpe, 1961.

Dearborn, Mary V. *Mailer: A Biography.* Boston: Houghton Mifflin, 1999.

Hemingway, Ernest. *Death in the Afternoon.* New York: Scribner's, 1932.

———. *Selected Letters, 1917–1961.* Ed. Carlos Baker. New York: Scribner's, 1981.

Lea, Tom. *The Brave Bulls.* Boston: Little, Brown, 1949.

Mailer, Norman. *Advertisements for Myself.* New York: Putnam, 1959.

———. *The Bullfight: A Photographic Narrative with Text.* New York: CBS Legacy Collection, 1967.

———. *The Deer Park.* New York: Putnam's, 1955.

Michener, James A. *Iberia: Spanish Travels and Reflections.* New York: Random House, 1968.

Mills, Hillary. *Mailer: A Biography.* New York: Empire Books, 1982.

Phelps, Ross A., Farrell Brody, and Dave Tuggle. *La Busca.* Winona, MN: W & C Printing, 2000.

Tynan, Kenneth. *Bull Fever.* New York: Harper, 1955.

# Works Cited (Companion to DIA)

Agustí Guerrero, María Dolores. *Roberto Domingo: Arte y trapío.* Madrid: Agualarga, 1998.

Álvarez de Miranda, Ángel. *Ritos y juegos del toro.* Madrid: Biblioteca Nueva, 1998.

Anderson, Sherwood. "The Work of Gertrude Stein." (Introduction to the 1922 ed. of *Geography and Plays*). Rpt. in *Geography and Plays,* by Gertrude Stein. Madison: U of Wisconsin P, 1993. 5–8.

Arendt, Hannah. *On Violence.* New York: Harcourt Brace, 1969.

Baker, Carlos. *Ernest Hemingway: A Life Story.* New York: Scribner's, 1969; New York: Collier / Macmillan, 1988.

———. *Hemingway: The Writer as Artist.* 3rd ed. Princeton: Princeton UP, 1963.

———, ed. *Hemingway and His Critics: An International Anthology.* New York: Hill and Wang, 1961.

Becker, Ernest. *The Denial of Death.* New York: The Free Press, 1973.

Beegel, Susan F. "The Death of El Espartero: An Historic Matador Links 'The Undefeated' and *Death in the Afternoon.*" *The Hemingway Review* 5.2 (1986): 12–23.

———. "Ernest Hemingway's 'A Lack of Passion.'" In *Hemingway: Essays of Reassessment.* Ed. Frank Scafella. New York: Oxford UP, 1991. 62–78.

———. "Eye and Heart: Hemingway's Education as a Naturalist." In *A Historical Guide to Ernest Hemingway.* Ed. Linda Wagner-Martin. New York: Oxford UP, 2000. 53–92.

———. *Hemingway's Craft of Omission: Four Manuscript Examples.* Ann Arbor: U of Michigan Research P, 1988.

———. "On Editing Hemingway Badly or Not at All: Cautionary Reflections." *Documentary Editing* 20.2 (1998): 29–34.

———. "'That Always Absent Something Else': 'A Natural History of the Dead' and Its Discarded Coda." In *New Critical Approaches to the Short Stories of Ernest Hemingway.* Ed. Jackson Benson. Durham: Duke UP, 1990. 73–95.

Benson, Jackson. *Hemingway, The Writer's Art of Self-Defense.* Minneapolis: U of Minnesota P, 1969.

Bilger, Martin. *Corrida, Corrida: The Meaning of "Death in the Afternoon."* DAI 55.07 (1955): 1951A.

Bloom, Harold. "Introduction." In *Ernest Hemingway*. Ed. Harold Bloom. New York: Chelsea House, 1985. 1–5.

Brand, Anthony. Interviews, August–October 2003.

Brasch, James D., and Joseph Sigman. *Hemingway's Library: A Composite Record*. New York: Garland, 1981.

Bredendick, Nancy. Email communication, 8 October 2003.

———. "*Toros célebres:* Its Meaning in *Death in the Afternoon*." *The Hemingway Review* 17.2 (1998): 64–77.

Brenner, Gerry. "Are We Going to Hemingway's *Feast*?" In *Ernest Hemingway: Six Decades of Criticism*. Ed. Linda W. Wagner. East Lansing: Michigan State UP, 1987. 297–311.

———. "A Compleat Critique: *Death in the Afternoon*." In his *Concealments in Hemingway's Works*. Columbus: Ohio State UP, 1983. 65–80.

———. *A Comprehensive Companion to Hemingway's "A Moveable Feast."* 2 vols. Lewiston, NY: Edward Mellen Press, 2000.

———. *Concealments in Hemingway's Work*. Columbus: Ohio UP, 1983.

Brickell, Herschel. "Introduction." In *Prize Stories of 1949: The O. Henry Awards*. Ed. Herschel Brickell. Garden City: Doubleday, 1949. ix–xxiv.

Broer, Lawrence R. *Hemingway's Spanish Tragedy*. University, AL: U of Alabama P, 1973.

Brogan, Jacqueline Vaught. "Hemingway's *In Our Time:* A Cubist Anatomy." *The Hemingway Review* 17.2 (1998): 31–46.

Bruccoli, Matthew J., ed., with the assistance of Robert W. Trogdon. *The Only Thing That Counts: The Ernest Hemingway–Maxwell Perkins Correspondence 1925–1947*. New York: Scribner's, 1996.

Burke, Sean. *The Death and Return of the Author*. 2nd ed. Edinburgh: Edinburgh UP, 1998.

Burwell, Rose Marie. *Hemingway: The Postwar Years and the Posthumous Novels*. New York: Cambridge UP, 1996.

*La Busca*. Publication of Taurine Bibliophiles of America, vols. 9 (1973), 12 (1976), 16 (1980), 20 (1984), and 30 (1994).

Byron, George Gordon (Lord Byron). "Childe Harold's Pilgrimage." In *The Complete Poetical Works of Lord Byron*. Ed. Paul Elmer More. Boston: Houghton Mifflin, 1905. 1–83.

———. *Don Juan*. Eds. T. G. Steffan, E. Steffan, and W. W. Pratt. New York: Penguin, 1987.

Capellán, Angel. *Hemingway and the Hispanic World*. Ann Arbor: U of Michigan Research P, 1977, 1985.

Castillo-Puche, José Luis. *Hemingway: Entre la vida y la muerte*. Barcelona: Ediciones Destino, 1968.

*Catálogo Núm. 9: Catálogo de libros, folletos, revistas y carteles de asuntos taurinos*. Madrid: Librería Rodríguez, 2002.

Clark, Ronald. *Einstein, the Life and Times*. New York: World Publishing, 1971.

Clearfield, Andrew. *These Fragments Have I Shared: Collage and Montage in Early Modernist Poetry*. Ann Arbor: U of Michigan Research P, 1984.

Coates, Robert M. "Bullfighters." Rev. of *Death in the Afternoon*. *The New Yorker* 8 (1 October 1932): 61–63. Rpt. in *Ernest Hemingway: The Critical Heritage*. Ed. Jeffrey Meyers. London: Routledge, 1982. 160–62.

Comley, Nancy R., and Robert Scholes. *Hemingway's Genders: Rereading the Hemingway Text*. New Haven: Yale UP, 1994.

Conrad, Barnaby. "Cayetano the Perfect." In *Prize Stories of 1949: The O. Henry Awards*. Ed. Herschel Brickell. Garden City: Doubleday, 1949. 110–22.

———. *The Death of Manolete*. Boston: Houghton Mifflin, 1961.

———. *Encyclopedia of Bullfighting*. Boston: Houghton Mifflin, 1961.

———. *La Fiesta Brava: The Art of the Bull Ring*. Boston: Houghton Mifflin, 1953.

———. *Fun While It Lasted*. New York: Random House, 1969.

———. *Gates of Fear*. New York: Crowell, 1957.

———. *Hemingway's Spain*. San Francisco: Chronicle Books, 1989.

———. *How to Fight a Bull*. Garden City: Doubleday, 1968.

———. *The Innocent Villa*. New York: Random House, 1948.

———. *Matador*. 1952. Santa Barbara: Capra Press, 1988.

———, comp. *Famous Last Words*. Garden City, NY: Doubleday, 1961.

———, trans. *My Life as a Matador*, by Carlos Arruza. Boston: Houghton Mifflin, 1956.

Cossío, José María de. *Los toros: Tratado técnico e histórico*. 12 vols. Madrid: Espasa-Calpe, 1943–1997.

Cowley, Malcolm. "A Farewell to Spain." *New Republic* 73 (30 November 1932): 76–77. Rpt. in *Ernest Hemingway: The Critical Heritage*. Ed. Jeffrey Meyers. London: Routledge, 1982. 164–69.

Crompton, Louis. *Byron and Greek Love: Homophobia in 19th-Century England*. Berkeley: U of California P, 1985.

Daniel, Alix Du Poy. "The Stimulating Life with Gertrude & Co." *Lost Generation Journal* 6 (1979): 16–18.

Davidson, Arnold E., and Cathy N. Davidson. "Decoding the Hemingway Hero in *The Sun Also Rises*." In *New Essays on "The Sun Also Rises."* Ed. Linda Wagner-Martin. Cambridge: Cambridge UP, 1987. 83–107.

Dearborn, Mary V. *Mailer: A Biography*. Boston: Houghton Mifflin, 1999.

"*Death in the Afternoon* sales description." *Scribner's Fall Books 1932*. New York: Scribner's, 1932. 6. Microfilm copy, South Carolina Library, U of South Carolina, Columbia, SC.

DeFazio, Albert John III. Email communications, September–October 2003.

———. *The "Hemhotch" Letters: The Correspondence and Relationship of Ernest Hemingway and A. E. Hotchner*. Ph.D. Dissertation, University of Virginia, 1992.

Delgado, José (Pepe-Hillo). *Tauromaquia o arte de torear*. 1796. Madrid: Turner, 1988.

Delling, Dianna. "Michael Reynolds: Getting Hemingway Right" (interview). *Book* (July / August 1999): 21–22.

Dewberry, Elizabeth. "Hemingway's Journalism and the Realist Dilemma." In *The Cambridge Companion to Hemingway*. Ed. Scott Donaldson. Cambridge and New York: Cambridge UP, 1996. 16–35.

Diamond, Stanley. *In Search of the Primitive: A Critique of Civilization*. 1974. New Brunswick, NJ: Transaction Books, 1987.

Díaz Arquer, Graciano. *Libros y folletos de toros: bibliografía taurina compuesta con vista de la biblioteca taurómaca de D. José Luis de Ybarra y López de la Calle*. Madrid: Vindel, 1931.

Diliberto, Gioia. *Hadley*. New York: Ticknor & Fields, 1992.

Doctorow, E. L. "Braver Than We Thought." *The New York Times Book Review* (18 May 1986): 1, 44–45.

Dolan, Marc. *Modern Lives, A Cultural Re-reading of "The Lost Generation."* West Lafayette, IN: Purdue UP, 1996.

Donaldson, Scott. *By Force of Will: The Life and Art of Ernest Hemingway*. New York: Viking, 1977.

———. "Dos and Hem: A Literary Friendship." In *Ernest Hemingway: Six Decades of Criticism*. Ed. Linda W. Wagner. East Lansing: Michigan State UP, 1987. 41–59.

———. *Hemingway vs. Fitzgerald: The Rise and Fall of a Literary Friendship*. Woodstock, NY: Overlook Press, 1999.

Dos Passos, John. *The Fourteenth Chronicle: Letters and Diaries of John Dos Passos*. Ed. Townsend Ludington. Boston: Gambit, 1973.

———. "Introduction." *Three Soldiers*. New York: Modern Library, 1932. v–ix.

Dowsett, J. Morewood. *The Spanish Bullring*. London: Bale, 1928.

Duffus, R. L. Rev. of *Death in the Afternoon*. *New York Times Book Review* (25 September 1932): 5, 17. Rpt. in *Ernest Hemingway: The Critical Reception*. Ed. Robert O. Stephens. New York: Burt Franklin & Co., 1977. 112–13.

Durán Blázquez, Manuel, and Juan Miguel Sánchez Vigil. *Historia de la fotografía taurina*. Vol. I. Madrid: Espasa-Calpe, 1991.

Eby, Carl P. *Hemingway's Fetishism: Psychoanalysis and the Mirror of Manhood*. Albany: State U of New York P, 1999.

Egan, Susann. "Lies, Damned Lies, and Autobiography: Hemingway's Treatment of Fitzgerald in *A Moveable Feast*." *Auto-Biography Studies* 9 (1994): 64–82.

Eisenstein, Sergei. *Film Form*. Trans. Jay Leyda. New York: Harcourt, Brace and Company, 1949.

———. *The Film Sense*. Trans. Jay Leyda. New York: Harcourt, Brace and Company, 1942.

———. "The Montage of Film Attractions." In *The Eisenstein Reader*. Ed. Richard Taylor. Trans. Richard Taylor and William Powell. London: British Film Institute Publishing, 1998. 35–52.

———. "The Problem of the Materialist Approach to Form." In *The Eisenstein Reader*. Ed. Richard Taylor. Trans. Richard Taylor and William Powell. London: British Film Institute Publishing, 1998. 56–64.

Eliade, Mircea. *The Sacred and the Profane: The Nature of Religion*. Trans. Willard R. Trask. 1957. New York: Harcourt, Brace and World, 1959.

Eliot, T. S. "Hamlet." 1919. *Selected Essays*. 3rd. ed. London: Faber and Faber, 1951. 141–46.

Fadiman, Clifton. "Ernest Hemingway: An American Byron." *The Nation* 136 (18 January 1933): 63–64. Rpt. in *Ernest Hemingway: The Critical Reception*. Ed. Robert O. Stephens. New York: Burt Franklin, 1977. 124–28.

"Fall Book Prices Are Lower." *Publishers' Weekly* 122: 20 (12 November 1932): 1866.

Fernández Salcedo, Luis. *"Diano" (o el libro que quedó sin escribir)*. Madrid: Librería Merced, 1959.

Fiedler, Leslie A. *The Return of the Vanishing American*. London: Granada-Paladin, 1972.

*La Fiesta Nacional: Ensayo de bibliografía taurina*. Madrid: Biblioteca Nacional, 1973.

Fleming, Robert E. "Perversion and the Writer in 'The Sea Change.'" *Studies in American Fiction* 14 (1986): 215–20.

Flora, Joseph M. "*Men without Women* as Composite Novel." *North Dakota Quarterly* 68.2–3 (2001): 70–84.

Ford, Richard. *Gatherings from Spain*. 1846. London: J. M. Dent, [1906].

Foster, Gretchen. "John Dos Passos' Use of Film Technique in *Manhattan Transfer* and *The 42nd Parallel*." *Literature / Film Quarterly* 14.3 (1986): 186–94.

Foucault, Michel. *Surveiller et punir*. Paris: Gallimard, 1975.

———. "What is an Author?" Rpt. in *The Book History Reader*. Eds. David Finkelstein and Alistair McCleery. London: Routledge, 2002. 225–30.

Frank, Waldo. *Virgin Spain: Scenes from the Spiritual Drama of a Great People*. New York: Boni and Liveright, 1926.

Fussell, Paul. *The Great War and Modern Memory*. New York: Oxford UP, 1975.

Genette, Gerard. *Paratexts: Thresholds of Interpretation*. Trans. Jane E. Lewin. Cambridge: Cambridge UP, 1997. Trans. of *Seuils*. Paris: Seuil, 1987.

Gerogiannis, Nicholas. "Introduction." In *Ernest Hemingway: Complete Poems*. Ed. Nicholas Gerogiannis. 1979. Rev. ed. Lincoln and London: U of Nebraska P, 1992. xi–xxviii.

Giger, Romeo. *The Creative Void: Hemingway's Iceberg Theory*. Bern: Francke Verlag, 1977.

Griffin, Peter. *Less than a Treason: Hemingway in Paris*. New York: Oxford UP, 1990.

Grimes, Larry. "Hemingway's Religious Odyssey: The Oak Park Years." In *Ernest Hemingway: The Oak Park Legacy*. Ed. James Nagel. Tuscaloosa: The U of Alabama P, 1996. 37–58.

Grosskurth, Phyllis. *Byron: The Flawed Angel*. Boston: Houghton Mifflin, 1997.

Hanneman, Audre. *Ernest Hemingway: A Comprehensive Bibliography*. Princeton: Princeton UP, 1967.

Hay, John. *Castilian Days*. With Illustrations by Joseph Pennell. 1871. London: William Heinemann, 1903.

Hemingway, Ernest. *Across the River and into the Trees*. New York: Scribner's, 1950.

———. "Bull Fighting Is Not a Sport — It Is a Tragedy." *Toronto Star Weekly* (20 October 1923): 33. Rpt. in *By-Line: Ernest Hemingway. Selected Articles and Dispatches of Four Decades*. Ed. William White. London: Grafton / Collins, 1989. 111–18; and in *Ernest Hemingway: Dateline: Toronto: The Complete "Toronto Star" Dispatches, 1920–1924*. Ed. William White. New York: Scribner's, 1985. 340–46.

———. "Bullfighting, Sport and Industry." *Fortune* 1 (March 1930): 83–88, 139–146, 150.

———. *By-Line: Ernest Hemingway: Selected Articles and Dispatches of Four Decades.* Ed. William White. New York: Scribner's, 1967.

———. *The Complete Short Stories of Ernest Hemingway.* Finca Vigía ed. New York: Scribner's, 1987.

———. *The Dangerous Summer.* New York: Scribner's, 1985.

———. *Dateline: Toronto: Hemingway's Complete Dispatches for "The Toronto Star," 1920–1924.* Ed. William White. New York: Scribner's, 1985.

———. *Death in the Afternoon.* New York: Scribner's, 1932.

———. Death in the Afternoon Manuscripts and Typescripts, Items 22–63a, Hemingway Collection, John F. Kennedy Library, Boston.

———. *Ernest Hemingway: Complete Poems.* Ed. Nicholas Gerogiannis. 1979. Rev. ed. Lincoln and London: U of Nebraska P, 1992.

———. *A Farewell to Arms.* 1929. New York, Scribner's, 1969.

———. "The Friend of Spain: A Spanish Letter." *Esquire* (January 1934). Rpt. in *By-Line: Ernest Hemingway, Selected Articles and Dispatches of Four Decades.* Ed. William White. New York, Scribner's, 1967. 144–52.

———. *The Garden of Eden.* New York: Scribner's, 1986.

———. *Green Hills of Africa.* New York: Scribner's, 1935.

———. *In Our Time.* New York: Boni and Liveright, 1925.

———. *In Our Time.* New York: Scribner's, 1930.

———. *in our time.* Paris: Three Mountains Press, 1924.

———. "Introduction." *Men at War.* Ed. Ernest Hemingway. New York: Crown, 1942. 5–20.

———. "A Lack of Passion." *The Hemingway Review* 9.2 (1990): 57–93.

———. *A Moveable Feast.* New York: Scribner's, 1964.

———. "Muerte en la tarde." Trans. of *Death in the Afternoon* by Lola Aguado. Illus. Pablo Picasso. *Gaceta ilustrada* 11.506–17 (18 June–3 September 1966).

———. *Muerte en la tarde.* Trans. of *Death in the Afternoon* by Lola Aguado. Barcelona: Planeta, 1968.

———. "My Own Life." (Subtitled segment: "The True Story of My Break with Gertrude Stein"). *New Yorker* (12 February 1927): 23–24.

———. "A Natural History of the Dead." *The Short Stories of Ernest Hemingway.* New York: Scribner's, 1938. 440–49.

———. "Necessary photographs." Unpublished Manuscript Item 30, Hemingway Collection, John F. Kennedy Library, Boston.

———. *The Nick Adams Stories.* Ed. Phillip Young. New York: Scribner's, 1972.

———. "Pamplona in July." *Toronto Star Weekly* (27 October 1923). Rpt. in *By-Line: Ernest Hemingway, Selected Articles and Dispatches of Four Decades*. Ed. William White. New York: Scribner's, 1967. 99–108.

———. "Pamplona Letter." *the transatlantic review* 2.3 (1924): 300–302.

———. "Remembering Shooting-Flying: A Key West Letter." *Esquire* (February 1935). Rpt. in *By-Line, Ernest Hemingway, Selected Articles and Dispatches of Four Decades*. Ed. William White. New York: Scribner's, 1967. 186–91.

———. "The Sea Change." 1933. *The Short Stories of Ernest Hemingway*. New York: Scribner's, 1938. 397–401.

———. "The Sea Change" Drafts. Unpublished Manuscript Items 222, 679, 680, 681, Hemingway Collection, John F. Kennedy Library, Boston.

———. *Selected Letters 1917–1961*. Ed. Carlos Baker. New York: Scribner's, 1981; London: Granada, 1981.

———. "Soldier's Home." 1925. *The Short Stories of Ernest Hemingway*. New York: Scribner's, 1938. 145–53.

———. "Some four hundred photographs." Unpublished Manuscript Item 48, Hemingway Collection, John F. Kennedy Library, Boston.

———. *The Spanish Earth*. With an Introduction by Jasper Wood and Illustrations by Frederick K. Russell. Cleveland: The J. B. Savage Company, 1938.

———. "Success, It's Wonderful!" Interview with Harvey Breit, *New York Times Book Review* (3 December 1950): 58.

———. *The Sun Also Rises*. 1926. New York: Scribner's, 1970.

———. "Tancredo Is Dead." *Toronto Star Weekly* (24 November 1923). Rpt. in *By-Line: Ernest Hemingway: Selected Articles and Dispatches of Four Decades*. Ed. William White. London: Grafton / Collins, 1989. 381–83.

———. "Then it was early June." Unpublished Manuscript Items 734, 734a, 735, 735a, Hemingway Collection, John F. Kennedy Library, Boston.

———. *The Torrents of Spring*. New York: Scribner's, 1926.

———. "World's Series of Bull Fighting a Mad, Whirling Carnival." *Toronto Star Weekly* (27 October 1923): 33. Rpt. in *Ernest Hemingway: Dateline: Toronto: The Complete "Toronto Star" Dispatches, 1920–1924*. Ed. William White. New York: Scribner's, 1985. 347–54.

———. Unpublished Manuscript Items 22, 24, 54, Hemingway Collection, John F. Kennedy Library, Boston.

———. Unpublished, Untitled Bullfight Manuscript Item 681a Hemingway Collection, John F. Kennedy Library, Boston.

Hermann, Thomas. *"Quite a Little About Painters": Art and Artists in Hemingway's Life and Work*. Tübingen: Francke, 1987, 1997.

Hernández, Rafael (RAFAEL). "Mr. Ernest Hemingway, el amigo de España." *La Libertad* (24 September 1933): 7.

Hicks, Granville. "Bulls and Bottles." *The Nation* 135 (9 November 1932): 461. Rpt. in *Ernest Hemingway: The Critical Heritage*. Ed. Jeffrey Meyers. London: Routledge, 1982. 162–64.

Hobhouse, Janet. *Everybody Who Was Anybody*. New York: Putnam's, 1975.

Hotchner, A. E. *Papa Hemingway: A Personal Memoir*. London: Weidenfeld and Nicolson, 1966.

Howard, A. E. "Ernest Hemingway." *New York Times Book Review* (9 October 1932): 25.

Hulme, T. E. *Speculations: Essays on Humanism and the Philosophy of Art*. London: Routledge and Kegan Paul, 1987.

Imbs, Bravig. *Confessions of Another Young Man*. New York: Henkle-Yewdale, 1936.

Jackson, Laura Riding. "The Word-Play of Gertrude Stein." In *Critical Essays on Gertrude Stein*. Ed. Michael J. Hoffman. Boston: G. K. Hall, 1986. 240–60.

Jameson, Fredric. *Marxism and Form: Twentieth-Century Dialectical Theories of Literature*. Princeton: Princeton UP, 1971.

———. *The Political Unconscious: Narrative as a Socially Symbolic Act*. London: Methuen, 1981.

Jamison, Kay Redfield. *Touched with Fire: Manic-Depressive Illness and the Artistic Temperament*. 1993. New York: Free Press, 1994.

John F. Kennedy Library. "Velázquez y Sánchez, José" in "Books." *Catalogue of the Ernest Hemingway Collection*. 2 vols. Boston: G. K. Hall, 1982. II: 704.

Josephs, Allen. "Beyond *Death in the Afternoon:* A Meditation on Tragedy in the Corrida." *North Dakota Quarterly* 65.3 (1998): 105–19.

———. "*Death in the Afternoon:* A Reconsideration." *The Hemingway Review* 5.2 (1986): 2–16.

———. "La Plaza de Toros: Where Culture and Nature Meet." *North Dakota Quarterly* 64.3 (1997): 60–68.

———. "Toreo: The Moral Axis of *The Sun Also Rises*." In *Modern Critical Interpretations: Ernest Hemingway's "The Sun Also Rises."* Ed. Harold Bloom. New York: Chelsea House, 1987. 151–67.

Junkins, Donald. "Hemingway's Old Lady and the Aesthetics of Pundonor." *North Dakota Quarterly* 62.2 (1994–95): 195–204.

———. "The Poetry of the Twentieth Chapter of *Death in the Afternoon:* Relationships between the Deleted and Published Halves." In *Hemingway in Italy and Other Essays*. Ed. Robert W. Lewis. New York: Praeger, 1990. 113–21.

Kahnweiler, Daniel-Henry. *Juan Gris: vida y pintura*. Trans. Concepción Falcón Rodríguez. Madrid: Patronato Nacional de Museos, D. L., 1971. Trans. of *Juan Gris. Sa vie, son oeuvre, ses ècrits*. Paris, Gallimard, 1946.

Kinnamon, Keneth. "Wright, Hemingway, and the Bullfight: An Aficionado's View." In *Richard Wright's Travel Writings: New Reflections*. Ed. Virginia Whatley Smith. Jackson: UP of Mississippi, 2001. 157–64.

Kvam, Wayne E. *Hemingway in Germany: The Fiction, the Legend, and the Critics*. Athens, Ohio: Ohio UP, 1973.

*La Lidia*. Madrid, 1914–1928.

Lamb, Robert Paul. "Hemingway and the Creation of Twentieth-Century Dialogue." *Twentieth Century Literature* 42 (1996): 453–80.

Lane, Steven M. "A River Runs Through It: Recollection, Return, and Renovation in Hemingway's *In Our Time* and Wordsworth's *Prelude*." International Hemingway Society, Sun Valley, Idaho, 20–27 July 1996. http://www.mala.bc.ca/~lanes/river.htm.

―――. "Child Hemingway's Pilgrimage: Byron, Hemingway, and Authority." International Hemingway Society, Bimini, the Bahamas, 3–9 January 2000. http://www.mala.bc.ca/~lanes/english/hemngway/ehbyron.htm.

LaPrade, Douglas. *La censura de Hemingway en España*. Salamanca: Universidad de Salamanca, 1991.

―――. "The Reception of Hemingway in Spain." *The Hemingway Review* 12.2 (1992): 42–50.

Lawrence, D. H. "*In Our Time:* A Review." 1927. Rpt. in *Hemingway: Seven Decades of Criticism*. Ed. Linda Wagner-Martin. East Lansing: Michigan State UP, 1998. 19–20.

Lea, Tom. *The Brave Bulls*. Boston: Little, Brown, 1949.

Leach, Henry Goddard. Letters to Ernest Hemingway, 28 June 1929 and 2 May 1930. Incoming Correspondence, Hemingway Collection, John F. Kennedy Library, Boston.

Lears, T. J. Jackson. *No Place of Grace: Antimodernism and the Transformation of American Culture, 1880–1920*. New York: Pantheon, 1981.

Leiris, Michel. *Manhood*. Preceded by *The Autobiographer as Torero*. 1946. Trans. Richard Howard. London: Jonathan Cape, 1968.

Levine, George, ed. *Realism and Representation*. Madison: U of Wisconsin P, 1993.

Lewis, Robert W. "The Making of *Death in the Afternoon*." In *Ernest Hemingway: The Writer in Context*. Ed. James Nagel. Madison: U of Wisconsin P, 1984. 31–52.

Lewis, Wyndham. "The Dumb Ox: A Study of Ernest Hemingway." In his *Men Without Art*. London: Cassel, 1934. 15–40. Rpt. in *Hemingway: The Critical Heritage*. Ed. Jeffrey Meyers. London: Routledge and Kegan Paul, 1982. 186–207.

———. "Tests for Counterfeit in the Arts" and "The Prose-Song of Gertrude Stein." In *Critical Essays on Gertrude Stein*. Ed. Michael J. Hoffman. Boston: G. K. Hall, 1986. 52–55.

Limon, John. *Writing After War: American War Fiction from Realism to Postmodernism*. Oxford: Oxford UP, 1994.

López Becerra, Aureliano (Desperdicios). *Los ingleses y los toros. El secreto de Uzcudun por Desperdicios y Asterisco*. 3rd ed. Bilbao: Editorial Vizcaína, 1926.

López Valdemoro y de Quesada, Juan Gualberto (Conde de las Navas). "Embollado. En beneficio de los extranjeros." *El Espectáculo más nacional*. Madrid: Rivadeneyra, 1899.

Lynn, Kenneth S. *Hemingway*. New York: Simon and Schuster, 1987; Fawcett Columbine, 1987.

Lyotard, Jean-Francois. *The Postmodern Condition: A Report on Knowledge*. Minneapolis: U of Minnesota P, 1984.

Mailer, Norman. *Advertisements for Myself*. New York: Putnam, 1959.

———. *The Bullfight: A Photographic Narrative with Text*. New York: CBS Legacy Collection, 1967.

———. *The Deer Park*. New York: Putnam's, 1955.

Maine, Barry. *Dos Passos: The Critical Heritage*. New York: Routledge, 1988.

Mandel, Miriam B. "The Birth of Hemingway's *Afición:* Madrid and 'The First Bullfight I Ever Saw.'" *Journal of Modern Literature* 23.1 (1999): 127–43.

———. *Hemingway's* Death in the Afternoon: *The Complete Annotations*. Lanham, MD: Scarecrow, 2002.

———. "Index to Ernest Hemingway's *Death in the Afternoon*." *Resources for American Literary Study* 23.1 (1997): 86–132.

———. *Reading Hemingway: The Facts in the Fictions*. Metuchen: Scarecrow, 1995.

———. "Realidad, historia y poesía: el arte de Ernest Hemingway." Conference on Hemingway: "75 años de *Fiesta*." Universidad Pública de Navarra, Pamplona, Spain, July 2001.

Manganaro, Marc, ed. *Modernist Anthropology: From Fieldwork to Text*. Princeton, NJ: Princeton UP, 1990.

Manning, Peter J. *Byron and His Fictions*. Detroit: Wayne State UP, 1978.

Marcoviç, Mihailo. "Violence and Human Self-Realization." In *Violence and Aggression in the History of Ideas*. Eds. Philip P. Wiener and John Fisher. New Brunswick, New Jersey: Rutgers UP, 1974. 234–52.

Martínez-Novillo, Alvaro. *El pintor y la tauromaquia*. Madrid: Turner, 1988.

McCarthy, E. Doyle. "The Sources of Human Destructiveness: Ernest Becker's Theory of Human Nature." *Thought* 56.220 (1981): 44–57.

McConnell, Frank. "Stalking Papa's Ghost: Hemingway's Presence in Contemporary American Writing." In *Ernest Hemingway: New Critical Essays*. Ed. A. Robert Lee. Totowa, New Jersey: Barnes & Noble, 1983. 193–211.

McCormick, John, and Mario Sevilla Mascareñas. *The Complete Aficionado*. Cleveland: The World Publishing Company, 1967.

McGann, Jerome J. *A Critique of Modern Textual Criticism*. 1983. Charlottesville: U of Virginia P, 1992.

McNab, Angus. *The Bulls of Iberia*. London: William Heinemann Ltd., 1957.

Mencken, H. L. "The Spanish Idea of a Good Time." Rev. of *Death in the Afternoon*. *The American Mercury* 27 (December 1932): 506–7. Rpt. in *Ernest Hemingway: The Critical Heritage*. Ed. Jeffrey Meyers. London: Routledge, 1982. 170–72.

Messent, Peter. *Ernest Hemingway*. Houndmills, Basingstoke: Macmillan, 1992.

———. "Slippery Stuff: The Construction of Character in *The Sun Also Rises*." Chap 3 in his *New Readings of the American Novel: Narrative Theory and its Application*. Houndmills, Basingstoke: Macmillan, 1990. 86–129.

Meyers, Jeffrey. *Hemingway: A Biography*. New York: Harper & Row, 1985.

———, ed. *Hemingway: The Critical Heritage*. London: Routledge and Kegan Paul, 1982.

Michener, James A. *Iberia: Spanish Travels and Reflections*. New York: Random House, 1968.

Mills, Hillary. *Mailer: A Biography*. New York: Empire Books, 1982.

Moddelmog, Debra A. *Reading Desire: In Pursuit of Ernest Hemingway*. Ithaca and London: Cornell UP, 1999.

———. "Re-Placing Africa in 'The Snows of Kilimanjaro': The Intersecting Economies of Capitalist-Imperialism and Hemingway Biography." In *New Essays on Hemingway's Short Fiction*. Ed. Paul Smith. Cambridge: Cambridge UP, 1998. 111–36.

Montes, Francisco (Paquiro). *Tauromaquia completa*. 1836. Madrid: Turner, 1983.

Mulvey, Laura. "Visual Pleasure and Narrative Cinema." *Screen* 16.3 (1975): 6–18.

*The National Union Catalogue Pre-1956 Imprints* and its Supplements. 754 vols. London: Mansell, 1971.

Norris, Margot. "The Animal and Violence in Hemingway's *Death in the Afternoon.*" In her *Beasts of the Modern Imagination: Darwin, Nietzsche, Kafka, Ernst, & Lawrence*. Baltimore: Johns Hopkins UP, 1985. 195–219.

"Un novillo de Conradi mata al diestro Alcalareño II." *ABC* (25 August 1931): 39.

Orts-Ramos, Tomás (Uno al Sesgo). *El arte de ver los toros: Guía del espectador*. Barcelona: Fiesta Brava, [1929].

———. *Los ases del toreo: Estudio crítico biográfico de los primeros diestros de la actualidad*. 48 pamphlets. Barcelona: Ediciones Lux, 1920–31.

———. "Bibliografía taurina." *Toros y toreros en 1933: Resumen crítico estadístico de la temporada taurina*. Eds. Tomás Orts-Ramos and Ventura Bagués (don Ventura). Barcelona: Talleres Gráficos Irández, 1933. 333–36.

———. "Libros de toros: Un rato a bibliografía, II." Rev. of *Death in the Afternoon (La muerte en la tarde)*. *La Fiesta Brava* (7 April 1933): 2–3.

Padilla, Guillermo Ernesto. *El maestro de Gaona*. Mexico City: Compañía Editorial Impresora y Distribuidora, S.A., 1987.

Patterson, Curtis. "The Ancients are Ancients." Rev. of *Death in the Afternoon. Town & Country* 87 (15 October 1932): 50. Rpt. in *Ernest Hemingway: The Critical Reception*. Ed. Robert O. Stephens. New York: Burt Franklin & Co., 1977. 118–19.

Penas Ibáñez, Beatriz. *Análisis semiótico de los aspectos taurinos de la obra de Ernest Hemingway*. Zaragoza: Prensas Universitarias de la Universidad de Zaragoza / Instituto de Estudios Riojanos, 1990. Microfiche.

———. "Looking Through The Garden's Mirrors: The Early Postmodernist Hemingway Text." *North Dakota Quarterly* 65.3 (1998): 91–104.

Perkins, Maxwell. *Editor to Author: The Letters of Maxwell E. Perkins*. Selected and ed. John E. Wheelock. New York: Scribner's, 1950.

Peterson, Richard K. *Hemingway: Direct and Oblique*. Paris: Mouton, 1969.

Phelps, Ross A., Farrell Brody, and Dave Tuggle. *La Busca*. Winona, Minnesota: W & C Printing, 2000.

Phillips, Christopher. "Introduction." In *Montage and Modern Life 1919–1942*. Ed. Matthew Teitelbaum. Cambridge: MIT Press, 1992. 20–35.

Phillips, Steven R. "Hemingway and the Bullfight: The Archetypes of Tragedy." *Arizona Quarterly* 29 (1973).

Plimpton, George. "The Art of Fiction: Ernest Hemingway." *Paris Review* 5 (Spring 1958): 60–89. Rpt. in *Conversations with Ernest Hemingway*. Ed. Matthew J. Bruccoli. Jackson: UP of Mississippi, 1986. 109–29.

Pondrom, Cyrena N. "An Introduction to the Achievement of Gertrude Stein." In *Geography and Plays,* by Gertrude Stein. Madison: U of Wisconsin P, 1993. vii–lv.

Pound, Ezra. "Small Magazines." *The English Journal* 19.9 (1930): 689–704.

Raeburn, John. *Fame Became of Him: Hemingway as Public Writer.* Bloomington: Indiana UP, 1984.

Redman, Ben Ray. Rev. of *Death in the Afternoon. Saturday Review of Literature* 9 (24 September 1932): 121.

Review of *Death in the Afternoon. Time* 20 (26 September 1932): 47.

Reynolds, Michael S. "Ernest Hemingway." In *Prospects for the Study of American Literature.* Ed. Richard Kopley. New York: New York UP, 1997. 266–82.

———. "Ernest Hemingway 1899–1961: A Brief Biography." In *A Historical Guide to Ernest Hemingway.* Ed. Linda Wagner-Martin. Oxford: Oxford UP, 2000. 15–50.

———. *Hemingway: An Annotated Chronology.* Detroit: Manly / Omnigraphics, 1991.

———. *Hemingway: The Final Years.* New York: Norton, 1999.

———. *Hemingway: The 1930s.* New York: Norton, 1997.

———. *Hemingway: The Paris Years.* New York and Oxford: Basil Blackwell, 1989.

———. *Hemingway's First War: The Making of "A Farewell to Arms."* 1976. New York and Oxford: Basil Blackwell, 1987.

———. *Hemingway's Reading 1910–1940, An Inventory.* Princeton, NJ: Princeton UP, 1981.

———. "'Homage to Switzerland': Einstein's Train Stops at Hemingway's Station." In *Hemingway's Neglected Short Fiction: New Perspectives.* Ed. Susan F. Beegel. Tuscaloosa: U of Alabama P, 1989. 255–62.

———. "Oak Park Before the Great War." In *Ernest Hemingway: The Oak Park Legacy.* Ed. James Nagel. Tuscaloosa: The U of Alabama P, 1996. 23–36.

———. "*The Sun* in Its Time: Recovering the Historical Context." In *New Essays on "The Sun Also Rises."* Ed. Linda Wagner-Martin. Cambridge: Cambridge UP, 1987. 43–64.

———. "A Supplement to *Hemingway's Reading: 1910–1940.*" *Studies in American Fiction* 14.1 (1986): 99–108.

———. *The Young Hemingway.* New York: Basil Blackwell, 1986.

Ridenour, George M. *The Style of Don Juan.* New Haven: Yale UP, 1960.

Rosenblum, Robert. "Cubism as Pop Art." In *Modern Art and Popular Culture: Readings in High and Low.* Eds. Kirk Varnedoe and Adam Gropnik. New York: Harry N. Abrams, 1990. 116–32.

Sáenz de Heredia, Cesáreo (El Bachiller Garrocha). *Las corridas de toros en la actualidad*. 2nd ed. Madrid: Impresa Hijos de Gómez Fuentenebro, 1914.

Sánchez del Arco, Manuel (Giraldillo). "Informaciones Taurinas: 'Los Toros' de José María Izquierdo a José María de Cossío." *ABC* (1 March 1944): 16.

Scafella, Frank, ed. *Hemingway. Essays of Reassessment*. Oxford: Oxford UP, 1991.

Scholes, Robert. *Semiotics and Interpretation*. New Haven: Yale UP, 1982.

"Scribner's advertisement." *Publishers' Weekly* 122.11 (10 September 1932): 826.

"Scribner's advertisement." *Publishers' Weekly* 122.12 (17 September 1932): 1007.

Serrano García-Vaõ, Manuel (Dulzuras). *Catecismo taurino: Breve compendio de conocimientos útiles a los aficionados a los toros*. Rev. ed. Madrid: Hijos de R. Álvarez, 1913.

Shubert, Adrian. *Death and Money in the Afternoon: A History of the Spanish Bullfight*. New York and Oxford: Oxford UP, 1999.

*Los Sitios Cubanos de Ernest Hemingway*. Videocassette. Cuba: N.p., n.d.

Smith, Paul. *A Reader's Guide to the Short Stories of Ernest Hemingway*. Boston: G. K. Hall, 1989.

Smith, Rex, comp. "The Album of Roberto Domingo." In *Biography of the Bulls: An Anthology of Spanish Bullfighting*. Ed. Rex Smith. New York and Toronto: Rinehart, 1957. 280–89.

———, ed. *Biography of the Bulls: An Anthology of Spanish Bullfighting*. New York and Toronto: Rinehart, 1957.

*Sol y Sombra*. "Días en que se celebran generalmente corridas de toros propiamente dichas en los principales circos taurinos de España, Francia y Portugal." *Vademécum taurino por la redacción de Sol y Sombra*. Madrid: Ginés Carrión, 1909. 255–59.

Sontag, Susan. *On Photography*. New York: Farrar, Straus and Giroux, 1977.

Spilka, Mark. *Hemingway's Quarrel with Androgyny*. Lincoln: U of Nebraska P, 1990.

Stallings, Laurence. Rev. of *Death in the Afternoon*. *New York Sun* (23 September 1932): 34.

Stanton, Edward F. *Hemingway and Spain: A Pursuit*. Seattle: U of Washington P, 1989.

Stein, Gertrude. *The Autobiography of Alice B. Toklas*. In *Gertrude Stein, Writings 1903–1932*. Eds. Catharine R. Stimpson and Harriet Chessman. New York: Literary Classics of the United States, 1998. 653–913.

———. *The Autobiography of Alice. B. Toklas*. New York: Vintage, 1933.

———. "Bibliography." *transition* 15 (February 1929): 47–55.

———. *Geography and Plays*. 1922. Madison: U of Wisconsin P, 1993.

Stein, Sally. "'Good fences make good neighbors': American Resistance to Photomontage between the Wars." In *Montage and Modern Life 1919–1942*. Ed. Matthew Teitelbaum. Cambridge: MIT Press, 1992. 128–89.

Stephens, Robert O. *Hemingway's Nonfiction, The Public Voice*. Chapel Hill: U of North Carolina P, 1968.

Stoneback, H. R. "'Mais Je Reste Catholique': Communion, Betrayal, and Aridity in 'Wine of Wyoming.'" In *Hemingway's Neglected Short Fiction: New Perspectives*. Ed. Susan F. Beegel. Ann Arbor, MI: U of Michigan Research P, 1989. 209–24.

Strychacz, Thomas. "'The Sort of Thing You Should Not Admit': Hemingway's Aesthetics of Emotional Restraint." In *Boys Don't Cry? Rethinking Narratives of Masculinity and Emotion in the U.S.* Eds. Milette Shamir and Jennifer Travis. New York: Columbia UP, 2002. 141–66.

Taylor, Richard. "Eisenstein: A Soviet Artist." In *The Eisenstein Reader*. Ed. Richard Taylor. Trans. Richard Taylor and William Powell. London: British Film Institute Publishing, 1998. 1–28.

Thomas, Hugh. *The Spanish Civil War*. New York: Harper and Row, 1961.

Thurston, Michael. "Gender, Genre and Truth in *Death in the Afternoon*." *The Hemingway Review* 17.2 (1998): 47–63.

Tomás, Mariano. *Los extranjeros en los toros*. Barcelona: Editorial Juventud, S.A., 1947.

Tyler, Lisa. "Passion and Grief in *A Farewell to Arms*: Ernest Hemingway's Retelling of *Wuthering Heights*." *The Hemingway Review* 14.2 (Spring 1995): 79–96.

Tynan, Kenneth. *Bull Fever*. New York: Harper, 1955.

Urquijo de Federico, Antonio, comp. *Catálogo de la biblioteca taurina de don Antonio Urquijo de Federico*. Madrid, 1956 or 1957.

Varnedoe, Kirk, and Adam Gopnik. *High and Low: Modern Art and Popular Culture*. Exhibition Catalogue, Museum of Modern Art, New York, 1990–1991. New York: Harry N. Abrams, 1990.

Vázquez, Leopoldo, et al. *La tauromaquia escrita por D. Leopoldo Vázquez, D. Luis Gandullo y D. Leopoldo López de Sáa bajo la dirección técnica del célebre diestro cordobés Rafael Guerra, "Guerrita."* 2 vols. Madrid, 1896.

Wagner-Martin, Linda. *"Favored Strangers": Gertrude Stein and Her Family*. New Brunswick, NJ: Rutgers UP, 1995.

———. "The Intertextual Hemingway." In *A Historical Guide to Ernest Hemingway*. Ed. Linda Wagner-Martin. New York: Oxford UP, 2000. 173–94.

———. "Racial and Sexual Coding in Hemingway's *The Sun Also Rises*." *The Hemingway Review* 10.2 (1991): 39–41.

———, ed. *Ernest Hemingway: Seven Decades of Criticism*. East Lansing: Michigan State UP, 1998.

———, ed. *Ernest Hemingway: Six Decades of Criticism*. East Lansing: Michigan State UP, 1987.

———, ed. *A Historical Guide to Ernest Hemingway*. New York: Oxford UP, 2000.

Warner, Charles Dudley. "The Bull-Fight." *The Century Magazine* 27.1 (November 1883): 3–13.

Warren, Robert Penn. "Ernest Hemingway." In *Ernest Hemingway*. Ed. Harold Bloom. New York: Chelsea House, 1985. 35–62.

Watts, Emily Stipes. *Ernest Hemingway and the Arts*. Urbana: U of Illinois P, 1971.

Weber, Ronald. *Hemingway's Art of Non-fiction*. London: Macmillan, 1990.

Welland, D. S. R. "Hemingway's Reputation in England." In *The Literary Reputation of Hemingway in Europe*. Ed. Roger Asselineau. New York: New York UP, 1965. 9–38.

Westbrook, Max. "Grace Under Pressure: Hemingway and the Summer of 1920." Rpt. in *Ernest Hemingway: Six Decades of Criticism*. Ed. Linda W. Wagner. East Lansing: Michigan State UP, 1987. 19–40.

White, Ray Lewis. *Gertrude Stein and Alice B. Toklas, A Reference Guide*. Boston: G. K. Hall, 1984.

White, William, ed. *Ernest Hemingway: Dateline: Toronto: The Complete "Toronto Star" Dispatches, 1920–1924*. New York: Scribner's, 1985.

Wilkinson, Myler. *Hemingway and Turgenev: The Nature of Literary Influence*. Ann Arbor: UMI, 1986.

Winterowd, W. Ross. *The Rhetoric of the "Other" Literature*. Carbondale: Southern Illinois UP, 1990.

Wolfson, Susan J. "'Their She Condition': Cross-Dressing and the Politics of Gender in *Don Juan*." *ELH* 54 (1987): 586–617. Rpt. in *Romantic Poetry: Recent Revisionary Criticism*. Eds. Karl Kroeber and Gene W. Ruoff. New Brunswick, NJ: Rutgers UP, 1993. 267–89.

Wood, Greg. "Blood, Sweat, Terror and a Whole Load of Macho Bull." *The Independent on Sunday*, "Sport" (6 August 2000): 14.

Woolf, Virginia. "An Essay in Criticism." 1927. Rpt. in *Granite and Rainbow*. London: Hogarth, 1958. 85–92.

Young, Philip. *Ernest Hemingway: A Reconsideration*. University Park: Pennsylvania State UP, 1966.

# Contributors

ANTHONY BRAND is an Independent Scholar with an eclectic background that includes television, film, photography, bullfighting, flamenco guitar, and taurine history. His photographs have appeared in a variety of journals and books, ranging from Barnaby Conrad's *Encyclopedia of Bullfighting* (1961) to Robert Ryan's *Trapío verde* (2001). He has served as consultant to several photographic archives and to numerous other projects, both print and film, involving Spain and the bullfight.

NANCY BREDENDICK was Professor of Spanish at Minnesota State University-Mankato before she joined the English Department of the Universidad Autónoma de Madrid in 1991. She was named Honorary Professor of the Department in 2003. Interested in the connections between Spanish and North American writing, she has written about the Madrid poems of John Dos Passos and on the meaning of *Toros célebres* in Hemingway's *Death in the Afternoon*. Most recently, she has edited *Mapping the Threshold: Essays in Liminal Analysis,* which contains her essay, "The Dynamics of Decadence in *Death in the Afternoon*" (forthcoming from The Gateway Press, Madrid).

HILARY K. JUSTICE is Assistant Professor of English and Literary Publishing at Illinois State University. Her essays have appeared in *The Hemingway Review, North Dakota Quarterly, Resources for American Literary Study,* and, most recently, in the collection *Hemingway and Women: Female Critics and the Female Voice* (2002). She is currently completing a book, tentatively titled *The Necessary Danger: Hemingway and the Problem of Publishing.*

KENETH KINNAMON is Ethel Pumphrey Stephens Professor Emeritus of English at the University of Arkansas, having previously taught at the University of Illinois and elsewhere. He is the author of *The Emergence of Richard Wright: A Study in Literature and Society* (1972) and *A Richard Wright Bibliography: Fifty Years of Criticism and Commentary* (1988) and the editor of *James Baldwin: A Collection of Critical Essays* (1974), *New Essays on "Native Son"* (1990), and *Critical Essays on Richard Wright's "Native Son"* (1997). He has also written numerous articles, book reviews, and encyclopedia entries in the field of African American literature. His longstanding interest in Hemingway and the bullfight has also produced numerous notes and articles.

MIRIAM B. MANDEL is Senior Lecturer in the English Department at Tel Aviv University, Israel. She has published articles on Jane Austen, Joseph Conrad, F. Scott Fitzgerald, A. E. Housman, and Katherine Mansfield, but her main interest is the work of Ernest Hemingway, about which she has published more than a dozen essays. Her books include *Reading Hemingway: The Facts in the Fictions* (1995, reissued 2001), *Hemingway's "Death in the Afternoon": The Complete Annotations* (2002), and *Hemingway's "The Dangerous Summer": The Complete Annotations* (forthcoming from Scarecrow Press).

PETER MESSENT is Professor of Modern American Literature at the University of Nottingham (UK). He is the author of *New Readings of the American Novel: Narrative Theory and Its Application* (1990), *Ernest Hemingway* (1992), *Mark Twain* (1997), and *The Short Works of Mark Twain: A Critical Study* (2001). He also works on crime fiction and is the editor of *Criminal Proceeding: The Contemporary American Crime Novel* (1997).

BEATRIZ PENAS IBÁÑEZ is Senior Lecturer in the Department of English and German at the Faculty of Arts of the University of Zaragoza, Spain. Her work on Hemingway has appeared in the *North Dakota Quarterly, The Hemingway Review,* and in two collections of essays: *Amor, Odio y Violencia en la Literatura Norteamericana* (1994) and *From Baudelaire to Lorca: Approaches to Literary Modernism* (1996). She is currently working on Hemingway's posthumously published work, *True at First Light*.

ROBERT W. TROGDON is an assistant professor of English at Kent State University and the assistant executive editor of the Cambridge Edition of Joseph Conrad. He is the editor of *Ernest Hemingway: A Literary Reference* (2002) and associate editor of *The Only Thing That Counts: The Ernest Hemingway / Maxwell Perkins Letters* (1996). His essays on Hemingway and Conrad have been published in *The Hemingway Review, Conradiana,* and *The Conradian*.

LISA TYLER is a professor of English at Sinclair Community College in Dayton, Ohio. She has published the *Student Companion to Ernest Hemingway* (2000) as well as two dozen articles in essay collections and in journals, including *Studies in Short Fiction, Pinter Review,* and *Woolf Studies Annual*. She is currently compiling a collection of essays on the teaching of Hemingway's *A Farewell to Arms*.

AMY VONDRAK is an assistant professor at Mercer County Community College in New Jersey. Her reading of modern American and British literature is colored by her training in film, film theory, gender theory, psychoanalytic theory, and popular culture. Her recently completed dissertation, "Strange Things: Hemingway, Woolf, and the Fetish" (Syracuse University), combines several of these interests. Her article on "*The Sun Also Rises* and the Practice of Gender Theory" appeared in *Teaching "The Sun Also Rises"* (ed. Peter Hays, 2003).

LINDA WAGNER-MARTIN is Hanes Professor of English at The University of North Carolina-Chapel Hill, where she teaches twentieth century American literature and women's literature. She has written and edited several books, her most recent being *Hemingway: Seven Decades of Criticism* (1998); *A Historical Guide to Ernest Hemingway* (2000); *The Sun Also Rises: A Casebook* (2002); *William Faulkner: Six Decades of Criticism* (2002); *Sylvia Plath, A Literary Life* (revised edition, 2003); and the *Penguin Portable Edith Wharton* (2003). Forthcoming in 2004 are her biographies of both Barbara Kingsolver (Chelsea House) and Zelda Sayre Fitzgerald (Macmillan, UK).

# Index

*ABC* (newspaper), 102, 219
*Across the River and into the Trees*. *See* Hemingway, Ernest, works by
Adams, James Truslow, 35, 241
Adams, Nick (character), 74 n. 8, 130–31, 267
Agassiz method, 79 n. 9
aggression, 151–52
Agüero, Martín, 203
Alcázar, Federico M., 104
Algabeño. *See* García Carranza, José
Allington, Floyd, 23
*American Mercury* (magazine), 36, 242, 252
analogies: between bull and man, 145, 146; between bullfighting and Spain, 147–48; between bullfighting and United States, 149–50; between Old lady and critics, readers, 247–48, 251; between Spain and United States, 8, 127–29, 133–34, 136–37, 157–58; between writing and bullfighting, 145, 238. *See also* transgression
Anderson, Sherwood, 60, 62–63, 261
androgyny. *See* transgression
Anlló, Juan (Nacional II), xv
anti-Semitism, 283
appendices. *See Death in the Afternoon,* various sections of
Aristotelian unity, 50–51
Armillita. *See* Espinosa, Fermín; *and* Espinosa, Juan
Arruza, Carlos, 287, 291, 295

art, artist, 237–38, 244. *See also* analogies; audience; censorship; collage; modernism; montage; movies; painters; photographs; transgression; *and* writing
*El arte de ver los toros*. *See* Orts-Ramos, Tomás (Uno al Sesgo), works by
*Los ases del toreo*. *See* Orts-Ramos, Tomás (Uno al Sesgo), works by
*The Atlantic Monthly* (magazine), 36
Aubier, Dominique, 294
audience, 167, 251–53
Aulnoy, Madame d', 81, 104–5
author, authorship, 237–39, 243, 246–53
authority, 245

Babbitt, Irving, 241
Baedeker, Karl, 105
Bagüés, Ventura, 105, 114
Bailador (bull), 292
Baker, Carlos, xvi, 11 n. 1
"Banal Story." *See* Hemingway, Ernest, works by
Barcelona, 293
Barker, Llewellys, 61
Becerra y Alvarez, José (Capotito), 82, 105
Beegel, Susan F., 9, 74 n. 9, 277 n. 32
Bell, Aubrey FitzGerald, 81, 85, 105
Belmonte, Juan, 266; in Conrad, 287, 288, 291, 294; in *DIA*'s published photographs, 168, 170, 173, 175, 176, 178,

179. *See also* Stein, Gertrude, works by
Belmonte y Campoy, Juan, 294–95
Benítez, Manuel (El Cordobés), 284, 298
Benlliure, Mariano, 79
Bergson, Henri, 161 n. 14
"Bibliographical Note." *See Death in the Afternoon*, various sections of
Bienvenida. *See* Mejías, Manuel
"Big Two-Hearted River." *See* Hemingway, Ernest, works by
Bilger, Martin, 13 n. 8
Bipolar disorder, 5, 54. *See also* Hemingway, Ernest, diseases of
*Birth of a Nation* (Griffith), 257, 267
Bizet, Georges, 79
Blanco y White, José María, 85–86
Blasco Ibáñez, Vicente, 105
Bleu, F., 105–6
Bohn Library, 27
Bombilla, 28
Bombita. *See* Torres Reina, Ricardo
Boni & Liveright, 22, 63
*Book Dial*, 36
book jacket. *See Death in the Afternoon*, dust jacket of
Book-of-the-Month Club, 25–26
*Borderline* (MacPherson), 266
Borrow, George Henry, 106
Bowen, True, 296
Brand, Anthony, 10, 84, 161 n. 10
Braque, Georges, 261, 262, 263
Brasch, James, 84
Bredendick, Nancy, 10, 56 n. 9, 84, 107, 117 n. 2, 117–18 n. 6, 273 n. 3
Brennan, Gerald, 298
Brenner, Gerry, 10, 11 n. 1
Brickell, Herschell, 288

Broer, Lawrence R., 13 n. 18
Bronchalo, Antonia, 288–89
Brontë, Emily, 45
Brujito (bull), 204
Brunel, Antoine de, 80, 86, 96
bullbreeders. *See under individual bullbreeders:* García Aleas, José; Martínez, Vicente; Mendoza y Montero, Agustín; Miura, Eduardo; Pablo Romero, Felipe; *and* Sánchez, Matías
bullfight, 144–50, 167. *See also* analogies *and* writing
*The Bullfighter* (Gris). *See Death in the Afternoon*, frontispiece of
"Bullfighting, Sport and Industry." *See* Hemingway, Ernest, works by
"Bullfighting a Tragedy." *See* Hemingway, Ernest, works by
"Bull-Fighting Is Not a Sport." *See* Hemingway, Ernest, works by
bulls, 148–49, 171–73; in photographs, 192–201, 203–4. *See also under individual bulls:* Bailador; Brujito; *and* Diano
*La Busca* (magazine), 84, 283
Butcher, Fanny, 71–72
*By-Line*. *See* Hemingway, Ernest, works by
Byron, George Gordon, Lord, 10, 43, 44–56, 106
Byron, George Gordon, Lord, works by: *Childe Harold's Pilgrimage*, 46; "The Destruction of Sennacherib," 44; *Don Juan*, 46–55; *English Bards and Scottish Reviewers*, 45; *The Prisoner of Chillon*, 44

Caen, Herb, 296
Cagancho. *See* Rodríguez, Joaquín

Calderón de la Barca, Pedro, 160 n. 5
Calle Victoria (Madrid), 28
Calvache, Antonio, 166
Calvache, José (Walken), 166
Calvo Martínez, Ricardo, 106
Camará, José, 288–89
Camisero. *See* Carmona, Angel
Campbell, Roy, 82, 106
Capellán, Angel, 13 n. 18, 124, 169–70
"The Capital of the World." *See* Hemingway, Ernest, works by
Carabanchel, 293
Carmona, Angel (Camisero), 82, 106
Carralero, José, 107
Carratalá, Angel C., xv
Castillo de las Guardas, 293
Castillo-Puche, J. L., 13 n. 18
"Cat in the Rain." *See* Hemingway, Ernest, works by
Cather, Willa, 267
censorship, 24–25, 31–32, 36, 239–42, 244, 250–51. *See also* language
*Century* (magazine), 124
Cervantes, Miguel de, 43, 107
Cervera, Manuel, 166
Chaplin, Charlie, 266
Charlevoix County (Michigan), 3
Charteris, Leslie, 295
Chicuelo. *See* Jiménez Moreno, Manuel; *and* Jiménez Vera, Manuel
*Childe Harold's Pilgrimage*. *See* Byron, George Gordon, Lord, works by
Chopin, Frederic, 61
Cintrón, Conchita, 291
*Circulation of the Blood* (Harvey), 27
*El Clarín* (magazine), 103, 218
Clarke, Edward, 87

"A Clean, Well-Lighted Place." *See* Hemingway, Ernest, works by
Clearfield, Andrew, 258, 264
Clifford, James, 127, 137
Coates, Robert M., 36
Cocteau, Jean, 43, 50, 65, 66
Cohen, Milton, xvi
Cohn Collection, Cohn-Hemingway Papers (University of Delaware), 8, 32, 39 n. 6
collage, 258–59, 261–62
Comley, Nancy, 9, 43, 113
Conde de la Corte. *See* Mendoza y Montero, Agustín
Conde de las Navas. *See* López Valdemoro y de Quesada, Juan Gualberto
Conrad, Barnaby, 80, 286–98
Conrad, Barnaby, works by: "Cayetano the Perfect," 288; *The Death of Manolete*, 296–97; *Encyclopedia of Bullfighting*, 297; *Famous Last Words*, 287; *La Fiesta Brava*, 290–92; *Fun While It Lasted*, 294; *Gates of Fear*, 292–96; *Hemingway's Spain*, 298; *How to Fight a Bull*, 297–98; *The Innocent Villa*, 287–88; *Matador*, 288–90; "The Writing of *Matador*," 289
*The Cooperative Commonwealth* (magazine), 6
*La Corrida* (magazine), 103
Corrochano, Gregorio, 102, 226
*Cosmopolitan* (magazine), 24
Cossío, José María de, 285, 292, 297
costume (fashion): of bullfighter, 145–46, 167, 173, 215; of audience, 167
Cowley, Malcolm, 160–61 n. 10, 251, 252
Crane, Stephen, 71
crossover. *See* transgression

Cuba, 4
cubism, 215–17, 257–72, 274 n. 11
cultural translation. *See* Spain; translation; *and* United States
culture (high and low), 214–17. *See also* transgression
Curling, E. V., 295
Cutter, Mrs. Norman, 88

*The Dain Curse* (Hammett), 218
*The Dangerous Summer. See* Hemingway, Ernest, works by
D'Annunzio, Gabriele, 45
Darwin, Charles, 151
Dashiell, Alfred, 24, 25
*Dateline: Toronto. See* Hemingway, Ernest, works by
"Dates on Which Bullfights Will Ordinarily Be Held." *See Death in the Afternoon*, various sections of
Davis, Robert Gorham, 283
Day, Henry, 80, 88
de Falla, Manuel, 79
Dean, Loomis, 298
death, 47–48, 131, 150–51. *See also* joy *and* suicide
*Death in the Afternoon*:
 advertising for, 33–37; analysis of chapter 1, 63–64; analysis of chapter 20, 153–55; audiences of, 251–53; as bullfight manual, 207–8; correspondence about, 21–28, 31–35, 165–67; cost and price of, xviii, 25–26, 37, 166–67; criticism and reviews of, 9–11, 36, 46, 79–80, 251–52, 297; dedication of, 206–7, 218–20; different texts of, xvii–xix; dust jacket, illustration of (*Toros*, by Roberto Domingo), 33, 206, 208–9, 211–14, 217, 261–62; dust jacket, text of, 33, 211, 212–13; footnotes of, 228; frontispiece of (*The Bullfighter*, by Juan Gris), xviii, 33, 206, 208, 214–17, 230 n. 12, 261, 262; and humor, 34, 182, 217, 248, 258; manuscripts and typescripts of, 8–9, 24, 221, 274 n. 9; metacritical agenda of, 237, 239–40, 249–53, 253–54 n. 1; "obscene" language of, 36; pedagogical agenda of, 168–70, 237–40, 243–44, 246–48; and repetition, 264; revisions of, 26–33; running heads of, 32, 228; sales of, 37, 38; table of contents of, 206–7, 220–24; title and title page of, 206, 208–10; translations of, 79–80, 225–26. For "A Natural History of the Dead," *see* Hemingway, Ernest, works by. *See also* genre *and* Old lady
*Death in the Afternoon*, various sections of (as listed in *DIA*'s table of contents), 205–7
 "Bibliographical Note," 206, 207, 220, 224–28
 "Dates on Which Bullfights Will Ordinarily Be Held," xviii, 220, 223
 "An Explanatory Glossary," xviii, 22, 206, 220, 222
 "Illustrations," xvii–xviii, xix n. 1, 2, 23, 24, 35, 165–82, 222, 261–62. *See also* painters *and* photographs
 "A Short Estimate of the American, Sidney Franklin, As a Matador," 31, 134, 220, 222–23
 "Some Reactions of a Few Individuals to the Integral Spanish Bullfight," xviii, 150, 216–17, 219, 220, 222–23
decadence, 65, 240, 247, 260, 265

dedication. *See Death in the Afternoon*, dedication of
defamiliarization, 216
DeFazio, Albert John III, xvi, 84
Delgado, José (Pepe-Hillo), 82, 214, 293
depression of 1930s. *See Death in the Afternoon*, cost and price of; *and* United States
"The Destruction of Sennacherib." *See* Byron, George Gordon, Lord, works by
Dewberry, Elizabeth, 6
Dewey, John, 241
diabetes. *See* Hemingway, Ernest, diseases of
Diamond, Stanley, 124
Diano (bull), 172
Díaz Arquer, Graciano, 82, 83, 84, 107, 226–27
didacticism. *See Death in the Afternoon*, pedagogical agenda of
Doctorow, E. L., 156
Domingo, Roberto, 165, 211, 212, 230 n. 10. *See also Death in the Afternoon*, dust jacket, illustration of
Domínguez, Manuel (Desperdicios), 293
Dominguín. *See* González Lucas, Luis Miguel; *and* González Mateos, Domingo
*Don Juan*. *See* Byron, George Gordon, Lord, works by
don Luis. *See* Uriarte, Luis
don Ventura, Ventura. *See* Bagüés, Ventura
Doolittle, Hilda (H. D.), 266
Dorman-Smith, Eric Edward, 14 n. 20
Dos Passos, John, 23, 24, 107, 266–67, 283; editorial suggestions of, 26–31, 72

Dos Passos, John, works by: *Fourteenth Chronicle*, 26–27, 31; *Manhattan Transfer*, 267; *Three Soldiers*, 39–40 n. 9; *U. S. A.*, 267
Dowsett, J. Morewood, 82, 107–8, 209–10
Dreiser, Theodore, 241
Drink, 47, 128. *See also* Hemingway, Ernest, diseases of
*Dubliners* (Joyce), 261
Duffus, R. L., 36, 252
Dumas, Alexandre, 43
dust jacket. *See Death in the Afternoon*, dust jacket of

Eby, Carl, 138 n. 14
*El eco taurino* (magazine), 103
Einstein, Albert, 241, 260–61, 269–70
Eisenstein, Sergei, 268–70
El Gallo. *See* Gómez Ortega, Rafael
Eliade, Mircea, 132
Eliot, T. S., 29, 43
Elliot, Frances, 80
Ellis, Havelock, 56 n. 8, 81, 108, 294
*English Bards and Scottish Reviewers*. *See* Byron, George Gordon, Lord, works by
epigraph, 217
Espinosa, Fermín (Armillita Chico), 186 n. 33, 286, 291
Espinosa, Juan (Armillita), 189
"An Explanatory Glossary." *See Death in the Afternoon*, various sections of

Fadiman, Clifton, 46
*A Farewell to Arms*. *See* Hemingway, Ernest, works by
Farrell, James Thomas, 283
fashion. *See* costume

Faulkner, William, 43, 52, 213, 230 n. 11
fear, 150–51
Fernández, Baldomero, 166
Fernández de Heredia, Antonio (Hache), 82, 109, 225
Fiedler, Leslie, 161 n. 11
Field, Henry M., 89
*La Fiesta Brava* (magazine), 103, 208
filmic montage, 266–71. *See also* montage *and* movies
Firbank, Ronald, 43, 50, 52, 65, 66, 75 n. 18
"The First Matador Got the Horn." *See* Hemingway, Ernest, works by
First World War. *See* war
Fitch, Noel, 84
Fitzgerald, F. Scott, 73 n. 1, 162 n. 17
Fleming, Robert, 241
Flora, Joseph M., 7
footnotes. *See Death in the Afternoon*, footnotes of
*For Whom the Bell Tolls*. *See* Hemingway, Ernest, works by
Ford, Ford Madox, 43, 73 n. 1
Ford, Richard, 82, 83, 209–10, 219
Ford, Richard, works by: *Gatherings from Spain*, 81, 89–90, 109; dedication of, 219
*The Handbook for Travellers in Spain and Readers at Home*, 90
*Fortune* (magazine), 21
*The Forum* (magazine), 36, 240–41
Foucault, Michel, 254 n. 2
*Fourteenth Chronicle*. *See* Dos Passos, John, works by
France, 295–96
Franco, Francisco, 287, 298
Frank, Waldo, 33, 43, 52, 82

Frank, Waldo, works by: *Virgin Spain*, 26–29, 32–33, 52, 83, 109, 219, 260
Franklin, Sidney, 31, 115, 220, 223, 228, 287, 296; in photographs, 180
Frazer, James George, 109
Freg, Luis, 167, 168, 172, 173, 178, 181, 201, 202
Freud, Sigmund, 43, 151
frontispiece. *See Death in the Afternoon*, frontispiece of; *see also* Gris, Juan
Fuentes Bejarano, Luis, 291
Fulton, John, 287

*Gaceta Ilustrada* (magazine), 221
Gallo family, 173, 178. *See also* Gómez Ortega, José; *and* Gómez Ortega, Rafael
Gallo, El Gallo. *See* Gómez Ortega, Rafael
Ganivet, Angel, 298
Gaona, Rodolfo, 85, 185 n. 24, 201, 291, 293
gap (between reader and text), 206–8, 220
García, Manuel (El Espartero), 166, 181, 182, 277 n. 32, 293
García, Manuel (Maera). *See* García López, Manuel
García Aleas, José (bullbreeder), 204
García Carrafa, Arturo, 110
García Carranza, José (Algabeño), 212
García López, Manuel (Maera), 25, 177, 179, 211–12, 263; Conrad mentions, 291, 298; in Hemingway's work, xiii, xiv, xiv, 8; as parallel to Hemingway, 66; in photographs, xix n. 1, 168, 173, 196, 197
García Lorca, Federico, 79, 284, 292

García Rodrigo, Ramón, 110
*The Garden of Eden. See*
  Hemingway, Ernest, works by
Gaskell, Mrs. William (Elizabeth
  Cleghorn), 62
*Gatherings from Spain. See* Ford,
  Richard, works by
Gautier, Theophile, 90–91
gender roles, 149–50. *See also*
  transgression
Genette, Gerard, 205, 209, 219,
  224, 229
genre, generic crossovers: in
  *Death in the Afternoon*, 1–2,
  11–12 n. 2, 137 n. 3, 205–6,
  208, 239–40, 252, 257–62,
  273 n. 5; in Hemingway's
  earlier work, 5–8. *See also* gap
  *and* transgression
*Geography and Plays. See* Stein,
  Gertrude, works by
Gerogiannis, Nicholas, xvi
Gide, André, 43, 50
Giles, Dorothy, 81, 110
Gingrich, Arnold, 209
Girón, César, 293, 296
Gitanillo de Triana. *See* Vega de
  los Reyes, Francisco
glossary. *See Death in the
  Afternoon*, various sections of
Gómez, José, 294–95
Gómez Ortega, José (Joselito),
  168, 170, 172, 173, 178–79,
  266; in Conrad's work, 292
Gómez Ortega, Rafael (El Gallo),
  25, 168, 173, 174, 181, 211; in
  Conrad's work, 291, 293
González, Rafael (Machaquito),
  293
González Lucas, Luis Miguel
  (Dominguín), 284, 288–89,
  291, 296, 298
González Mateos, Domingo
  (Dominguín), 185 n. 24, 201
Gordon, Jan and Cora, 91

Goya y Lucientes, Francisco José
  de, 29, 79, 82, 110, 165;
  mentioned, 149
Granados, José (Veneno), 175
Granero, Manuel, 172, 173
Gray, Julian, 298
El Greco, 29, 50
*Green Hills of Africa. See*
  Hemingway, Ernest, works by
Griffin, Peter, 44, 45, 46
Griffith, D. W., 257, 268. *See also*
  movies
Grimes, Larry E., 3
Gris, Juan, 165, 263. *See also
  Death in the Afternoon*,
  frontispiece of
Guerra, Rafael (Guerrita), 82,
  105–6, 110, 114, 116, 166,
  214, 293
Guzmán, Félix, 286

H. D. (Hilda Doolittle), 266
Haba, Antonio de la (Zurito),
  131
Haba, Manuel de la (Zurito), 175
Hache. *See* Fernández de Heredia,
  Antonio
Hall-Hemingway, Grace (mother
  of E. H.), 2–7, 59–60
Hammett, Dashiell, 43, 218
*Harper's Monthly*, 36
Harris, Frank, 91
Hart, Jerome, 91–92
Harte, Bret, 92
*Harvard Psychological Review*, 61
Harvey, William, 27
Havelock, Ellis, 108
Hay, John, 81, 110
Heap, Jane, 13 n. 12
Hemingway, Clarence Edmonds
  (Ed, father of E. H.), 3–8
Hemingway, Ernest: artistic
  development of, 143; attacks
  authors, critics, 52–54, 59–63;
  and authenticity, 123–24;

biographies of, 5; childhood and family of, 2–4; diseases of, 4–5, 54; education of, 44, 61, 143; and heroism, Romantic tradition, 45–47, 53–54, 131; iceberg theory of, 133, 156–58, 268–69; as insider, outsider in Spain and bullfighting, 207–8, 124–26, 133–39, 153–54; as journalist, 6–7, 59; and money, 134–36, 166–67, 273 n. 2; as public figure, brand name, 44–45, 238–39; reading of, 81–84, 102–17; repetitions of, 7, 265; and superstition, 32; travels of, 1, 4; unpublished work of, xv–xvi; use of pronouns, 6, 221–22, 224, 243, 245–47, 249; use of sources, 10, 43, 45, 50, 81–84, 102–17, 225–28, 273 n. 3, 277 n. 3. *See also under individual sources and influences:* Byron, George Gordon; Orts-Ramos, Tomás; *and* Stein, Gertrude

Hemingway, Ernest, works by:
*Across the River and into the Trees,* 45–46
"Banal Story," 8
"Big Two-Hearted River," 63, 259
"Bullfighting, Sport and Industry," 8, 21
"Bullfighting a Tragedy," 7
"Bull-Fighting Is Not a Sport," 8
*By-Line* (ed. William White), 1
"The Capital of the World," 298
"Cat in the Rain," 7
"A Clean, Well-Lighted Place," 145
*The Dangerous Summer,* xiv, 1, 298
*Dateline: Toronto* (ed. William White), 21
*A Farewell to Arms,* 1, 24, 74 n. 8, 81, 131, 240, 267–68; critical and financial success of, 30, 36, 38, 71, 212–13, 253
"The First Matador Got the Horn," 7–8
*For Whom the Bell Tolls,* xiii, 1, 292, 298
*The Garden of Eden,* 5, 55 n. 1, 150, 259
*Green Hills of Africa,* 38, 148, 270
*The Hemingway Reader* (ed. Charles Poore), 21–22
"Homage to Switzerland," 260–61, 266, 270
"Indian Camp," 7
*in our time* (1924), 261
*In Our Time* (1925), 7, 22, 168, 212–13, 261
*In Our Time* (1930), 22, 148, 170
"Judgment at Manitou," 12 n. 8
"A Lack of Passion," 49, 168
"The Last Good Country," 45
"Maera Lay Still," 8
"A Matter of Colour," 12 n. 8
*Men at War* (ed. Ernest Hemingway), 55 n. 1, 71
*Men Without Women,* 12–13 n. 1, 55 n. 4
"The Mother of a Queen," 8
*A Moveable Feast,* 63
"Mr. and Mrs. Elliot," 22
"A Natural History of the Dead," 23, 29, 34, 61, 66–67, 130–31, 209, 240, 242, 260, 264–65
*The Old Man and the Sea,* 13 n. 16, 145

"On the Quai at Smyrna," 7, 22, 260
"Pamplona in July," 7
"Pamplona Letter," 8
"The Poem Is By Maera," 8
"Refugees from Thrace," 7
"The Sea Change," 23, 150, 240, 241
"Sepi Jingan," 12 n. 8
"The Short Happy Life of Francis Macomber," 55 n. 1, 150
"A Silent, Ghastly Procession," 7
"The Snows of Kilimanjaro," 273 n. 2
"Soldier's Home," 7
"[Someday when you are picked up . . .]," 13 n. 13
"The Soul of Spain with McAlmon and Bird the Publishers," 13 n. 13
*The Spanish Earth* (film), 125
*The Sun Also Rises,* xiii, 1, 7, 8, 74 n. 8, 134, 135, 169; in Conrad's work, 292, 293–94, 298; referred to but not named, 290
"Tancredo is Dead," 8
"The Three-Day Blow," 7
*Three Stories & Ten Poems,* 7
*To Have and Have Not,* 1
"To a Tragic Poetess," 13 n. 13
*The Torrents of Spring,* 45, 267
*True at First Light,* 145
"The Undefeated," 8, 168, 277 n. 32
"Up in Michigan," 61
"A Very Short Story," 22
"Wanderings," 7
"Wine of Wyoming," 145
"World's Series of Bull Fighting a Mad, Whirling Carnival," 8
Hemingway, Grace. *See* Hall-Hemingway, Grace

Hemingway, Gregory (son of E. H.), 23
Hemingway, Hadley Richardson (first wife of E. H.), 59, 74 n. 13
Hemingway, John Hadley Nicanor (son of E. H.), 168, 218
Hemingway, Mary Welsh (fourth wife of E. H.), 74 n. 13
Hemingway, Patrick (son of E. H.), 260
Hemingway, Pauline Pfeiffer (second wife of E. H.), 23, 74 n. 13, 218–19
Hemingway Collection (at John F. Kennedy Library), xvi–xvi, 8, 189
*The Hemingway Reader. See* Hemingway, Ernest, works by
Henry, O., 43
Hernández, Rafael, 208
Hernandorena, Domingo, 246, 253, 269
Hicks, Granville, 251, 252
Hollywood, 273 n. 2. *See also* movies
"Homage to Switzerland." *See* Hemingway, Ernest, works by
homophobia, homosexuals. *See* transgressions
Horace, 50
Horton Bay (Michigan), 3, 4
Hotchner, A. E., 162 n. 17
Howells, William Dean, 93
Hudson, W. H., 43
Hulme, T. E., 161 n. 14, 162 n. 19
Hume, Martin, 81
humor. *See Death in the Afternoon,* and humor
Huxley, Aldous, 43, 62, 213, 249–51

iceberg theory. *See* Hemingway, Ernest, iceberg theory of
Idaho, 4
"Illustrations." *See Death in the Afternoon,* various sections of
"Indian Camp." *See* Hemingway, Ernest, works by
individual, and the state, 148–49. *See also* art
innatism, 151
insider. *See* Hemingway, Ernest, as insider, outsider in Spain
*In Our Time. See* Hemingway, Ernest, works by
Irving, Washington, 81, 111, 295
Ivens, Joris, 125. *See also* movies

Jackson, Laura Riding, 65
James, Henry, 43, 50, 63–64
James, William, 61
Jameson, Fredric, 138 n. 13
Jamison, Kay Redfield, 5, 54
Jerez de la Frontera, 293
Jiménez Moreno, Manuel (Chicuelo), 49, 211; in fiction, 168; in painting, 262; in photos, 167, 168, 172, 173, 179–80, 193–95
Jiménez Vera, Manuel (Chicuelo), 185 n. 28
Jones, Tom, 111
Joselito. *See* Gómez Ortega, José
Josephs, Allen, 13 n. 18, 259, 298
joy, of creating and killing, 152–55
Joyce, James, 261
"Judgment at Manitou." *See* Hemingway, Ernest, works by
Junkins, Donald, 12 n. 3, 13 n. 18, 14 n. 19, 262
Justice, Hilary, 11

Keith, Arthur, 241
Kemp, Lysander, 295
Kenya, 4

Key West (Florida), 4, 27
killing. *See* death *and* joy
Kinnamon, Keneth, 11, 13 n. 18
Knudsen process, xvii

"A Lack of Passion." *See* Hemingway, Ernest, works by
Lalanda, Marcial, 167, 168, 173, 180, 211
Lamb, Robert Paul, 43
Lane, Steven M., 45
language, 36, 53. *See also* censorship *and* decadence
Lanham, Charles, 14 n. 20
"The Last Good Country." *See* Hemingway, Ernest, works by
Lawrence, D. H., 7, 111–12, 295
Lawrence, T. E., 45, 274 n. 8
Layman, Richard, 84
Lea, Tom, 288, 299
Leach, Henry Goddard, 240–42
Lee, Harper, 296
Lee, Sidney, 80
Leiris, Michel, 132
Lengle, William, 24
Lewis, Robert W., 9, 14 n. 19, 165
Lewis, Wyndham, 65, 160–61 n. 10
*La Libertad* (newspaper), 208
*La Lidia* (magazine), 103
*Life* (magazine), 298
liminality (threshold), 205. *See also* genre *and* transgression
Linares, 289
Longfellow, Henry Wadsworth, 43, 94, 218
Lope de Vega, Félix, 43
López, Hank, 286
López, Luis (Chanito), xv
López Valdemoro y de Quesada, Juan Gualberto (Conde de las Navas), 82, 112, 225
lost generation, 258
Lowell, James Russell, 94

Luján, Nestor, 292
Lynn, Kenneth, 267

Machaquito. *See* González, Rafael
macho image, 283
MacLeish, Archibald, 21, 24, 267
MacPherson, Kenneth, 266. *See also* movies
Madariaga, Salvador de, 81, 112, 298
Madrid, 176, 293
Maera. *See* García López, Manuel
"Maera Lay Still." *See* Hemingway, Ernest, works by
Maestranza (bullring), 289–90. *See also* Seville
Mailer, Norman, 283–86
Mailer, Norman, works by: *Advertisements for Myself*, 284; *The Bullfight: A Photographic Narrative*, 284–86; *The Deer Park*, 284
*The Making of Americans*. *See* Stein, Gertrude, works by
Málaga, 295
Mandel, Miriam B., xvi, 11 n. 1, 259, 262
Manet, Edouard, 165
Manganaro, Marc, 127
*Manhattan Transfer*. *See* Dos Passos, John, works by
Manning, Peter, 52, 53
Manolete. *See* Rodríguez, Manuel
Manzanares, 292
Marín, Ricardo, 165
Marlowe, Christopher, 43, 50
Márquez, Antonio, 186 n. 33, 193
Martín-Caro, Juan (Chiquito de la Audiencia), 49
Martínez, Vicente (bullbreeder), 184 n. 17, 185 n. 29
Marvell, Andrew, 29, 43
Marx, Karl, 151
Mateo, Manuel, 166

"A Matter of Colour." *See* Hemingway, Ernest, works by
Maugham, W. Somerset, 81, 112
Maupassant, Guy de, 43
Mazquiarán, Diego (Fortuna), 266, 293
Mazzantini, Luis, 166, 293
McBride, Robert Medill, 112
McCormick, John, 80, 298
McGann, Jerome, 253–54 n. 1
McNab, Angus, 80
Meier-Graefe, Julius, 43, 81, 83, 113
Mejías, Manuel (Manolo Bienvenida), 168, 169, 173, 180
memory. *See* nostalgia
*Men at War*. *See* Hemingway, Ernest, works by
*Men Without Women*. *See* Hemingway, Ernest, works by
Mencken, H. L., 36, 241, 242, 251–52
Mendoza y Montero, Agustín (Conde de la Corte, bullbreeder), 211
Mérimée, Prosper, 95–96
Messent, Peter, 10
metacriticism. *See Death in the Afternoon*, metacritical agenda of
metatextual, 51, 74 n. 8
Mexico, 296
*Mexico City Daily News*, 296
Meyer, Wallace, 284
Millán, Pascual, 113, 225
Mills, Hilary, 286
Minguet y Calderón de la Barca, Enrique (Pensamientos), 113
Miura, Eduardo (bullbreeder), 211
Moddelmog, Debra, 136
modernism, 2, 11, 158. *See also* cubism; Einstein, Albert; Eisenstein, Sergei; *and* time

modernity. *See* Spain, as antidote to modernity
money, and publication, 166–67, 245–47. *See also Death in the Afternoon,* cost and price of; *and* Hemingway, Ernest, and money
Monroe, Harriet, 7
montage, 258–59, 262–63. *See also* filmic montage
Montana, 4
Montes, Francisco (Paquiro), 113, 214, 215, 226, 293
Montherland, Henri de, 113
Moore, Thomas Ewing, 96
Morris, James, 298
mortality. *See* death
"The Mother of a Queen." *See* Hemingway, Ernest, works by
*A Moveable Feast. See* Hemingway, Ernest, works by
movies, 125, 257, 266–70. *See also* Hollywood
"Mr. and Mrs. Elliot." *See* Hemingway, Ernest, works by
Muñoz Díaz, Eugenio (Eugenio Noel), 114
Mürnsterberg, Hugo, 61

Nacional II. *See* Anlló, Juan
narrator, 50, 221–22
"A Natural History of the Dead." *See* Hemingway, Ernest, works by
*New York Herald,* 36
*New York Sun,* 36
*The New York Times Book Review,* 36, 37–38
*The New Yorker,* 36
Niño de la Palma. *See* Ordóñez, Cayetano
Noel, Eugenio. *See* Muñoz Díaz, Eugenio
Norris, Margot, 13 n. 8

nostalgia (and memory), 128–30, 138 n. 10, 139 n. 21, 152–53, 259, 260

Oak Park (Illinois), 2–3, 4, 252
Ojibway, 3
Old lady, 59–62, 64–69, 221–22, 239–43, 246–49, 264–65; added in galleys, 28, 29, 72; mentioned, 291. *See also* analogies
*The Old Man and the Sea. See* Hemingway, Ernest, works by
Olmos, Rosario, 173, 211
"On the Quai at Smyrna." *See* Hemingway, Ernest, works by
*One of Ours* (Cather), 267
Ordóñez, Antonio, 284, 296, 298
Ordóñez, Cayetano (Niño de la Palma), 29, 169, 198, 199, 290, 291
Ortega, Domingo, 103, 169, 173, 180
Ortega, Enrique (Almendro), 181
Orts-Ramos, Tomás (Uno al Sesgo), 83, 208
Orts-Ramos, Tomás (Uno al Sesgo), works by: *El arte de ver los toros,* 114, 227; *Los ases del toreo,* 223; *Toros y toreros en . . .,* 114

Pablo Romero, Felipe (bullbreeder), 211
Pacheco, Juan (Vandel), xvii, xviii, 103, 166, 225
*Pagan Spain* (Wright), 11
painters. *See under individual painters:* Domingo, Roberto; Goya; Greco; Gris, Juan; Manet, Edouard; Marín, Ricardo; Peirce, Waldo; Picasso, Pablo; Ruano Llopis, Carlos; *and* Velázquez, Diego. *See also Death in the Afternoon,*

frontispiece of; *Death in the Afternoon*, various sections of: "Illustrations"; *and* photographs
Pamplona, 59, 155, 167, 176; in Conrad's work, 291, 293–94, 298; in photos and film, 200, 267
"Pamplona in July." *See* Hemingway, Ernest, works by
"Pamplona Letter." *See* Hemingway, Ernest, works by
Paquiro. *See* Montes, Francisco
paratexts, 205–6, 208. *See also* gap
Paris, 7
Park, Mungo, 43, 260
Patterson, Curtis, 36, 251
pedagogical agenda. *See Death in the Afternoon*, pedagogical agenda of
Peirce, Waldo, 165, 189
Penas, Beatriz, 10
Penfield, Edward, 97
Pensamientos. *See* Minguet y Calderón de la Barca, Enrique
Peña y Goñi, Antonio, 114
Pepe-Illo. *See* Delgado, José
Perea, Daniel, 82, 115
Pérez Lugín, Alejandro, 225
Perkins, Maxwell, 23, 31–32, 327 n. 2. *See also Death in the Afternoon*, correspondence about
Peru, 296
Pfeiffer, Gustavus Adolphus (Gus), 218, 245
Pfeiffer, Pauline. *See* Hemingway, Pauline Pfeiffer
phenomenological approach, 143
Phillips, Christopher, 13 n. 8, 259
photographs and photography: cameras, 165–66; correspondence about, 23, 24, 165–66; cost and payment of, 38, 166–67; not published in *Death in the Afternoon*, 189–204. *See also under individual photographers:* Calvache, Antonio; Calvache, José (Walken); Cervera, Manuel; Dean, Loomis; Fernández, Baldomero; Pacheco, Juan (Vandel); Rodero, Aurelio; Serrano, Juan José; *and* Vaquero, Manuel. *See also Death in the Afternoon*, various sections of: "Illustrations"
Picasso, Pablo, 165, 258, 261, 262, 263
*Pilar* (boat of E. H.), 264
Plotkin, Stephen, 137–38 n. 5
*The Plumed Serpent* (Lawrence), 111–12, 295
"The Poem Is By Maera." *See* Hemingway, Ernest, works by
*Poetry: A Magazine of Verse*, 7
Poore, Charles, 21–22
Portugal, 295
Pound, Ezra, 50, 155
Prado Museum, 212, 267
Primo de Rivera, Miguel, 244
*Princeton Alumni Weekly*, 36
*The Prisoner of Chillon. See* Byron, George Gordon, Lord, works by
Pritchett, V. S., 298
Procuna, Luis, 296
pronouns, 6, 221–22, 224, 243, 245–47, 249
*Publishers' Weekly*, 25, 36
Puerto de Santa María, 293

Quintana, Juan, 228

Rabelais, François, 27
Radcliffe College, 61
Radiguet, Raymond, 43, 50, 65, 66, 75 n. 17, 265
Ramírez, Amado, 285
reader (dramatized), 221–22

*The Red Badge of Courage* (Crane), 71
Redman, Ben Ray, 36
Redondo y Zuñiga, Ladislao, 115
"Refugees from Thrace." *See* Hemingway, Ernest, works by
*Reglamento* (taurine code), 23, 31, 297
Rejoneo, 147, 295
*Retail Bookseller*, 36
Reynolds, Michael, xvi, 1, 7, 11, 72, 84, 260–61
Rodero, Aurelio, xvii, xviii, 166, 181, 225
Rodríguez, Félix, 181
Rodríguez, Joaquín (Cagancho), 168, 175, 177, 179, 180–81; Conrad meets, mentions, 287, 291, 292
Rodríguez, Manuel (Manolete), 287–91, 296–97
Roger, José (Valencia), 186 n. 32
Roger, Victoriano (Valencia II), 29
Roman Catholicism, 147–48, 290. *See also* Spain *and* Spanish Inquisition
Romero, Pedro, 273 n. 4, 293
Rosa, Juan Luis de la, 128
Roth, James, xv
Ruano Llopis, Carlos, 165, 286

Sáenz de Heredia, Cesáreo (El Bachiller Garrocha), 115, 227
Sánchez, Matías (bullbreeder), 185 n. 29
Sánchez de Neira, José, 82, 116, 225
Sánchez Mejías, Ignacio, 168–69, 177, 284, 292
Sand, George, 61
*Sangre y arena* (magazine), 103
*Sangre y arena* (Blasco Ibáñez), 105
Santayana, George, 61, 65

Sappho, 49
*The Saturday Review of Literature*, 36
Scholes, Robert, 9, 43, 113
*Scribner's Magazine*, 23, 24, 25, 36
Scribner Archives (Princeton University), 13 n. 17, 39 n. 1
"The Sea Change." *See* Hemingway, Ernest, works by
Sebastian, St., 49
Sedgwick, Henry Dwight, 81, 116
Segura, Vicente, 85
self-reflexivity, 137–38 n. 5, 224
"Sepi Jingan." *See* Hemingway, Ernest, works by
Serrano, Juan José, 166
Seville, 167, 294–95, 415. *See also* Maestranza
Shakespeare, William, 43, 50, 55 n. 1
Shelley, Percy Bysshe, 44
"A Short Estimate of the American." *See Death in the Afternoon*, various sections of
"The Short Happy Life of Francis Macomber." *See* Hemingway, Ernest, works by
Sigman, Joseph, 84
"A Silent, Ghastly Procession." *See* Hemingway, Ernest, works by
Silveti, Juan, 202, 212, 296
Skinner, Cornelia Otis, 292
Slater, Ernest (Paul Gwynne), 99
Smith, Paul, xvi, 7, 240
Smyrna, 259, 265
"The Snows of Kilimanjaro." *See* Hemingway, Ernest, works by
*Sol y sombra* (magazine), 103
"Soldier's Home." *See* Hemingway, Ernest, works by
"[Someday when you are picked up . . .]." *See* Hemingway, Ernest, works by

"Some Reactions of a Few Individuals." *See Death in the Afternoon,* various sections of
"The Soul of Spain with McAlmon and Bird the Publishers." *See* Hemingway, Ernest, works by
sources. *See* Hemingway, Ernest, use of sources; *and* writing
Southey, Robert, 51–52
Spain, 8, 125, 147; as antidote to modernity, contrast to United States, 8, 127–33, 148–49; and bullfights, 131–34, 157. *See also* analogies
Spanier, Sandra, 11 n. 1
Spanish Civil War. *See* war
*The Spanish Earth. See* Hemingway, Ernest, works by; *and* movies
Spanish Inquisition, 147–48
Spilka, Mark, 9, 45
Stallings, Laurence, 36
Stanley, Edward (Bishop Stanley), 43
Stein, Gertrude, 7, 10, 43, 50, 59–63. *See also* Old lady
Stein, Gertrude, works by: "Accents in Alsace," 69, 71; *Geography and Plays,* 60, 69, 72; "I Must Try to Write the History of Belmonte," 69, 72–73, 116; "In the Grass (On Spain)," 69; "Johnny Green," 69–70; *The Making of Americans,* 60; "Mallorcan Stories," 69; "Sacred Emily," 69; "Susie Asado," 69; *Tender Buttons,* 60; *Three Lives,* 60; "Tourty or Tourtebattre," 69
Stein, Leo, 60
Steinbeck, John, 283, 298
Stendhal (Marie Henri Beyle), 43
Stephens, Robert O., 11
Stewart, Donald Ogden, xv

*Still-Life with Chair Caning* (Picasso), 258
Stoddard, John L., 81, 116
Strater, Mike, 7
Strychacz, Thomas, 9
subject and object, 146
subtitle, 209
suicide, 294. *See also* death
Sumner, John S., 32
*The Sun Also Rises. See* Hemingway, Ernest, works by

table of contents. *See Death in the Afternoon,* table of contents of
*Tabula* (magazine), 6, 7
Talavera de la Reina, 178, 292
"Tancredo is Dead." *See* Hemingway, Ernest, works by
Taurine Bibliophiles of America (TBA), 84, 283
*Tender Buttons. See* Stein, Gertrude, works by
*Three Lives. See* Stein, Gertrude, works by
Three Mountains Press, 261
*Three Soldiers. See* Dos Passos, John, works by
*Three Stories & Ten Poems. See* Hemingway, Ernest, works by
"The Three-Day Blow." *See* Hemingway, Ernest, works by
threshold, 205. *See also* genre *and* transgression
Thurston, Michael, 9, 230 n. 11
Ticknor, George T., 100
time, 259–61, 266. *See also* nostalgia
*Time* (magazine), 36
title. *See Death in the Afternoon,* title and title page of
Todó, Isidoro, 218–19
"To a Tragic Poetess." *See* Hemingway, Ernest, works by
*To Have and Have Not. See* Hemingway, Ernest, works by

"To His Coy Mistress" (Marvell), 29
Toklas, Alice B., 7, 60–63, 70
Tolstoy, Leo, 43
*El Toreo* (magazine), 103
*Torerías* (magazine), 103
*El Torero* (*The Bullfighter*, Gris). See *Death in the Afternoon*, frontispiece of
*Le Torero* (magazine), 104
*Toreros y toros* (magazine), 104
*Le Toril* (magazine), 104
Torón, Saturio, 200
*Toronto Star*, 6–7, 59, 298
*Toros*. See *Death in the Afternoon*, dust jacket, illustration of
*Toros célebres* (Carralero and Borge), 83, 107, 226
*Toros y toreros en . . . .* See Orts-Ramos, Tomás (Uno al Sesgo), works by
*The Torrents of Spring.* See Hemingway, Ernest, works by
Torres, Enrique, 175
Torres Reina, Ricardo (Bombita), 293
tourism, tourists, 133–35. See also Hemingway, Ernest, as insider, outsider in Spain
*Town & Country* (magazine), 36
transgression (crossover): in terms of fact and fiction, 13 n. 16; in terms of gender, sex, 5, 45, 47, 49–50, 65, 68, 149–50, 243; in terms of literature and film, 257, 262–67, 271–72; in terms of speech and writing, 264–65. See also culture (high and low); gender roles; genre, generic crossovers; liminality; *and* translation
translation: of culture, rituals, 123–30, 136–37; of *Death in the Afternoon*, 79–80, 225–26; of *Reglamento*, 23, 31, 39 n. 2, 297. See also analogies
*Trapeze*, 6, 7
Trelawny, Edward John, 44
Trevelyan, G. M., 14 n. 20
Trogdon, Robert W., xvi, 9
*True at First Light.* See Hemingway, Ernest, works by
Turkish War. See war
Tyler, Lisa, 10, 45, 83
Tynan, Kenneth, 292, 295

"The Undefeated." See Hemingway, Ernest, works by
United States: Civil War of, 2; in 1910s, 2–4; depression of 1930s, 25; Gilded Age of, 160 n. 8; represented via bullfight, 148–49. See also analogies; Hemingway, Ernest, as insider, outsider in Spain; *and* nostalgia
*El Universal* (newspaper), 104
Uno al Sesgo. See Orts-Ramos, Tomás
"Up in Michigan." See Hemingway, Ernest, works by
Uriarte, Luis (don Luis), 116
*U. S. A.* See Dos Passos, John, works by

Valencia. See Roger, José
Valencia II. See Roger, Victoriano
Vandel. See Pacheco, Juan
Vaquero, Manuel, 166
Varé, Manuel (Varelito), 168, 172, 173
Varelito. See Varé, Manuel
Vázquez y Rodríguez, Leopoldo, 116
Vega de los Reyes, Francisco (Gitanillo de Triana), 25, 29, 175, 209, 291
Velázquez, Diego, 29

Velázquez Sánchez, José, 116, 225
Veneno. *See* Granados, José
Venezuela, 296
Ventura, don Ventura. *See* Bagüés, Ventura
Vera, Carlos (Cañitas), 287
"A Very Short Story." *See* Hemingway, Ernest, works by
Villa, Antonio de la, 295
Villalta, Nicanor, 49, 167, 168, 177, 192
Vindel, Pedro, 82, 117
*Virgin Spain*. *See* Frank, Waldo, works by
Vondrak, Amy, 11
*La Voz de Navarra* (newspaper), 104

Wagner-Martin, Linda, 83, 273 n. 3
Wagner-Smith, Linda, 10
Walken. *See* Calvache, José
"Wanderings." *See* Hemingway, Ernest, works by
war: American Civil War, 2; First World War, 130–31, 259, 263–64; Spanish Civil War, 13 n. 16, 54–55, 125, 134, 147; Turkish War, 59, 259–60
Warner, Charles Dudley, 101–2, 123–24
Warren, Robert Penn, 46
Weber, Ronald, 11
Wertenbaker, Charles, 298
West, Ray B., 288
White, Gilbert, 43
Whitman, Walt, 43, 50
Whittier, John Greenleaf, 43, 67
Wilde, Oscar, 43, 50
Wilson, Edmund, 22
"Wine of Wyoming." *See* Hemingway, Ernest, works by
*Winesburg, Ohio* (Anderson), 261
Wister, Owen, 268

Woolf, Virginia, 43, 50, 62, 66, 150
Wordsworth, William, 45, 51
World War I. *See* war
"World's Series of Bull Fighting a Mad, Whirling Carnival." *See* Hemingway, Ernest, works by
Wright, Frank Lloyd, 12 n. 5
Wright, Richard, 11
writing: about bullfight, after *Death in the Afternoon*, in English, 11, 283–99; before *Death in the Afternoon*, in English, 80–82, 84–102, 208–10; in Spanish, 208, 214–15, 225–26. *See also* Hemingway, Ernest, reading of; Hemingway, Ernest, use of sources; *and* Hemingway, Ernest, works by

Yale University, 286
*The Yale Review*, 36

*Zig-Zag* (magazine), 104
Zurito. *See* Haba, Antonio de la

www.ingramcontent.com/pod-product-compliance
Lightning Source LLC
Chambersburg PA
CBHW022008300426
44117CB00005B/88